D1334404

YUGOSLAVIA
THE ADRIATIC COAST

THE BLUE GUIDES

YUGOSLAVIA
THE ADRIATIC COAST

Edited by

STUART ROSSITER

M.A.

Atlas and 32 Maps & Plans

1969

LONDON: ERNEST BENN LIMITED
CHICAGO: RAND McNALLY & COMPANY

FIRST EDITION 1969

Published by Ernest Benn Limited
Bouverie House · Fleet Street · London · EC4

Rand McNally & Company
Chicago · Illinois 60680 · USA

© Ernest Benn Limited 1969

Printed in Great Britain
by Fletcher & Son Ltd, Norwich

510–02505–6

PREFACE

The Balkans, notorious until well into the twentieth century as the most politically backward part of Europe, have recently come into their own touristically as the least spoiled. Yugoslavia, with one of the loveliest coastlines and a great diversity of cultural remains, has increased steadily in popularity in the ten years during which its once doctrinaire régime has become more moderate. Indeed, this very popularity had begun to encourage speculative development on the Montenegrin coast that threatened to spoil just those features that were most to be prized. The need for planning and control if the fate of Spain were to be avoided has been appreciated in time, and with the assistance of the United Nations Development Programme, the Yugoslav government sponsored in 1967 a comprehensive Physical Development Plan for the South Adriatic Region (Projekt Južni Jadran). Its first public report, issued a week before this preface was written, was well received and offers hope that future changes will be reasoned and appropriate.

The present guide to the Adriatic Coast will, it is hoped, play its part in fostering an intelligent interest in this lovely region. For centuries Dalmatia has maintained a position between East and West, now dominated by one culture, now by another, becoming an amalgam epitomized in the oft-quoted cliché about the Federal Republic of Yugoslavia that six republics, five peoples, four languages, three religions, and two alphabets have been crystallized in one nation. The contrasts and contradictions increase its fascination but require a key for their comprehension, to which end the guide is equipped with two short lucid essays by experts in their fields on the historical background and the artistic heritage.

The guide proper is based on a series of routes, arranged from North to South, by which the traveller by road or sea can explore not only the major places during a single tour, but also—if he so desires—the lesser-known areas in some depth. The by-ways of Istria, for example, and many of the islands are here described in detail, and various inland excursions farther south are suggested in the hope that coastal sun-seekers may be encouraged to discover different beauties and meet the Yugoslav people.

In the compilation the Editor is indebted in the first instance to **Mr. Michael Scammell** for travelling extensively throughout the area in the service of the guide. His previous experience of Yugoslav life and his fluency in several Balkan languages enabled him to tap written Slav sources and obtain the cooperation of many local scholars. Throughout the long preparation of the book his industry and enthusiasm have beaten many problems. The Editor is not the less indebted to him for his forbearance when parts of his text were torn apart, pruned, extended, or recast to conform with the particular requirements of the Series.

The cartography has been entrusted to **Mr. John Flower,** who has improved upon the style he initiated for the Editor in the Blue Guide to Malta to produce an atlas and a complement of town plans not only clear, detailed, and accurate, but also attractive in appearance.

Gratitude must be warmly expressed to the Turistički Savez Jugoslavije (Yugoslav Tourist Association) for generous assistance, both moral and material, to Mr. Scammell in his travels in 1965 and 1967, for a copious supply of printed sources, and for general advice to the Editor concerning his visits to Yugoslavia in 1966, 1967, 1968 (twice), and 1969. Of particular assistance were the Association's representatives in London: Mr. Ante Sorić, followed by Mr. Zlatko Uzelac and his assistant, Mr. Dejan Živojinović. Among local representatives deserving special mention are Dr. Mitja Gorec, Foreign Tourism Secretary of the Tourist Association of Slovenia, Mr. Igor Pelan of Koper, Mr. Vlado Zarić of Opatija, Mr. Hektor Kamalić of Rijeka, Mr. Božo Frgačić of Krk, Mr. Petar Halović of Rab, Mr. Mate Solis of Cres, Mr. Franjo Fattuta of Lošinj, Mrs. Nerina Čorić of Zadar, Mrs. Edita Piler of Šibenik, Messrs. Ivo Dragičević, Zdravko Draganja, and Miroslav Bonačić, and Prof. Armando Moreno of Split, Messrs. Kruno Butković and Kazimir Cukar of Brac, Mrs. Marija Carić of Hvar, Mr. Martin Vojvodić of Korčula, Mr. Radovan Radović of Kotor, and Mr. Bogoljub Radjenović of Budva.

The Editor also wishes to acknowledge the invaluable help given to Mr. Scammell by various specialists in the field, notably Miss Ksenija Radulić, Director of the Institute for the Conservation of Monuments at Zadar, who not only read the draft MS but assisted with discussion of many difficult points, specific suggestions and information, and introductions to fellow scholars in Dalmatia. For assistance with particular sections of the text, thanks are due to Prof. Ante Šonje (Poreč and inland Istria), Dr. Štefan Mlakar (Pula and southern Istria), Dr. Ante Glavičić (Senj), Prof. Franjo Matejčić (Krk), Prof. Slavo Grubišić (Šibenik), Dr. Tomislav Marasović (Split), Dr. Raden Vučenović (Trogir), and the late Dr. Lukša Beritić (Dubrovnik). In addition special thanks should go to Dr. Duško Kečkemet, Director of the Town Museum at Split, for reading the text for that city and offering valuable suggestions; to Dr. Niko Duboković-Nadalini for reading and correcting the text of Hvar; to Dr. Juraj R. Arnerić for his indefatigable assistance towards obtaining an accurate description of Korčula and reading the proofs; and to Prof. Jovan J. Martinović both for help on the spot in Kotor and for reading the text in proof.

The general kindness accorded to the Editor by Yugoslav citizens up and down the coast may be exemplified by Dr. Donko Mirković and Dr. Ivica Barović of Dubrovnik, whose generous and efficient assistance have nullified problems and saved endless time. In London Mr. Carlo Novak and Mr. Erik Helbling have given friendly encouragement as well as practical advice on many aspects of Yugoslav affairs. Finally particular thanks are due to young friends in Korčula (Branko Šeparović) and Trogir (Davor Lovrić and Boris Burić) without whose help the plans of those towns and of Šibenik would be far less accurately drawn.

Even with the help received from all quarters, it is not to be supposed that all the difficulties experienced in describing this area have been satisfactorily solved. The polyglot nomenclature of Dalmatian artists defies consistency and the Index of Artists is only a modest aid to a complexity of little-known names, barely yet studied by scholars. The most far-reaching editorial difficulties since the upheaval of the Second World War are being caused by the Vatican's encyclical enjoining changes in the celebration of Mass. Scarcely a sanctuary throughout the Roman Catholic world has not been modified in arrangement to allow mass to be said facing the congregation, with consequent removal to a new position of many an altarpiece or reredos.

No one is better aware than the Editor of the difficulty of avoiding errors both of omission and commission, and suggestions for the correction or improvement of the Guide will be gratefully welcomed.

CONTENTS

MAPS AND PLANS

ISTRIA AND DALMATIA

A Historical Sketch

by LOVETT F. EDWARDS

A glance at the map of the Yugoslav Adriatic coastline is enough to give one a general idea of its history. The cities cut off from the hinterland by high ranges of mountains, with only occasional passes leading into the interior, have always looked outward towards the sea rather than inward towards the continent. Before the coming of modern communications, less than a century ago, the inland caravan routes were difficult and dangerous. The overlordship of continental rulers was always distant, often transient and frequently almost nominal. Raids and incursions were common, but permanent conquest was almost always dependent on the slow processes of demographic change. On the other hand, access by sea was easy. The many deep fjords were, in Dalmatia at least, sheltered by the islands. For many centuries political change and political conquest came from the sea. After the coming of the Illyrians, the formative influence of the coastal cities came from overseas, from Greece, from Rome, and from Venice. Slav penetration into the coastlands was slow, though permanent. Even when the coastal cities became almost purely Slav, they still maintained the classical and medieval concept of the city-state. The main cities of the coastland remained separate units, even though acknowledging the overlordship of distant masters, Croatian kings or Venetian Senate. There was constant strife between the autonomous or semi-autonomous cities and tribes and the powerful invaders from across the sea.

The people of the eastern Adriatic coast, Illyrians and Slavs, carried on a constant and often very successful struggle against their overseas enemies. This struggle continued, culturally and socially, until comparatively modern times. When the countryside had become wholly Slav, the nobles and upper classes in many of the cities held tenaciously to their Latin or Venetian way of life, which was closely linked with power and privilege, even in cities like Biograd-na-Moru or Trogir where the people soon became racially Slav and spoke Croatian.

Therefore the history of Istria, Dalmatia, and the Montenegrin coast is a mosaic of city chronicles and continual strife. It is not possible to think of it as a whole, save in very early times or from the beginning of the last century after the final defeat of Napoleon and the dissolution of his Illyrian province, and the suppression of the ancient Republic of Dubrovnik (Ragusa). Then the whole coastline came under the control of a single power for the first time since the Roman conquest—the Austro-Hungarian monarchy. It was a century of somnolent and unenterprising decay. It is only within living memory, just after the First World War, that Dalmatia and Montenegro became part of a unified Yugoslav state. Istria had to wait even longer; it became Yugoslav only after the Second World War.

Throughout their history therefore the peoples of Dalmatia were merchants and sea-raiders. From Roman times they were formidable pirates. They fought the Romans as they fought the Venetians. When finally defeated by Venice, they became her staunchest guardians and most skilful pilots, as the name of the Riva dei Schiavoni in Venice bears witness. Only the merchant republic of Dubrovnik maintained its independence and was for a time a formidable rival to Venice herself.

Before the Illyrians. Although one of the earliest ancestors of man, Homo Krapinensis, was found in Croatia, little was known of early man on the Adriatic coast until recent years. But discoveries in the Grapčeva cave on the island of Hvar show that man lived in Dalmatia more than five thousand years ago and at least as early as Neolithic times had found a way of reaching the offshore islands. These men had reached a comparatively high standard of civilization. They made efficient weapons and beautiful ceramics; on one fragment found in the Grapčeva cave is the earliest picture of a boat discovered in Europe. It is not a luxurious barge like those used by the early Egyptian rulers but an ordinary transport craft probably used on voyages to and along the coast.

Ruins of stone-built forts from the Bronze Age have been found in Istria, near Labin, Poreč, and Pula, on the Brioni islands and on the shores of the Kvarner Gulf.

The Illyrians. Illyrian is a convenient term for the mass of comparatively unorganized tribes which lived in the Adriatic coastlands at the time when the first Greek voyages were being made along the coasts, and which had formed some sort of confederation about the time when the Roman republic was becoming the Roman Empire. It is an important term, because it has impressed itself on later generations and acquired a sort of mystique; Napoleon called his short-lived Adriatic conquests the Illyrian province and the first tentative approaches to a Yugoslav cultural unity were known as the Illyrian movement.

Only a few of these tribal names have any real importance in history. The Histris and Dalmates gave their names to the present Istria and Dalmatia, and the Liburnians, who lived mainly around the Kvarner Gulf, developed the swift Liburnian galleys whose design was later adopted by the Romans for their fleets. They were very fast, with sleek hulls and steep sides, with a sharp underwater beak at the prow. A number of these *Liburnas* took part in the battle of Actium and ensured the victory of Octavian over Antony and Cleopatra.

It is now that the Dalmatians and Istrians come into written history, first with the Greeks and then with the Romans. Diodorus Siculus, writing with the aid of earlier documents now lost, describes the Greek struggles with the Illyrian islanders, and a Greek *Periplus*, or pilots' manual, describes the coasts of Dalmatia and Istria about the 4th century B.C.

Greek ships had been trading in the Adriatic for many years before that, but the first permanent Greek settlement appears to have been on the island of Vis (Issa) and was built by the Syracusan general Dionysios the Elder about 390 B.C. A few years later the Parians seized the island of Hvar to use as a base to protect their commerce and extend their power in the Adriatic. Later both became independent states, minted their own coins and maintained their own fleets.

There was violent reaction from the people of Hvar. They attacked the Greek garrison and killed many of them. Greek power in the Adriatic was saved only by massive help from Vis. The description of the revolt (by Diodorus Siculus) is the first written account of Dalmatian history.

Greek commercial and political influence lasted nearly a hundred and fifty years. It spread rapidly. Greek trading-posts were established not only on the islands but along the coasts, sometimes on the site of existing Illyrian settlements: Tragurion (Trogir), Epetion (Stobreč), Salona (Solin), and many other places.

The Illyrians reacted. All the written history that we possess was compiled by their adversaries who describe them as bandits and pirates, which they probably were. But they were able to combine sufficiently to form a powerful state, or at least a confederation of tribes, under a leader, Agron, who captured Hvar and drove the Greek outposts from many of their bridgeheads on the mainland. His widow, Teuta, continued the struggle, besieged Dürres (Durazzo in Albania) and even invested the island of Corfu. Vis remained the last stronghold of Greek naval power. Seapower in the Adriatic was almost entirely in Illyrian hands.

Now a new enemy took the field—Rome. The Roman wars against the Illyrians lasted for nearly two and a half centuries, from the defeat of Teuta's armies in 228 B.C. to the Pannonian and Dalmatian Triumph of Tiberius in A.D. 12.

Roman discipline and military organization won victory after victory. There were several Illyrian Triumphs in Rome, one of which displayed the captive Illyrian king, Gentius (167 B.C.). The military title Dalmaticus was won by several generals. For a time Julius Caesar was proconsul of Illyria (one of his least successful ventures). The Emperor Octavian celebrated a Dalmatian Triumph. The Illyrian leader Bato (perhaps not a proper name but a title) revolted and his armies passed the Italian frontiers and caused consternation in Rome. The future Emperor Tiberius led the Roman armies. In the Triumph, Bato was paraded through the streets of Rome and the famous Gemma Augustea was minted to commemorate the victory. Suetonius referred to the war as "the most difficult of all the external wars, with the exception only of the Punic Wars".

The remarkable thing about these wars was not the Roman victory; that was almost a foregone conclusion. It was the astonishing power of recovery shown by the Illyrian tribes in defence of their personal, perhaps even their national (to borrow an expression which was probably almost meaningless to the tribes themselves) freedom. The final curtain of the Illyrian wars was the terrible siege of Arduba (Knin) where, after the garrison had been slaughtered, the women threw themselves and their children into the flames of the burning citadel rather than fall into the hands of the Romans.

The Illyrians, in the cities at least, became Romanized. They were to give several emperors to Rome, notably Diocletian the great reformer of the Empire. Pannonia, with which Dalmatia was closely allied geographically and racially, became in practice the nerve-centre of the

Empire, operating from Sirmium (Sremska Mitrovica in Croatia). Still later, Julius Nepos, one of the last pretenders to the throne of the western emperors, had his capital at Salona (Solin, near Split). At first the fighting spirit of the Illyrians was both feared and respected by the Romans. Octavian Augustus, after his Illyrian Triumphs, forbade Illyrian slaves to be sold in the border areas and no Illyrian could buy his freedom until he had been a slave for thirty years.

For several centuries Istria and Dalmatia were an important and prosperous part of the Roman Empire. Salona was one of its most important cities, celebrated by Lucan; another was Pula (Pietas Julia) where to this day the walls of the great Roman amphitheatre (preserved in the Middle Ages from pillage and destruction by the Venetian Senator Guglielmo Emo) dominate the harbour and the city. At Pula Gallus, the unfortunate brother of Julian the Apostate, was judicially murdered by his uncle. Diocletian's palace, "the noblest dwelling-place ever erected for a single man", still exists. For centuries its powerful walls sheltered the infant city of Split. Another of many important cities was Poreč (Colonia Julia Parentium).

It seemed that the eastern Adriatic coast was at long last at peace. But its prosperity was first disturbed and then destroyed by three great events which changed the whole course of European history: the division of the Empire, the advent of Christianity, and the coming of the Slavs.

Early Christianity and the division of the Empire. One reason why Dalmatia is an excellent region in which to study early Christianity is closely connected with its history. When the Roman Empire of the West collapsed under the weight of the barbarian invasions, Salona in particular was a centre of early Christianity. Some of the finest early Christian churches are to be found there. The invaders were, however, pagans and country dwellers. As a rule they did not live in the great cities after they had destroyed them (as also happened, in a smaller way, at St Albans in England). Therefore what has been left from the earliest Christian centuries has been little changed by subsequent rebuilding. Many of the ancient sites were not reoccupied, as at Salona, and remained empty and deserted for centuries. The main damage to them was the work of local masons, pilfering stones for their dwellings, or local military leaders, afraid lest the once mighty ruins shelter enemies or rebels.

Rome was notoriously tolerant in matters of religion and eagerly welcomed new gods. So at first Christianity flourished almost unchecked. It was only after the exclusiveness and intolerance of the new sect began to show political overtones that serious and organized persecution began. Instead of being merely another mystical Oriental sect, like the worship of Osiris, Christianity emerged as a moral force capable of undermining the foundations of empire.

The persecutions, at first haphazard, local and sporadic (as Nero's at Rome), became violent and almost universal after Diocletian's edict of A.D. 303. Diocletian, whose favourite residence was at Split, dreamed of a universal empire governed by a hierarchy of Augusti, Caesars and lesser officials, under a single paternal control. His edict against these unco-operative sectaries was rigorously applied in Dalmatia and Pannonia. The number of victims was large, though not as large as medieval Christian apologists like to claim. Many of these victims, some historical and others purely imaginary, were later proclaimed saints. One such saint from Dalmatia was Domnius, Bishop of Salona, who is still honoured under the later Slav corruption of his name—Sveti Duje.

This most efficient and protracted persecution ended after the Edict of Milan in 313. Christianity triumphed, the emperor Constantine became a Christian, and instead of being persecuted the Church itself became a persecutor.

The Dalmatians and Istrians, always independent and intolerant of control, provided a fine crop of heretics. The greatest of the heresiarchs, Arius of Alexandria, was excommunicated after the Council of Nicaea and banished to Illyria, where he lived for some time and preached his creed. The tenets of Arianism were formulated at Sirmium (Sremska Mitrovica in Croatia) and were at once supported by the bishops of Mursa (Osijek) and Singidunum (Belgrade).

The tenets of Arianism are no part of this essay and, indeed, are only understood with difficulty by a non-theological age. But they had immense political influence. Many of the barbarian nations were converted to Christianity in its Arian form. The consequent religious wars between catholic and heretic, especially Arian, Christians bedevilled European history and profoundly influenced events not only in the Balkans but also in western Europe, particularly in Italy and France.

Dalmatia and Istria had their heretics but they also had their saints, including one of the fathers of the Church, the peppery and controversial Sophronius Eusebius of Stridon, better known as St Jerome. Stridon was somewhere in Illyria, but it is not certain where; it may have been in Istria (Zrenj) or in the Bosnian mountains (Bosanska Kostajnica). St Jerome's greatest work was the preparation of the standard Latin translation of the Bible—the Vulgate. His fiery and contumacious character is best summed up in his own despairing plea: "Pardon me, O Lord, for I am a Dalmatian!"

Diocletian's magnificent scheme for organizing the empire of the Mediterranean world foundered on the personal rivalries and ambitions of his successors. The spheres of influence of Rome and Byzantium depended on the abilities of the emperors in power. The Adriatic was, roughly speaking, the dividing line. Both empires claimed it. In 437 it was annexed by the Byzantine Empire.

But though Byzantine influence was important in Dalmatian (and Italian) affairs for centuries to come, Byzantine power was too far away and often too weak to give adequate defence against external enemies. Attacked and harried by the Vandal pirates from Africa, the Dalmatian general Marcellinus declared the country independent and refused obedience to either empire. It maintained this rather shaky isolation until the fall of the Western Empire in the 5th century. Then the Dalmatian leaders claimed the imperial title themselves. It was a flamboyant but useless gesture. For fifteen months Julius Nepos, nephew of Marcellinus, claimed an uneasy and unenforceable sovereignty of the Western world from his capital at Salona. He seems to have had some moral support from Byzantium but had to struggle against other pretenders, one of whom was the Bishop of Salona, Glycerius. It was a puppet-show upon which Odoacer was to ring down the curtain. Julius Nepos was murdered in his palace in 480 by Glycerius, who was raised, perhaps as a result of this crime, to the Archbishopric of Milan. The last pretender was a certain Ovid, of whom we know practically nothing, but who called himself King of Dalmatia for a year before he was overthrown by Odoacer.

Now, however, a vast movement in the heart of the continent was to change the entire map of Europe and the whole history of Dalmatia and Istria.

The coming of the Slavs. At first the advent of the Slavs into Central Europe and the Balkans was scarcely noticed by the writers of the Empire. They came mainly as allies or confederates of the invading Avars and Antes, two conquering peoples which have entirely disappeared from history. The Slavs are mentioned in a Byzantine military handbook of the 6th century, which says that they cannot be induced to bow their necks to slavery or subjection, that they are brave and capable of great endurance and that they are extremely hospitable to strangers (*Mauricii Strategikon*). Procopius says that they lived under a government of elders and had no kings or princes. Originally pastoral and agricultural, they were forced by the conditions of the times to become soldiers, to unite in tribal federations and to choose war leaders. The names of some of these have come down to us: Mesimir, Radogost, Mužok, etc.

By the middle of the century the Slav raiders had reached the Adriatic where they spent the winter of 550–51 "as if they were in their own countryside" (Procopius) and then retreated across the Danube with their plunder. They did not attack the fortified cities.

By the beginning of the next century their tactics had changed. They again entered the Balkans with the Avars, who had probably subdued a number of Slav tribes. They took Sirmium after a three-year siege in 582 and marched almost to the gates of Constantinople. The Avars after four years in the Balkans withdrew across the Danube; but the Slavs, whether as subjects, allies or enemies, remained. Their attacks on the cities increased. Albona (Labin) records a Slav attack in 610.

Meanwhile the Romanized inhabitants of the coastal cities were involved in civil strife and religious controversy. In Istria the clergy took a leading part in the obscure heresy of 'The Three Chapters', about which Gibbon remarks: "It has filled more volumes than it deserves lines." In Salona, Bishop Natal, "an ignorant and little-read man" and a notorious drunkard, "wasted his time in banquets and drinking parties". None the less he remained bishop until he died of old age in 592. He was succeeded by Maxim, the last bishop of Salona.

It was to Maxim that Pope Gregory I wrote his famous letter in 600, in which he said: "I am highly distressed and deeply concerned with the threat posed to us by the Slavs . . . they have already started to encroach upon Italy through Istria." The letter, however, also reproached Maxim for irregularities in his election and the indignant bishop had it torn to pieces in public.

The Slavs were by now deeply entrenched in the Balkans and the Byzantine line of defence collapsed. A Slavo–Avar army broke into the bay of Split and in 614 the city of Salona was taken. The chroniclers of the time are vague and uncertain, but it seems that not all the Roman cities fell into Slav hands. Trogir, Zadar, and some of the Istrian cities seem to have held out. It was about this time that the inhabitants of ancient Epidaurus (modern Cavtat) fled across the bay to the cliffs on the farther side and there founded the famous city of Dubrovnik (Ragusa). Even now on Italian maps Cavtat is marked as Ragusa Vecchia. Other groups of Roman inhabitants fled to the islands, particularly Hvar, Brač, and Šolta.

At this point in time the histories of Istria, Dalmatia, Dubrovnik and the Montenegrin coastland become more and more individual and diverse. It is no longer possible to treat them as a single narrative. Only in very recent years is it possible to return to the Adriatic coastland as a homogenous whole.

Istria in the Middle Ages and the Renaissance. After the break-up of the Roman Empire, Istria was a frontier province which suffered continually from the passage of armies to and from Italy. It remained under the Byzantine Exarchate of Ravenna until its downfall, when it was joined to the Lombard Kingdom in 752. For a time it was part of Charlemagne's Frankish Empire.

In Istria the mountains form less of a barrier between the coastal cities and the hinterland so that it is more open to invasion from the landward side. When the central power was finally abolished, save in far-off Byzantium, it fell under the sway of the Patriarchate of Aquileia, whose bellicose prelates were such a thorn in the flesh of infant Venice. Then it became the patrimony of the Marquises (later Counts) of Istria. The central and mainly Slav-inhabited parts became feudal fiefs while the seaboard cities retained their municipal freedom.

This freedom did not mean very much. They were continually torn by hostile factions, in which the people looked towards Venice, and the nobles to their various feudal overlords. They were an easy prey to invasion from the sea, where the greatest power was that of Venice. Venice was none too eager to take over the responsibility for these fractious foster-children, some of which, like Pula or Poreč, might become rivals. For years, indeed for centuries, Venice was satisfied if they remained *fideles*, paid tribute and contributed to the Venetian fleet. They only became *subjectos* in the 13th century and remained so until the fall of Venice in 1791.

At first this loyalty to Venice cost them dear. In the 14th century, during the war of Chioggia, they were sacked by the Genoese. Also, they were continually raided by the Croatian pirates, either the Kačići of Omiš or (later) the freebooters of Senj.

Wars, factions, revolts, piratical raids and plague almost depopulated Istria on several occasions. In the 16th and early 17th centuries Pula, whose population in Roman times (and again today) was more than thirty thousand, was reduced to three hundred souls. Poreč was left with one hundred and it is said that the few remaining local boys amused themselves by snaring birds in the central square.

Such weak and bloodless suppliants were of no value to Venice. Great immigrations were encouraged from the other Slav territories under Venetian rule, parts of Bosnia and Hercegovina, Dalmatia and even Montenegro. Their task was to populate the deserted countryside. These immigrations went on from 1376 until the end of the 17th century and finally completed the Slavization of Istria, except for the few Italians remaining in the cities. These, considering themselves more refined and civilized than the Slavs, which at that time they probably were, regarded the immigrants as wild and savage men and tried to confine their settlements to the barren karst. At their request immigrants were brought in from regions which they considered more civilized, from Greece and the Levant.

Nevertheless these 'barbarians' evolved a very distinctive art and way of life of their own, despite the onerous demands of their feudal lords. It owed little or nothing to the municipal life of the seaboard cities and showed only too clearly the division between Latin and Slav. One has only to compare Carpaccio, born perhaps in Istria, with the fresco painters of the inland churches, men like Vincent of Kastav, whose work can still be seen in the fortified churches of Istria, such as Beram or Hrastovlje. In both these churches there is a Dance of Death where, it is noteworthy, Death takes toll of prince, baron, bishop and feudal lord but leaves the miserable serfs to their labours in the fields.

The fortifications, incidentally, were only partly against feudal faction. They were mainly a defence against raiding Turkish bands from Bosnia.

An interesting by-way of history is the spread of Protestantism in Istria. This was a consequence of the close relationship between the Church and the feudal lords, almost all of them foreigners, which drove the downtrodden serfs to revolt. Their protest was not social and military as in Croatia and Hungary (the peasants' revolts of Dózsa and Matija Gubec) but religious. For a time Istria was a centre of Protestantism and it is interesting that the movement spread even to the coastal cities, another proof of their progressive Slavization. In 1534 the Papal Nuncio in Venice bewailed the fact that "the majority of the people of the city of Piran are Lutherans together with their most distinguished citizens", while an Italian writer, Pio Paschini, reports that "almost all the citizens of Pula and Vodnjan are Lutherans, and even boys, shepherds and farm labourers discuss religious topics". It was a revolt of the spirit. At least two of the leaders of the Reformation came from Istria, though their fame is part of Venetian and German history. They were Father Baldo Lupetina from Labin and his follower and pupil Matija Vlačić, better known by his Latin name of Flaccus Illyricus.

Istria, or at any rate the Slav population of Istria, had always rejected the temporal claims of Rome. Istrians had taken a vigorous part in the Glagolitic controversy and Glagolitic books and inscriptions existed up till the 17th century. They were frequently accused of being tainted with Bogumilism (of these two controversies we shall have more to say later). There is still existent near Pula a mysterious cemetery, mentioned by Dante, which may well have been Bogumil.

Baldo Lupetina was a friar from Labin. In 1542 he was arraigned for Lutheranism and taken to the prison of the Inquisition at Venice. A detail of his interrogation says that he was accused of converting the whole island of Cres to the new faith. Even in a prison cell regularly flooded at high tide he refused to recant and preached his doctrines to his fellow prisoners. He was sentenced "to be brought to the pillars on St Mark's Square, his head be cut off there, his corpse burned in that same place and his ashes thrown into the sea". But the Venetians had no love of the Holy Office and the Doge commuted his sentence to life imprisonment. Lupetina, however, still refused to recant and was drowned in 1562.

His pupil and relative, Matija Vlačić, was also born at Labin, in 1520. A very brilliant scholar, he left Istria for Germany where he became professor of Hebrew and Greek at the University of Wittenberg in 1544. He was then twenty-four years old. Vlačić carried on the struggle for Protestantism even further than Luther, whose friend he was. He was the spirit behind the Magdeburg resistance to the imperial armies. In thirty years he wrote more than three hundred books and pamphlets, in some of which he quoted the Croatian Church as one which had never accepted the Roman liturgy. It is interesting that his enemies, probably because of his origin, referred to him as a Manichaean and a Bogumil.

The Croats in Dalmatia. About the beginning of the 9th century the Slavs of Dalmatia began to form their own state and church. The bishopric of Nin (near Zadar) was founded and, for a time, Nin was the centre of Croat power. The Frankish Empire of Charlemagne, which in any case had had little more than nominal sovereignty, was breaking up and the Croats filled the power gap thus created in Dalmatia. Most of them were still pagans, with a hierarchy of nature gods—Perun, Vid, Lel and others—of which we know little. Some were later converted into Christian saints; Perun the Thunderer became St Elias, Vid became St Vitus, etc. There was no Christian equivalent for Lel, the god of love.

It was about this time that the first written documents in Slav appear, mainly inscriptions. The earliest so far found—probably dated about 800—refers to a Croat ruler Godesav. Other inscriptions, sometimes written in Latin, also refer to early Croat kings: Trpimir, Zdeslav, Branimir, and Mutemir. Some of these may have been tributaries of the Franks.

The Croats occupied most of the Dalmatian coastland, though some of the larger and more powerful cities remained municipally independent with a somewhat shadowy allegiance to Byzantium: Split, Zadar, Trogir, and Dubrovnik, as well as a few lesser ones. But contact with the Roman tradition soon led the Croats to build in stone rather than in wood, that is to say to build for permanent residence. Purely Croat cities were founded. Usually they were the capital, for all the Slav rulers were peripatetic and wherever they lived, even were it only for a short time, became their capital. Šibenik, Nin, Knin and Biograd-na-Moru were such cities.

At this time the Croat Church was Roman Catholic, used the Latin liturgy and was in general dependent on the Archbishopric of Split. This did not last long. The association of the Roman Church with the

Romanized cities and consequently with the nobles, and its continual territorial claims, soon brought it into conflict with the Croats who were now beginning to consider themselves a nation with a tradition of their own. The first Croatian state soon forced the cities under Byzantine rule (with the exception of Dubrovnik) to pay tribute to them; and the Croat navy, often in alliance with the pirate ships of the still pagan Neretljani (around the river Neretva), was master of the Adriatic. The Pope addressed the Croatian ruler as "Our dear son and famed Prince of the Slavs".

Squabbles which were as much political as religious soon broke out between Split and Nin. These were greatly complicated by the war of the alphabets. Two monks from Salonika, Cyril and Methodius, who had formerly lived among the Slavs, wished to convert them to Christianity and decided that the task would be easier if the Word of God were preached to them in their own language. They therefore devised an alphabet, based on Greek with an occasional Hebrew letter, which was suitable for Slav phonetics. There is a lot of argument about the original form, date and even compiler of this alphabet. It appears that Cyril and Methodius first used a very complicated script known as Glagolitic and that their disciples Kliment and Naum later devised the alphabet that bears Cyril's name, the Cyrillic, which in a more simplified form is still the alphabet of the Serbs, the Bulgarians, and the Russians. The Glagolitic alphabet developed very slowly as a literary form but was used for church books for many centuries.

The Croats accepted the Glagolitic script for church use and with it a Slavonic liturgy. This brought down upon them the thunders of the Roman Church and an accusation of heresy. Political aims were mingled with religious, and the two parties contended vigorously. At the height of the conflict the Croat King Tomislav was no longer a mere tribal ruler; according to Constantine Porphyrogenitos he could raise an army of a hundred thousand footmen and ninety thousand cavalry. His navy had eighty large and a hundred smaller warships.

Political aims complicated the religious quarrel which was more or less a pretext since it seems that at one time the Pope had been willing to accept the Slavonic liturgy. The archbishops of Split broadcast a story that Sv. Duje, whose relics are supposed to be buried in the cathedral at Split, had been a disciple of St Peter himself and that therefore the archbishopric was apostolic and had rights over the whole Adriatic. Naturally, this could not please the Church of Nin or the Croatian kings.

The champion of this battle of the alphabets, according to Croat tradition, was Bishop Gregory (Grgur) of Nin who defended the Croat view at the Council of Salona. Since we know very little about him, it is better to accept the tradition. It has been perpetuated in stone by Ivan Meštrović, whose colossal statue of Grgur Ninski is to be seen at Split.

But the idea of an independent Croatian Church was destroyed at the Council of Split in 925, despite the passionate opposition of Grgur Ninski. The decision was only partly religious; it also had political and social implications, as the bulk of the nobles were Latinists. Since then Croatia has always been, outwardly at least, Roman Catholic, though the Glagolitic books and services continued in out-of-the-way places until the late 18th century. This decision had, however, little effect on the hostility of the Croats to Rome or to the Latins, that is the Venetians, who often cynically claimed to be the emissaries of Rome whenever it suited them to do so. There were continual revolts and rebellions, often in the name of the Croat Church. During one of them the energetic Pope Gregory VII even asked a Danish king for help against the Croats: "Not far from us there is a very rich country by the sea, now ruled by vulgar and base heretics; we should like one of your sons to be its ruler. . . .' The contest went on until the Croat King Dmitar Zvonimir became a vassal of the Pope. For what reason we do not know, but a folk tradition says that King Zvonimir was cut to pieces by an infuriated crowd in 1089.

Before leaving this thorny alphabetic and ecclesiastical question, it is worth mentioning that the Serbian Orthodox Church, which uses the Cyrillic alphabet, has never maintained a permanent foothold on the Dalmatian coast. But there are Orthodox churches and monasteries in the Boka Kotorska and Orthodoxy is the creed of the Montenegrins.

The Yugoslavs (for in this the Croats and the Montenegrins are coupled) alone among the Slavs, who are inland peoples, have built up a great seafaring tradition. Perhaps it was a triumph of environment over heredity; perhaps it was an echo of the Liburnian tradition. Skilled seamanship, coupled with a tradition of raiding, soon made them the pirates of the Adriatic.

Pirates lived and flourished along the coast, in certain cities and on some of the islands (on one island at least there is a church to Our Lady of the Pirates). The Neretljani lived around the estuary of the Neretva. Later the tribe or family of the Kačići lived at Omiš, where their fleets could rest and careen in the impregnable and land-locked harbour of the Cetina. Lastly the Uskoks whose centre was at Senj, which became an independent republic and sent its representatives to the courts of Europe. Their depredations are still remembered in the phrase: "Beware the hands of Senj."

Until the end of the 9th century the Croat navies were the naval force of a powerful kingdom, which rivalled Byzantine Zadar for the mastery of the eastern Adriatic. The main battlefield was the Pašman channel, whither the Croat capital—Biograd-na-Moru—was transferred. A great sea battle won by Prince Mioslav in 839 confirmed their mastery of the seas. For a hundred and sixty years the Croat navy ruled supreme, more and more a thorn in the flesh of the growing power of Venice. But in A.D. 1000 the combined navies of Venice, Rab, Krk and Zadar completely defeated the Croats. It was in memory of this victory that the famous ceremony of the Bucintoro was established in Venice. The Doge went down to the sea in his great gilded barge and threw a ring into the sea with the words: "I wed thee, O sea, in sign of our full and complete mastery over thee." It was carried out regularly until 1757.

Croats and Venetians then fought for mastery of the Dalmatian cities, which changed sides many times. While the Venetians were involved in the Crusades the Croats managed to capture almost all of them. But when the Doge returned, he besieged Biograd: "Let this infernal spot which menaces Venice be razed to its foundations."

The threat was carried out. Biograd was burnt and systematically destroyed. The citizens fled to Šibenik and Dolac, and the site remained waste for two hundred years. Venetian raids on Dalmatia became more and more frequent and more and more effective. In 1116 the Doge Ordelato Falieri captured Šibenik and ordered that that city too be destroyed. But the destruction was not so complete as at Biograd. In a few years the city had revived.

Venice grew stronger and more powerful, especially at sea. The Croatian kingdom, on the other hand, after the personal union of the Croatian and Hungarian crowns, grew weaker. The Hungarians soon became the dominant partner and remained so until after the First World War. Croatian ambitions turned landward and continental Zagreb became their capital. Dalmatia became a frontier province, more and more dependent on a few powerful feudal lords, such as those of the Šubić (Zrinjski) and Frankopan families.

Zadar, which had been a faithful ally of Venice in the earlier naval wars against the Croats, was now the most powerful city in Dalmatia (Dubrovnik was an independent republic). It was under Croatian–Hungarian rule. An old French chronicler reports the Doge as saying, at the start of the Fourth Crusade: "The King of Hungary has taken away from us Zadar in the land of the Slavs, one of the best fortified places in the world. We shall never recapture it with our own forces." He, the Doge, therefore proposed that the Crusaders on their way to the Holy Land should first conquer Zadar and hand it over to Venice in payment of their debts to the Most Serene Republic. The fight was a bitter one. After it, not enough people were left alive in the city to bury the dead.

Venice had achieved her aim. She was now the most powerful force in the eastern Adriatic. But she still had powerful enemies to contend with. These were the sea-raiders of Omiš and other Dalmatian cities, regarded by the western nations as pirates and by the Slavs as upholders of their ancient tradition. They had staunch supporters even in metropolitan Split. In 1180 they murdered the Archbishop of Split, Raineri, in a dispute over land tenure. The Pope joined with the Croatian–Hungarian king in a war against "the impious Kačići, those most bitter enemies of Christ". It had little effect.

It is probable that this war had a religious as well as a commercial and political reason. Behind the mountains, in the hinterland of Bosnia and Hercegovina, the heretic sect of the Bogumils ("Those dear to God") had become exceedingly powerful. Its tenets and development are marginal to the history of Dalmatia, but it had many adherents or sympathizers there, possibly including the Kačići who at best were luke-warm Catholics. The sect started in Bulgaria, was powerful in Macedonia and became an organized state and semi-organized church in Bosnia. Its influence spread far to the west; the Patareni of Milan adopted the Bogumil creed, as also the Albigenses of southern France. It greatly influenced the Lollards in England. The Bogumils preached a sort of Manichaeanism, an eternal struggle between the equally powerful principles of good and evil, one spiritual and bodiless, the other bodily and visible. They rejected all church administration, though in fact they were compelled to create one, and the Cathari or Pure Ones rejected the visible world and all its manifestations, including marriage. Those who could not aspire to perfect purity could be reconciled or 'consoled' before death to the spirit of good. Despite these beliefs there were among them able administrators and formidable warriors.

They were regarded as heretics both by the Roman Church and the Orthodox Church. Thus most of what we know of them we know only from their enemies who accused them of every possible theological error and natural or unnatural vice. Our word 'bugger' originally meant a Bulgarian heretic, i.e. a Bogumil.

Association with the Hungarian crown meant the rapid disintegration of the old Croatian tribal tradition (a similar tradition was maintained much longer among the Serbs and Montenegrins) and the adoption of the feudal system with its strict gradation of classes. This led at first to popular revolts. There were risings of the common people in Trogir, Šibenik, and Split. The most violent and successful was at Hvar (1510–14). About six thousand peasants besieged and took the city, killing many of the nobles. The revolt was only put down by the aid of a punitive expedition from Venice led by Vicenzo Capello.

Split too was rebellious. There were constant uprisings, some of which were aided by the Kačići. Some of the dukes of Split appear to have been tainted with Bogumilism, and religious strife was added to civil strife.

A curious side-effect of Bogumilism was the development of the slave trade. This inhuman practice, generally alien to the Slav temperament, was mainly directed against the Bogumils who, being heretics, were considered beyond the pale of normal consideration. Slave lists are still extant, with names and prices; a large proportion of the slaves were young women. There were slave markets in Venice, in Dubrovnik and in other Dalmatian cities. The slaves were sent to many parts of Italy, to Spain, and North Africa. But it is to the credit of the Dalmatian cities, especially Dubrovnik, that this trade was soon abolished, many years before the more profitable trade in African slaves was abolished in western Europe (in Dubrovnik its worst excesses were modified in 1312 and it was finally abolished in 1416).

Another scourge, which only slightly effected Dalmatia, was the Mongol invasions of the 13th century. These ruthless horsemen were more at home in the vast central European plains and the appearances of their armies on the coast were usually forays in search of booty or in pursuit of some fugitive. Such a fugitive was the Hungarian King Bela IV. The king first sought refuge at Split but, evidently not feeling safe there, fled to Trogir. Still fearful, he moved to the island of Čiovo. But the Mongol horsemen were not experienced in the subjugation of fortified cities and were too far from their base to obtain supplies and reinforcements. Split, Trogir, and Klis held out and the Mongol forces withdrew into Russia when they got the news of the death of Ogudai, their leader.

The Mongol forays were not intended as a conquest. They were little more than devastating raids in search of booty and vengeance. But the skirmishes between the Croatians and the Venetians continued. Many cities changed sides, some by conquest, some by purchase. Finally, in 1409, Venice purchased for a hundred thousand ducats all the sea-coast estates of Ladislas of Naples, one of the pretenders to the Croatian–Hungarian throne. They included Zadar, Vrana, Novigrad, and Pag.

Venice now had a stranglehold on the eastern Adriatic, though she had still to break the opposition of many of the cities—Kotor, Split, Trogir, and Omiš—and several of the island strongholds—on Brač, Hvar, Vis, and Korčula. Venice had by far the most powerful navy in the Adriatic and by the end of the century almost all the Dalmatian cities were subject to her. In the north a few cities still held out, the most important of which was the pirate stronghold of Senj. The Republic of Dubrovnik (Ragusa) kept its independence.

With the exception of Senj and Dubrovnik the history of Dalmatia now becomes a part of the history of Venice. It was a period of political stagnation but artistic exuberance which lasted until the fall of Venice in 1797. In all the Istrian and Dalmatian cities (except Senj) the victorious Lion of St Mark can still be seen on all the more important state and municipal buildings. It was often placed on buildings built earlier by the Croatians, as at Split. Only in a few rare cases was that amiable animal with its peaceful message replaced by a more ferocious beast with a harsher message aimed at rebellious subjects, or with its book closed; for example at Trogir and Piran.

Venetian artists, architects, and engineers came to Dalmatia and impressed on the cities the outward veneer of Venetian civilization; but it was a two-way infiltration. There were many well-known Italian painters of Dalmatian origin. Usually they can be identified by the sobriquet Schiavone (Slav). Carpaccio, perhaps the greatest of the Venetian painters, probably came from Istria. But as far as we know he was not a Slav.

Dalmatia under the Venetians. The ignominious purchase of Dalmatia by the Venetians had certain material advantages for the coastal cities. It put an end to the continual faction fights and shifting allegiances of parties supporting Croatian, Hungarian, and Venetian claims. It was also a period of artistic renaissance. But the cities retained a certain amount of local independence and consequently of local patriotism. Only one threat continually lowered over Dalmatia—the menace of the Turks, who swallowed up the Slav states of the Balkans one by one, ending with the total subjection of Bosnia in 1463. The Bosnian nobles, most of whom were Bogumils, accepted Islam; and a vigorous and warlike Moslem power, filled with the zeal of the newly-converted, hovered on the Dalmatian borders and not infrequently made successful raids on the sea-coast. The Dalmatian cities were always conscious of this menace and were only granted respite by the Turkish invasion and conquest of Hungary. None the less, in 1540, almost all Dalmatia except the cities and the Ragusan republic was under Turkish overlordship.

By the 17th century the tide of Turkish power was beginning to ebb. Kara Mustafa was thrown back from the walls of Vienna and internal maladministration weakened the central power at Constantinople. The Treaty of Požarevac (Passarovitz) in 1718 confirmed Venetian possession of Dalmatia. From that time until the fall of the Venetian republic in 1797 Dalmatia shared in the torpor that affected Venice herself.

During this period of internal peace and Turkish menace two events took place which were important for the history of Dalmatia. In 1618 the city of Senj was captured, the Uskok ships destroyed and the Uskoks themselves forcibly transported inland to Karlovac, where they became part of the Austrian Military Frontiers, a defence line against the Bosnian Moslems. The other event was that the mass of refugees from the Turkish raids on the countryside soon made Croatian the common speech of the cities and completed their Slavization. Indeed, even the defence of the Dalmatian cities was entrusted to Croatian rather than Venetian troops, and as early as 1574 the Venetian representative at Split wrote to the Signoria at Venice: "The principal defence of their own country ought to be committed to those brave people who verily have no care for their own lives against the Turks, but set on them like mad bulls; and truth compels me to say (albeit with grief) that we have been vanquished in more than one important skirmish through the cowardice of the Italian infantry."

Dubrovnik. Dubrovnik, known throughout the Middle Ages as Ragusa, was originally settled by refugees from Epidaurus across the bay after the Slav invasions. The memory of this event is kept alive by place-names; in Serbo-Croat Epidaurus is Cavtat (Civitas Vetus—the old city) and in Italian it is still known as Ragusa Vecchia (Old Ragusa). Its romantic history is also enshrined in an English word—argosy. Today this word is used in poetry as a treasure-ship of valiant merchant-adventurers. Originally it simply meant 'a ship of Ragusa' (Dubrovnik).

The new settlement was in two parts, divided by a shallow creek, now filled in, which has become the main street of the city, the Stradun. On the one side was the ancient Romanized city of Ragusa and on the other the Slav settlement of Dubrovnik. The two grew side by side, but did not begin to merge until the end of the 13th century when for the first time Slav names appear in the roll of the nobility, mainly those of women. The two settlements were enclosed within a single system of fortifications in 1272. By the 15th century the city was almost Slavized and the nobles used two names, one Latin or Italian, the other Slav. It was still known as Ragusa. After the disasters of 1667 the name Dubrovnik came into common use.

At first Dubrovnik was nominally subject to a foreign overlord—Byzantium or Venice. But the Byzantine *strategos* lived in Zadar and the Venetian *podestà* was by choice of the citizens themselves, to avoid internal faction fights. The city was well able to fend off an attack by the Arabs without outside aid. In alliance with the great Venetian Doge Pietro Orseolo it drove off a Croatian attack in A.D. 1000.

But the Dubrovnik nobles were not great warriors. Their city was too small and their enemies too numerous. Also they lived for trade, and war is bad for trade. They became bold merchants and consummate diplomats. By the late 13th century Dubrovnik was signing treaties with great, if transient, empires in the name of the republic. It was on friendly terms with the powerful Bulgarian Tsar Michael Asen (1252) and later with the Serbian Nemanja dynasty.

Dubrovnik developed into a republic controlled by an oligarchy. The nobles, almost all of them merchants, held absolute power. Neither Venetian *podestà* nor Ragusan Rector in the days of complete independence had any real power. Never was any outsider allowed to interfere in internal affairs. The power was always in the hands of the Council of Nobles. Its executive instrument was the Minor Council.

Dubrovnik's great test of diplomatic skill was at the time of the Turkish invasion of the Balkans. What remained of the Serbian Empire was practically destroyed at the battle of Kosovo in 1389. The Serbian Despotate existed for another half-century, but the Despot himself, George Branković, had to flee to Dubrovnik as a suppliant. The Turkish sultan, Murad II, ordered him to be handed over. The Minor Council replied: "We men of Dubrovnik have nothing but our faith and, by our faith, we would have acted towards you in the same way had you come hither."

However, while proudly upholding their civic liberties, the nobles of Dubrovnik concluded two treaties, one, as a sort of insurance, with the distant king of Hungary, the other with the Turkish sultan. They realized that the Ottoman Empire had come to stay and that it would shortly become the most powerful state in Europe. So when the Turks finally conquered the Balkans, Dubrovnik was an ally and not an enemy. Her merchants had a near monopoly of trade between the Turkish Empire and the rest of Europe, and the Dubrovnik merchants had their privileged caravanserais in Skopje, Sofia, Belgrade and many other cities. It is true that Dubrovnik had to pay the sultan a form of tribute, but the Dubrovnik nobles considered it as a sort of tax on trade and the annual tribute caravan was almost like a triumphal procession. No Turkish officials ever lived within the city walls.

As long as the Turkish state was expanding and victorious the traders of Dubrovnik did well. But when the long centuries of Turkish decline set in, Dubrovnik too had her troubles. Venice became a more and more jealous rival. In 1520 there was an earthquake and in 1527 a serious visitation of the plague. The decisive blow came in the next century, on Easter Day 1667. A terrific earthquake shook the city, The walls were broken. More than two-thirds of the inhabitants were killed. Bands of looters and brigands added to the confusion. The few remaining nobles guarded the treasury, sword in hand. Few of the city's buildings remained intact. The great cathedral, built partly with funds provided by a grateful refugee, Richard Coeur-de-Lion, King of England, was destroyed. The treasury was depleted to rebuild the city.

Thenceforward the city became almost purely Slav. Indeed it became the centre and source of Croatian literature. New citizens were brought in from the surrounding villages and islands. Slav names became more and more frequent in the roll of the nobles.

Then came the worst crisis in Dubrovnik history. The Turkish Grand Vizier, Kara Mustafa, intent on his dream of conquering Vienna, demanded double tribute. In case of refusal, the Pasha of Bosnia was ordered to make war on the Republic. Four nobles volunteered to go and appease the Grand Vizier and the Pasha. The mission meant almost certain death.

Marojica Gozze-Gučetić and Nikola Bona were to go to the Pasha, Marojica Kaboga and Djura Bućić to the Vizier. Those who went to the Vizier were at once thrown into prison, whence they did not emerge until the arrival of the tribute caravan in the following year. Those who went to the Pasha were sent to the Ottoman armies in the Danube delta. Bona died there of fever, but Gučetić managed to survive. But in the meantime the Ottoman armies were defeated before Vienna and Kara Mustafa sentenced to the bowstring. Gučetić was then able to return. The usual figure of the tribute was maintained.

The city was rebuilt and continued to trade profitably for another century. But it was now too small and too weak to compete with the great states of Europe. Of the great city-states only Venice survived. Dubrovnik was now a little city, weak and divided by faction. It was in no state to defend itself against Napoleon's marshals in 1806. On New Year's Day 1808 Marshal Marmont, ironically created Duc de Raguse, seated himself beside the last Rector, Sabo Georgić, and declared the ancient republic at an end.

A last few flickers of independence flared up in Austro-Hungarian times but were quickly suppressed. Proud Dubrovnik became a sleepy, decaying and out-of-the-way provincial town, only to reawaken under Yugoslav rule as a city of beauty, history, and art.

The Boka and the Montenegrins. South of Dubrovnik the people change and the history changes also. Until the 15th century, when the fjord of the Boka became a Venetian lake, Venice enters little into its history. Before that time the main influences were Byzantine and Serbian. Kotor was the chief seaport of the Slav state of Zeta, ancestor of Montenegro. It was on close and friendly terms with the greatest of the Serbian emperors, Stefan Dušan the Mighty, who referred to the city as "our most loyal, well-beloved and glorious". The greatest of Serbian churchmen and diplomatists, St Sava, founded monasteries in the Boka. Even today the people of the Boka are of mixed creed, Catholic and Orthodox. As befits a people of seafarers, religious controversy was less bitter. There were, and are, churches with one Catholic and one Orthodox altar under the same roof.

In Venetian times too the Boka was distinct from Dalmatia. Kotor became the seat of the Grande Provveditore of the Venetian province of Albania. In it were several small but rich merchant cities. Some, like Kotor, still exist; others, like Perast, are in ruins with only a few fishermen living in the walls of former marble palaces.

The men of the Boka were famous as skilful and daring master-mariners and pilots. At the famous battle of Lepanto in 1571 the pilots of the Venetian galleys were the men of Perast.

For a time the Boka was in Spanish hands and the fortress above Hercegnovi is still known as the Spagnuola.

South of the Boka and as far as the Albanian frontier the physical and historical scene once more changes. There are no more islands and the coastline is open, backed by rugged mountains. The people are Monte-negrins (with a few Albanians, especially at Ulcinj). All through the Middle Ages they had a sort of tribal independence, overawed by the ancient fortified city of Budva. There was a constant effort to unite with the Montenegrins but the great powers, Byzantium, Venice, Turkey, and later Austria-Hungary, were unwilling to let the Montenegrins come down to the sea-coast and for most of the time the frontier, still studded with castles, ran along the mountain ranges, in sight of but cut off from the sea. The little peasant republics maintained a remarkable degree of independence in internal affairs, but had to rely on some more powerful external protector, usually Venice. The most important of these was the republic of the Paštrovići, whose descendants still retain a great tribal pride.

Only in comparatively recent times did the Montenegrins manage to get a foothold on the coast. In 1878 they took Bar, now the main sea-port of southern Yugoslavia. The old city of Bar was almost destroyed; what remains of it (Stari Bar) is a romantic contrast to the present busy port.

The southernmost port on the Yugoslav Adriatic, Ulcinj, has a dis-tinct history of its own. Originally a city of the Montenegrin–Albanian princes (the Balšići and others), it was conquered by the corsairs of the Barbary coast and became a Moslem pirates' nest. The remains of their mosques can still be seen in the ruined Balšić citadel (rather reminiscent of a battered Dubrovnik) and until just before the Second World War there was a considerable colony of Serbian- and Albanian-speaking negroes, descendants of the corsairs' slaves.

A century of stagnation. The Congress of Vienna, which rearranged the map of Europe after the battle of the Nations and the internment of Napoleon on the island of Elba, granted Dalmatia and Istria to the Austro-Hungarian monarchy. The grant included the lands of the Re-public of Dubrovnik. Kotor and Pula became Austro-Hungarian naval bases. Dalmatia sank into an uneasy sleep.

However, much was happening in the rest of Yugoslavia (for although Yugoslavia as such was not to exist for another century the idea of Yugoslavia now became an important factor). Two events in particular were of crucial importance. The first was the emergence of Serbia as an independent state after the insurrection against the Turks, though un-fortunately bedevilled by dynastic quarrels between the families of Obre-nović and Karageorgević. This meant that the Yugoslavs now had an independent state of their own, which gave coherence and hope to the idea of a union of the South Slav (Yugoslav) peoples.

Almost as important, though less dramatic, was the unification of the Yugoslav literary language by a group of scholars, of whom the most important was Vuk Stefan Karadžić. The various local dialects con-tinued to exist but there was now a single flexible and comprehensible means of easy communication for almost all Yugoslavs akin to modern Serbo-Croat. The Slovenes, however, retained their separate language. The Macedonian dialect, differing grammatically from Serbo-Croat, but close enough to it for mutual comprehension, became a fully developed literary language only in the present century.

The second great event was the creation of a literary and political common Yugoslav front. The history of this is outside the scope of this essay, although Dalmatians took a leading part in it. First known as the Illyrian Movement it later adopted the term Yugoslav. One of its greatest figures was the Croat bishop of Djakovo, Josip Juraj Štrosmajer, a great churchman but also a great patriot. It was he who founded the Yugoslav Academy of Sciences at Zagreb. He even toyed with the idea of a rebirth of the ancient Croatian Church.

The events of the revolutionary upheavals of 1848 were, at first, disastrous for Croats and Serbs alike (for not all the Serbs were in Serbia; many were in the Austro-Hungarian Empire). The Hungarians, it is true, won their battle for their national ideals, at least for a time. But the Croats and Serbs learnt by bitter experience that nothing could be won from Vienna. They would have to rely on themselves alone.

Yugoslav societies were formed throughout the Yugoslav lands; sometimes they were idealistic and literary, sometimes revolutionary. It was the members of one such society, Mlada Bosna (Young Bosnia), who organized the assassination of the Austrian Archduke Franz Ferdinand at Sarajevo in July 1914 which led to the First World War. It is little wonder that the man who fired the shots, Gavrilo Princip, has become a national hero.

The Yugoslav movement aroused first the suspicion and then the organized hostility of the Austro-Hungarian authorities. Repression became the order of the day and the Slav districts of the Dual Empire became a police state, its full rigour only modified by its comparative inefficiency.

One immediate effect of this, as far as Dalmatia was concerned, was official encouragement of the Italian minority and the Italian language. The authorities in Vienna liked the Italians no better than the Slavs (the police régime in Austrian Italy was even harsher than in Dalmatia), but the Italians were less of a political risk and, above all, there were not so many of them. Aided by the visible memorials of Venetian rule, the Austrians did everything possible to encourage the idea that Dalmatia was Italian and for many years they were moderately successful. It has taken the present century to redress the balance.

First World War. Save for naval skirmishes in the Adriatic, Istria and Dalmatia were not greatly involved in the devastation of the First World War. After the initial victories of the Serbs, the Serbian armies were forced to retreat through the then roadless mountains of Albania. They were rallied on the island of Corfù and finally made their victorious return through Salonika and what Churchill called the 'soft underbelly' of the Balkans.

But in the meantime Yugoslav political action went on. Thousands of Yugoslav soldiers serving in the Austrian armies deserted and joined their kinsmen in Serbia or in Russia and fought against the hated Austrians. Treason and sabotage, now become patriotic, were the order of the day. Croat politicians were able to join the Serbian king and the

Serbian armies on Corfù and on 20 July 1917 a declaration was signed there envisaging the creation, after the war, of a Kingdom of the Serbs, Croats and Slovenes (SHS). It came into being on 4 December 1918. King Alexander changed the name to Yugoslavia in 1929.

Between the World Wars. The decision had been taken to form a unified state of Serbs, Croats, and Slovenes. But it was far more difficult to put into practice. For one thing, Istria and a large part of Dalmatia had been promised to the Italians in 1915 as a reward for their participation in the war. This, however, cut right across President Wilson's demand for the self-determination of peoples. There could be no possible doubt that Dalmatia was Slav. When the Italian armies tried to enter Yugoslav territory to take what they claimed to have been promised them by treaty, there was no force to oppose them save the Serbian armies. Moreover, the only organized administration available was the Serbian one. Inevitably, it had to take to control. Equally inevitably it aroused opposition among the Croats. It was one of the causes of the hostility and rivalry that bedevilled the internal politics of Yugoslavia for thirty years.

As far as Istria and Dalmatia were concerned the peace created an uneasy compromise pregnant with trouble for the future. In Istria, it is true, the Italian minority was larger than in Dalmatia but it was still a minority. Istria was given to Italy and the *condottiere* exploits of D'Annunzio for a time focused world attention on Rijeka (Fiume). In Dalmatia the Italians retained an enclave at Zadar (Zara) and control over some of the islands. These prospered, not because of their administration but, in the old Dalmatian tradition, as highly competent smugglers' bases.

There were occasional flare-ups in the Yugoslav coastal cities, mostly caused by changes in policy and administration sponsored by Belgrade. But, broadly speaking, the tribal rivalry of Serbs and Croats affected them little. They developed a mercantile marine and a small, but efficient, navy. In Slovenia there was a constant ferment, since large numbers of Slovenes (and, for that matter, Croats) had remained under Italian rule in Istria and Venezia Giulia. They suffered many restrictions and privations, especially after Italy came under fascist rule.

Thus at the beginning of the Second World War Yugoslavia was politically in a sorry condition. The Serbo-Croat dispute had been settled, at least on paper, but the slackening of internal tension came too late. Externally the country was almost surrounded by enemies. The army, though courageous, was badly led and was still suffering from tribal dissensions. In April 1941 Hitler ordered the bombing of Belgrade, followed by invasion. Organized resistance ceased within a fortnight.

All Yugoslavia's enemies took advantage of her collapse. Slovenia and parts of Dalmatia were shared out between Italy and Germany. Bulgaria annexed a large slice of Macedonia. The rich farmlands of the north had a mixed German–Hungarian administration. Albania, with Italian assistance, claimed the province of Kosovo where there is a large Albanian minority. In Montenegro the Italians tried to set up an independent state under the Petrović–Njegoš dynasty (of which the Italian queen was a member). In Croatia the anti-Serb extremists seized power under Ante Pavelić, who had been involved in the murder of King Alexander of Yugoslavia at Marseilles in 1934.

Second World War: The Resistance. Resistance movements sprang up everywhere. Two of them became nation-wide and of great importance. One, the Četniks, was led by an army officer, Draža Mihailović, and was at first regarded as the more important. Draža was supported by the Allies and by the Yugoslav government-in-exile in London. But his movement was too Serbian nationalist in spirit and was regarded with hostility and suspicion by all the other Yugoslav peoples, especially the Croats. The other movement, the Partisans, was mainly organized by the communist party. Its leader was Josip Broz Tito. It had the great advantage of being unconnected with any specific nationalist interest. It was open to Serbs, Croats, and Slovenes alike. Tito himself is a Croat; many of his principal lieutenants were Serbs, Slovenes, and Macedonians.

Yugoslavia was in the unhappy position of having two hostile resistance movements facing at least four enemy armies: the Germans, the Italians, the Bulgarians, and the Ustaša-Croatians.

Various attempts were made to get the two movements to unite, but the hostility and suspicion between them was too great. It soon became clear that the Četnik movement was sporadic, inefficient, and without cohesion. Indeed, many of Draža's regional leaders made private pacts with the enemy, often against the Partisans. It ceased to have much value as a military force. On the other hand the Partisans, despite some serious reverses at first, rapidly developed their fighting forces and soon controlled large areas of the country, especially in Bosnia. Furthermore, they were actively and continuously fighting the enemy. Allied assistance was transferred from the Četniks to the Partisans and a military mission was sent to Marshal Tito's headquarters during the great battle for the crossing of the R. Neretva in May 1943. After the Allied invasion of Italy, the British set up supply depots to aid the Partisans, at Bari and on the Dalmatian island of Vis.

In Bosnia, after some striking Partisan victories, the plan for a new Yugoslavia was drawn up at Jajce in 1943 by the AVNOJ (Antifascist Council of the National Liberation of Yugoslavia).

Immediately after the war the military rivalry between Četniks and Partisans was transferred to the political field. Prolonged and acrimonious discussions took place between the Yugoslav government-in-exile in London and the Communist administration in Yugoslavia. The Communist administration triumphed. King Peter II was not permitted to return to the country and the Federal Democratic People's Republic of Yugoslavia was proclaimed (later the word 'Democratic' was dropped, leaving the present FNRJ).

There is little point in pursuing Yugoslav history any further, since what remains must be well known to any reader of the newspapers. But there are two things to be remembered. One is that the Yugoslavs liberated themselves. It is true that they received help in the west from the Allies and in the east from the Soviet armies, but they created their own army and fought their own battles. This makes it easier to understand the independent attitude of Yugoslavia in recent years, particularly towards the Soviet Union, and her present role as one of the leaders of the group of uncommitted nations. The other point concerns the revision of the western Yugoslav frontiers. Yugoslavia obtained Istria and certain areas in Venezia Giulia; she also obtained the enclave of Zadar and the islands formerly occupied by the Italians. The frontier is now, ethnologically speaking, as just as it is possible to be. Let us hope that the wars, rebellions, intrigues and treacheries of more than three thousand years of history have at last come to an end.

ISTRIA AND DALMATIA: ART AND ARCHITECTURE
by BERNARD COX

The historical and geographical background already described is the key to an understanding of the artistic heritage of the Adriatic coast of Yugoslavia. The common tendency to adopt a condescending attitude towards all the Balkan countries except Greece can only be sustained by a very short-sighted view of history; in the late Classical and Early Christian eras they were near the centre of the civilized world, on the crossroads between Rome, Athens, and Constantinople. Despite the vicissitudes and fragmentation which followed the break-up of the Roman Empire, Classical traditions survived in the coastal city-states nourished by continuing contact with Italy. During late Medieval and Renaissance times they shared in the wealth and artistic flowering of Venice. It was only from the 17th century onwards, with the decay of Venice, the Turkish menace and Habsburg rule, that a decline set in.

Dalmatia and Istria are formed of limestone. The stone of Brač was used for Roman buildings throughout Dalmatia and for much of Venice. With such a material to hand, it is not surprising that architecture and sculpture are the dominant arts. Painting is never as important as in medieval Serbia and Macedonia, which followed the Byzantine tradition in preferring painting to any three-dimensional form of decoration. An exception is the Montenegrin coast, which is culturally linked with Serbia but remote from the main artistic centres.

The unique works of art of the Yugoslav Adriatic coast are not individual monuments but complete cities. The siting and shape of the city may well be Greek, as at Trogir and Korčula, and the layout of streets is often Roman, as at Split, Zadar, and Poreč (where even the Roman street names are retained), while the pattern of Medieval and Renaissance planning is either superimposed, as at Split, or forms the basic layout of the city, as is clearly seen at Dubrovnik. Each of these cities still has a central core free of vehicular traffic and rich in old houses, some even Romanesque and many Gothic, Renaissance, or Baroque. The houses are built and the streets are paved with the same stone. Towns on the islands are smaller but still less altered by modern accretions.

The region also has much to offer of ethnographical interest and in vernacular domestic architecture, though these are beyond the scope of this essay.

Greek and Roman. Greek reliefs have been found at Trogir, and pottery was imported from Greece and later from Magna Graecia. But the Greek imprint is most apparent in the characteristic siting of such towns as Trogir, Korčula, and Cavtat.

The Roman period is of prime importance and has left not only the remains of a string of Roman towns from the Italian frontier to Split, but also a lasting effect on the art of later centuries. The chief Roman towns of Istria, Pietas Julia (Pula), and of Dalmatia, Salona (Solin), met with very different fates. Pula has been continuously built over and retains remarkably intact monuments in an urban setting, while Solin was destroyed by the Avars and Slavs in the 7th century and is now an archaeological site in open fields. The Roman amphitheatre is still the most prominent structure in Pula, although only the external walls are standing. Of the twin temples of Augustus and Rome, one has been enclosed in later buildings but the other is among the best preserved of Roman temples, tall and narrow, with refined Corinthian capitals and entablature. The Sergii arch is also Corinthian and of modest dimensions, but richly decorated with every device of Roman ornament. Other Roman sites are at Zadar (the recently excavated forum), Poreč, Veli Brion, Osor, Krk, and Nin, and there are mosaic floors *in situ* at Pula and Krk. Roman sculpture can be studied in the museums at Pula, Zadar, and Split, the latter housing the finds from Solin. The realism of Roman sculpture is well illustrated in sarcophagi, and sepulchral and public monuments. Many Solin inscriptions are in Greek, and there is evidence of the practice of Eastern religious cults, including Mithraism as well as Christianity, all showing the cosmopolitan nature of the city.

The same mixture of Eastern and Latin elements is repeated in Diocletian's palace at Split. Not only is it unprecedented in Roman architecture, but no other building in Yugoslavia has played such a significant role internationally. Diocletian's palace marks the end of the Classical era of Greece and Rome. The break with Classical rules is most evident in the North or Golden Gate, where blind arcading on colonettes carried on corbels is probably the earliest of its kind, and in the Peristyle, where arches are turned from capital to capital, with no entablature. The only structures remaining intact at street level are the Emperor's mausoleum and the Temple of Jupiter (owing their preservation to Christian use as cathedral and baptistery), but recent excavations in the southern part of the palace have thrown new light on the private and state apartments of Diocletian. Here, owing to the slope of the ground, the main floor was supported by a basement, of which all the walls remain and show the precise plan of what was above it. Running the full length of the façade was the Cryptoporticus, a magnificent gallery directly above the sea, and behind it were ranged a series of rooms of varying size and plan, including basilican halls and others of elaborate shape with internal apses.

Diocletian's palace was a fertile source of inspiration for later buildings. Dalmatian architecture inherited the fine tradition of craftsmanship in stone and a continuing love of the barrel vault and the round arch (especially when placed above a flat lintel, as in the palace gateways). The planning of halls with internal apses is repeated in Croatian pre-Romanesque churches. The Renaissance went further and copied both structure and ornament, as in the coffered barrel vault in a chapel of Trogir cathedral, modelled on the Temple of Jupiter. Famous architects came to Split to study the domestic architecture of the ancients, including Palladio, Fischer von Erlach, and Robert Adam, who spent five weeks recording the palace and in 1764 published his 'Ruins of the Palace of the Emperor Diocletian at Spalatro in Dalmatia', one of the most influential architectural books of the century.

Early Christian and Byzantine. Solin ranks among the few important Early Christian archaeological sites of Europe. The ornamentation of the numerous sarcophagi is essentially Roman, only distinguished by the introduction of Christian symbolism. Architectural remains are principally of basilicas of the 4th to 6th centuries. The one intact Byzantine basilica on the coast is that of Bishop Euphrasius at Poreč, which is contemporary with and in no way inferior to the 6th-century churches of Ravenna. Indeed the Poreč basilica is unique in retaining its atrium, octagonal baptistery, remains of external mosaics, and the original arrangement of the bishop's throne and presbyters' bench in the apse. The apse shows Byzantine decoration at its most opulent, with opus sectile below and mosaics above, culminating in the earliest central placing of the Virgin and Child in the semi-dome of the apse, flanked by angels and saints against a glowing background of gold mosaic.

Pre-Romanesque. After the destruction of Solin, Jadera, the modern Zadar, became the most important town in Dalmatia, and pre-Romanesque and early Romanesque are best studied here. The Croats, who probably came from a region of timber buildings, found a great tradition of stonework and the massive remains of Roman civilization. We know practically nothing of Croatian architecture of the 7th to the 9th centuries and nothing of their domestic buildings, but a surprising number of small churches of the 9th to 11th centuries are scattered along the coast and among the islands. These vary greatly in design, including basilicas and domed cruciform churches of Byzantine type, and others with many internal apses, no doubt derived from Roman examples. The stonework is rough, earlier columns are often incorporated, and the squinch is used instead of the pendentive to support domes and semi-domes; their preservation is due to the use of stone vaulting. All these churches are miniature in size except Sveti Donat at Zadar, a galleried circular building of the same type as San Vitale at Ravenna and Charlemagne's octagon at Aachen. The original Zadar cathedral was also large, a basilica of which the apse was retained in the Romanesque rebuilding. Nin, a Slav outpost which resisted Latin domination until the 15th century, is said to have once had sixteen churches. Of those remaining, Sveti Križ (9th or, more probably, 11th century) is well-preserved and representative, cruciform and with a central dome, very small and roughly built, the three internal apses perhaps suggested by structures from Roman Aenona. The Archaeological Museum at Zadar and the Early Croatian finds at Split give a comprehensive view of the sculptural decoration and furnishing of pre-Romanesque churches. Stonework is carved with the plaited ornament of interwoven bands common to the Mediterranean region at the time, either alone or used to frame figure sculpture in the low relief which had replaced classical forms. One such slab in the baptistery at Split shows an enthroned Croatian ruler.

No doubt the churches had wall paintings, of which one important example has survived at Sveti Mihajlo, a tiny chapel with no less than nine apses, on top of a hill near Ston. The paintings are Byzantine in style with provincial variations, and include figures of saints and the royal donor.

Romanesque. The Roman tradition made Dalmatia receptive to the Romanesque and reluctant to replace it by later styles. Zadar can show Romanesque buildings from around 1100 and at least into the 14th century. The earliest is the Convent of Sveta Marija (which suffered severe war damage). The Romanesque structure of the church is concealed by Baroque plasterwork, but more remarkable is the chapter house, containing the tomb of the Abbess Vekenega, who died in 1111. The barrel-vaulted hall is plain and dignified, and has an undoubted affinity with the Romanesque of Apulia. The same is true of Trogir cathedral, especially the south façade, although T. G. Jackson in his 'Dalmatia, the Quarnero and Istria' (still the best book on its subject) traces a resemblance to Hungarian churches. On the other hand, the two most spectacular Romanesque exteriors at Zadar are decorated with blind arcading on colonettes, immediately recalling the churches of Tuscany; they are the façade of the cathedral, completed very late but the best of its kind in Dalmatia, and the east end of the church of Sveti Krševan, which is not inferior to the best Italian work. No doubt there was an interchange of artists with Italy, in both directions, but research is needed to uncover the historical evidence. The typical Romanesque church is basilican, with nave and two aisles and absidal east end. Rab has both the most spectacular group of Romanesque towers and the finest single tower, that of the cathedral, outstanding for its simple dignity and subtle disposition of windows. Neighbours at Split are the earliest Romanesque campanile—the tiny one perched above the Iron Gate; and the latest—the over-restored bell-tower of the cathedral, built just after 1300 and already Gothic in feeling, although round-arched. Complete Romanesque houses, a rarity anywhere in Europe, are to be found in Split, Trogir, and Poreč.

Trogir and Split have important Romanesque figure sculpture. The earliest is a surprising survival of wood carving from 1214, the doors of Split cathedral. The sculptor was Andrija Buvina, who used the same combination of figure sculpture (New Testament scenes) with plaited ornament as in pre-Romanesque work. There is similar carving on the choir stalls, but with figures from secular life. An inscription below the lunette of the great west doorway of Trogir cathedral gives the date of 1240 and the Croatian name of the master-sculptor, Radovan. Besides a wealth of sculpture in relief, there are large figures in the round, the two lions and, more remarkable, the life-size Adam and Eve, among the earliest nudes since Classical times. Instead of the demons and monsters usual on Romanesque portals, the relief sculptures show scenes from everyday life, acutely observed and portrayed with a realism absent from European art since the Roman sculpture which must have been known to Radovan. At Split, some of the sculpture on the cathedral campanile is attributed to the school of Radovan, but the most aesthetically satisfying of all this work is by the unknown sculptor of the hexagonal pulpit. At Zadar there are traces of 12th-century wall paintings of true Romanesque character, but the 13th century brought a reversion to the Byzantine manner, as in the apse of Sveti Krševan. Istria has wall paintings ranging from the 11th to the 16th century, but the earlier ones are fragmentary.

Gothic. The coastal cities give the impression of a wealth of Gothic architecture, though more through sheer quantity than any striking originality. All of it is late and the emphasis is strongly on secular buildings, indeed the only major ecclesiastical structures are the earlier part of Šibenik cathedral and the fine tower of Trogir cathedral, completed only in 1598. All secular buildings are in the style called Venetian Gothic, though it should be remembered that the whole Adriatic enjoyed great commercial prosperity at the time, many 'Schiavoni' found their way to Venice, and influences penetrating from the East are at the root of Venetian art. The most important single building is the Rector's palace at Dubrovnik, clearly a Dalmatian version of the Doges' palace, although successive rebuildings have left only one Gothic capital of the façade arcade. The near-by Sponza palace also combines Gothic and Renaissance work, and this is characteristic of other cities besides Dubrovnik (where the earthquake of 1667 accounted for extensive reconstruction). Dubrovnik still retains the street plan, greatly admired by modern planners, from this period of her greatest prosperity as an independent state. Koper has an especially fine group of late Gothic buildings. Practically every city still has its municipal loggia, an open hall used for public trials. At Trogir and Zadar the stone table and bench used by the judges are still in place. The palaces of noble families are numerous in the coastal cities and in the district west of Dubrovnik. Among the finest are the Papalić palace (now the town museum) at Split and the Cipiko palace at Trogir, both with arcaded courtyards. Windows with ogee heads and stone balconies are a familiar sight in Koper, Piran, Rab, Šibenik, Trogir, Split, Hvar and many smaller towns.

The favourite type of doorway is flanked by pilasters and has a stone lintel with an arch above, as in Roman times except that the arch is pointed. On the tympanum is carved the arms of the owner, often already Renaissance in character while the form remains Gothic, a manner associated with the foremost Dalmatian architect and sculptor of the 15th century, Juraj Dalmatinac. Dalmatinac was born at Zadar and studied in Venice. The Papalić palace is his work, and other houses in Split and Šibenik are by him or his collaborators. He is seen at his most realistic in the remarkable portrait heads which form a frieze around the apse of Šibenik cathedral. Of two fine altar-pieces he carved at Split, one has been removed to the church at Kaštel Lukšić; the other, in the cathedral, is Gothic in outline and decoration but encloses figure sculpture which foreshadows the Renaissance, especially the highly accomplished Flagellation panel. Among other late Gothic sculptors were two Italians, Bonino da Milano (in Split and Šibenik), and Onofrio de la Cava (in Dubrovnik).

Castles and fortifications are to be seen the length of the coast from Socerb castle, looking down on Trieste, to the Byzantine and Turkish walls of Ulcinj. Most are in ruins and a number are post-medieval, including a rectangular type with corner towers, such as the Nehaj castle

at Senj and the fine 17th-century castle of the Frankopan counts at Kraljevica (one of a whole series built by them in northern Dalmatia). By
far the most important fortifications are those which make Dubrovnik
one of the most impressive walled cities of Europe. The massive walls
and towers vary in date from the 12th century onward, but we see them
today substantially as left when repaired after the 1667 earthquake.
Dubrovnik was also responsible for constructing the complete system of
fortifications at Ston, with walls enclosing both the town and the hill
behind it, an arrangement also to be seen at Kotor and Hvar.

A special feature of the furnishing of Dalmatian churches is the ciborium or baldachino, not often found elsewhere except in Apulia. The
baldachino in Rab cathedral is pre-Romanesque, though altered later.
The 13th-century example at Poreč has mosaics and reused earlier
columns. Those in the cathedrals of Kotor and Trogir have canopies
with diminishing tiers of arcades, still Romanesque in pattern though of
14th century date, not far from contemporary with the splendid Gothic
baldachino in Zadar cathedral. Zadar cathedral also has the best of a
series of 15th-century choir stalls, others being at Poreč, Rab, Cres,
Trogir, Split, and in two of the Zadar churches; all are of similar design
to those in the Frari church at Venice.

The treasuries of Dalmatian churches are rich in precious objects of
gold and silver, ornamented with enamels and jewels. Zadar and Dubrovnik were important centres of the goldsmith's art, and the cathedrals
of these two cities have especially notable collections, both including
reliquaries with Byzantine enamels in later settings. There are reliquaries or other items of great value in the treasuries at Split, Rab,
Trogir, Nin, Korčula, Kotor, and Hvar. The most celebrated single
object is the silver-gilt coffin or ark of Sveti Simun, in the church of the
same name at Zadar, completed in 1380 for the Hungarian Queen
Elisabeth, with reliefs of the saint's life and also of historical events at
Zadar, showing fascinating details of life at the time. Silver-gilt altar-
pieces are preserved at Kotor, Poreč, and Krk.

Late Gothic painters were active at Dubrovnik, Šibenik, Kotor, and
Trogir, one of the most prominent being Blaz Jurjev Trogiranin. Painted
crucifixes, some of earlier date, are found especially at Zadar and Split.
For a Catholic country, Dalmatia is surprisingly rich in icons. There are
many in the Zadar churches, including at least two of the 13th century,
and they show the Byzantine element progressively modified by Italian-
ate influences. Hvar cathedral also has early icons. A large number of
Cretan icons were brought home by the seamen of Korčula. The Boka
of Kotor, always closely associated with Serbia and still partly Orthodox,
produced a late school of icon painters, well represented in the art gallery at Split and best described as Byzantine-Baroque.

At Beram, a typical Istrian hill-top village, the chapel of Sveta Marija
contains the most important late Gothic wall paintings of the coastal
region, which belong to the Austrian or Alpine tradition and are related to other work in Slovenia. They are dated 1470 and signed by
Vincent of Kastav, although the hand of at least one other painter can
be traced. The complete decoration of the nave is preserved and consists mainly of New Testament scenes. Except for Christ and the

Apostles, all figures are shown in contemporary dress and against a background of Istrian life and landscape. Although archaic and unpolished, the paintings have a naïve charm and directness, with a realism new to the Gothic tradition. Similar paintings are in the little Romanesque church at Hrastovlje, up to twenty years later in date and by Ivan of Kastav (probably the son of Vincent). Both at Beram and Hrastovlje the usual Last Judgement is replaced by the more popular Dance of Death.

Gothic to Renaissance. The foremost architects in the Gothic and Renaissance styles were employed in succession on the building of Šibenik cathedral. Juraj Dalmatinac was responsible for the lower part of the building and the apses, and may have designed the vaults and dome, though their construction was undertaken by Nikola Firentinac (Nicholas of Florence), who had worked under Dalmatinac and took charge of the work after his death in 1475. Firentinac, a pupil of Donatello, introduced the full Renaissance style to Dalmatia and was its most accomplished exponent. There is no architecture on the coast which can rival the modelling of the exterior at Šibenik, with the great curves of the barrel vaults building up to the dome at the apex of the crossing. Using no material but the stone of Dalmatia, it epitomises the essential spirit of building throughout the region.

Renaissance architecture and sculpture were readily accepted, though no other work is on the same scale as at Šibenik. The chapel of the Blessed Ivan Ursini at Trogir cathedral, for which Firentinac was the main architect and sculptor, is a work of the highest quality. It has a vault of Roman inspiration and richly decorated walls with free-standing statues in niches. The baptistery, by Andrija Aleši, shares the same purity of Renaissance detail in stonework. The rounded gable and wheel-window of Šibenik cathedral were repeated in a series of smaller façades, such as that of Sveti Spas, Dubrovnik. Renaissance motifs are seen in many secular buildings, used in a very free manner.

In the 15th and 16th centuries artists were continually crossing the Adriatic in both directions. It is believed that the Carpacci brothers were of Istrian origin; the sculptor Ivan Duknović, of Trogir, and the architect Lucijan Laurana, of Zadar, undertook important commissions in Italy. There is hardly a painter of the Venetian school, from Gentile Bellini to Tiepolo, to whom paintings are not attributed in Istria or Dalmatia. Most of the attributions are suspect, and there is no painting which can rank among the masterpieces of Venetian art. A more interesting study is the work of native schools, of which the most important was at Dubrovnik, with others at Kotor, Šibenik, and Trogir. The leading Dubrovnik painters were Nikola Božidarević and Mihajlo Hamzić (a pupil of Mantegna), whose work can be seen in the Dominican church and the art gallery.

Mannerist and Baroque. From the 16th century onwards Italian artists are increasingly predominant. The distinguished Mannerist architect Michele Sammichele was employed by Venice in the building of fortifications to repel the Turks, and he designed the Land Gate at Zadar in the same rusticated Doric as the gates of Verona. Baroque altar-pieces are numerous, looking ill-at-ease in Dalmatian interiors, and stucco was introduced for the first time. Dubrovnik has many Baroque buildings. The two main churches are by Italian architects, the cathedral essentially Roman Baroque and Sveti Vlaho Venetian. But the most authentic interpretation of the Baroque spirit is the stairway known as Uz Jezuite, leading up to the church of St Ignatius and reminiscent of Sta Trinità dei Monti in Rome. Baroque is most at home in Dalmatia when assimilated into the vernacular idiom, in stone doorways and balconies. There are many of these in such places as on the Boka of Kotor, which had a period of maritime prosperity in the 17th and 18th centuries. Perast is largely a Baroque town and was the birthplace of the painter Tripo Kokolja. But much Baroque painting is by Italians, the most notable being Jacopo Palma the Younger, whose many pictures in Dalmatia stand out from the generally mediocre standard. Except for minor secular work, sculpture is also mainly by Italians.

19th and 20th centuries. The stagnation of the 18th and 19th centuries was not an ummitigated evil, for it at least saved the centres of the maritime cities from the unsightly rebuilding which has spoiled so many historic towns. An exception is Rijeka, the largest town on the coast, which began to grow from a small medieval core in the 18th century. For the most part, 19th-century art and architecture shows a dependence on the main European schools. Paintings of the Classical and Romantic epochs are influenced by Vienna and Munich, but those later in the century follow the successive developments of the school of Paris. The art gallery at Split has a representative collection of works by the best Dalmatian painters of the late 19th and early 20th centuries. Among artists worthy of special note are Celestin Medović (1857–1920), a talented painter of academic subjects, and Emmanuel Vidović (1870–1953), who applies sure and sensitive handling of sombre colours to paintings of his native Split and neighbourhood.

Ivan Meštrović (1883–1962), the only Yugoslav artist who has achieved a world-wide reputation, was born in Dalmatia, and that he should be a sculptor is in the tradition of his native soil. He was an artist of great versatility, at home in stone, bronze, or wood. His earlier work shows the influence of Rodin, to be followed by a patriotic phase in which he sculptured large-scale figures from South Slav history and folklore. With the political achievement of national unity he turned to less heroic themes, some religious but all marked by symbolism and never far removed from the monumental. The well-known Grgur Ninski is the largest of several figures standing in the open at Split, and the full range of his work is displayed at his own villa, now the Meštrović gallery. The architecture of the house itself (and of the Račić mausoleum at Cavtat) falls short of his essential genius as a sculptor, which is exemplified at its most moving in twenty-eight reliefs of the Life of Christ, carved in walnut on the walls of the Kaštelet chapel. Meštrović was the dominating but not the only figure in a revival of sculpture in the first half of the 20th century. Toma Rosandić, another leading sculptor from Split, worked in a more romantic vein, as at the Petrinović mausoleum at Supetar, and shows a special mastery of carving in wood.

Liberation after the Second World War introduced a short-lived phase of Socialist Realism, seen in some Partisan memorials, to be followed by a reversion to symbolic and abstract compositions. From its revival at the end of the 19th century, painting has continued in line with modern trends, possibly because of its affinity with France. Soviet formalism has left hardly a mark on Yugoslav architecture, which is unmistakably modern and international. The skyline of Split has been transformed by tall buildings to serve the needs of industry and housing, but planning controls have been applied wisely to the centre around Diocletian's palace. Zadar has been faced with major rebuilding after war damage, but all tall blocks have been excluded from the island site of the old town, where the new buildings are well in scale though economic stringency has limited the materials used. In 1967 the setting up of a planning commission with wide powers to control future development of the Southern Dalmatian and Montenegrin coastline was a cause of great satisfaction to all who realize the wisdom of conserving this priceless asset. It is to be hoped that money will also be found to halt the dilapidation which threatens many fine buildings in towns which do not share the prosperity brought by industry or tourism.

PRACTICAL INFORMATION

I APPROACHES TO THE YUGOSLAV COAST

The eastern Adriatic shore may be reached directly from Britain at relatively few points. By air there are direct scheduled services (in summer only) to Dubrovnik, though there are connections viâ Zagreb all the year round (but not every day) to both Dubrovnik and Split. Split may be reached direct by train (through coaches) from Ostend (Tauern Express). The most agreeable way to arrive is by steamer from Venice from which the international service calls at main ports between Rijeka and Bar. By car, entry can be made from Austria by several mountain passes, or having traversed the Alps into Italy, from Trieste without recourse to further mountain roads. The farthest point attainable by car-sleeper express (from Ostend) is Ljubljana. Alternatively the coast may be approached across the Adriatic from farther s. in Italy by car-ferry from Ancona to Zadar, from Pescara to Split, or from Bari to Dubrovnik or Bar.

Travellers who wish to save the bother of making their own reservations will be advised to do so through a **Travel Agent,** choosing a reputable member of the Association of British Travel Agents. These organizations, for a small fee, obtain travel tickets, make hotel reservations, deal with the problems of visas, V-forms, and foreign currency, and, if desired, arrange tours for individuals or parties. A selection of agents in London is given below; several of them have branches in other towns.

Thomas Cook & Son, 45 Berkeley St., W.1, and many branches; *American Express*, 6 Haymarket, S.W.1, 89 Mount St., W.1; *Dean & Dawson*, 81 Piccadilly, W.1; *Frames' Tours*, 25 Tavistock Place, W.C.1, 42 Albemarle St., W.1, 80 Southampton Row, W.C.1, etc; *Global Tours*, 318 High Holborn, W.C.1, 191 Regent St., W.1, etc; *Poly Travel Ltd*, 40 Edgware Rd., W.2, 311 Regent St., W.1.

Specializing in Yugoslav holidays are *Yugotours Ltd*, Chesham House, 150 Regent St., W.1; and *Pilgrim Tours Ltd.*, 21 Maddox St., W.1.

General information may be obtained from the Yugoslav National Tourist Office, 143 Regent St., London W.1; also 509 Madison Av., New York 22. Travellers who enjoy planning their own journey can work out their schedules with the aid of the timetables listed below and purchase tickets at the relevant addresses given.

TIMETABLES. *Cook's Continental Timetable* (monthly; 10s. 6d.) is the leading international timetable for railway and main steamer services; it is not easy to obtain information in Britain about local steamer and bus services (even in Yugoslavia the *Red Vožnje*, a supposedly comprehensive timetable, is seldom seen and difficult to use). The *A.B.C. World Airways Guide* (monthly; 30s.) is the most comprehensive air-travel guide published in England.

Air Services between London and Yugoslavia are maintained by *J.A.T.* (Jugoslovenski aerotransport) in association with British European Airways. Full information may be obtained from *B.E.A.*, Dorland Hall, Lower Regent St., S.W.1. Flights in 1969 are as follows: from London (Heathrow) daily to Zagreb, with connections for Split and Dubrovnik (also twice weekly for Zadar).—Charter flights are organized by Yugotours, etc, to Pula and to Tivat (for Budva).

Railway Services. The Tauern Express from Ostend offers through coaches to Split viâ Ljubljana. The Simplon Express from Paris affords the best connection (at Pivka) for Rijeka, though in high summer the Rijeka Express operates direct from Ostend. It takes however no longer and is much pleasanter if going by rail to complete the last stage (from Venice or Trieste, or even Ancona) by sea.

BY RAIL AND SEA. *Jadrolinija* operate **Steamer Services** weekly from Venice to Rijeka—Rab—Split—Hvar—Korčula and Dubrovnik; also twice weekly from Trieste to Istrian ports—Mali Lošinj—Silba—Zadar —Šibenik and Split.

Motoring. British drivers taking their own cars by any of the multitudinous routes across France, Belgium, Luxembourg, Switzerland, Germany, Austria, and Italy need only the vehicle registration book, a valid national driving licence (with, in Italy, a translation of its provisions into Italian; or an international driving permit), and an International Insurance Certificate (the 'Green Card'). A nationality plate (e.g. GB) must be affixed to the rear of the vehicle so as to be illuminated by the tail lamps. Motorists who are not owners of the vehicle should possess the owner's permit for its use abroad.

The continental rule of the road is to drive on the right and overtake on the left. The provisions of the respective highway codes in the countries of transit, though similar, have important variations, especially with regard to priority, speed limits, and pedestrian crossings. Membership of the *Automobile Association* (Fanum House, Leicester Square, London W.C.2), The *Royal Automobile Club* (83 Pall Mall, London S.W.1), or the *Royal Scottish Automobile Club* entitles motorists to many of the facilities of affiliated societies on the continent and may save trouble and anxiety. The U.K. motoring organizations are represented at most of the sea and air ports, both at home and on the continent, to assist their members with customs formalities. In Yugoslavia membership of the neighbouring European organizations carries the same privileges.

Car Ferries are operated by British and French Railways from Dover to Calais, Boulogne, and Dunkirk and from Newhaven to Dieppe; also by Townsend Ferries from Dover to Calais; by British Rail and Zeeland Steamship Co. from Harwich to Hook of Holland; by Belgian State Marine from Harwich to Ostend and from both Dover and Folkestone to Ostend. A hovercraft service operates from Ramsgate to Calais. In London full particulars are available from the A.A., R.A.C., or British Rail, all at the *Continental Car Ferry Centre*, 52 Grosvenor Gardens, S.W.1.

Between Italy and Yugoslavia drive-on car ferries operate daily in summer between Ancona and Zadar, less frequently between Pescara and Split (an Italian service), and between Bari and either Dubrovnik or Bar.

Air Ferries for cars are run by *British United Air Ferries* (Portland House, Victoria, London S.W.1) from Southend, Lydd, or Coventry to Calais, Le Touquet, Ostend, Rotterdam, etc.

The easiest overland approaches to the Adriatic coast are viâ Italy, crossing into Yugoslavia by any of several frontier points E. of Trieste or Muggia according to destination; or from Austria by the Gross

Glockner Pass to Villach, thence viâ Tarvisio (Italy) to Rateče (Yugoslavia), whence the coast is reached by Ljubljana and Postojna.

A CAR SLEEPER EXPRESS operates in summer from Ostend to Ljubljana (outward Sun, back Fri). It is also possible to reach Milan or Rimini similarly if crossing by one of the Adriatic ferry routes.

In Yugoslavia no additional motoring documents are necessary, and a national driving certificate is valid (international permit for driving a hired car). Petrol stations on the Adriatic Highway are now numerous but the tank should not be allowed to get too low. The superior grade of petrol (98 octane) costs 1·80 *din* per litre (c. 6s. per gallon). Petrol coupons may be bought at the frontier (or, e.g. through the automobile clubs in London) giving a discount. Imported oils are expensive and a spare can is advisable. The principal variations in the Yugoslav regulations are an absolute speed limit of 100 km. per hour and some very low speed limits (e.g. 20 km.) applied in specially hazardous places. Trams and buses have no right of way in town traffic (but tend to expect it to be accorded them nevertheless).

Drivers using the Adriatic Highway (Magistrala) should take particular care at blind corners, not only because the locals (and continentals generally) drive near the crown of the road, but because of the prevalence of rock falls. A dangerous hazard in certain seasons is the 'Bora', a violent cross wind; some particularly susceptible areas of road are equipped with wind-socks at exposed corners. In sudden storms it may prove impossible to continue because of blinding rain, when at night it is too hazardous to drive off the road; a flashing red lamp, held in readiness in an easily accessible position inside the car, and placed in the rear window, affords a modicum of additional protection from accident.

An emergency service is organized by *Auto-Moto Savez Jugoslavije* with yellow vehicles bearing the sign 'Pomoć-Informacije' (available 8 a.m. to 8 p.m., 9 p.m. on Sundays), and assistance can be summoned by telephone from the Automobile clubs in Pula, Rijeka, Zadar, Šibenik, Split, Makarska, and Dubrovnik.

Cars may be hired through *Auto-Tehna* (agents for Avis), *Kompas* (agents to Hertz), *Putnik*, or *Inex*, one or other of which has an agency in most coastal towns of importance.

Passports are again necessary for all British and American travellers entering Yugoslavia and must bear the photograph of the holder. British passports (30s.), valid for five years, and renewable for five years more (fee 4s. per year), are issued at the Passport Office, Clive House, Petty France, London S.W.1 (9.30–4.30, Sat. 9.30–12.30), or may be obtained for an additional fee through any tourist agent. In International Tourist Year (1968) the necessity for a passport was abolished. At the moment of going to press (May '69) the requirement of a visa has again been abolished.

Currency Regulations. The allowance permitted by the British Government for pleasure travel per yearly period (beginning on 1 Nov) varies from time to time. In 1969 it is £50 for each person, all of which may be held in foreign notes. An additional £25 for a car (or £15 for a motor-cycle) may be allowed on application. In sterling notes no more than £15 may be taken out of Great Britain by British or American travellers. The complicated regulations, which lay down even what you may spend your money on in countries not subject to British law, are set out in the Foreign Office leaflet 'Notice to Travellers'. Not more than 50 new dinars may be brought out of Yugoslavia in notes.

Money. The monetary unit is the New Dinar (ND) divided into 100 paras. The current exchange value is 30 ND to the pound, making the dinar worth 8*d*. There are coins of 5, 10, 20, and 50 paras and 1 dinar, notes of 5, 10, 50, 100, and 500 new dinars. Older notes still circulate and are valid, so that care should be exercised since 100 old dinars is the equivalent of 1 ND.

Custom House. Provided that dutiable articles are declared, travellers will find the Yugoslav customs authorities courteous and reasonable. The following are admitted without formality (beyond an oral declaration) for personal use (but may not be disposed of in Yugoslavia): one pair of skis, field glasses, tennis racket, camping equipment, one sporting gun, one fishing rod, two cameras of different type with five rolls of film each, cine-camera, typewriter, gramophone with a 'reasonable' number of records (or tape-recorder), portable radio and/or television, bicycle, sports boat or kayak with or without motor. Quantities beyond these may be admitted duty-free but must be declared in writing.

Returning travellers may be reminded that all articles purchased abroad are now dutiable or forbidden in Britain, but 200 cigarettes or ½ lb. of tobacco, a bottle of wine and a bottle of spirits, a small bottle of perfume and a small bottle of toilet water, one cigarette lighter, and souvenirs to the value of £5 are usually passed free, if declared. Foreign reprints of copyright English books may be confiscated.

Souvenirs bought in Yugoslavia may be exported free of duty, but special permits are necessary for original objects of cultural, artistic, archaeological, ethnographic, historical or scientific value.

II HOTELS AND RESTAURANTS

Hotels. No hotel categories have been indicated in the present guide because at the time of going to press a complete re-classification of hotels was being undertaken by the Yugoslav authorities. In general, however, Yugoslavia employs four categories: A, B, C, and D, which more or less correspond to similar categories in other European countries. Up till now local variations and flexibility in interpreting the rules have led to considerable differences within a given category, and the present revision is intended to enforce more rigid standards and a more uniform system of classification. The majority of hotels on the coast are relatively new, having been built during the tourist boom of the past 15 years, and these include most of the A and B category hotels. The difference between them is that in A category hotels all rooms are equipped with a bathroom and telephone; in B category hotels about three quarters of the rooms have their own bathroom, while telephones are not always provided. A hotels also have more public rooms. The number of C and D hotels, by contrast, is quite small, consisting mainly of older buildings and frequently situated in the old quarters of towns. C category hotels usually have running water in rooms and bathrooms on each floor, while those in category D have only cold water and a slightly lower standard of amenities generally. It may be noted that the attraction of mass tourism to the coast of Yugoslavia has had a marked effect on the hotel pattern. In general there is a preponderance of seaside hotels often quite far from the centres of towns, while less pretentious institutions within a town are more difficult to find.

Hotel charges in Yugoslavia having been hit by domestic inflation are not quite so low as in earlier years, but efforts are being made to hold them steady and they still compare favourably with most other countries in Europe. The charges current in any particular year are listed annually in *Hotelske Cene* (Hotel Prices), a bulletin issued in several languages (including English) by the Zavod Savezne privredne Komore za ekonomski publicitet (Publicity Office of the Federal Chamber of Economy) and are usually given in dollars. Hoteliers are bound to conform to the prices given in this bulletin and are required to display the official cost of each room on a notice fixed to the inside of the door. A sliding scale operates in all cases, the higher rates being charged during the tourist season (July, August, and sometimes September), and low rates in the winter, with an intermediate rate for May, June, and October. Service charges are included, but not the visitors' tax, which ranges from 0·60 to 2 *New Dinars* per day according to the amenities of the town. Full board in Yugoslavia includes Continental breakfast, lunch, and dinner, but is not available for stays under three days.

In addition to hotels there is now a growing number of *Pensions* (pansioni), classified in three categories: I, II, and III. Category I corresponds roughly to a B category hotel in the quality of its installations, Category II to a C hotel and Category III to a D hotel. The standards of the pensions vary considerably, particularly since this is a transitional period in Yugoslavia. Until now all pensions have been communally owned, but with the recent passing of new laws relating to private ownership of boarding houses there has been a mushroom growth and a certain prudence should be exercised for the time being in making of choice. Pensions take guests only for full board.

Consideration should be given while travelling in Yugoslavia to the wide-spread availability of *Private Rooms* (privatne sobe). These are graded like pensions and hotels but are considerably cheaper, and thanks to the inborn hospitality of the Yugoslavs and efficient supervision, offer excellent value for money. Meals, except breakfast, are not normally provided, but such accommodation offers an unrivalled opportunity of acquiring a more intimate knowledge of the country and the people. Private rooms can be booked either on the spot or in advance through the local *Turističko drustvo*.

CAMPING in Yugoslavia is organized on normal European lines. The local term of *autocamp* has been used throughout this guide to indicate where the main sites are and these are also shown on standard tourist maps of the country. The minimum provisions are running water, electricity, and parking space, but the main sites offer all the amenities usually associated nowadays with this form of accommodation. A more recent development is the building of *motels* (the same word is used), of which over 70 are now in existence. They are graded in three categories (I–III), usually have a petrol station nearby, and are to be found along the main highways.

There are relatively few *Youth Hostels* in Yugoslavia, though the number is increasing. They are administered by the *Ferijalni savez Jugoslavije*, from whom details and a full list may be obtained (Moše Pijade 12/IV, P.O.B. 726, Belgrade). Students may take advantage of *Student Hostels* (studentski domovi) and *International Youth Centres*, of which there are three on the coast. Details may be obtained from the Travel Department of the *Biro za medjunarodnu razmenu omladine i studenata*, Moše Pijade 12 I, P.O.B. 374, Belgrade, which also organizes its own tours.

Restaurants (*restorani*, Slov. *restavracije*) operate on similar principles to those prevailing in other European countries. Fixed price meals (*menu*, pronounced and sometimes spelt *meni*) are generally obtainable in hotel restaurants and are spreading rapidly to other establishments, but are not yet the rule. Most restaurants display a bill of fare, together with prices, outside, to which a service charge of 10% is automatically added. It is customary when settling the bill to round up the amount to the nearest 50 *paras*, the small change going to the waiter; a larger tip is also acceptable to show appreciation for exceptional service. There is rarely a cover charge.

A less expensive place to eat is in the *gostiona* or *gostionica* (Slov. *gostilna*), where the dishes are traditionally chalked up on a board or else recited by the waiter, though menus are also appearing now. The food is simple and the number of dishes limited, but the quality is often excellent. *Gostione* usually specialize in national dishes. Rather more impersonal are the modern self-service restaurants (*samoposlužnirestoran*, Slov. *samopostrežna restavracija*) that are springing up in many places, while simple food may also be obtained in snack bars (*bife*), where it is often eaten standing up. Breakfast, consisting of rolls, butter, doughnuts, and coffee or hot milk, are to be had cheaply in dairy restaurants known as a *mljećni restoran* (Slov. *mlečna restavracija*), some of which in the bigger towns are able to provide more ambitious menus.

Meals compare favourably in price with those in England and are usually of a higher standard, bearing in mind the Mediterranean preference for spices and an abundance of olive oil. A simple three-course lunch or dinner can generally be had in a restaurant for the equivalent of about 10s., including wine, while this may be reduced further in cheaper establishments. Breakfast in general follows the continental pattern, though cold meats, bacon, eggs, cheese, etc may be ordered if desired. White coffee is generally to be avoided. The main meal of the day is lunch (*ručak*, Slov. *kosilo*), consisting of soup, a main dish based on meat or fish, together with vegetables and usually a salad, and dessert. Dinner (*večera*, Slov. *večerja*) is similar, but usually substitutes an hors d'oeuvre for soup and is generally lighter.

Red or white table wine (*crno* or *bijelo vino*, Slov. *črno* and *belo*) is the usual accompaniment to meals, the wine being strong and natural and able to stand dilution. Water is readily available, except on some of the smaller islands, and the Yugoslavs are very fond of mineral water (*mineralna voda*), of which some of the best known varieties are *Radenska* and *Rogaška* in the north and *Bukovička* in the south. Beer (*pivo*) is also readily available, being usually of the lager variety preferred on the continent.

Food and Wine. Yugoslav cooking as represented on the Adriatic coast has no national characteristics that set it off completely from the cuisine of other nations, but consists rather of a distinctive blend of Mediterranean and Austrian elements, together with a selection of Serbian, Bosnian, and Macedonian dishes of basically Greek and Turkish origin. Meat (*meso*) is invariably fresh and plentiful and first-rate, particularly the lamb (*janjetina*) and veal (*teletina*); salads (*salate*) and fruit (*voće*, Slov. *sadje*) are outstanding; the cooked vegetables (*variva*) are more variable and, like all food in Yugoslavia, depend heavily on the season; desserts, except where oriental dishes are introduced, are uninspired; the cheeses (*sirevi*) also vary but can offer some pleasant surprises (*Bohinjski, Paški sir; Kačkavalj* from Serbia). As is to be expected, fish is plentiful and available in great variety, also squid (*kalamar*), octopus (*hobotnica*), and a rather limited selection of shellfish (*školje*). A tendency in recent years for Yugoslav restaurants to lean too heavily in the direction of featureless 'international' dishes and ignore their local cuisine, seems to be changing again in favour of national dishes.

Some oriental dishes, such as *sarma* (stuffed cabbage or vine leaves), *djuveč* (a rich casserole with meat, rice paprikas, etc), *kapama* (lamb stewed with spinach, shallots, and yoghourt) or *musaka* are highly recommended, while the Yugoslav predilection for grilling and spit-roasting finds expression in numerous kebabs (*ćevap*) and shashliks (*šašlik*) of which the best known are the ubiquitous *ćevapčići* (grilled balls of minced beef) and *ražnjići* (grilled slices of veal and pork), both served with chopped raw onion and cayenne pepper. Popular variations on this formula are *pljeskavice* (grilled balls of minced veal and pork) and *ćulbastija* (grilled pork cutlets). Finally a word should also be said for the fine *pršut* (smoked ham) of Istria and Dalmatia and the Gavrilović *salama* (salami) from Serbia.

The **Wines** in Yugoslavia are generally of good standard without being brilliant; they rarely travel well and, with a few exceptions, are usually to be found only within a small area. Many of them are referred to in the text. In Slovenia and the northern part of Istria it is a good idea to try *teran* or the lighter *refoško*, both red, and the white wine *rebula*, while the sweet *malvazija* (Malmsey) is found all over Istria. Farther down the coast the red wines tend to predominate, the best being the *opoli* (almost a rosé) from mainland Dalmatia, the full-bodied *plavac* from the south Dalmatian islands and *dingač*, a very strong and fruity wine from the Pelješac peninsula. Among the best known white wines are *pošip, vugava, grk*, and *maraština*. The ubiquitous *prošek*, made from dried fermented grapes, may be too sweet for many palates but varies considerably from place to place. Also available in many restaurants are some of the better known wines from other parts of Yugoslavia: *silvanac, traminac, rizling, žilavka, blatina, prokupac, Fruškogorski biser*, and *kavadarka*. Those with a taste for liqueurs should try the national specialities of *šljivovica* (plum brandy), the well known *maraschino*, a sweet after-dinner liqueur made from morello cherries, and the cherry brandy.

The following MENU includes many dishes that are likely to be met with:

JELOVNIK (Slov. *Jedilnik*) — MENU

Doručak (Slov. *Zajtrk*) — Breakfast

Doručak komplet — Continental breakfast
Kruh, hleb — Bread
Pecivo, kifla — Roll
Maslac, puter — Butter
Džem, marmelada — Jam
Crna kava (or kafa) — Black coffee
B(ij)ela kava — White coffee
Turska kava — Turkish coffee
Čaj sa ml(ij)ekom — Tea with milk
Čaj sa limunom — Tea with lemon
Čokolada — Drinking chocolate
Šunka sa jajem, (h)emendeks — Ham and eggs

Ručak i obed ili večera (Slov. *Kosilo i Večerja*) — Lunch and dinner

Hladna predjela (Slov. *Narezek*) — Cold hors d'oeuvre

Kavijar, ajvar — Caviar
Pašteta — Pâté
Hladni narezak — Cold cuts
Dalmatinski pršut sa sirom — Smoked Dalmatian ham with cheese
Ruska jaja — Hard-boiled eggs with Russian salad
Sardine u ulju — Sardines in oil
Masline — Olives

Topla predjela (Slov. *predjed*) — Warm hors d'oeuvre

Špageti na milanski, bolonjski način — Spaghetti alla milanese, bolognese
Omlet sa šunkom, sirom, povrćem — Ham, cheese, 'Spanish' omelet
Srpska jaja — Omelet with tomatoes, paprikas and cucumber
Kajgana — Scrambled egg
Meko, tvrdo, kuvano jaja — Soft, hard, boiled egg
Špargle sa sirom — Asparagus with cheese
Kranjska klobasa, kobasica — Pork sausages from Kranj (Slovenia)

Juhe, supe, čorbe — Soups

Supa od povrća — Vegetable soup
Govedja juha — Consomme
Juha od rajčice, paradajza — Tomato soup
Supa od kokošijeg mesa s knedlama od džigerice — Chicken soup with liver [dumplings
Riblja čorba, Čorba od morske ribe — Fish soup
Govedja juha sa graškom — Pea soup

Ribe — Fish

Brodet na Dalmatinski, Bokeljski način — Dalmatian, Boka Kotorska fish stew
Bakalar na mornarski način — Smoked cod, sailor's style
Barbun, trlja u pergamentu — Striped mullet in waxed paper
Pečena kečiga — Baked Sterlet
Orada s paradajzom — Bream baked with tomatoes
Rizoto od kalamara — Squid risotto
Pohovan file od smudja — Fried perch fillets
Smudj sa pečurkama — Perch fried and then baked with mushrooms
Kuvane skuše — Boiled mackerel
Pržena pastrva, pastrmka, (postrv) — Fried trout

Pijani šaran iz Skadarskog jezera — Baked Skadar carp
Jastog — Lobster
Kamenica, oštriga — Oyster
Školjka, kapica — Clam
Rak, rakovica — Crab
Bjelica, kesiga — Whiting
Oslić — Hake
Zubatac — Dentex
Cipalj — Mullet
Tuna, tunj — Tunny
Pic, špic — Sheepshead bream
Murina — Moray eel
Ugor, grunj — Conger eel
List — Sole
Sardele — Fresh sardines

Gotova jela (Slov. *jedi*) — Plats du jour

Punjeni plavi patlidžani — Baked stuffed aubergines (eggplants)
Pasulj sa suvim jezikom — Beans with smoked pork
Bosanski lonac — Bosnian casserole cooked in white wine
Teleći rizoto — Veal risotto
Pileći paprikaš sa noklicama — Chicken stew with dumplings
Pašta i fažol — Macaroni with beans
Kelerabe nadevene mozgom — Cabbage stuffed with brains
Pilav od ovčetine — Mutton pilaff
Svinjski paprikaš s kiselim kupusom i pavlakom — Pork stew with sauerkraut and
Punjeni papadajz — Stuffed tomatoes   [cream
Punjene paprike, tikvice — Stuffed paprikas, courgettes
Kuhana govedina — Boiled beef
Teleće grudi punjene spanaćem — Breast of veal stuffed with spinach
Govedji gulaš — Beef goulash

Specijaliteti na ražnju i roštilju — Grills and Roasts

Pečeno pile, pečena patka — Roast chicken, roast duck
Svinjsko, teleće pečenje — Roast pork, veal
Pečena ćurka nadevena pečurkama — Roast turkey stuffed with mushrooms
Pečena guska sa limunom — Roast goose with lemon
Džigerica (*jetra*), bubrezi, srce na žaru — Grilled liver, kidneys, heart
Jagnjeći šašlik — Lamb shashlik
Šiš-ćevap — Shish-kebab
Hajdučki ćevap — Kebab of mixed meats

Jela po narudžbi (Slov. *Jedi po naročilu*) — Dishes to order

Biftek sa jajem — Steak with a fried egg on top
Ramstek — Rump steak
Šatobrian — 'Chateaubriand'—double steak garnished with vegetables
Svinjski kotlet — Pork chop
Naravni odrezak, (*zrezek*) — Escalope of veal
Zagrebački odrezak — Escalope of veal stuffed with ham and cheese
Bečki, (*Dunajski*) odrezak, šnicel, (*zrezek*) — Veal fried in bread-crumbs (Wiener
Srpska plošća   ⎫   [schnitzel]
Mešano meso na žaru   ⎬ Mixed grill
Prepelice na lovački način — Stewed quail, chasseur
Prepelice s pirinčem, rižom — Quail casserole with rice
Jarebice na žaru — Grilled partridges
Pečeni fazan — Roast pheasant

Povrće (Slov. *Zelenjava*) — Vegetables

Mrkva, šargarepa — Carrots
Grašak — Peas
Pasulj — Red or kidney beans
Boranija — French beans
Bobovi — Broad beans
Krompir (kuhani, pečeni) — Potatoes (boiled, roast)
Prženi krompir, pomfrit — Fried potatoes, chips

Spanać, špinat — Spinach
Kupus, (*zelje*) — Cabbage
Kiseli kupus, (*kiselo zelje*) — Sauerkraut
Prokelji — Brussels sprouts
Cvetača, karfiol — Cauliflower
Pirinač, riž — Rice
Paprika — Paprika
Patlidžan, (*melancan*) — Aubergine
Pečurka — Mushroom
Celer — Celery
Repa — Turnip
Luk, (*čebula*) — Onions
Ren — Horseradish
Šparga, špargle — Asparagus
Tikva, (*buča*) — Pumpkin, marrow
Tikvica — Courgette (Zucchini, squash)

Salate — Salads

M(ij)ešana salata — Mixed salad
Zelena salata — Green salad (lettuce)
Paradajz, rajčice, (*paradižnik*) — Tomato
Krastavac (kiseo), (*kumarica*) — Cucumber (gherkin)
Cikla, (*pesa*) — Beetroot
Rotkva, rotkvica — Radish

Poslastice, Kolači (Slov. *Slaščice*) — Desserts

Sladoled — Ice cream
Šerbet — Sherbet
Palačinka sa džemom, čokoladom — Jam, chocolate pancake
Strudla, savijača od jabuka, (*jabučni zavitek*) — Apple strudel
Torta — Gâteau
Medenjaci — Honey cakes
Istarske fritule — Istrian fritters, a form of crêpes suzettes made with Maraschino
Pita — A kind of paper-thin pastry that can be filled with fruits, nuts or cheese
Ratluk — Turkish delight
Kompot — Stewed fruit (generally cold)

Voće (Slov. *Sadje*) — Fruit

Voćna, (*sadna*) salata — Fruit salad
Grožđe — Grapes
Smokve — Figs
Trešnje, (*češnje*) — Cherries
Višnje — Sour cherries
Jabuke, (*jabolke*) — Apples
Kruške — Pears
Šljive — Plums
Jagode — Strawberries
Breskve — Peaches
Marelice, kajsije — Apricots
Narandže, naranče, pomarandže — Oranges
Limuni — Lemons
Dinja — Melon
Lubenica — Watermelon

Sir(ev)i — Cheese

Paški, Krčki sir — Sheep's milk cheese from the islands of Pag and Krk
Primorski, granički sir — The same made near Rijeka
Trapist — 'Trappist', one of the best cow's milk cheeses in Yugoslavia. International varieties can also be found under their usual names (Bel paese, gorgonzola, edam, etc.)
Zdenka — Processed cheese
Kačkavalj — A hard cheese of sheep's or sheep's and cow's milk mixed
Gibanica — Cheese pie
Pogačice od sira 'kačkavalja' — Kačkavalj cheese biscuits
Štruklji — Slovenian cheese pie

Miscellaneous

So, (*Sol*) — Salt	Šalica, šolja, (*skodelica*) — Cup
Biber, (*poper*) — Pepper	Tanjurić — Saucer
Ulje — Oil	Čaša, (*kozarec*) — Glass
Sirće — Vinegar	Čačkalica, (*zubotrebec*) — Toothpick
Senf, muštarda, (*gorušica*) — Mustard	Stolica, (*sto*) — Chair
Beli luk, (*česenj*) — Garlic	Sto, (*miza*) — Table
Šećer, (*sladkor*) — Sugar	Stolnjak, (*prt*) — Table cloth
Sendvič — Sandwich	Ubrus, salvet, servijeta — Napkin
Nož — Knife	Konobar, kelner, (*natakar*) — Waiter
Vilica — Fork	Račun — The bill
Kašika, (*žlica*) — Spoon	Plaćati! — May I pay the bill!
Tanjir, (*krožnik*) — Plate	Napojnica, (*napitnina*) — Tip

III TRANSPORT

Steamers play a large part in Adriatic transport. The regular services are run by *Jadrolinija*, the principal Yugoslav passenger shipping line, with headquarters at Rijeka and agencies in every port where tickets may be booked in advance. In high summer cabins are well booked, but it is rarely that a deck passage cannot be obtained. Fares are comparatively cheap.

An express service serves main ports daily in summer (4 times weekly in winter) on route Rijeka—Rab—Zadar—Split—Hvar—Korčula—Dubrovnik. One day a week this starts from Venice.

Another service (twice weekly) from Trieste serves Koper — Poreč — Rovinj — Pula — Mali Losinj — Silba — Zadar — Šibenik and Split. There is also a weekly service from Rijeka viâ Silba — Zadar —Biograd — Šibenik — Primošten — Split — Hvar — Korčula — Dubrovnik — Cavtat — Hercegnovi — Tivat to Kotor.

The main ports are connected by local services with their neighbouring islands. These services run all the year round. Being mail boats and market boats or school boats, they run at the times most convenient to the local users, often involving very early starts and late arrivals to the outlying ports (the opposite to what tourists expect). An indication of connected points and of frequency is given in the text but inquiry should always be made at the local Jadrolinija office. Weather conditions permitting, the services are regular, punctual and well organized, and printed timetables may be obtained.

Buses. Regular services connect all the principal places on the coast. The long-distance vehicles (some by night) have aircraft-type seats; more local services (e.g. between Zadar and Biograd; Split and Trogir; Rijeka and Opatija) are frequent and often crowded. Fares are moderate.

Railways are not of great use to visitors, though very slow lines reach the coast from inland, affording services from Ljubljana to Rijeka; from Zagreb to Rijeka, Split or Zadar; from Sarajevo to Ploče (and with a change, to Dubrovnik); and from Titograd to Bar. The only coastal line, from Dubrovnik to Hercegnovi, has recently been scheduled for closure.

Local **Air Services** connect Split and Dubrovnik (not very conveniently). Between all other coastal points it is necessary to fly viâ Belgrade or Zagreb.

IV GENERAL HINTS

Season. Generally speaking, July and August are the hottest months on the Adriatic coast and are to be preferred by those in search of sun, though southern Montenegro may be found rather too hot at this time of year. June and September are easier to bear everywhere and often provide periods of almost perfect weather, but it should be borne in mind that they also include the equinoxes, when unsettled spells of about 7–10 days are usually the rule. May and October may be relied upon as excellent months for travelling, while the sea is warm enough in both months, and sometimes even into November, for comfortable bathing to be possible. In the remaining months many hotels are closed and tourist facilities in the smaller places are reduced or non-existent, but the larger resorts are encouraging winter visitors and a high proportion of warm sunny days makes this an excellent time for sightseeing and getting to know the local populace. The climate is in general not severe throughout the winter and snow and frost are both rare occurrences.

Language. English is fairly widely spoken in towns, but elsewhere is less well known than Italian or German, while French is a popular language in Montenegro. It cannot be expected that many people will take the trouble to master the Yugoslavs' own language, but the acquisition of a few basic phrases will do wonders to smooth the visitor's path and creates a favourable impression out of all proportion to the effort needed to acquire them. Apart from the closely similar language of Slovenian, which in the area covered by this guide is spoken only in the north of Istria, the language of the coast is Serbo-Croatian, so named for the two closely related dialects of the Croats and Serbs. This language has the great advantage of possessing a completely phonetic alphabet, so that once the sounds are mastered it may be pronounced, save for some stress difficulties, with impunity by beginners and foreigners alike. Some hints for pronunciation follow.

Consonants are roughly the same as in English, but with the following exceptions: c has the sound of ts as in Betsy; h is more guttural, as in German, than in English; j is like consonantal y as in yard. Certain additional consonants are denoted by letters with diacritical marks: č has the sound of ch as in church; ć has the sound of t as in vulture; đ (also written as dj) has the sound of d as in verdure; š has the sound of sh as in shell; ž has the sound of s as in measure; dž has the sound of j as in jug.

Vowels are all open and pure in Serbo-Croatian as in Italian and have their full value; there are no diphthongs. In addition there is a vocalic r which need present no difficulties if approached with a cool head. Its sound is like the Scottish rolled r as in kirk.

Stress is not fixed, but generally speaking tends to be towards the beginning of words.

In Montenegro the Cyrillic alphabet is officially in use and although signposts, street names, and official signs are supposed to show Latin equivalents, this does not always occur in practice. It is desirable, therefore, when visiting that region, to have a knowledge of the alphabet for reference purposes. A full list of letters follows, together with their Latin equivalents.

Cyrillic		Latin		Cyrillic		Latin	
А	а	A	a	Н	н	N	n
Б	б	B	b	Њ	њ	Nj	nj
В	в	V	v	О	о	O	o
Г	г	G	g	П	п	P	p
Д	д	D	d	Р	р	R	r
Ђ	ђ	Đ Dj	đ, dj	С	с	S	s
Е	е	E	e	Т	т	T	t
Ж	ж	Ž	ž	Ћ	ћ	Ć	ć
З	з	Z	z	У	у	U	u
И	и	I	i	Ф	ф	F	f
Ј	ј	J	j	Х	х	H	h
К	к	K	k	Ц	ц	C	c
Л	л	L	l	Ч	ч	Č	č
Љ	љ	Lj	lj	Џ	џ	Dž	dž
М	м	M	m	Ш	ш	Š	š

Manners and Customs. The manners of the Yugoslavs can be informal to the point of abruptness when dealing with one another, but usually take on a more formal character when foreigners are addressed. In shops and offices a certain amount of self-assertion is taken for granted, since queues are not the general rule and it is incumbent on the inquirer or customer to get himself a hearing. Nevertheless, requests for service, information or advice should normally be prefaced by *molim* or *molim Vas* (please)—or *prosim* in Slovenia—and it is appreciated (though not expected) if such transactions are concluded with *hvala* (thank you) or the more fulsome *hvala Vam l(ij)epo*—in Slovenia *hvala lepa* (thank you very much). The almost universal response to thanks is again *molim* or *prosim* (don't mention it) and this is also used when asking someone to repeat a phrase that has not been properly heard. In buses or crowded places it is helpful to say *izvinite* (excuse me) when pushing past other people, while an apparent breach of manners is best apologized for by *oprostite* (forgive me). In Slovenia *oprostite* is used on both these occasions.

As in most parts of the continent, it is customary in Yugoslavia to shake hands with people not only on first meeting them but at each subsequent separate meeting, and in homes to shake hands on rising and before retiring. To this should be added the appropriate greeting of *dobar dan* (good day), *dobro veče* (good evening) or *laku noć*—in Slovenia *dober dan*, *dober večer*, and *lahko noč*. General greetings are rendered by *zdravo* (hello) and this is frequently accompanied by the inquiry *kako ste* (how are you?), to which the normal reply is *dobro*, *hvala*, *kako ste Vi* (very well, thank you, and how are you?). The word for welcome is *dobrodošli*, for goodbye *do vidjenja* (Slovenian *na svidanje*); yes is *da* (Slovenian *ja*) and no *ne* (a difficult adjustment to make when crossing into Yugoslavia from Greece!).

The Yugoslavs are an intensely hospitable people and the code of hospitality is treated with some seriousness, particularly away from the big towns. On entering a private house one is invariably offered Turkish coffee together with a liqueur of some kind—usually *šljivovica* (plum brandy) or one of its cousins. One or the other of these may be refused, but not both, without giving offence. The cup or glass will then be replenished as soon as it is empty, so it is essential to leave some in until the end of the visit if one wishes not to continue drinking. In Montenegro may also be experienced the Balkan custom of offering preserves with coffee and water; in such a case it is usual to take one spoon of preserves and sip or drink the water before drinking the coffee. A stranger is rarely permitted to play host to a native and will experience some difficulty in repaying debts of hospitality. Needless to say, payment in kind is the only method acceptable and the best course is to offer small gifts for the household or children or to bring flowers. At meals one is usually wished *dobar* (Slovenian *dober*) *tek* beforehand, to which the reply, if one's companions are also eating, is *hvala, i Vam takodje* (thank you, and the same to you).

The '*corzo*' or evening parade is universal and takes place usually between about 6 and 8 p.m. in summer and slightly earlier in winter. It is usually confined to certain streets or a particular street in larger towns (often itself named the *corzo*) and traffic is barred for its duration.

Photography. There are few restrictions on photography in Yugoslavia, but permission is necessary to photograph the interiors of churches and museums and may sometimes be withheld. Care should also be taken before photographing individuals such as soldiers or policemen or peasants from the interior, some of whom may feel insulted and protest. Moslems in particular may not be photographed without their permission unless in groups and from afar. Photography is normally forbidden near military and naval installations and this is indicated by a sign consisting of a picture of a camera with a cross over it.

Churches are normally closed for a considerable period during the middle of the day (12 to 3, 4 or 5), while smaller churches and chapels open only for a few hours in the morning or perhaps only on saints' or feast days. In the case of the former the sacristan may usually be found by inquiring locally, but the keys of the smaller churches are frequently kept in episcopal or parish offices or by local conservationists or museum curators and sometimes take a considerable time to obtain, particularly in country districts. Once a church is open access can normally be had to sacristies, closed chapels and paintings without any difficulty and only the smallest gratuity is necessary (and even so may be rejected) to the person bringing the key. In the cities an entrance fee is becoming customary for admission to treasuries, bell towers, etc. In Catholic churches visitors may move about during services (except during high mass), provided they do not approach the altar(s) in use, but at all times are expected to cover their legs and women are expected to cover their heads. In Orthodox churches moving about during services is not encouraged and women are not allowed in the sanctuary.

Museums are usually open six days a week, the commonest closing day being Monday. Typical opening hours are from 8–12 and 4–7, though these may vary slightly from place to place and with the size of the museum. A few museums are open only in the morning, while in small places museums are often opened on request. Entrance fees are generally small.

Public Holidays. The main public holidays in Yugoslavia are as follows: 1 and 2 Jan. (New Year), 1 and 2 May (Labour Day), 4 July (Partizans Day), 29 and 30 Nov. (Day of the Republic). In addition each constituent republic has its own national day, of which four are relevant to this guide: Slovenia (22 July); Croatia (27 July); Bosnia and Hercegovina (27 July), and Montenegro (13 July). The observance of patron saints' days and major Christian festivals is ill-defined owing to the disestablished nature of the church in Yugoslavia, but most cities on the coast contrive at least an informal holiday to coincide with Christmas, Easter, the Assumption, and the patronal festival.

Amusements. The organized entertainment that most visitors are likely to patronize is the cinema, of which there is at least one in all places of any size and up to a dozen or more in the larger cities. A wide selection of up-to-date foreign and domestic films is shown, usually in the original versions with subtitles, and cinemas may be indoors or in the open-air. Performances occur once, twice or sometimes thrice nightly and tickets may be purchased at the cinema box office between 10–12 during the day or one hour before the performance begins. Admission prices are extremely modest.

Details of the annual international FESTIVALS held in Split, Dubrovnik, and Pula, are indicated in the text: their programmes are widely publicized in advance (*The Times*, etc.). EXHIBITIONS of folk dancing and local handicrafts are organized during the tourist season and locally publicized. Other local entertainments are indicated in the text.

Newspapers. Foreign newspapers and magazines, including English, are readily obtainable in the larger towns from kiosks or shops specializing in them, but rarely elsewhere. The principal national newspapers are *Borba* and *Politika* (published in Belgrade), *Vijesnik* (Zagreb), and *Delo* (Ljubljana).

Working Hours. Government and business offices usually work from 7–2 daily except Sundays. School hours are either 8–1 or 2–7 (Mon–Sat). Banks and official exchange offices are open to the public from 7–11 and 5–8 in summer and from 8–12 and 4–7 in winter, except on Sundays and national holidays. Most restaurants are open from 6 a.m. till midnight.

Weights and Measures. The metric system is used in Yugoslavia, with basically the same terminology as in other countries. The unit of length is the *metar*, of weight the *gram*, of land measurement the *ar*, and of capacity the *litar*. Greek-derived prefixes (deka, hekto, kilo) are used with these names to express multiples, Latin prefixes (deci, centi or santi, mili) to express fractions (dekogram = 10 grama, santimetar = 10 milimetara). In measures of weight 100 kilograma = 1 quintal and 10 quintala = 1 tona.

TOPOGRAPHICAL GLOSSARY

Aerodrom — Airport
Banja — Spa
Bedem — Wall
Biskupija — Bishop's palace
Blato — Pond, swamp
Brdo — Hill, mountain
Cesta — Road, street
Crkva — Church
Dolina — Valley
Donj-i, a, e — Lower
Draga — Cove, inlet
Dvor, Dvorac — Palace
Fortica — Fortress
Gat — Pier, mole
Gledališče (Slov.) — Theatre
Gora — Hill, mountain
Gornj-i, a, e — Upper
Grad — Town, city
Groblje — Graveyard
Istok, Istočni (adj.) — East
Jadran, Jadransko — Adriatic
Jezero — Lake
Jug, Južni (adj.) — South
Kamen — Stone
Kamenolom — Quarry
Kanal — Channel
Kapela — Chapel
Katedrala — Cathedral
Kazalište — Theatre
Kuča — House
Kula — Tower
Kupalište — Bathing place
Loža — Loggia
Luka — Harbour
Mal-i, a, e — Small
Manastir — Monastery
More — Sea
Most — Bridge
Muzej — Museum
Nov-i, a, o — New
Obala — Shore, quay
Opatija — Abbey
Otok — Island
Palača, Palata — Mansion, town house

Pjaca — Square
Placa — Square
Planina — Mountain
Plaža — Beach
Poljana — Square
Polje — Field, meadow
Poluotok — Peninsula
Pozorište— Theatre
Pristaništ — Jetty
Prolaz — Passage, cut
Put — Road, street, path
Rijeka, Reka — River
Rt, Rat — Headland, point
Rudnik — Mine
Samostan — Monastery, nunnery
Selo — Village
Sever, Seven-i, a, o — North
Slap — Waterfall
Spilja — Cave
Spomenik — Monument
Star-i, a, o — Old
Stolnica (Slov.) — Cathedral
Svet-i, a, o — Saint, holy
Šetalište — Promenade
Tjesnac — Narrows
Toranj — Tower
Trg — Square
Trgovina — Shop
Tržnica — Market
Tvrdjava — Fortress
Ulica — Street
Ušće — River mouth
Uvala — Small bay
Vel-, Velik-i, a, o — Big, large
Vijećnica — Town Hall
Vrata — Strait, gate
Vrh — Peak, summit
Zaljev — Bay
Zapad, Zapadn-i, a, o — West
Zgrada — Building
Zid, Zidina — Wall
Zvonik — Bell tower, belfry

EXPLANATIONS

TYPE. The main routes are described in large type. Smaller type is used for branch-routes and excursions, for historical and preliminary paragraphs, and (generally speaking) for descriptions of greater detail or minor importance.

ASTERISKS indicate points of special interest or excellence.

DISTANCES are given cumulatively from the starting-point of the route or sub-route. Yugoslav road distances are measured and signposted in kilometres and it was felt that motorists would prefer the motoring distances recorded in the guide to conform, especially since it is expected that in the 1970s Gt Britain will change to metric measurement. On the other hand, particularly for short distances British readers (and American readers) habitually think in feet, yards, and miles, so that mountain heights and short walking distances have been expressed in the old familiar form (and total route distances given additionally in miles), a somewhat awkward compromise which, it is hoped, has the merit of convenience.

POPULATIONS are given in round figures according to the census of 1961.

ABBREVIATIONS. In addition to generally accepted and self-explanatory abbreviations, the following occur in the guide:

Abp = archbishop	Pl. = plan
Adm. = admission	r. = right
Bp. = bishop	R = room(s)
C = century	Rest. = restaurant
c. = circa	Rfmts. = refreshments
fl. = floruit (flourished)	Rte = route
km. = kilometres	Slov. = Slovene
l. = left	Sv. = sveti (saint)
m. = mile(s)	ul. = ulica (street)
min. = minutes	

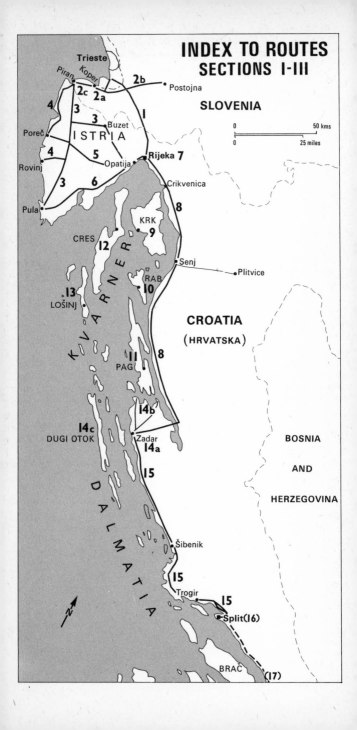

INDEX TO ROUTES
SECTIONS I-III

SLOVENIA

Trieste
Piran
Koper
2b ● Postojna
2c 2a
1
4
3
Poreč 3 Buzet
ISTRIA
4 3
5
Rovinj 4 Opatija Rijeka 7
3 6
Pula Crikvenica
8
KRK
9
CRES 12
Senj ● ● Plitvice
RAB
13 10
LOŠINJ
CROATIA
(HRVATSKA)
11
PAG 8
14b
14c
DUGI OTOK Zadar
14a
15
BOSNIA
AND
HERZEGOVINA
Šibenik
15
Trogir 15
Split(16)
BRAC (17)

DALMATIA

KVARNER

N

0   50 kms
0   25 miles

I ISTRIA

Geographically Istria is the roughly triangular peninsula that projects southward from a line joining Trieste and Rijeka. For much of its history, it has been linked with Venice and always had the largest Italian minority of the E. Adriatic littoral. Nowadays the northern part is administered by the Federal Republic of Slovenia, and the larger southern part by the Federal Republic of Croatia.

1 FROM TRIESTE TO RIJEKA

ROAD, 77 km. (48 m.), crossing the frontier. 17 km. *Kozina.*—27 km. *Markovščina.*—37½ km. *Podgrad.*—67 km. *Jušići.*—77 km. **Rijeka.** BUSES, c. 4 times daily, usually viâ Opatija, in c. 3 hrs.

RAILWAY, 102 km. (63 m.) in 3½ hrs, viâ Poggioreale then after crossing the frontier viâ *Sežana, Divača, Pivka* (where a change is necessary) and *Ilirska Bistrica.*

Trieste (Slovene and Serbocroat, *Trst*), see the 'Blue Guide to Northern Italy'. The road runs viâ (10 km.) *Basovizza* to (14½ km.) the frontier (customs, exchange, petrol coupons). The first Yugoslav village is (17 km.) *Kozina*, where we cross a main road linking Postojna (l.; see Rte 2B) and Ljubljana with Koper and the Istrian coast (see Rte 2A). Our road (asphalted but ill-kept) leads across typical karst countryside, characterized by green pastureland in the foreground stretching away on either side to a bare rocky landscape, intersected by long hilly ridges and deep ravines, and with high mountains rising to the N.E. and S.W. The limestone is honeycombed with underground rivers and caverns, and the turf forms only the thinnest of coverings on its surface.

27 km. *Markovščina.* Here a guide and key may be found to the cave of *Dimnice*, ½ m. N. on the way to Slivje. The cave extends nearly a mile with stalagmites and stalactites.—At (52 km.) *Rupa* we join the main Ljubljana–Rijeka road.—67 km. *Jušići.* Near by, in the hamlet of Jurdani, are two small limestones caves, *Sparožna pečina* and *Crljenčina pečina.*

Kastav, a charming and historic small town, stands 3 km. from Jušići on the old Trieste–Rijeka highway (frequent buses from Rijeka), which also provides a good alternative route to the busier main road. As a Roman settlement, *Castra*, from which its name derives, it was a strategic junction of the Roman roads from Tergeste (Trieste) and Pola (Pula) to Tarsatica (Rijeka) and the province of Liburnia. Later, as a border town between Austria-Hungary and Italy, it belonged to the Habsburg family. It is known for its barrel-making and for traditional vintage customs. The only remaining Roman traces are fragmentary walls near the cemetery, but six towers of the medieval fortifications still stand.

Kastav was the home of the 15C fresco painters Vincent and Ivan of Kastav, thought to have been father and son. Vladimir Nazor (1876–1949), the Croatian author, lived and taught here for many years, and Milan Marjanović, the critic, was born here. Their houses are marked by plaques.

At the entrance to the town a fine 16C *Loggia* faces Lončarija, a tree-shaded square where the colourful feast of Bela nedeja is celebrated each year (first week of Oct). The small Renaissance church of *Sv. Sebastijan* has an attractive painted ceiling. Inside the medieval *Town Gate*, bearing Jesuit arms, the narrow main street leads to the LOKVINA, or main square. In the centre a well bears a locally famous incription describing how Morelli, an unpopular and repressive governor, was drowned here by the outraged citizens. In the disused 15C Gothic church of *Sv. Trojica* (Holy Trinity) frescoes have been discovered.

On the N. side of the town the arcaded parish church of *Sv. Jelena*, in an 18C Baroque style, has carved choir stalls. The view from the detached bell tower (1237 ft) extends s. over the Kvarner Gulf and islands, and E. to Mts. Obruč (4400 ft) and Snježnik (5800 ft) and the Gorski Kotar. On the E. side of the town rise the walls of an enormous church started by the Rijeka Jesuits in the 18C and never finished.

From Jušići the main road descends through Matulji and Zamet (comp. Rte 6) to the shore of the Bay of Rijeka.—77 km. **Rijeka,** see Rte 7.

2   SLOVENE ISTRIA

A. From Trieste to Koper

ROAD, 25 km. (15½ m.), crossing the frontier. 15 m. *Albaro Vescova/Škofije* (frontier).—25 km. **Koper.** Frequent buses in 1 hr, though the pleasantest way is by local steamer (45 min).

We thread the s. suburbs of *Trieste* and, leaving the road to Muggia on our right, cross (15 km.) the frontier at *Albaro Vescova*, known to the Yugoslavs as *Škofije.*—19 km. *Križišče Ankaran* crossroads. To the right lies Ankaran (4 km.; see below); to the left the main road goes to Kozina and Postojna (see Rte 2B) and to Ljubljana. We keep straight on and at the main gate of Koper bear left for the waterfront.

25 km. **KOPER,** a thriving town (12,000 inhab.) situated on a small peninsula that was formerly an island, is the principal town of Slovene Istria and the chief port of Slovenia. Still perhaps better known by its former name *Capodistria*, it combines the distinct personalities of a typical Venetian coastal settlement of narrow streets and old houses, with a bustling and rapidly growing modern seaport and expanding industries.

Hotels. In town: **Triglav** (a), 100 R, dancing, night club, kavarna; **Galeb** (b). Across the causeway in *Semedele*: **Žusterna**, 170 R, swimming pool, beach, dancing. —In *Ankaran* (comp. above): **Adria**, 255 R, in converted Benedictine monastery and chalet annexes in grounds, beach, dancing.

Autocamp at Ankaran.

Restaurants. *Ribja restavracija* (fish), Titov trg; *Emona*, Gallusova ul.; *Taverna*, Carpacciev trg.

Kavarnas. *Loža*, Titov trg; and at Hotel Triglav.

Post Office, Muzejski trg.—INFORMATION OFFICES, Pristaniški trg, and Kidričeva ulica.

Buses from Pristaniški trg. Frequent services to all parts of Istria and to Trieste; long distance to *Belgrade*, *Zagreb*, and *Ljubljana*, and in the season to *Graz*, *Vienna*, and *Venice*.

Steamers from Staro pristanište, near bus station. Frequent connections with all places between Trieste and Pula; twice weekly in season to chief towns in Dalmatia.

Beach, Nabrežje jugoslovanske mornarice. Also in front of Hotel Žusterna and at Ankaran; all pebble and sand.—WATER POLO at Hotel Žusterna.—SAILING from Jadralni klub, Pristaniški trg.

Festival of National Folklore last week in July, tickets locally or in advance through Kompas travel agency.

History. Situated on or near the site of the Greek *Aegida*, mentioned by Pliny the Elder, Koper derives its present name from the later Roman *Capris*. During the 7C it was settled by the Slavs, in 788 became part of the Frankish empire, and from the 10C came under increasing Venetian influence, acknowledging Venetian sovereignty in 1279. The town then flourished under the name of *Capodistria* (from Caput Histriae), reaching the height of its prosperity in the 15–16C, when it was the chief town of Istria. Five of its podestà-captains became Doge of Venice. It was incorporated into Napoleon's Province of Illyria in 1797, became Austrian after the Congress of Vienna, and from 1918 till the Second World War (in common with the rest of Istria) was occupied by Italy. After the war Koper was the chief town in the internationally administered Zone B of the Free Territory of Trieste and in 1954 was joined to Yugoslavia as a result of the London Agreement.

From the bus station on the waterfront, we take Kidričeva ul., to the E., passing (r.) a former salt warehouse (15–16C) that now serves as a restaurant. Behind lies CARPACCIEV TRG where St Justina's column, erected in 1571, commemorates the battle of Lepanto, to which Koper contributed a galley. In the far corner of the square the house in which Benedetto Carpaccio reputedly lived provides the entrance to the night club Triglav. The tradition that Benedetto (d. 1560) and even his more famous father, Vittore, were natives of Capodistria is not proven. Continuing along Kidričeva ul. we pass Sv. Trojica and Sv. Nikolaj, two small Renaissance churches both closed, and reach the 16C Baroque *Palača Totto*, the ground floor of which has been converted into shops. Inside a Baroque staircase and portal have been preserved, while set in the outer wall is a winged lion of St Mark, brought here from a former Venetian fortress that guarded the causeway. Opposite are medieval houses with protruding upper stories resting on exposed beams.

The large irregular Muzejski trg extends N. on the site of a demolished Italian prison in which Marshal Tito was once incarcerated. On the right is the handsome Baroque *Palača Belgramoni-Tacco*, built at the end of the 16C with fine balustrades. The main portal has an iron grille in the tympanum enshrining a medusa's head, and a bronze door-knocker in the form of Venus rising from the Waves, by Tiziano Aspetti. The palača houses the **Okrajni Muzej za zgodovino in umetnost** (Art and Historical Museum; daily 9–12, 3–6) in a new arrangement since 1965.

VESTIBULE. Escutcheons of former Koper nobles and a 15C Gothic font, with a relief of the Madonna. A lapidary collection (1.) includes Roman mosaics and two Romanesque columns from the first cathedral of Koper.—FIRST FLOOR. In the Banqueting Hall a good collection of 16–18C paintings includes a Nativity by *Correggio* and works by Padovanino, Fiamminghini, Romanino, and the schools of Ben. Carpaccio and Iac. Bassano. Other rooms contain Venetian icons, porcelain figurines, modern Slovene and Italian paintings, a reconstructed Istrian kitchen of the 18C, and the study of Angelo Calafati, governor of Istria under Napoleon.—SECOND FLOOR. Historical memorials of Koper, a musician's gallery, and the armoury, with a 17C ceiling and wall paintings.

Kidričeva ul. ends at *TITOV TRG, a beautiful old square and Koper's principal attraction, though its appeal is impaired by traffic and parked vehicles. Immediately on our left is the fine **Loža** in Venetian Gothic, built in 1462–63 by Nikola of Piran and Tomaso da Venezia. It was restored in 1698 and now houses a pleasant kavarna. Set in its walls are a Madonna, a lion of St Mark, and the arms of former mayors. Verdijeva ul., to the left of the loggia, leads to the summer theatre and cinema.

The **Stolnica**, or *Cathedral of Sv. Nazarij* (St Nazarius), on the E.

side of the square, displays a mixture of styles. The lower story built at
the beginning of the 15C, is in decorated Venetian Gothic, with a w.
door (no longer used) flanked by twin-canopied alcoves containing effigies of saints (attr. to Domenico da Capodistria) and blind arcading. A
fresco of St Nazarius fills the tympanum. The upper story was completed
about a century later in Renaissance style, with Corinthian pilasters and
a wheel-window filled with stained glass. At the s.w. corner the massive
Romanesque *Campanile*, planned as a watch-tower at the beginning of
the 13C, was completed when the present cathedral was built, and the
belfry (view) added in 1660.

INTERIOR. The cathedral is entered through one of the doors on the s.
side, which were constructed of 15C materials garnered when the interior
was reconstructed in the Baroque style in 1714 by Giorgio Massari.
Notable are the ceiling of the apse, the 16C sarcophagus of St Nazarius
behind the high altar, the walnut choir stalls, and the bishop's throne.

Above the throne are two paintings by Vitt. Carpaccio. The Massacre of the
Innocents appears to be only a half, while the Presentation at the Temple derives its
shape from having been painted for an organ door; until 1959 both hung in a single
frame. Other paintings include a Madonna with saints, also by Vitt. Carpaccio
(1516), and the same subject in less detail by Ben. Carpaccio.
The *Treasury* (apply to sacristan) includes a fine Byzantine casket (12C), silver
crucifixes and a silver monstrance (15C).
Just behind the cathedral, on the N. side, is the *Rotunda Carmine*, a 13C Romanesque edifice with a Baroque interior, that serves as the baptistery.

Across the square the *Town Hall* occupies the 16C Venetian barracks,
with a Renaissance doorway in the s.w. corner. The **Pretorska palača,**
former residence of the mayor and of the Venetian podestà, fills the
fourth side of the square and now houses the law courts. It is an impressive but cluttered building, half in Venetian Gothic, with a pleasing four-
light window, and half in Renaissance style.

Originally there were two separate mansions, erected in the 13C, with the town
loggia between them. In the mid-15C the loggia was moved to the other end of the
square (comp. above) and the two parts joined. Later in the same century the
centre and w. wing were given a Renaissance façade, and in 1664 the decorative
battlements were added. The façade is incrusted with medallions, inscriptions, escutcheons and busts of successive governors, and a large lion of St Mark. In the
centre of the parapet a curious statue represents Justice: the body is Roman, the
head Gothic, and the limbs Venetian Baroque.

An arch in the E. wing of the Pretorska palača leads into picturesque
narrow Čevljarska ul., the town's main shopping street. Beneath the
arch (r.) the 'bocca del leone' for anonymous denunciations still bears
its Venetian inscription. About thirty paces down on the right a narrower arch admits to the courtyard of the *Palača Orlandini* (1774) with a
Baroque staircase and balustrade and a painted ceiling at the head of the
stairwell. We leave Čevljarska ul. by Župančičeva ul., passing (l.) the
17C *Palača Carli*. In Prešernov trg an ornate Renaissance well, erected
in 1423 and twice restored in the 17–18C, has a bridge-like superstructure modelled on the arms of the Podestà Lorenzo da Ponte. On the far
side are the plain Renaissance church of Sv. Basso and the *Vrata Muda*,
the former main gate of the town (1516). Outside begins the main road
to Trieste and Ljubljana by which we approached the town.

Turning back we take Tominčeva ul. and, bearing left and right, reach
Gimnazijski trg, dominated by the *Gimnazija*, a 17C school for the sons

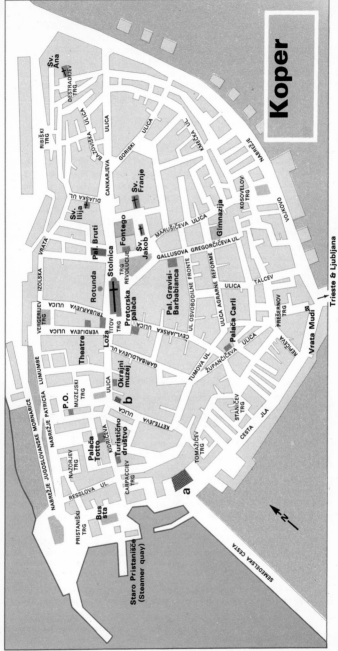

of Venetian noblemen (now the Italian grammar school). We continue down Gallusova ul., where, on our left in Ul. osvobodilne fronte, opposite the new Koper radio station, are the 17C *Palača Tarsio* and *Palači Gravisi-Buttorai*. In Gallusova ul., a little farther on, the *Palača Gravisi-Barbabianca*, also 17C, has a good Baroque façade but suffered by use as barracks during the war. It now houses a music school and entry is easily gained to the striking banqueting hall, with trompe l'oeil murals and ceiling paintings.

We reach the spacious TRG REVOLUCIJE, also known as the *Brolo*, at the s.e. end of the cathedral. The E. side of the square is dominated by the *Fontega*, a former grain warehouse built in Venetian Gothic in 1392. A fine classical pediment was added in 1529, and the façade bears the escutcheons of various podestà of Koper. Flanking it are the small 14C Gothic church of *Sv. Jakob*, now deconsecrated, and the 17C *Palača Vissch-Nardi*, while to the rear are the abandoned monastery of Sv. Klara and 13C church of *Sv. Frančiško* with a Gothic w. door and apse and 17C painted ceiling. On the N. side of the square the heavy Baroque *Palača Bruti*, by Massari, is occupied by the public library.

Leaving the square by Cankarjeva ul. we pass the former Catholic Seminary, a 19C imitation of Venetian Gothic, and make for the oldest corner of the town. Our street and its side streets are lined with Renaissance houses, including the late-15C *Palača de Belli*, and in Dijaška ul. is the Romanesque Rotunda of *Sv. Elijo* (?9C) with 17C additions. A five-minute walk brings us to Destradijev trg, with the former Franciscan monastery and church of *Sv. Ana* (apply to the sacristan for admission). The monastery is used as a prison, but the church includes in its small collection of paintings, a Madonna Enthroned with Saints by Girolamo da Santacroce, a polyptych by G. B. Cima (1513) and pictures by Palma Giovane. Behind Destradijev trg is the quaint old *Fishing Quarter* centred on Ribiški trg, with a number of houses dating from the 14C and in continuous occupation to this day.

B. From Koper to Postojna

ROAD, 62 km. (39 m.). 12 km. *Rižana* (for Hrastovlje, 3 km.).—29 km. *Kozina.* —35 km. *Divača* (for Škocjan, 3 km., and **Lipica**, 6 km.).—62 km. **Postojna.** Frequent buses in the season; also special excursions to *Hrastovlje, Škocjan, Lipica,* and *Postojn.*—RAILWAY only from *Kozina* to *Postojn.*

Leaving Koper by Ljubljanska cesta, we take the main road as far as (5 km.) *Križišče Ankaran* (comp. Rte 2A) and turn right towards Ljubljana, following the course of the river Rižana. In this valley Charlemagne's emissaries called a popular assembly in 804 to settle grievances between the Slavonic rural population of Istria and the Romanic inhabitants of the towns. Shortly beyond (12 km.) *Rižana* a branch road (r.) leads to Rižana Park (3 km.) and Hrastovlje (6 km.) with its famous church.

Rižana Park (Chalet Motel with rest.), a pleasant oasis amid the karst, surrounds the second source of the Rižana. Its true source is some 20 km. to the E., but for fifteen of these the river flows underground before re-emerging here. An experimental beaver farm was once established in the park and some animals have been retained in an enclosure. There is also a pheasant farm, a small aviary, and a collection of native mammals including deer. The river is stocked with trout, a speciality of the restaurant; fishing licences may be obtained at the inn (gostilna) in the village.

Beyond the park macadam gives place to gravel. After 1 km. we branch left along another gravel road (unsignposted) that descends into the *Dolina gradov* (Valley of the Castles), so called from a legend that nine castles stood here; the ruins of three remain on the far ridge. On a hill beside the rustic village of **Hrastovlje**, the church of Sv. TROJICE (Holy Trinity; open 10–5 in season, otherwise key from house No. 30. Recorded commentary in Slovene and planned in English) was constructed in a primitive Romanesque style on the basilican plan, probably in the 13C. Its best feature is the plain Romanesque tower. The main door dates from 1727. The fortifications built around 1500 to protect it from the Turks still stand.

The Interior has the most complete and best preserved *Frescoes of the Istrian school extant. They are in a rustic Gothic style and were painted, according to a Latin inscription, by Ivan of Kastav (Johannes de Kastua) in 1490. Traces of earlier frescoes can be seen underneath in places, also glagolitic inscriptions. The frescoes illustrate the history of the world in terms of the Old and New Testaments. Of particular interest are the twelve apostles in the main apse; the Life of Christ, on the w. wall and the upper part of the s. wall; the monumental Genesis Cycle on the roof of the nave; the months of the year in medallions on the roofs of the aisles; the Journey of the Magi on the N. wall; and the Dance of Death on the lower part of the s. wall, a fine example and one of the only two in Istria. In the sacristy, entered from the s. apse, are preserved 15C and 17C reliquaries.

Continuing along the main Ljubljana road, we climb a barren karst plateau and pass through (17 km.) *Črni Kal* and (19 km.) *Gornji Črni Kal*, which has a handsome leaning church tower, with views left across the Osp valley and the city of Trieste to the sea.—At (22 km.) the next crossroads a macadamized road leads left to the village of *Kaštelec* (1 km.) and the 14C castle of *Socerb* (3½ km.) on the very border with Italy. Inside the castle (restaurant, open all the year) is a carved well-head. The terrace provides excellent views of the Julian Alps, the Dolomites, Trieste and its bay. About 100 yds from the castle is a limestone cave in which St Socerb (2–3C) reputedly lived; a rude altar that stood here was destroyed during the Second World War.

Beyond (29 km.) *Kozina*, where we cross the main Trieste–Rijeka road, we come to (35 km.) **Divača**, where about 50 yds from the railway station there is a limestone cave, *Kačna jama*, descending to a depth of 1000 ft. At Divača we may diverge left to Lipica, the famous stud for Lipizaner horses, or right to the Škocjan Caves.

To LIPICA, 8 km. we take the road towards Sežana and then immediately left again along the Lokev road. After 1 km. there is another cave, *Divaška jama* (ask at the railway-line keeper's house for directions), and in 3 km. we reach the village of *Lokev*. Just outside the village is the cave of *Vilenica* (guide and key from A. Umek in Lokev or the Jamarski Klub, 'Iskra', Sežana), which achieved fame in the 19C and whose visitors' book, containing many illustrious names, is preserved in the village. The cave, now little frequented, is varied and beautiful and can be explored for about half a mile.

Lipica is the original stud farm where the Lipizaner horses were bred for the Spanish riding school in Vienna. It was founded by the Archduke Charles, son of the Emperor Ferdinand, in 1580, and the Lipizaners were bred by crossing Andalusian thoroughbreds with the native ponies of the Karst region. Owing to wars the Lipica stud has been moved and divided many times, so that there are now also studs for breeding Lipizaner horses in Austria, Hungary, Czechoslovakia, and Italy. Guided tours (entrance fee) take place throughout the year, twice daily (10 and 3) in Nov–March and five times daily (8, 10, 12, 3, and 5) in high season; exhibition of riding (free) every Tuesday. There is a restaurant, open to all, and accommodation for those who have arranged to ride (own equipment necessary).

From Divača the *Škocjan Caves (Škocjanske jame)* are reached viâ the hamlet of *Matavun* or on foot (c. 1 hr) along a well-marked shady footpath through *Dolnje Ležeče*. Just beyond this village (l.) a side path leads to Razgledišče (see below). The caves were discovered at the beginning of the 19C but, despite their wildness and grandeur, are less well-known than Postojna (p. 9) and have at times been closed to the public. They

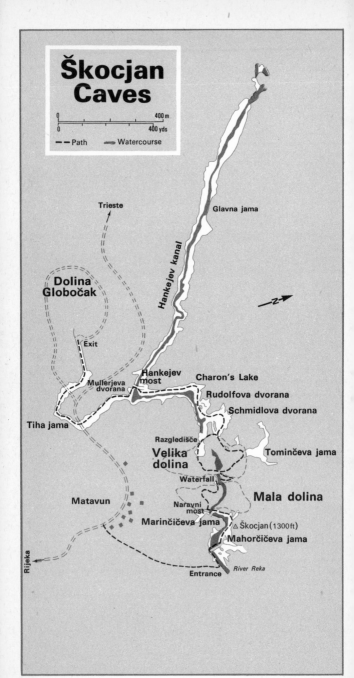

owe their existence to erosion by the river Reka and extend for c. 5 km. along its course, of which about two-thirds is accessible.

Guided tours daily in Nov–March at 10; in Apr, May, and Oct at 10 and 3; in summer at 10, 1, 3, and 5. Special visits can also be arranged.

The tour begins at Matavun, whence a steep footpath leads down and across the foaming river into *Mahorčičeva jama* (Mahorčič cave). We then descend to a small lake and pass by rapids into the gloomy *Mariničeva jama*. Ahead, where the light glimmers, is a narrow passage by which we attain the *Naravni most* (Natural Bridge) and pass into the open *Mala dolina* (Little Swallow-hole), with breathtaking views at the end of it of the *Velika dolina* (Great Swallow-hole) and of the Reka, which plunges in a waterfall into the lake below. At periods of full flood this fall can raise three-foot waves in the lake. We recross the river by another bridge and find ourselves in the *Velika Dolina*, whose perpendicular cliffs rise nearly 500 ft on either side. At the top of them, at the far end, can be seen Razgledišče, while all around us is a rich and varied flora, including Karstic, Mediterranean, Illyrian, Pontic, Baltic, and Central European species. Following a footpath cut in the side of the rock, we continue to *Tominčeva jama* (Tominc Cave), the first to be discovered and opened to the public (1823). Excavations here show the caves to have been inhabited in the Stone Age. Hence we proceed to the majestic *Schmidlova dvorana* (Schmidl Chamber), with magnificent stalactites and stalagmites, the *Rudolfova dvorana*, even larger, and into the long water-filled cave known as *Jezero Haron* (Charon's Lake). At its narrowing far end is *Hankejev most* (Hanke Bridge), whence we gain a view of the mysterious gorge leading to the mile-long Hankejev kanal and further caves beyond; this section is open only to experienced speleologists. After the bridge we leave the course of the river and walk through *Müllerjeva dvorana* to the long well-named *Tiha jama* (Peaceful Cave) and the swallow-hole *Globočak*, whence a road leads back to Matavun.

From the hamlet of *Škocjan* (1300 ft) there are excellent views over the surrounding karst and of Mt. Snežnik (5400 ft) to the E., as well as into the 300 ft-deep gorge of Okroglica. *Razgledišče*, a noted vantage point, commands similar views and a superb aerial view of the Velika and Mala dolina and the Reka waterfall.

From Divača the main Ljubljana road runs direct to (62 km.) **Postojna** (*Kraš, Javornik*; motel; restaurants), a thriving small town that makes an excellent centre from which to explore the whole karst region. In the main square an 18C mansion houses the *Notranjski muzej* (Regional Museum), with ethnographical and archaeological exhibits, and on the first floor the *Institut za raziskovanje kraša* (Karst Exploration Institute), with an exhibition illustrating the peculiarities, history, and development of the region.

The ****Postojna Caves** (*Postojnska jama*; also known under the Italian name POSTUMIA and the German ADELSBERG), one of the finest systems of limestone caves in Europe, lie about a mile from the town centre along the well-signposted road to Veliki otok (parking, restaurants, exchange and information offices). Discovered in 1818, the caves are estimated to be two million years old (beginning of Pleistocene age) and have been formed by the erosive action of the river Pivka. Recent explorations have shown them to be part of a unified system extending for some 21 km.; the Postojna section comprises 16¼ km., while other sections have become known under different names (comp. map) and are visited separately (see below).

The part open to the public, comprising the largest and most spectacular chain of caverns, extends for c. 4 km., while a further 3 km. of side passages are open only to speleologists. The main caves are open all the year. Guided tours (English commentary) daily in Nov–March 9.30 and 3; in Apr, May, and Oct 8.30, 10.30, 1.30, 4, and 6; in summer also at 12.30; entrance fee. The normal tour, partly effected by a small electric railway, takes 1¾ hrs, and it is advisable to take advantage of the special clothing offered at the start. The average temperature of the caves is 47–48°F. Elderly or infirm visitors should also bear in mind that though the railway extends for 2 km., a further 2 km. are covered on foot over quite difficult terrain.

The entrance gallery is completely denuded of stalagmites and stalactites and its walls are smoke-blackened, the result of guerrilla action during the Second World War when a German fuel and ammunition dump here was sabotaged by the Partisans. Our first halt is in the *Velika dvorana* (Great Hall), of impressive size (397 ft long, 165 ft wide and 116 ft high) but whose walls have also suffered from wartime damage. Leading off this hall is the *Imenski rov* (Tunnel of Names) with names carved on its walls dating back to the 15C. The gallery then narrows. We pass a barred tunnel on our right where Postojna's first Biospeleological Institute was founded by Andrej Perko in 1910, then a stalactite formation known as the *Slonova glava* (Elephant's Head), and come to the caves *Zvrnjena ladja* (Capsized Boat) and *Gotska dvorana* (Gothic Hall). We now fork right along the gallery *Snežnik* (Snow Mountain) and enter the spacious *Plesna dvorana* (Ballroom), where dances and festivals have been held regularly since the first half of the 19C. At the entrance to the cave is a plaque dedicated to two of Postojna's leading explorers, Jeržinovič and Schmidl.

We next traverse a series of cleverly lit galleries and caves displaying outstandingly beautiful stalactite and stalagmite formations, including *Želvi* (The Tortoises), *Pralnica* (The Wash House), *Palmi* (The Palm Trees), *Oglarske kope* (The Charcoal Piles), *Mumije* (The Mummies), *Vodnjak* (The Well), *Senene Kopice* (The Haystacks) and arrive at a large hall called *Razpotje* (The Crossroads). The tour now forks right through the *Stare jame* (Old Grottoes) and past the *Mali baldahin* (Little Canopy) and *Cipresa* (Cypress) to the *Baldahin* (Canopy), a marvellously delicate drapery formation. The railway ends by a forest of stalagmites and stalactites, many of them picturesquely named, upon an enormous rift formation, 150 ft high, known as *Velika gora* (Big Mountain) or *Kalvarija* (Mount Calvary), caused by the collapse of the roof of one of the largest chambers.

We continue on foot and cross the *Russian Bridge*, built by Russian prisoners of war during the First World War, to the *Lepe jame (Beautiful Grottoes), so named for the delicate shapes of their stalagmites and and stalactites and their extraordinary range of colour. We have now reached the farthest point of the Postojna Caves.

A man-made tunnel stretches right to *Črna jama* (Black Cave, see below), but we turn back to the *Zimska dvorana* (Winter Hall), pass the pillar called *Briljant* (The Brilliant) and find ourselves once more by the railway terminus. Here we turn right down yet another gallery, pass-

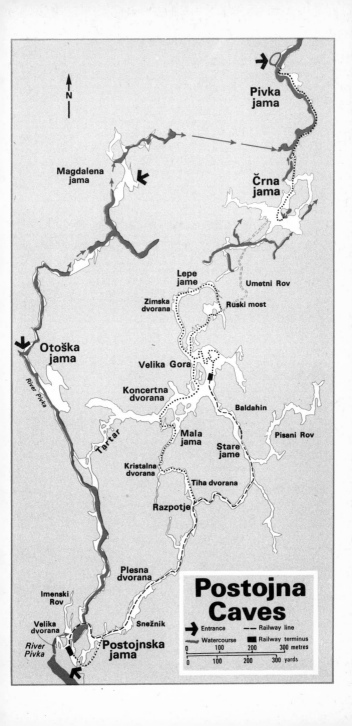

Pivka jama

Črna jama

Magdalena jama

Lepe jame

Umetni Rov

Zimska dvorana

Ruski most

Otoška jama

Velika Gora

Koncertna dvorana

Baldahin

Pisani Rov

Mala jama

Stare jame

Kristalna dvorana

Tiha dvorana

Razpotje

Plesna dvorana

Imenski Rov

Velika dvorana

Snežnik

River Pivka

Postojnska jama

River Pivke

Tartar

Postojna Caves

➤ Entrance   - - - Railway line

〰 Watercourse   ■ Railway terminus

0   100   200   300 metres

0   100   200   300 yards

ing on the right the long gallery known as *Tartarus* that connects with Otoška jama (see below), and come to the prodigious *KONCERTNA DVORANA (Concert Hall), the largest cave in the system. Covering an area of 30,000 sq ft and with a roof 165 ft high, this cave is said to accommodate over 10,000 people for concerts. In the season it contains a restaurant and a special post office accepting cards. Here a tenarium and two aquaria contain specimens of cave fauna, including the extraordinary Proteus Anguinus, or 'man fish' (named for the peculiar texture of its skin), thought to be a survivor from the Tertiary period.

After a pause for refreshment and card writing the guide now leads us through the beautiful *Mala jama* (Little Grotto), the *Kristalna dvorana* (Crystal Hall), and the *Tiha dvorana* (Hall of Silence) and back to the crossroads, whence the train returns to the entrance.

Near Postojna a number of smaller caves are linked with the Pivka river system. The nearest is *Otoška jama*, just outside the village of *Veliki otok* and c. ½ hr walk away.—At 5 km. by asphalt and gravel road is *Pivka jama* (guided tours twice daily in 1½ hrs; adm. fee), a well-lit cave reached by descending 256 steps. The cave is set in a pleasant wooded park with restaurant, shop, camp site, and chalet bungalows set among the trees. Fresh trout are usually available. Included in the entrance fee and 10 min walk away is *Črna jama* (Black Cave), the most beautiful of the smaller caves, with 3 km. of galleries.—At the village of *Planina*, 10 km. N. of Postojna on the road to Ljubljana, is the *Planinska jama* (guide on request), at the underground confluence of the Pivka and the Rak. A subterranean lake and many underground streams necessitate the use of a boat for much of the tour (1½ hrs).

From Postojna a good asphalt road (bus 3 times daily) leads to (9 km.) the cave and castle of *Predjama* (adm. 2,50 *din.*; children 1 *din.*). Strikingly situated in the mouth of a huge cavern in the hillside, the present Renaissance castle was built in 1570 by Johannes Cobenzl, later Austrian ambassador to Moscow and governor of Carniola. An earlier castle, built higher inside the cave, was reputedly the scene of a legendary siege of Erasmus Lueger, a 15C Robin Hood. The castle is interesting for its 'impossible' situation and the skilful way in which it is grafted on to the rock, rather than for any architectural nicety. Inside are exhibited archaeological finds, furniture, armour, and, in the small chapel, a 15C Gothic Pietà. The local parish church (1449) acquired its façade in the 17C.

Enthusiasts may inquire at Postojna about the caves at *Rakek* in the beautiful Rak valley and at *Lož*, also for the celebrated disappearing *Cerkniško jezero* (Cerknica Lake), which commonly dries up in summer.

C. From Koper to Piran

ROAD, 18 km. (11 m.). 7 km. *Izola.*—14 km. **Portorož.**—18 km. **Piran.** Frequent local buses and steamers.

We quit Koper by the causeway, passing through the suburb of *Semedele*. The road, close to the sea, traverses the Izola plain, flat fertile country noted for strawberries and Refoško wine.

7 km. **Izola** (*Zora; Riviera*) is a small coastal town (7500 inhab.) having, like Koper, a dual Venetian and modern character, but less historical interest. Founded by refugees from Aquileia, it passed to Venice, Austria, Italy, and with the rest of Zone B to Yugoslavia in 1954. In Gregorčičeva ul. the *Palača Besenghi degli Ughi*, a Rococo mansion of

1775–81, with a lavish interior, is now the music school. Near by are the *Palača Manzioli* (1470) in Venetian Gothic and the 16C *Palača Lovisato*. In *Sv. Mavro* (St Maurus), the 16C parish church, hang Madonnas by Girol, da Santacroce, and Zorzi Ventura; Palma Giovane, Entombment; Ant. Carneo, St Lawrence distributing alms; the sacristy contains a 15C monstrance, three illuminated antiphonaries, and eight large paintings by Peter of Koper (1473).

Climbing through pinewoods, we pass the *Hotel Belvedere*, the terrace of which commands a superb view over the Bay of Trieste. Below, a pleasant beach is backed by an autocamp for 100 cars. We descend to the valley and village of *Strunjan*, where Tartini (comp. below) had a villa, surmount another ridge and descend by hairpin turns.

14 km. **Portorož**, a pleasant sophisticated resort (2000 inhab.) in riviera style, quadruples its population in summer. Set in an amphitheatre of olive-clad hills and fruit trees, and planted with exotic shrubs, the town still preserves a mildly Austrian atmosphere.

Hotels, Riviera, 130 R, dancing, swimming pool, beach; Lucija, 210 R, beach; Palace, 220 R, casino, thermal baths, dancing, beach; Central, Jadranka, Planinka, Slovenski dom; Bristol, Virginija, Istra, Dora, Orion, Piran, Helios.
Autocamp. *Lucija*, 200 cars, restaurant, beach, 2 km. E.
Restaurants. *Jadran; Ribja restavracija* (fish).
Kavarnas. *Suzana; Jadran; Lucija.*
Buses (in the season) to *Piran* every 10 min; daily to towns in Istria and Slovenia. Excursions to *Škocjan; Postojna; Hrastovlje.*
Beach, cemented foreshore, sand.—SAILING from Jadralni klub (rowing boats for hire also).—TENNIS at Hotel Palace.
Sculpture Exhibition ('Forma Viva'), annual competition in July–Aug.—The FESTIVAL OF FOLKLORE (see Koper) opens at Portorož.

Portorož dates from at least the 12C, though nothing remains of the old settlement where Doge Dandolo took refuge with his fleet in 1202, and where in 1380 Carlo Zeno, admiral of Venice, did the same. The Emp. Conrad IV stayed here in 1252. In the late 19C, under Austria, Portorož salt was discovered to have healing properties and a spa came into being.

A pleasant brief excursion may be made on foot past the bus station and s.e. along the shore to the hamlet of *Sečovlje*. The road runs through salt-flats where wind-pumps having two rectangular sails on a wooden frame raise sea-water into the beds for evaporation. About 1 km. beyond the autocamp (comp. above) is a cypress-shaded park with a permanent exhibition of sculpture comprising pieces donated after the annual competition.

18 km. **PIRAN** (*Piran; Sidro*), just round the headland from Portorož on a narrow-jutting peninsula, is a small town (5500 inhab.) of Venetian type, one of the best preserved and most fully restored on the Adriatic coast. After a turbulent early history, it passed to Venice in 1283 and thereafter shared the fortunes of its neighbours. It is the most popular of the Slovene resorts and crowded in summer.

The focal point of the town is the spacious TARTINIJEV TRG, facing the harbour, which occupies the position of an older inner harbour (filled in 1893–94). In the centre stands a monument by Antonio dal Zotto (1896) to Giuseppe Tartini (1692–1770), the famous Piran violinist and composer after whom the square is named; his birthplace stands on the E. side (plaque). Beside it stands the church of *Sv. Petar* (1818), with a Madonna by Polidoro da Lanciano (?), a pupil of Titian, and in the N.E.

corner, a 15C mansion in Venetian Gothic, known as the *Beneška hiša*, or Benečanka, with lovely windows and balconies; the tourist office occupies the ground floor. Continuing round the w. side of the square we come to the *Art Gallery* (soon to be transformed into the town museum) and the Kavarna Galerija; the imposing *Town Hall* (Mestna hiša; 1879), with a lion of St Mark built into its façade and incorporating the Post Office; and the *Law Courts* (Sodišče; 1874), in the Tuscan style, into which are incorporated two 17C Baroque portals. Adjoining this on the harbour side is the former town gateway of *Sv. Nikola*, erected in 1663, while beyond the harbour on the s. side of the square stands the Hotel Sidro.

The two stone flagpoles standing in the s.w. corner of the square date from 1466 and were moved here in 1895 when the old town hall was destroyed. The city flag-pole bears a relief of St George on horseback and the inscription "By our prayers you remain safe, land of Piran"; the other, for the Venetian flag, bears the lion with the inscription "Behold the winged lion who spans the earth, the seas and the stars", the arms of Piran, and various medieval measures of length.

From the s.e. corner of the main square Cankarjevo nabrežje leads past the harbour to the yacht-club and an open-air cinema and thence along the shore to Portorož. At the near end, facing the harbour, is the **Mestni muzej** (Town Museum), housed in the former Gabrielli Mansion (1860). Here the town and maritime museums are combined until the new premises are opened (see above).

The museum (open 8–11, 4–7 in the season, one hour earlier Apr–June and Sept–Oct) is entered by a vestibule flanked by two 18C statues of Venetian sailors ('schiavoni'). Showcases on the wall illustrate the development of marine small arms (continued up the stairs) while the engravings opposite are by A. Tischbein (Piran, Devin, Koper, 1842), and Poncheimer (Trieste, 1840). Leading off right are rooms illustrating the history of the Piran salt mines and a small lapidary collection, including three 15–16C well-heads.

The most interesting exhibits are on the FIRST FLOOR. *Room 5.* Archaeological remains from prehistoric to early Slavonic times. *Room 6* illustrates the maritime activities of the Slovenes in the navies of Austria and Venice by three outstanding model ships: a 17C Venetian galley, an Austrian sloop, and the Austrian Admiral's ship, both of the 18C, all made by students of the Gruber Naval Academy in Ljubljana (1765–75). There are 17C engravings on the wall. *Room 7* is dominated by the monumental canvas *The City Council of Piran at Prayer by *Jac.* and *Dom. Tintoretto* (1578), painted when they were working in Piran. Also here are a 17C Venetian painting of Neptune, 18C seascapes, and local Istrian sea chests.

In the corridor (*Room 8*) *Padovanino*, Madonna; *Bon. Veneto*, Last Supper; two 17C still-lifes with roses by an unknown artist; and works of the school of Tinto-retto. *Room 9.* Relics of early Piranian notables, charming little votive pictures painted at sea by mariners and presented to local churches, and a pair of paintings by an anonymous Montenegrin artist depicting a naval battle between the French and British off Piran in 1812. In tiny *Room 10* are a wooden figure of St Anne (c. 1500), and a 17C ship's figurehead depicting the Virgin. *Room 11* is the Tartini room, with some of the composer's relics (the displayed violin is a copy of his origi-nal Amati), and the Baroque Paduan furniture (1720) of his bedroom. *Room 12.* Paintings and statues of the 18–20C.

The SECOND FLOOR is devoted to Slovene maritime history of the past hundred years and to the national liberation struggle during the Second World War.

A little behind Cankarjevo nabrežje and parallel to it, the narrow vaulted Ul. svobode leads from Tartinjev trg to the *Vrata Marciana*

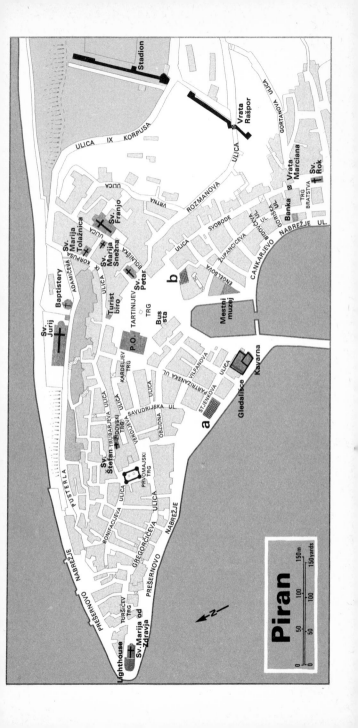

Piran

Lighthouse

Sv. Marija od Zdravja

PREŠERNOVO

TURŠIČEV TRG

PREŠERNOVO

NABREŽJE

PUSTERLA

BONIFACIJEVA ULICA

GREGORČIČEVA

NABREŽJE

ULICA

Sv. Štefan

TRUBARJEVA ULICA

ŽIDOVSKI TRG

VERDIJEVA

SAVUDRIJSKA UL

OBZIDNA UL

PRVOMAJSKI TRG

KARDELJEV TRG

ULICA

Sv. Jurij

Baptistery

ADAMIČEVA ULICA

IX KORPUSA

ULICA

Sv. Marija Tolažnica

Sv. Marija Snežna

Sv. Franjo

BOLNIŠKA ULICA

Sv. Petar

Turist biro

TARTINIJEV TRG

P.O.

Bus sta

STJENKOVA ULICA

PARTIZANSKA UL

VILANOVA ULICA

Gledališce

a

Kavarna

Mestni muzej

b

ENGELSOVA

ŽUPANČIČEVA UL

ULICA

SVOBODE

ROZMANOVA

VRTNA ULICA

ULICA

ULICA IX KORPUSA

Stadion

Vrata Rašpor

ULICA

GORTANOVA ULICA

CANKARJEVO NABREŽJE UL.

BIDOVČEVA UL

GORIŠKA UL

Banka

Vrata Marciana

Sv. Rok

TRG BRATSTVA

NABREŽJE UL.

—N—

0   50   100   150m

0   50   100   150 yards

(1553), originally the main entrance to the town, with a lion of St Mark set over it. Just outside is the small Baroque chapel of *Sv. Rok* (1649). Of the **Walls,** erected in 1475–1534 to protect Piran on the landward side, about 300 metres remain. These can be reached by ascending the steps that fork left from Gortanova ul. (alternative routes lead from Tartinijev trg via Ul. IX korpusa or Rozmanova ul.). Seven handsome crenellated lookout towers extend from Vrata Rašpor to the top of the hill; the furthest one, standing on the highest part of the peninsula, can be climbed for excellent views of the town and bay of Piran and, to the N.E. of Koper, Trieste and the Julian Alps.

Descending by Ul. IX korpusa, we turn left down the steps of Bolniška ul. to reach the **Franciscan Church and Monastery** (now a home for the aged). The foundation was established by Bishop Manolesso of Koper at the beginning of the 14C, but the church was enlarged a century later and the adjoining cloister rebuilt in the Renaissance style in the 16C (restored 1951) when the bell tower was also constructed. The first of the three chapels added on the s. side, in the shape of a baldachino (1518), is outstanding. The 15C pulpit is carved and there is a painting of Mary Magdalene by Palma Giovane. The altar-piece by Carlo Caliari replaces a celebrated earlier one, by Vitt. Carpaccio, removed to Italy during the war and not returned.

Opposite is the small church of *Sv. Marija Snežna,* originally Gothic (1404) but reconstructed in the Baroque style in the 17C and restored in 1967. Inside are paintings attributed to the Piran artist Tomaso Gregolin (1660) and a recently discovered 15C crucifixion by an unknown Italian artist. The narrow Istrska ul. leads in a few paces to the attractive little Baroque church of *Sv. Marija Tolažnica,* where the paintings include a 14C Venetian icon and four pictures either by Fontebasso or G. Angeli (18C). A little higher up Ul. IX korpusa, steps mount to **Sv. Jurij** (St George) in an imposing position on a hill above the town. The church was founded in the 14C but the present Baroque structure dates from 1637. Within, above the N. door, is a curious equestrian figure of St George. Adjoining are a detached *Campanile* (1607–8) by Giacomo de' Nodari, modelled on that of St Mark's in Venice, and a hexagonal *Baptistery* (1637), with a font adapted from a 2C Roman sarcophagus (relief showing Cupid riding on a dolphin), a 14C Gothic painted crucifix in wood ('the tree of life'), and a small painted pietà in stone (c. 1450). Set into the exterior wall is an early Croatian Romanesque transenna. In the treasury (apply sacristan) are two 17C Baroque statuettes of St George in silver and contemporary candlesticks, all the work of local smiths.

Lying to the w. of Tartinijev trg is the picturesque and peninsular *Old Quarter of Piran beloved of visitors, a maze of winding narrow streets crowded with houses painted in pastel colours and well supplied with cafés, inns, and bathing places. Obzidna ul., one of the oldest streets in Piran, leads w. through the ancient gateway of *Vrata Delfin* (1483). Here part of the town's inner walls dating from the 15C are surmounted by overhanging houses of a slightly later period. The central PRVOMAJSKI TRG is almost entirely occupied by the great Baroque *Cistern* (1776), which once supplied the town with water. Two female statues flanking the s. staircase represent Law and Justice, and the upper stairs are flanked by cherubs holding fish. On the N. side of the square a Baroque mansion houses the town *Pharmacy*, established in 1682. On Kidričevo nabrežje beside the harbour are a small *Aquarium* (open 8–11, 4–7), the *Gledališče* (theatre; guest performances in the summer), and the Kavarna Tartini. Beyond, the Prešernovo nabrežje leads past the Hotel Piran and cafés to the *Punta* at the tip of the peninsula. Here stands a lighthouse adjoined by the tiny 17C church of *Sv. Marija od Zdravja* (main altar by Gasper Albertini). The promenade leads back along the opposite waterfront past a small open-air summer theatre to the parish church (see above).

3   FROM PIRAN TO PULA VIÂ BUJE

ROAD, 94 km.—3 km. *Portorož.*—19 km. **Buje.**—50 km. *Baderna* (for Poreč).—64 km. *Brajkovići* (for Rovinj).—73 km. **Bale.**—84 km. **Vodnjan.**—94 km. **Pula.** Buses up to four times daily in 3 hrs.

The main road follows the shore of the Piran peninsula as far as *Portorož* (see Rte 2c), skirts the salt pans of Sečovlje (r.), and follows the river Dragonja as far as (11 km.) the border between Slovenia and Croatia. We are now entering that part of Istria known as Red Istria from the colour of its soil, which is rich in bauxite deposits. It also produces an excellent variety of the sweet white wine, Malvasia.

The road affords access to a series of inland Istrian towns standing on hill sites which have been in continuous occupation since at least Illyrian times. Their history parallels that of the better known coastal towns with the difference that during the Middle Ages they remained longer under the control of the Patriarch of Aquileia. Subsequently they came under the sway of local Istrian bishops and the feudal nobility, and passing to Venice correspondingly later, were subjected to considerable less Venetian influence. At first the inland towns flourished under Venice, despite being remote from the sea and forced to maintain elaborate defences first against Austria and later against the Turks. But in the 16C and early 17C plague decimated the population reducing the region to indigence. Settlers were introduced from Cyprus, Turkey, Greece, S. Italy and particularly the rest of the Balkans, where the indigenous Slav population was constantly in flight from the Turks. The towns themselves succeeded in assimilating most of the newcomers and retaining the Venetian language, but the surrounding countryside remained overwhelmingly Slavonic, a situation that bred more recent conflicts in this area between Italy and Yugoslavia. It also led, after the Second World War, when Istria became part of Yugoslavia, to the precipitate departure of almost all the Italian-speaking inhabitants to Italy, resulting once again in depopulation of the towns.

The towns are for the most part highly picturesque with many features of architectural interest but they are isolated on remote and mainly bad gravel roads, and except for infrequent local buses can be reached only by car. Hotels, for the moment, are non-existent and restaurants few and rather primitive. It is planned to revitalize some of the more accessible places and local inquiries should be made before setting out.

The road climbs out of the Dragonja valley passing (13 km.) the crossroads where a right turn leads to Savudrija, Umag and the coast road (see Rte 4) and brings us to (19 km.) **Buje** (*Zora*) a charming small town in an elevated position that earned it the sobriquet of 'the spy of Istria'. A Roman settlement under the name of *Bullea*, it later belonged to the Patriarchate of Aquileia and then to the counts of Weimar–Orlamunde, before passing to Venice in 1412. In appearance the town is entirely medieval, with fortifications still intact (renewed 15C and 17C) and a maze of narrow streets. In the central square are grouped a fine 15C palača in Venetian Gothic with painted façade, a Venetian loggia

(16C), a medieval measuring column and the 16C parish church of *Sv. Servolo* (rebuilt in the Baroque style in the 18C). The church walls contain fragments and inscriptions from a Roman temple that once occupied the site and on the w. end is a Romanesque relief of an angel; inside are 14–15C Gothic statues in wood. The detached 16C campanile (view), patterned on that at Aquileia, bears the arms of local nobles. Just outside the town walls near the main entry is the 15C church of *Sv. Marija* with a contemporary Madonna in wood, Renaissance gates in iron, a 15C Pietà (artist unknown) and eight biblical scenes by the Venetian, Gaspare Vecchio (1711).

Momjan, 6 km. N.E., the next nearest hill-town, has ruins of a 14C castle built into the rock face, a 16C parish church and Baroque houses. More interesting is **Grožnjan**, 9 km. S.E. of Buje, in a superb position overlooking the Mirna valley, almost 1000 ft up. The small town clustered tightly on its hilltop takes its plan from the Venetian military settlement established here in 1359, when Grožnjan became the seat of one of two military captains of Istria. Parts of the ramparts from this period still stand, together with a 15C town gate and loggia (inset with Roman fragments) and bell tower. On the far side of the town overlooking the valley is the small church of *Sv. Kuzma* (1554) with loggia added in the 18C. The large Baroque parish church of *Sv. Marija, Vid, i Modest* and most of the domestic buildings also date from the 18C. Mid-way along the attractive main street, the Renaissance *Palača Biriani* (1597) has been taken over by a group of Slovene and Croatian artists who work here in the summer and maintain a permanent exhibition gallery (ask neighbours for key if closed).

Continuing s. from Buje we pass immediately on our right the turning for Umag and Novigrad (see Rte 4) and descend to (31 km.) the MIRNA, Istria's largest river.

Thirty miles long, the river has its source in the hills S.E. of Buzet and has been known since ancient times. Its first recorded name was *Nengon* and to the Greeks it was known as the *Ister* (also the Greek name for the Danube), from which the name Istria is probably derived. On either side of the river to the N. and W. of Motovun (see below) stretch the *Motovun Woods*, which were placed under state protection by Venice as early as 1452 and were one of the Republic's principal sources of timber for shipbuilding. Below Motovun the valley in places attains up to a mile in width and is subject to extensive flooding, the resulting alluvial plain being rich in truffles.

To Motovun, Oprtalj, and Buzet by the Mirna Valley, 44 km. (with diversions). At the point where our road crosses the river a gravelled road leads left up the right bank. At (8 km.) *Livade*, a village on the Mirna, the ways divide.

Motovun (Ital. *Montona*), the finest of the Istrian hilltop towns, stands at 900 ft, 3 km. s., and is reached by a zigzag road or by some 1000 steps. We enter by an 18C outer gate and proceed through the newer part of the town to a Gothic *Gateway*; over it is set the town arms and a lion of St Mark, with open book, and inside another lion with book closed. To the right, just outside, stands an 18C Baroque *Loggia* (view). The gate forms part of the RAMPARTS (comp. below) dating from 1350 though later renovated, which encircle the old town; they are embellished on the s. side with Gothic arches. Through the inner gateway is the main square with the Renaissance church of *Sv. Stjepan* (1614), whose design is attributed to Palladio. A statue of St Lawrence by Giov. Bonazza (1725) adorns the high altar, and the choir stalls are 18C Baroque. The treasury (apply to sacristan) includes a silver processional cross and gold chalice (both 15C); a 14C altar cloth, once the property

of Bart. Colleoni, was later presented to the church (1509) by Bart.
Alviano. Adjoining the church is a crenellated bell tower (1442) with a
clock. The *Town Hall*, built originally in the 13C, was in continuous use
until the Second World War, though almost completely reconstructed
in the last century. Behind the Town Hall (l.) access may be had to the
ramparts (comp. above) which can be circled in their entirety (*Views
w. over Motovun Woods, N. to the Ćićarija mountains and E. to the
Učka Massif rising to 4600 ft). Motovun was the birthplace of Andrea
de Antiquis (Andrea Antico), composer and printer, who in the first
half of the 16C was a pioneer in the printing of music. It was also the
home of Veli Jože ('Big Joe'), a well-known 'giant' of Istrian folklore,
whose exploits were chronicled by Vladimir Nazor'and others.

From Motovun the gravelled road continues s. past the village of Rakotole (see
p. 21) and (7 km.) *Karojba* to join (16 km.) the main Poreč–Pazin highway.

From Livade, an alternative road (left) climbs by more vertiginous
bends to (7 km.) **Oprtalj** (1200 ft), with 17C Venetian loggia and Town
Hall. It was a centre of Italian resistance during Austrian rule. The
early 16C Gothic parish church of *Sv. Juraj* (St George), with a Renaissance w. front added in the 17C, has a fine fan-vaulted ceiling with
carved bosses and corbels. The statues of SS Anthony of Padua and
Francis of Paola on the high altar are by Giov. Bonazza and the painting
of the Trinity attended by Saints is by a pupil of Ben. Carpaccio. In the
treasury are 15–16C chalices, a Gothic monstrance and a Renaissance
pax. The 15C Gothic church of Sv. MARIJA (lengthened in the 18C) is
noted for its *Frescoes, the work of four artists of the Istrian School.
The best are on the triumphal arch: Annunciation (top), a group of
saints (below), and prophets with two saints (soffit of arch); and (s. wall,
top left) the Virgin protecting members of the guild whose church this
was, signed by Clerigin of Koper ('CLERIGINVS DE IVSTINOPOLI')ᵢ and
dated 1471.

The remaining frescoes, unsigned, are also from the 15C. Those completing the
top sector of the s. wall, by a second hand, have been almost obliterated. Those on
the s. wall (below) and on the w. end of the N. wall, showing scenes from the life of
Christ, are by a third artist; and the remainder of the N. wall, completed by a fourth
artist, depicts five saints and the Virgin and Child.
The tiny Romanesque chapel of *Sv. Jelena* (St Helen) just off the road ½ m. s,
of Oprtalj, contains frescoes by another Clerigin of Koper (thought to be the grand-
father of the artist responsible for Sv. Marija). These date from 1400, and depict
(triumphal arch) the Annunciation and (apse) Christ with the four symbols of the
Evangelists, Agnus Dei and SS Helen and Nazarius.—Other frescoes are to be
found in the churches of *Sv. Rok* (by Anton of Padova, early 16C) and *Sv. Leonard*,
in which there is also an altar painting by Zorzi Ventura of Zadar (17C).
The road continues N. from Oprtalj to (26 km.) Rižana Park and Hrastovlje (see
Rte 2B) and joins the main Koper–Ljubljana highway at (29 km.) *Rižana.*

From Livade the main road continues E. along the valley of the Mirna
to (15 km.) *Sv. Stjepan*, a tiny spa and curative centre. The sulphur
springs, known as *Istarske Toplice*, are considered the second most radio-
active in Europe. We pass under the shadow of towering Mt. Zvenje
(1350 ft) where Istrian stone has been quarried for centuries; on the
right is the main pipeline for Istria's water supply.

24 km. **Buzet** is another small Istrian hill town. Owing to its situation
on the Mirna and its links with the interior, Buzet has been a communications centre from earliest times, its Roman name, *Piquentum*,

becoming *Pinguente* under Venice and Italy. Here for a time the Venetian governor of Istria had his seat. The town is still medieval in character and atmosphere, though only fragments of its fortifications remain, notably the *West Gate* of 1592. The pleasant parish church and bell tower are 18C Baroque and *Sv. Juraj* (St George) has paintings by the school of Carpaccio. The adjacent house (No. 5) is arranged as a small ethnographic exhibit, and there is a town *Museum* (opened on request) with a small lapidary collection. View from the ramparts over the Ćićarija Mts. and Mirna valley.

Beyond Buzet a pitted asphalt road that quickly gives way to gravel winds in hairpin bends to the lower slopes of the *Ćićarija Mountains* (view down the Mirna valley and over Buzet).

The name Ćićarija derives from the Ćić people who at the invitation of Venice settled here in the 15C and 16C to escape from the Turks. They are Wallachian in origin and speak a Romance dialect cognate with modern Rumanian. Today they are concentrated in villages on the w. slopes of the Učka Massif between Pazin and Mošćenice.

31 km. Roč, a village on or near the site of the Roman settlement of *Rotium*, of which few traces remain. Of the three churches in the village the parish church of *Sv. Bartolomej* (restored 18C) contains a 16C Venetian painting of the Madonna and Saints together with the Doge of Venice and his consort. The tiny Romanesque chapel of *Sv. Rok* retains 14C frescoes of the Istrian school in its apse. *Sv. Antun* is 14C Gothic. Remains are visible of Venetian fortifications dating from 1420.

An excursion may be made to the tiny fortified town of *Hum*, 7 km. s. of Roč along a narrow track. In the cemetery, below the ruined fortress, is the 12C Romanesque chapel of *Sv. Jerolim*, whose interior is decorated with *Frescoes. Though damaged, these are among the oldest and best in Istria, dating from the late 12C and showing strong Byzantine influence. Note particularly the Annunciation in the apse and on the s. wall the Crucifixion, the Deposition, and the Entombment. The picture of St Antony adjoining the Crucifixion is a 16C addition.

Beyond Roč the road winds through increasingly barren karst scenery to (36 km.) *Ročko polje*, where it converges with the Divača–Pazin–Raša railway line, and (46 km.) *Vranja*, on the road from Pazin to Opatija and Rijeka (see Rte 5).

On the far side of the Mirna the road climbs steeply to (36 km.) *Vižinada*, a sadly neglected little town (view over the Mirna valley to Motovun).

From Vižinada a good, straight, but little used gravel road forks right, following the route of the Roman Via Flavia, to (19 km.) Poreč (see Rte 4). At 3 km. and about ½ m. off the road (r.) on the outskirts of the village of *Božje Polje*, is the 15C Gothic church of *Sv. Marija* (key in Labinci, see below). The church, which once belonged to a now defunct Franciscan monastery, contains a fine rib-vaulted ceiling decorated with contemporary frescoes of the Istrian school. A further 4½ km. down the road in the village of *Labinci* the tiny 13C Romanesque chapel of Sv. Trojica (Holy Trinity) likewise contains frescoes (15C) of the Istrian school (key in village, or at Turističko društvo, Poreč).

Continuing s. from Vižinada we come (41½ km.) to crossroads. To the right a gravel road runs to Poreč (15½ km.; see Rte 4) viâ (3 km.) *Višnjan* where the chapel of Sv. Antun contains 16C frescoes showing scenes from the life of Christ.

To the left another gravel road runs to Karojba where it divides for Motovun (N.; see p. 18) or Pazin (S.; Rte 5). About 2 km. E. of the Karojba–Motovun road is the village of *Rakotole*. In the graveyard the Romanesque church of *Sv. Nikola*, erected in the 14C by the Venetian nobleman Barbo of Motovun, contains frescoes (scenes from the life of St Nicholas) by two unknown Italian artists.

At (51 km.) *Baderna* we cross the main Poreč–Pazin road (Rte 5).—55 km. **Lovreč** (also known as *Sv. Lovreč Pazenatički*, or St Lawrence of Pazin), a historic town, stands on a rocky eminence girdled by its walls (partly 10–11C). As the seat of the Venetian governor of Istria, Lovreč once extended far beyond its present limits and had considerable importance. After the government was transferred elsewhere in the 15C its position declined. Its name derives from the tiny 8C chapel in the cemetery, but the main feature of architectural interest is the Romanesque basilica of SV. MARTIN, dating from the 9–11C, though the W. front was added in 1838. The two original windows of the N. and S. apses are filled with carved stone transennae with an interlacing pattern. The plain interior is divided by two irregular arcades with debased Byzantine capitals. The large Baroque altar was worked in oak by a 16C local sculptor. The apses are decorated with 11C frescoes in the Byzantine style, overlaid in the N. apse by 14C work in the Italian style. Adjoining the church is a 15C Venetian *Loggia* and opposite it a pillory column of like date, while the Romanesque campanile rests on one of the former town gates. There is a handsome main square. The chapel of *Sv. Blaž* by the main gate is in a rustic Gothic style dating from 1460, with traces of frescoes in the interior. The war memorial, erected in 1961, is by Nenad Krivić.

The road continues due S., leaving on the right a narrow gravel road for Vrsar and Poreč (Rte 4) and rises to (59 km.) a rocky eminence overlooking the LIMSKI ZALIV (also called *Limski kanal*), a narrow inlet extending six miles in from the sea. Steep banks, rising in places to a height of 400 ft, give it the appearance of a canyon or small fjord, but it is the submerged end of the valley of Limska draga which descends for 55 km. from Pazin. The river Lim flows into it only in winter. It is a rich fishing ground and has extensive oyster and mussel beds administered by the Oceanographical Institute in Rovinj. Its mouth has been colonized by central European naturists (comp. Rte 4).

Where the main highway bends sharply left a narrow track runs (r.) parallel with the inlet, offering excellent views. This leads to *Kloštar* (c. 1 m.) a village with ruins of an 11C Benedictine monastery. The monastery was founded by Romualdo, a hermit, who had lived, according to legend, in one of the many limestone caves that line the banks of the Limski zaliv. The small church of *Sv. Mihovil* dates from the 6C but was rebuilt by the Benedictines. The monastery church proper contains 11C frescoes in the Central European Benedictine style which, with those at Peroj (p. 28), are the oldest known frescoes in Istria.

Descending in a zigzag to the floor of the valley (*Motel* at the head of the inlet) we climb again on the far side, passing beneath the Pazint–Rovinj railway line, to (64 km.) *Brajkovići*, where a main road forks right to Rovinj (see Rte 4) and a minor road left to Kanfanar, Žminj and Pazin (see Rte 5) from Brajkovići to Pula we again follow the course of the Roman Via Flavia.—73 km. **Bale** (Ital. *Valle*), a hill town (450 ft) on the site of a Roman castrum. The 15C *Kaštel Bembo*, named for the noble family to whom it passed from the Soardo in 1618, has a graceful façade in Venetian Gothic with a double set of beautiful four-light windows adorned with balconies. Entering through the Gothic main gate we quickly come to the main square where the parish church of *Sv. Julian* (1880) retains a 13C Romanesque campanile. Within, on the s. side a late 12C Gothic crucifix surmounts the w. altar; the adjoining altar has a 15C wooden screen carved and painted in the Venetian style. The altar in the s. apse containing the relics of St Julian Cesarello, Bale's patron saint, is surmounted by an 11C Byzantine Madonna and Child carved in wood. On the N. side a niche at the w. end contains an ornamented pre-Romanesque sarcophagus (650). Steps left of the high altar descend to the crypt, where we find a stone altar and altar rail constructed of 6C and 8C fragments from an earlier church and decorated with Romanesque motifs, and the 14C sarcophagus of St Julian. Also in the main square are a Venetian loggia and fontego (grain warehouse) and the former *Pretorska palača* (Captain's Residence), now a school. In the little churches of *Sv. Duh* (Holy Spirit) and *Sv. Antun* (on the road to Pula) traces of 15C frescoes have been discovered (not yet cleaned); the Romanesque bell tower of *Sv. Ilija* (on the Rovinj road) is said to be one of the oldest in Istria (11 or 12C).

Bale is a centre of the Istriots, a people directly descended from the original Roman population of this area who speak a Romance dialect of their own. Many of them live in a large, distinctive type of homestead called a *štancija*, which houses several families together and has a ground floor for animals. These, in general, are built to extremely high standards.

84 km. **Vodnjan**, another Istriot town and road junction. Called *Dignano* in Italian, it passed to Venice in 1331, became independent in 1382 and apart from being sacked in 1413 by King Sigismund of Hungary has had a peaceful and prosperous past. Consequently it is one of the best preserved of Istrian towns. The attractive main street, UL. 1 OG. MAJA, lined with houses dating mainly from the 17–18C and with a notable Gothic town-house at the far end, leads into Narodni trg, the main square. The former *Palača Bradamante* (17C), on the S. side, is now the town hall. To the w. of this square lies the old quarter, a picturesque huddle of narrow streets and houses dating back to the 15C. In the first of two small squares stands the 15C *Kaštel* (formerly Palača Bettica) in Venetian Gothic; in the second, is the parish church (18C) with three Romanesque reliefs built into the w. wall and a detached bell tower (view to the coast and Brioni Isles). In the church the high altar is flanked by two pictures, the Last Supper by G. Contarini (1598) and a 14C polyptych (school of Paolo Veneziano); in the N. aisle is a Renaissance marble custodial dating from 1451. The treasury (apply to sacristan) contains a 15C Gothic reliquary ornamented with miniatures.

From Vodnjan roads lead N. to *Svetvinčenat*, *Žminj*, and *Pazin* (see Rte 5), E. to *Barban*, *Raša*, and *Marčana* (see Rte 6), S.E. to *Gali žana* and S.W. to *Peroj*, and *Fažana* (see below).

94 km. **PULA**, now the chief and largest town (37,000 inhab.) of Istria and seat of the Kotar (regional) administration. A major port and industrial centre, it is being intensively developed to the S. and E. as a tourist centre, with new hotels, camps, and beaches. The principal attraction for the visitor is its Roman remains.

Railway Station, Ul. Vladimira Gortana 7, with services to *Divača* on the main Trieste–Ljubljana line (3–3½ hrs); through coaches nightly to Zagreb.—AIRPORT. A near-by military airfield receives charter flights.

Hotels. **Riviera** (a), Splitska ul., 115 R, in town.—About 2 km. s.: **Verudela**, 325 R in main building and chalets, beach, night club, tennis; **Central**, 95 R; **Ribarska koliba**, 95 R; and **Zlatne stijene** 325 R, all with beach, dancing, kavana.

Autocamp at *Zlatne stijene* for 150 cars, restaurant, showers, beach; *Ribarska koliba* for 200 cars, restaurant, showers, beach. Also at *Medulin* 9 km. s. of Pula, for 400 cars, beach, etc.

Kavanas. *Jadran*, Trg bratstva i jedinstva; *Kavana na obali*, Obala Maršala Tita 14.

Post Offices. General, Trg narodne revolucije; branch, Ul. Jugoslavenske narodne armije 7.

Information. *Turist biro* and *Generalturist*, both in Trg bratstva i jedinstva.

Buses. Local buses every quarter of an hour from Trg bratstva i jedinstva to the tourist centre at *Veruda* and the town beach at *Stoja*. Bus station for all country buses in Trg oslobodjenja.

Steamers connect with Trieste and with all major towns on the Yugoslav Adriatic coast. Local steamers call at Istrian coastal towns.—BOATS may be hired to explore the harbour and offshore islands.

Beaches at *Zelenika* (1 m.) and *Stoja* (1½ m.). UNDERWATER FISHING at *Premantura* and *Medulin*. Sailing and tennis at *Verudela*.

Entertainments. THEATRE. Gradsko kazalište, Ul. Matka Laginje 5.—FILM FESTIVAL annually (Oct) in the Roman amphitheatre.

History. According to legend *Pula*, otherwise *Pola*, was founded by the Colchians after their unsuccessful pursuit of Jason and the Golden Fleece. Archaeological evidence shows that there was an Illyrian settlement here from at least 500 B.C. Pliny refers to the place as *Pietas Julia*; it is thought to have been refounded as a Roman colony by Augustus c. 40 B.C. and named in this way in honour of Julius Caesar. Its full name was *Colonia Julia Pollentia Herculanea*. Under the Romans, Pula flourished as a commercial and business town and the administrative centre of Istria. Its population is estimated to have reached 25–30,000 and the many remaining monuments testify to its wealth and importance. In the 2C A.D. Rasparaganus, the banished king of the Roxolans, found refuge here with his son, Publius Aelius Peregrinus; and in 326 Crispus, son of Constantine the Great, was brought here and killed on the orders of his father. Pula passed to the Ostrogoths and then to the Exarchate of Ravenna, under which it became a bishopric. In 788 it was joined to the kingdom of the Franks and became the seat of the elective counts of Istria. These gave way to hereditary margraves who remained in Germany, and Pula steadily declined, particularly when, after siding with Pisa against Venice, it was raided and sacked by the Venetians.

In 1230 Pula, together with the rest of Istria, came under the Patriarchate of Aquileia but 28 years later was able to purchase its autonomy. Future prospects were, however, dissipated in internecine struggle, particularly between the monarchical party, led by the Sergi family, and a popular party led by the Ionatasi. The Sergi family, also known as the Castropoli from the castle (Castrum Polae) they occupied, were descended from the Roman family whose name appears on the triumphal arch still standing in Pula. They supported the patriarch in Aquileia, but most of the clan was massacred by the Ionotasi and their allies on Good Friday, 1271. In the struggle between Genoa and Venice, Pula sided with Genoa and was sacked for her pains. In 1331 she submitted to Venice and the Sergi-Castropoli were banished from the town. Now Genoa exacted revenge by raids in 1354, 1374, and 1380. Decline and stagnation followed. The ancient monuments were pillaged, abbeys and churches rifled. In 1630 the Venetians, employing the French engineer Antony de Ville, used the stones of the old Roman theatre to build a fort overlooking the harbour. Plague and malaria were rampant and in 1631 Pula had only 350 inhabitants. Renewal came only under Austria, which in 1866 proclaimed Pula the chief naval port of the empire. Extensive fortifications were built on every hill and island surrounding the harbour, a dockyard and naval arsenal were established, the railway extended from Slovenia and a new centre built, much as it remains today. By 1914 the population had climbed to 60,000. Then, in 1918, came another sharp turn of fortune. Istria passed to Italy. Pula, on the very frontier with Yugoslavia, lost its importance and declined. During the Second World War it was subjected to heavy allied bombing and was occupied by Anglo-American forces until 1947 pending a frontier agreement between Italy and Yugoslavia.

Pula has links with Dante, who is presumed to have stayed here. James Joyce taught at the Berlitz School from Oct 1904 to March 1905.

The outstanding Roman monument is the magnificent ***Amphitheatre,** known locally as the *Arena* (open 8–7 in the season). It is the sixth largest of the surviving Roman amphitheatres, ranking in size just below Arles and Catania, and is in some ways the most interesting example of all. The ellipse of the amphitheatre lies upon an axis running from N.W. to S.E. with a diameter of 436 ft, while the transverse diameter is 346 ft. The arena itself measures 222 ft by 132 ft. The outer wall reaches 97 ft at its highest point. There were 15 entrances, of which that from the south nearest the town was the grandest, and the amphitheatre is estimated to have seated c. 23,000 spectators.

Probably built by Augustus during the early years of the 1C A.D. and enlarged by Claudius, the edifice achieved its present form c. A.D. 80 in the reign of Vespasian. In the Middle Ages almost the entire interior was removed, much of it to Venice. A plan to dismantle the exterior wall and re-erect it on the Lido at Venice was frustrated (comp. below). Modern archaeological interest started with the excavations of Marshal Marmont in 1810.

EXTERIOR. The building was situated just outside the limits of the old Roman town beside the Via Flavia which led to Parentium (Poreč), Aegida (Koper), and Tergeste (Trieste). Some of the original flagstones of the Via Flavia can still be seen at the foot of the amphitheatre wall. The exterior wall is in a remarkably fine state of preservation and can be approached on all sides. It varies in height from four stories on the seaward side to two opposite, where the slope of the terrain was used to support the seating. On the seaward side there is a lower story of massive monumental arches supported by rectangular piers extending for about half the total circumference. Above this is an arcade of equal length. A third arcade of 72 arches encircles the entire building. The topmost story of 64 rectangular apertures is surmounted by an unusual stone balustrading. The four shallow rectangular towers placed to the four cardinal points were part of a system of waterworks, unique to this amphitheatre, that supplied the building from a neighbouring spring. The water was stored at the top of the towers, and carried around the amphitheatre by a channel in the balustrading round the perimeter. The lower part of the towers contained spiral staircases that gave access to the upper tiers of seats. On the external wall of the W. tower a plaque, placed in 1584, expresses gratitude to Gabriele Emo the Venetian senator, who successfully protested against the scheme for transporting the amphitheatre to Venice.

Admission (fee; guide available) to the amphitheatre is gained through the S. tower.

INTERIOR. The first impression is of emptiness, for almost the entire contents have been removed over the centuries. The present banked seating was built by the Italians between the two world wars. This sharp contrast with the condition of the exterior was made possible by the complete separation of the two parts in the original construction. The gap between the outermost ring of seats and the perimeter was spanned only by wooden flooring, and the holes for the joists can still be seen in the masonry. The history of the Pula amphitheatre is exactly the reverse of that at Verona, where the outer wall has disappeared, while the interior remains intact.

Around the arena is an excavated passage along which the animals used to run.

Their dens beneath the arena now house lighting equipment. At the s.e. end a line of broken-off rectangular pillars shows the extent of the smaller amphitheatre built by Augustus. A grassy bank at the N.W. end affords an excellent view of the interior; for those with a head for heights, the top of W. water tower provides an even better vantage point from which the town and harbour are also seen. Here the balustrading and its water channel may be examined. The amphitheatre, once used by the local commandery of Knights of St John for jousting, now serves for open-air opera productions and for the Annual Festival of Yugoslav Films.

From the amphitheatre Ul. Matije Gupca takes us to the local bus station in Trg Oslobodjenja, behind which is located *Karolinin izvor* (Caroline Spring) built in the 18C on the site of a former Roman nymphaeum. Beyond the trg is a small *Park* containing a bronze monument to the fallen of the last war, by V. Radauš. The central figure is typical of the socialist realism era, but the pleasant bas-reliefs on either side portray a traditional theme from Yugoslav folklore.

Ul. Gorana Kovačića marks the N. boundary of the old Roman town and brings us to the **Cathedral of Sv. Tomo,** a building that has suffered much during its long history. The original Byzantine basilica was erected in the 6C, possibly on the site of a temple of Jupiter or of thermal baths, and incorporated much Roman material in its structure. In the 15C after heavy damage in raids by both Venice and Genoa, the building had to be almost completely reconstructed, although much earlier material was re-used. In the s. wall, is embedded a lintel dated 857 and bearing the monogram of Bp. Handegis, with an inscription recording his donation of a doorway to the cathedral. In the 16C a Renaissance w. front was added and in the 17C a bell tower, into the foundations of which were incorporated a quantity of seats from the amphitheatre.

The cathedral is entered through a loggia built as a war memorial by the Italians after the First World War against the wall of a Franciscan nunnery. The striking late Gothic lintel over the entrance dates from 1456 and was brought here from the defunct Benedictine church of Sv. Mihovil, whose site is now occupied by the city hospital.

The INTERIOR preserves the basilican plan with the main apse slightly shortened and squared off. The columns dividing the nave from the aisles are a hodge-podge of Roman, Byzantine and other work, while the majority of the capitals date from the 15C reconstruction. Many bear heraldic emblems of the craft guilds that donated them. Fragmentary Byzantine mosaics remain just inside the entrance door and in front of the high altar. The altar consists of a 3C Roman sarcophagus and is reputed to contain the relics of the Hungarian King Solomon (d. 1074).

Opposite the cathedral the narrow Rasparaganov Uspon leads up to the **Kaštel** that crowns the hill in the centre of the old town. This was the site of the original Illyrian settlement and of the Roman capitol, which was destroyed in the 13C for the first castle of the Sergi family. Their fortress was completely reconstructed in 1630–31 by the Venetians according to plans by the French military engineer Antony de Ville and restored first by Napoleon and then (1840) by Austria. Today it houses the *Pula Museum of the National Liberation Movement* (adm. 8–7; 1 *din.*).

Steps on the far side of the Kaštel lead down to the Archaeological Museum and Pula's two Roman gateways (see below).

Passing the small square at the cathedral's w. end, beyond which can be seen the harbour and naval headquarters, we continue along Ul. Gorana Kovačića past attractive houses to the Trg republike, or *Piazza Foro*, the site of the Roman Forum. At the N. end of the square are two small 1C temples of which the ***Temple of Augustus** (*Augustov hram*) is an outstanding example, with high, narrow proportions, delicately carved Corinthian capitals (some restored) and a handsome entablature. The *Temple of Diana* (alternatively attributed to Hercules) can only be perceived in outline from the rear, for at the end of the 13C it was bodily incorporated into the Gothic *Vijećnica* (Town Hall). This later became the seat of the Venetian rectors, but was badly damaged by the Genoese in 1379, and later almost completely destroyed. Most of the present building dates from a renewal in 1653; only the E. façade remains from the original structure.

From the Trg republike the main street of the old town, the Corso, now named *Ul. 1 maja*, leads through the busy shopping centre. In the first street to the left, the steep, Uspon Balde Lupetine, are the Franciscan church and monastery. **Sv. Franjo** was built at the end of the 13C in the restrained Gothic style characteristic of the Adriatic seaboard. A curiosity is the double pulpit with one part projecting into the street for preaching to an overflow congregation. The ornate w. portal, decorated with unusual shell motifs, is surmounted by a rose window. Within are a beautiful 16C screen of gilt and painted wood behind the high altar, and a 15C Gothic polyptych by Jakob of Pula. To the left of the church is the early 14C cloister (restored), with a small lapidary collection, including a 6C mosaic of saints and the gravestone of the 11C Hungarian King Solomon. Leading off it is a tiny Gothic chapel in which more mosaics have recently been discovered.

In the courtyard of No. 16 Ul. 1 maja (entrance from the rear through small park) is a large and complete Roman *Mosaic Floor* attributed to the 1C B.C.; part of a Roman villa urbana revealed by bombing, it depicts the punishment of Circe by the sons of Antiope. In the S.E. corner of the park stands a tiny cruciform chapel, the last remaining fragment of *Sv. Marija Formosa*, a monumental Byzantine basilica (also known as Santa Maria in Canneto).

The basilica, built by St Maximian, Abp. of Ravenna in 546, was one of the most sumptuous buildings of the Adriatic, with marble columns, mosaic floors and a profusion of Byzantine sculpture. In the 14C it was sacked by the Genoese and through succeeding centuries its treasures were removed to Venice. Four exquisite columns of Oriental alabaster from this church can still be seen behind the high altar of St Mark's in Venice and are famous for their transparency. The remaining chapel, one of two that originally flanked the basilica, served as a mausoleum and resembles that of Galla Placidia at Ravenna; its principal feature is a small Byzantine panel carved in stone, set into the wall over the door. Within are fragments of a 6C mosaic and 15C frescoes.

Ribarska ul. leads back to the main street whence its continuation, Ul. Jana Husa, brings us to the Orthodox church of *Sv. Nikola*. Although the exterior dates from the 6C, the interior has been largely reconstructed. Continuing along Ul. 1 maja we pass through the Trg narodne revolucije, with the church of *Sv. Milosrdje* (Holy Mercy) and the *General Post Office* on our left, and come to the **Sergi Arch** (*Sergijev slavoluk*), which stands just inside the former Porta Aurea of the Roman town. Facing inwards, it consists of a single large arch flanked by paired

columns of the Corinthian order. The faces and inner walls of the piers are richly decorated with vine and acanthus leaves and the coffered intrados, ornamented with rosettes, bears a bas-relief showing a snake and eagle locked in combat. In the spandrels are winged victories.

The ornamented frieze carries an inscription attesting that the donor was Salvia Postuma, of the Sergi family, while inscribed plinths surmounting the entablature show that the arch was a memorial to three members of the family, whose statues presumably adorned it. The arch is attributed to the 1C B.C. and was studied by Michelangelo, Fra Giocondo, Battista da Sangallo, and Palladio and also drawn by Piranesi and the Englishmen Thomas Allison and Robert Adam.

Ul. Matka Laginje, beyond the arch, traverses the site of the Roman necropolis thought to have inspired Dante's comment on Pula in the 'Inferno' (Canto IX, 113–16), and ends at a Roman theatre, of which only traces remain.

Turning N. from the arch we skirt parts of the town walls, whose base and inner side are still to some extent Roman, till we reach TRG BRAT-STVA I JEDINSTVA, the main square of modern Pula, a busy centre of banks and tourist offices. In the s.w. corner is *Hercules' Gate* (Herkulesova vrata), the oldest remaining component of the Roman walls, dating from the 1C A.D. At its apex are relief carvings of a club and the head that gives the gate its name. A little beyond are the *Twin Gates* (or Porta Gemina), dating from the 2C A.D., a double arch with a highly decorated cornice but no frieze. Excavations opposite, at the foot of a modern block of flats, have uncovered the foundations of an octagonal Roman mausoleum.

Within the Twin Gates a large Austrian-built structure in eclectic *fin de siècle* style houses the Research Library and **Arheološki muzej**, with extensive prehistoric, Roman and medieval collections. Behind the museum, on the hillside leading up to the Kaštel, are the excavated remains of a second *Roman Theatre* dating from the 2C A.D. Like the amphitheatre, it was so placed as to make the best use of the slope for the cavea.

A pleasant excursion (8 km.) may be made by the asphalted coast road N.W. to the fishing village of **Fažana** (restaurant, swimming, fishing). The small 12C church of *Sv. Marija od Karmela* (rebuilt 15C, loggia added in 16C) contains well-preserved frescoes in the Gothic manner (undergoing restoration). The Gothic parish church of *Sv. Kuzma i Damjan* has traces of Renaissance frescoes on its side walls, while the sacristy is decorated with 16C frescoes by an unknown Friulian artist (Crucifixion, Pietà). On the N. wall hangs a Last Supper (1578) by Zorzi Ventura of Zadar. On the E. side of the village is the tiny Romanesque chapel of *Sv. Elizej*, attributed to the 8C or 9C, with a polygonal apse and carved stone transennae in the windows.

Beyond Fažana a narrow gravel road continues to *Peroj* (3 km.), a village founded in 1645 by Montenegrin immigrants. Most of the inhabitants retain their Montenegrin dialect and customs. Of the two churches Sv. Spiridon is Orthodox and contains icons of the 16–18C, while the Catholic church of Sv. Stjepan is Romanesque and has fragmentary 13C frescoes.—*Sv. Foška*, another Romanesque church, 3 km. farther N., has frescoes in the Byzantine manner that are among the oldest in Istria (12C). A large Ascension has been uncovered in the apse; elsewhere a later layer awaits restoration.

About 1 m. offshore from Fažana are the Brijuni or **Brioni Islands**, of which *Veliki Brioni*, the largest, is the summer residence of President Tito. Foreigners are at present forbidden to visit the islands.

Off the road to Labin (Rte 6), beyond (11 km.) Valtura is Glavica, site of Roman *Nesactium*. Once the chief town of the Illyrian tribe of Histra, Nesactium was sacked by the Romans in 177 B.C. when they defeated Epulo, last of the Illyrian princes. It was later rebuilt by them but did not survive the collapse of the Roman Empire. Extensive archaeological investigation is in progress and intending visitors should contact the Arheoloski muzej in Pula for information and possibly a guide.

4 FROM PIRAN TO PULA VIÂ THE COAST

ROAD, 140 km. (87¼ m.). 27 km. *Savudrija.*—35 km. **Umag.**—51 km. **Novigrad.** —67 km. **Poreč** (*Vrsar*, 9 km.).—106 km. **Rovinj.**—140 km. **Pula.** Buses frequently in 3–5 hrs.

Following Rte 3 to (13 km.) the crossroads beyond the Dragonja valley, we turn right along a narrow asphalted road and pass through flat featureless country to (27 km.) *Savudrija* (Moj Mir; autocamp) a small fishing village and quiet resort set in pine woods and with a rocky shore. The local fishermen's custom of hoisting the boats out of the water on davits when not in use is unique on the E. Adriatic coast. The lighthouse (120 ft), the tallest in Istria, also marks the westernmost tip of the Balkan peninsula (view of Piran, Portorož, and the Bay of Piran). A plaque in the parish church commemorates the defeat here in 1177 of Otto, son of the Emp. Frederick I (Barbarossa), by the Venetian fleet under Doge Seb. Ziani and Nic. Contarini.

From Savudrija the road turns s. to follow the coast, passing (31 km.) the site of Roman *Siparis*, later Sipar, destroyed in the 9C by the Neretvan corsair Domagoj. We now enter the main wine-producing region of Istria, extending s. to Vrsar and notable for the white wine, Malvasia, and the red Teran.

35 km. **Umag** (*Adriatic*, 140 R with bath, beach, dancing; *Beograd*, beach; *Sipar; Park; Zagreb; Jadran; Plitvice*) a bustling small resort town (2660 inhab.) is quickly modernizing itself, and affords facilities for sailing and water-skiing.

Known as *Humagum* in Roman times, Umag passed to the bishopric of Trieste in the early Middle Ages and to Venice in 1268, where it remained until the fall of the Republic. Legend has it that the ship carrying the body of St Mark to Venice stopped in Umag en route. It was sacked by the Genoese in 1370. Since passing to Yugoslavia in 1953 the town has been developed as a resort, and light industries established here include a cement factory and a cannery.

The tourist settlement developed on the N. side of the town affords a view of the picturesque old quarter typically placed on a low narrow peninsula. The parish church of *Sv. Pelegrin* has a 14C relief of St Peregrinus Laziosi built into the s. wall and, within, a 15C polyptych on wood, by an anonymous Friulian artist. Houses from the 12C to the 17C survive, particularly in Riječka ul.

BUSES to all parts of Istria and the main towns of Yugoslavia. STEAMERS daily to all points N. as far as Trieste.
From Umag a good asphalted road runs 13 km. E. to *Buje* (see Rte 3).

Continuing s. we follow the coast road to (46 km.) the hamlet of *Dajla*, passing (just off the road, r.) a Neo-classical mansion and Baroque church erected in 1839 on the site of a Benedictine monastery. The adjoining farm buildings are an excellent example of the Istrian štancija and the complex is now worked as a co-operative farm. We catch glimpses across rolling vineyards of Novigrad on its peninsula.

51 km. **Novigrad** (*Emonia*; *Stella Maris*, beach; *Trst*, on quayside) a sleepy little town (1500 inhab.) of great charm with a history of unbroken continuity from Roman times.

Possibly *Aemona* in Roman times, the town was refounded in the 8C under Byzantium as *Neapolis*. This became *Cittanova* under Venice and Italy and finally

Novigrad under Yugoslavia. Novigrad had a bishop from the 6C until 1831, and prospered after passing to Venice in 1270, mainly owing to its position at the mouth of the river Mirna which provided an outlet for timber from Motovun (see p. 18). In 1687 the town was sacked by the Turks. After the Second World War, Novigrad marked the southern limit of the disputed Zone B, which passed to Yugoslavia in 1954.

The parish church (formerly cathedral) of **Sv. Pelagij** (St Pelagius) is a handsome Baroque structure of complicated ancestry. The church was totally reconstructed in the 15–16C. The Baroque interior dates from 1754, while the exterior and campanile result from 19C alterations. Beneath the high altar, a late-Romanesque crypt remaining from an 11C basilica, contains the relics of St Pelagius, a boy martyred in Istria c. 283 under Numerian. In the Trg slobode is a small Venetian town hall with clock tower and in Ul. Josip Milovac, leading out of it, the 18C Urizzi mansion containing an excellent lapidary collection and small museum (key from tourist office). Noteworthy are the Romanesque reliefs, showing a rich variety of ornamentation, taken from the original basilica.

BUSES to all parts of Istria and the major cities of Yugoslavia. STEAMERS daily to all points N. as far as Trieste.

Immediately s. of Novigrad we cross the wide shallow estuary of the river Mirna (see p. 18) by a causeway and climb through pinewoods viâ (58 km.) *Tar* to Poreč.

67 km. **POREČ**, a town of great antiquity, is celebrated for its 6C basilica and fine mosaics. Poreč (2990 inhab.) preserves in exceptional purity the urban plan of a Roman municipium, with the two main arteries, the decumanus maximus and the cardo maximus not only still in use but still bearing their original names. The forum too is still preserved in name and outline at the w. end of the town in the large open space known as the Marafor (Mars' Forum).

Hotels. In the town: *Riviera* (a); **Jadran** (b). On the island of *Sv. Nikola* (200 yds offshore): **Istra**, 234 R, in converted mansion and modern chalets, beach, dancing—To the N. (1 mile): *Pical*, 360 R. in bungalows.—To the s. (2 miles): **Bellevue Villas**, 360 R. in bungalows, beach; (3 miles) **Plava Laguna**, 420 R., beach, dancing.

Autocamp on s. side of town.

Restaurants. *Riblji restoran* (fish), Obala Maršala Tita; *Mirna*, Trg Joakima Rakovca; *Centar*, Trg slobode.

Kavanas. *Parentino*, *Riviera*, both on Obala Maršala Tita.

Post Office, Trg slobode.—INFORMATION. Obala Maršala Tita and Trg slobode.

Buses run locally in season between hotels Riviera and Plava Laguna. Buses for Istria and the rest of Yugoslavia, from Trg slobode. To *Trieste* and *Graz* in the season.—Car hire available.

Steamers to all the coastal towns of Istria and also to Zadar and Dubrovnik.

Beach near the autocamp (rock and pebble). *Water-skiing* at Plava Laguna; *Skin diving* at Pical; *Sailing* from Jedriličarski klub.

Concerts in season in the Basilica.

History. *Poreč* (Ital. *Parenzo*) is known to have existed in 200 B.C. as a centre of the Illyrian tribe of Histra. Its name is one of the few thought to be derived from Illyrian. It became Roman in 35 B.C. under the name of *Parentium*, and was raised to the dignity of a colonia in the 2C A.D. With the fall of the Western Roman Empire, Poreč passed to the Goths, then in 539 to Byzantium, during whose rule a bishopric was founded and the present basilica built. Short intervals of Lombard and Frankish rule followed in the 8C, during which time the Slavs began to arrive. After a period of violence and disorder Parenzo became in 1267 the first Istrian town to submit to Venice, under whom it remained for five centuries. As a result of local disputes and plague its fortunes declined sharply, until in the mid-17C the population had been reduced from over 3000 to less than 100. The town was resettled mainly by Croats with some Greeks and Albanians. In 1797 Poreč passed to Napoleon, in 1815 to Austria, and in 1861 became the principal town of Istria and seat of an Istrian Assembly. Like the rest of Istria it was occupied by Italy in 1918 and during the Second World War for a short while by the Germans, when a large part of the town was destroyed by allied bombing. Poreč was joined to Yugoslavia in 1945.

One of the outstanding buildings of the Adriatic littoral is the ****Basilica of Euphrasius** (*Eufrazijeva bazilika*), a 6C Byzantine cathedral with mosaics in the tradition of Ravenna. Jackson describes it as "inferior to the churches of Ravenna in size alone; in beauty of execution it is quite their equal, while in the completeness of its plan with atrium and baptistery it surpasses them". The basilica is approached by way of either Zagrebačka or Ljubljanska ul.

HISTORY. The complexity of the basilica can best be understood if considered in four stages (see plan). It is thought that the earliest Christian building in Poreč was the so-called 'Oratorium' of St Maurus (Sv. Mauro), who was probably the first bishop. It was probably part of the Roman house (pl. A), dating from the 3C A.D., in which Maurus lived. After the Edict of Milan (313) a small basilica (pl. B; known as the 'Original Basilica') is thought to have been raised on this spot together with a catechumeneum (pl. C) on the N. side and a martyrium (pl. D) to the south. The martyrium probably held relics of St Maurus. In the first half of the 5C this was superseded by a larger church (known as the 'Pre-Euphrasian Basilica') consisting of a rectangular non-apsidal structure flanked on the N. by a consignatorium. Finally, the present building was erected in 543–53 on the foundations of the previous one by order of Bp. Euphrasius. It is the earliest known Byzantine church where the place of honour in the conch of the centre apse is given to the Virgin and Child, not the Pantokrator.

EXTERIOR. The basilica is entered through an ATRIUM, consisting of an open courtyard surrounded by a covered ambulatory, with three arches on each side. The marble columns probably derived from some local Roman building and support Byzantine basket-shaped capitals of the type found at Ravenna. The atrium was partially restored in 1869 and now has fragments of antique, Romanesque, and Gothic masonry embedded in its walls, while on one side of the courtyard is a 9C stone throne.

On the w. side opens the octagonal BAPTISTERY (upper part and roof restored in 1881 and again in 1935). The stone inscription on the s. wall comes from the sarcophagus of St Maurus, which was found under the basilica's main altar, and refers to the transfer of the saint's remains to the newly built martyrium. Within is an 18C marble font by the Venetian sculptor Melchior Caffa. Behind the baptistery stairs give access to the *Campanile*, built in 1592 and unusually alined on the axis of the church.

To the N. of the Atrium is the *Bishop's palace*, originally dating from the 6C though the present structure dates from 1694 and is used by the church as offices (no adm.).

The *West Front* of the basilica is best seen from the baptistery door. This façade was once entirely decorated with mosaics of which only the lower part (restored 1897) remains. Here the wall is pierced by three windows flanked on the outside by two pairs of saints. On the piers between are depicted the seven candlesticks of the seven churches of the

Book of Revelation. Three marble portals open into the basilica. The lintel of the centre door bears the ornate monogram of Euphrasius.

INTERIOR. The perfect tripartite basilica adheres to the classical Byzantine plan, its restrained beauty wonderfully set off by the rich mosaic in the apse. The NAVE has twin arcades of ten semicircular arches. The columns, like those in the atrium, were probably taken from classical buildings, but the capitals were specially carved and surmounted by the monogram of Euphrasius. The soffits of the N. arcade are covered in stucco decorated with coffered geometrical patterns; they probably date from the original construction of the church. Those on the S. arcade were destroyed by earthquake in 1440, when the wall above was given inappropriate Gothic windows.

The APSE, polygonal without and semicircular within, is lighted by four Romanesque windows, which has the unusual effect of placing a pier in the central position. Round the apse is the synthronon in white-veined marble with the cathedra in the centre; the walls and semi dome are covered with *Mosaics and inlay.

Above the sedilia is a sumptuous Dado made of inlaid porphyry, serpentine, onyx, alabaster, glass, burnt clay and mother-of-pearl, the latter used to particularly striking effect to reflect an opalescent light over the curved wall. The panels that make up the dado contain eight varieties of geometrical pattern, arranged symmetrically in pairs. In the centre, above the bishop's throne, a single panel is inlaid with a gold cross on a ground of serpentine and mother-of-pearl, and surmounts a dome between lighted candlesticks. A cornice of acanthus leaves moulded in stucco then separates the dado from the mosaics, which are on a level with the four windows.

The central pier is occupied by an angel holding an orb; the piers between the windows by (l.) St Zachary and (r.) St John the Baptist. In the wall spaces beyond the windows are represented (l.) the Salutation of Mary and Elizabeth and (r.) the Annunciation. The magnificent centre-piece of the whole composition occupies the semi-dome. On a golden ground the Virgin holds the Infant giving a blessing. To either side are an angel and further figures. On the right St Maurus, holding an urn, Bp. Euphrasius holding a model of his church, together with his son, and the Archdeacon Claudius, holding a book. Those on the left are thought to be early patron saints of Poreč. Below these figures is a large inscription running the full width of the semi-dome, testifying in thirteen hexameters that Bp. Euphrasius had pulled down the former church and erected this new basilica for the worship of Christ.

The soffit of the triumphal arch is filled with twelve medallions within wreaths, each portraying a female saint. At the summit of the arch is the Euphrasian monogram in coloured plaster. On the E. wall above the triumphal arch, Christ in majesty and the Twelve Apostles. A thin red line marks off the original upper part from the restored portion below.

The altar frontal is of silver gilt and dates from 1452, though the figures of the Virgin and saints on it date from after 1669, when the originals were stolen. The magnificent *Ciborium, dating from 1277, rests on four marble columns, probably from an earlier building, with capitals of a Byzantine type carved in the 13C. The four sides are decorated with Venetian mosaics that are more expressive and natural than the mosaics of the apse, but inferior in artistic design and execution. The front shows the Annunciation, while the other three sides bear medallions containing the heads of saints.

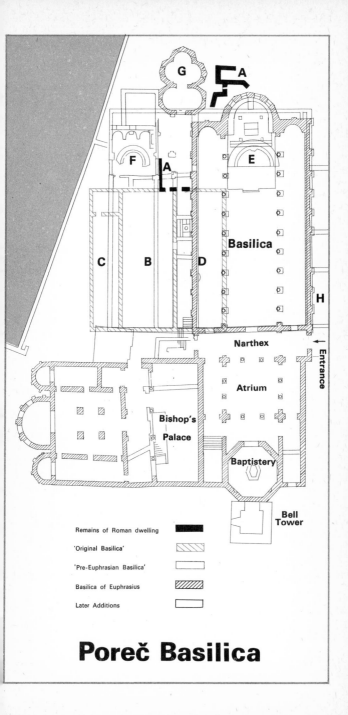

G

A

F

E

A

C B D Basilica

H

Narthex

Entrance

Atrium

Bishop's Palace

Baptistery

Bell Tower

Remains of Roman dwelling

'Original Basilica'

'Pre-Euphrasian Basilica'

Basilica of Euphrasius

Later Additions

Poreč Basilica

The sculptured panels enclosing the sanctuary are of 6C origin but were restored and replaced in their present position in 1837. Immediately in front, protected by trapdoors (usually standing open, if not, apply to sacristan), survive portions of the *Mosaic Floor* (pl. E) of the pre-Euphrasian Basilica, at a depth of about two feet below the present floor. Their 5C local workmanship shows a strong Roman tradition. Other parts of this floor (not usually seen) have been discovered just inside the main entrance and beneath the sacristy in the former consignatorium.

The mosaics in the N. and S. apses were badly damaged in the 15C when new windows were pierced. The N. apse shows the Face of Christ above clouds as he hands a martyr's crown to each of two saints, while the superior S. apse, though in a worse condition, shows a fine unbearded Christ crowning SS Cosmas and Damian. A 6C altar in the N. apse bears an inscription stating that Bp. Euphrasius ordered the Basilica to be built in the eleventh year of his episcopate.

On the S. side of the church are three chapels, added at a later date. In the largest, dedicated to *Sv. Križ* (The Holy Cross), are walnut *Choir Stalls* (1452) carved in the Gothic style. A curious group of three little chapels is entered from behind the high altar. The first, rectangular, is used as a vestry; the second, oval, with the remains of 15C frescoes, forms the sacristy. It contains a Last Supper by Palma Giovane and a small enamel 18C cross, made on Mt. Athos (apply to sacristan to view). The third, the Cella trichora (pl. G), is clover-shaped and has remains of mosaics on its floor. It is thought to have been the martyrium of Eu-phrasius's basilica or possibly a mausoleum for Euphrasius. Here a 13C sarcophagus, constructed of 6C fragments, contains relics of St Maurus.

Excavations were in progress in 1968 just N. of the main building. Admission (fee) is gained from the Atrium by a door just right of the stairs leading into the Bishop's palace. Here are the remains of the three halls of the 'ORIGINAL BASILICA', consisting of (from N. to S.) the catechumeneum, the basilica proper and the martyr-ium. In the martyrium we find the oldest *Mosaic of the entire complex, dating from the 3C and a relic of the Roman dwelling that once stood here. In its centre is a fish (ichthys), symbol of Christ, which was inserted into the Roman mosaic probably in the 4C. The remaining mosaics (greatly restored) also date from the 4C.

On the W. side of the MARAFOR are the scanty remains of two Roman temples. The larger of them, popularly known as *Martov hram* (Temple of Mars), is of unknown date and attribution, and although its original dimensions make it the largest Roman temple so far discovered in Istria, all that remains are parts of the stylobate, a few columns and capitals and a reconstructed architrave. The smaller *Neptunov hram* (Temple of Neptune), erected in the 1C A.D. by Vice-Admiral Titus Abudius Verus of Ravenna, stood opposite; only a few fluted columns from the portico remain but the altar is preserved in the museum (see below).

Beyond the Baroque fountain we take DEKUMANSKA ULICA and pass right a striking 13C Romanesque house with an unusual projecting wooden balcony. In July–Aug it houses 'Anale', an exhibition of con-temporary Yugoslav painting and sculpture. Opposite are the remains of a gateway belonging to the former Roman *Comitium*. Further down Dekumanska ul., on the same side, is an attractive block of late 14C Gothic town houses and, at the crossroads where Dekumanska is crossed by Ul. Cardo Maksimus, a cluster of 15C houses in Venetian Gothic, including the *Palača Zuccato*, with the family escutcheon on the wall, and the Palača Radojković.

The UL. CARDO MAKSIMUS leads (l.) to the abandoned 13C Franciscan church, in plain Gothic with an 18C Baroque interior, which is being restored as a museum, and to Ljubljanska ul., on the corner of which is the 15C portal of the former bishop's palace. Ljubljanska ul. in turn takes us past the 18C *Palača Vergotini*, with pleasant courtyard, to the entrance to the Basilica (see above). The **Canonica**, just to the S. of the Basilica, is a rare and outstanding example of secular Roman-esque architecture, dating from 1251. Although reduced in size the remaining part has been well preserved and restored and has a simple but harmonious frontage with two-light windows, each carved out of a single block of stone.

Continuing along Dekumanska to the next crossroads we come to the Baroque *Palača Sinčić* (1719) now occupied by the **Gradski muzej** (Town Museum; open daily, 9–12 and 5–8). The ground floor houses Roman architectural fragments, including an altar (1C A.D.) from the Temple of Neptune. In a side room prehistoric finds include a ritual cup and knife from the Early Bronze Age and Etruscan pottery. Upstairs are further Roman and Greek objects including mosaics found at near-by Črvar and a small head of Zeus. The pictures are mainly of a local noble family named Carli.

Continuing E. we reach Poreč's small shopping centre. On the right No. 5, dating from 1497, is a fine example of Venetian Gothic with three-light windows. The pentagonal *Kula* (Fortress Tower, 1448), at the far end of the street marks the end of the old town. Most of the medieval walls have been destroyed, but a good idea of them can be had in Ul. Nikole Tesle on the N. side of town.

Beyond the tower is the modern part of Poreč where the cinema, the bus station and the information bureaux are situated. Also here are the 18C Baroque church *Gospa od Andjela* (Our Lady of the Angels) and a memorial to People's Hero Joakim Rakovac. In the Trg slobode is a pleasant round tower, erected in 1475, that houses a café dansant. In Beogradska ul., notable among a number of 13–15C houses, a 13C Romanesque house known as *Dva sveca*, has an unusually large archway on the ground floor (now used as a shop).

From Poreč the coast road continues S. for 9 km. to *Vrsar* (Roman Ursaria), a fishing village recently much affected by tourism. The Tourist Settlement Anita (May–Oct) consists of a large hotel with annexe, chalet-bungalows, etc. (full pension only). The *Kaštel Vergotini*, the 18C summer palace of the bishops of Poreč (now abandoned), overlooks the village from its highest hill. The 12–13C parish church of Sv. Marija is Romanesque. Traces of former town walls remain, particularly the W. gate, and a 4C early-Christian basilica with mosaic floor is undergoing investigation. Beyond Vrsar an asphalt road continues to the mouth of the Limski Kanal, where there is a naturist autocamp; the offshore island of *Kuvrsada* (also naturist) can be reached by boat direct from Vrsar.—A moderate gravel road leads directly from Vrsar to the main Piran–Pula highway, but most motorists will prefer to return to Poreč and use the asphalt road.

From Poreč our road runs E. to (80 km.) *Baderna*. Hence we follow Rte 3 to (94 km.) *Brajkovići*, where we fork right on asphalt to return to the coast at Rovinj.

106 km. **ROVINJ** (*Katarina, Monte Mulini, Park, Lone, Jadran*, Pl. a; *Crveni Otok*; autocamp), a popular and growing resort (8000 inhab.), occupies a typical rocky promontory rising from the sea. The town has a large Italian minority and is the centre of Italian studies in Istria. The outstanding natural beauty of its surroundings, particularly to the south, has attracted a colony of artists; to the N. in 1968 the International Naturist Federation opened a settlement (Val Alta).

First mentioned in the 8C, *Rovinj* (Ital. *Rovigno*) follows the pattern of other Istrian coastal towns in its early history. It came under the sway of Venice in 1283 and in the days of sail was a trading port for timber and bauxite. With the coming of steam it was eclipsed by Trieste and Rijeka.

Trg Maršala Tita, the main square, opens from the harbour. On the corner stands the 17C Baroque *Vijećnica* (old town hall), with a clock tower, and opposite it the fine Baroque *Vrata Sv. Križa* (Holy Cross Gate), by Balbi (1680), one of three remaining gates that lead into the old Venetian quarter of the town. The *Gradski muzej* (daily, 9–11, 6–9), housed in a Baroque mansion adjoining the gate, contains pictures by Bonifazio, portraits of the Hütteroth family, a library, furniture, and, on the top floor, paintings by modern Yugoslav artists.

Just within the gate (l.) are the *Narodni odbor* (new town hall) and administrative offices. We may regain the shore by the *Vrata pod zidom* (Old Wall Gate) and continue by Obala Pino Budicin to the *Vrata Sv. Benedikta*, the oldest of the three (1554) which adjoins a small chapel also dedicated to St Benedict. A little farther on, in Obala jugoslavenske mornarice, the pretty little *Loža* (1592) overlooks the sea. The rocky foreshore beyond is used for bathing. Steps lead up to the parish church.

The church of *Sv. Eufemija*, built in the Baroque style in 1736, dominates the town. A 14C marble relief of St Euphemia flanks the side door and within stands the 6C sarcophagus of the saint (adapted in the 15C). The lofty bell tower (197 ft) was built to plans by A. Manopole in 1677, in imitation of St Mark's in Venice and affords excellent views over the harbour and neighbouring islands.

Behind the main square, in Trg Valdibora, are the market and a striking monument to the fallen of the Second World War, by I. Sabolić (1956). A small *Etnografski muzej* occupies a former bakery in Ul. Silvano Chiurco. The Obala palih boraca leads to the *Marine Biological Institute* (responsible for the oyster beds in the Limski kanal) with an aquarium, then to the hospital and *Railway Station*. On the E. side of the town a modern quarter has developed round the curious heptagonal chapel of *Sv. Trojstvo* (Holy Trinity), a 13C Romanesque baptistery that has survived its former church. The N.W. window has early Gothic decoration.

The islands just off the coast are beautiful and repay exploration (boats may be hired). The closest is *Otok Katarina*, the site of Rovinj's best hotel and a favourite spot for bathing or evening entertainment. Also popular is *Crveni Otok*, sometimes known as Sant' Andrea from its church. Here the Hütteroth Mansion, once a 13C Benedictine monastery, has been converted into a hotel. There are a number of pebbly beaches, one frequented by naturists, while round about are the smaller islets of *Otok ljubavi* (Island of Love), *Banjole*, *Sv. Ivan*, with lighthouse and church, and *Scurado*.

On the mainland opposite, s. of Rovinj and extending between the twin headlands of Punto Auro and Punta Corrente, is an extensive park shaded with Mediterranean pine. Along the shore here are Rovinj's main beaches and hotels, while the rocky coast to the s. is excellent for underwater fishing. Beyond the park is an international student centre.

From Rovinj we can return to the Piran–Pula highway at (118 km.) *Brajkovići*, and thence join Rte 3 to (147 km.) *Pula*. The gravel road direct to (120 km.) *Bale* (see Rte 3) cuts off c. 7 km.—140 km. **Pula** (see Rte 3).

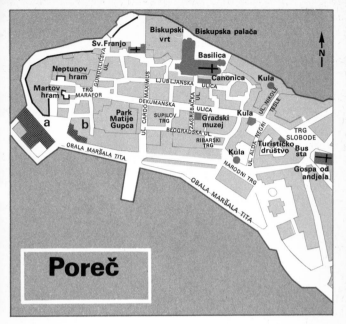

Poreč

Map labels: Biskupski vrt, Biskupska palača, Sv. Franjo, Basilica, Neptunov hram, Canonica, Kula, Martov hram, TRG MARAFOR, GUNDULIĆEVA UL., LJUBLJANSKA, UL. CARDO MAXIMUS, DEKUMANSKA, ZAGREBAČKA UL., ULICA, UL. NIKOLE TESLE, Kula, Park Matije Gupca, SUPILOV TRG, Gradski muzej, UL. ALDA NEGRI, TRG SLOBODE, BEOGRADSKA UL., RIBARSKI TRG, Kula, Turističko društvo, Bus sta, OBALA MARŠALA TITA, NARODNI TRG, Gospa od anđela, OBALA MARŠALA TITA, a, b

Rovinj

Map labels: Lighthouse, Bathing, ULICA, VLADIMIRA, Ljetna pozornica, Sv. Eufemija, ŠTURE ZA TVRBNE, ŠALBE, BREGOVITA UL., SILVANO CHIURCO, Spomenik, TRG VALDIBORA, OBALA PALIH BORACA, Rly station, Etnografski muzej, Kazalište "Gandusio", Bathing, GRISIA, CAŠALE, GRISIA, GRISIA, CAŠALE, Tržnica, ZD ENAŠ, ULICA PIETRO IVE, GARIBALDI, AUGUSTO FERRI, DE AMICIS, JUGOSLAVENSKE, MONTALBANO, TREVISOL, GARZOTTO, STARI TRG, Gradski muzej, Kavana, VL. GORTANA, Loža, MORNARICE, Sv. Benedikt, Narodni odbor, TRG MATTEOTTI, Vrata Sv. Križa, BEOGRADSKA UL., TRG PIGNATON, P.O., Pula, Jadrolinija, Vrata, OBALA PINO BUDICIN, Vijećnica, a, OBALA ALDO RISMONDO, Beach and Auto camp, N

5 FROM POREČ TO PAZIN AND RIJEKA

ROAD, 91 km. (56 m.).—13 km. *Baderna.*—27 km. *Beram.*—32 km. **Pazin.**—54 km. *Boljun.*—58 km. *Vranja,* beyond which the road becomes bad, narrow, and mountainous.—73 km. *Veprinac.*—81 km. *Matulji.*—91 km. **Rijeka.**
BUSES to *Pazin,* but not beyond. Pazin is on the Divača–Pula–Rovinj railway.

A good asphalt road runs E. to (13 km.) *Baderna* on the main Piran–Pula highway (comp. Rte 4), and to (21 km.) *Tinjan,* where a poor gravel road branches right to the village of *Sveti Petar u Šumi,* with 13C Benedictine monastery (Romanesque and Renaissance cloister) and fine Baroque church, and Kanfanar (see p. 40). At the next junction (27 km.) another gravel road forks left for Karojba and Motovun (see p. 18).

27 km. **Beram** stands on a hill (1000 ft) above the main road (l.) and should be visited for its frescoes. A great Illyrian necropolis was discovered here by the Austrian archaeologist Pulcher at the end of the last century. In the Middle Ages Beram was fortified. The parish church of *Sv. Martin* has a Gothic sanctuary (1431) with contemporary frescoes and a glagolitic inscription on the font. A number of glagolitic manuscripts discovered in the church are now in the University Library at Ljubljana. In the cemetery, ½ m. outside the village, is the guild church of *Sv. Marija na Škriljinama* with the best cycle of *Frescoes in Istria, by Vincent of Kastav (thought to be the father of Ivan of Kastav, responsible for the frescoes at Hrastovlje, see p. 7). The original 15C church was altered in the 18C when the triumphal arch was removed, the rib-vaulted ceiling replaced by a wooden one, and windows pierced in the walls. The outstanding fresco sequences are the *Dance of Death over the w. door and the *Adoration of the Magi on the upper part of the N. wall.

Also on the upper part of the N. wall is a Last Supper, while the panels on the lower wall depict (l. to r.) the Temptation of Christ, a trio of saints (Apollonius, Leonard, and Barbara), St Martin, St George, the Entry into Jerusalem, Christ Praying on the Mount of Olives, and (beyond the window) the Kiss of Judas. On the s. wall are fourteen panels arranged in two tiers. Those in the upper tier, depict (l. to r.) the Birth of Mary, Mary's Offering in the Temple, Mary's Betrothal, the Annunciation, the Journey to Bethlehem, the Birth of Christ, and the Infant Christ in the Temple. Shown in the lower tier are (r. to l.) the Massacre of the Innocents, the Flight into Egypt, St Sebastian, St Michael, Christ Disputing in the Temple, the Baptism of Christ, and SS John and Florian. The name of the painter and the date of completion are indicated in a Latin inscription just above the door in the s. wall.

Returning to the main Poreč–Pazin road we pass the obelisk and memorial to the native hero Vladimir Gortan, shot by the Italians in 1929. A plaque marks his birthplace.

The road climbs steeply in a series of hairpin bends till we appear above the deep chasm into which the river Fojba plunges to vanish underground for the rest of its way to the sea.

32 km. **Pazin** (3000 inhab.) stands dramatically on the cliffs (250 ft) that overhang the Fojba gorge. Strategically placed, on an important road junction in the centre of the Istrian peninsula, Pazin (Ital. *Pisino*; Ger. *Mitterburg*) marked for centuries the boundary between Venetian and Frankish (later Austrian) territory and was the seat of the counts of Pazin.

History. *Pazin* is first mentioned in 983 in a charter of the Emperor Otto II granting the town to the bishops of Poreč. In the 12C it passed to Maynard of Schwarzenburg, who became its first count. In 1248 the title passed by inheritance to the counts of Gorica (Gorizia) and, in 1374, to the Habsburg dynasty, although the town was briefly occupied by Venice in 1344 and again in 1508. In 1766 the title passed to Antonio Laderchi, marquis of Montecuccolo, near Modena, with whom it remained until the Second World War. In 1825–61 Pazin was the administrative centre for all Istria.

The garrison commander of Pazin in the 15C was Leonhart Herberstein, father of Sigismund von Herberstein (fl. 1549), the diplomat and writer. The castle and some of the turbulent history of Pazin have been described by Jules Verne in 'Mathias Sandorff' and by the Croatian novelist, Vladimir Nazor, in 'Krvavi dni' (Time of Blood).

Dominating the town is the massive KAŠTEL, founded in the 9C and so many times reconstructed in the 13–16C that architecturally it is interesting only for individual details. In the interior is an *Ethnographic and Historical Museum* (open 10–1, 4–6) with a collection of bells of the 12–18C. The front courtyard and battlements afford views into the Fojba gorge and to the Učka Massif in the east.

In the Prelaz Jurja Dobrile is the parish church of *Sv. Nikola*, founded in 1266, but largely reconstructed in the Baroque style in 1714, when the separate bell tower was erected. The vaulted ceiling of the sanctuary (1441) is decorated with frescoes, notable for their fine colouring and realism; the work of an anonymous Tyrolean artist, they depict scenes from Genesis and the life of Christ.

FROM PAZIN TO PULA, 47 km. The good gravel road runs s. along the old border between Venice and Austria to (6 km.) *Lušetići*, a hamlet whence a poor gravel road forks right to Sv. Petar u Šumi (4 km.; p. 38). Continuing s. we come to (14 km.) **Žminj** (1200 ft), once a thriving small border town, though now reduced to less than 500 inhab., which commands a multiple road junction. The 16C parish church of *Sv. Mihovil* (restored 18C) contains Venetian paintings of the 16–18C, a Baroque pulpit in marble and, among its ancient vestments (apply to sacristan), a 16C red damask cope. Next to the church the small chapel of the *Sv. Trojstvo* (Holy Trinity) has frescoes of 1471. Gothic in manner and painted by an anonymous Tyrolean artist, the majority are badly damaged. On the N. wall, Last Supper; W. wall above the door, the Flight into Egypt; and, upper part of the E. wall, the Ascension. Older frescoes, also damaged, adorn the guild church of *Sv. Antun Opat* (St Antony Abbot), a tiny Gothic structure built by the mason Armirigus in 1381. Painted under Venetian influence, the best preserved of them are in the apse.

From Žminj a by-road runs s.e. to *Barban* (14 km.) on the main Pula–Rijeka road (Rte 6).

21 km. **Svetvinčenat** is another old frontier town. The *Main Square rivals that of Koper as the finest in Istria. At its far end the 16C Renaissance church of the *Navještenje* (Annunciation) contains in its 19C interior a Madonna and Saints attributed to Palma Giovane and an Annunciation by an unknown 16C Venetian artist. The pulpit dates from the same period. To the left of the church is the *Kaštel Grimani*, a handsome rectangular fortress founded in 1485 and rebuilt in the Renaissance manner in 1589. The interior was badly damaged during the Second World War. Right of the church are the Renaissance *Vijećnica*

(town hall) and *Loggia*, probably 15C, flanked by a number of contemporary town houses.

In the town cemetery is the unusual 12C Romanesque church of *Sv. Vincent*, with three apses but no aisles. The walls are decorated with frescoes painted in the 13C by Ognobenus of Treviso (OGNOBENUS TRIVISANUS) under Byzantine influence. The best preserved, depicting (l. to r.) the Baptism of Christ, Christ Enthroned, and the Mother of God Enthroned, are in the conches of the three apses.

The road continues straight to join the main Piran–Pula highway at (37 km.) *Vodnjan* (see Rte 3).

FROM PAZIN TO ROVINJ, 40 km. We follow the road to (14 km.) *Žminj* (comp. above) and turn s.w. to (20 km.) **Kanfanar,** a small railway junction where the branch line to Rovinj leaves the main Divača–Pula railway. The town grew up mainly in the 17–18C as a result of the evacuation of Dvograd (see below). The parish church of *Sv. Silvestar* (1696) contains objects brought from the basilica at Dvograd, notably a 13C Gothic pulpit decorated with reliefs of St Sophia holding twin towns in her hands and, on the inner wall, of the Madonna. The lectern is supported by a single slender column. Notable also are a 14C painted door, a pair of wooden statues dating from the 15–16C and, among illuminated manuscripts (apply to sacristan), a 15C Liber anniversariorum. Beside the road to Barbat and Lovreč (see p. 21), 2 km. N. of Kanfanar, is the small 11C chapel of *Sv. Agata*, with Romanesque frescoes decorating the apse and triumphal arch.

In the valley of Limska draga, 3 km. w. of Kanfanar, is the ruined and deserted town of **Dvograd** (or Dvigrad) which is reached by a rough narrow track. Its foundation dates from Illyrian times when fortifications were set up on twin mounds controlling the passage through the valley. In the Middle Ages the twin towns were known as *Moncastello* and *Parentino* and were later joined under the name Duecastelli (or Docastelli), whence the modern Croatian form. The town belonged to the Patriarchate of Aquileia until the 15C, when it passed to Venice. It was sacked by the Genoese in 1381 and by the Uskoks (see p. 58) at the beginning of the 17C. In 1630 it was assailed by a virulent epidemic of malaria and its population hastily evacuated to Kanfanar.

The ruins stand in a romantic situation in the deserted valley and give a remarkable impression of the town as it was when abandoned. Two fortified gates and a ruined tower guard the entrance, but the main object of interest is the excavated foundations of the 11–12C basilica of *Sv. Sofija*. The innumerable holes in the ruins are said to have been dug by treasure seekers and testify to a curious local legend. The village of *Morgani* (or Mrgani), 2 km. w. of Dvograd, is supposed to have been named after Captain Henry Morgan, the pirate Governor of Jamaica, and it was widely believed for a time that his treasure was buried in Dvograd.

Just outside the town beside the road from Kanfanar is the ruined 10C Benedictine abbey of *Sv. Petronilla*. On the other side, on the road to Morgani, the Romanesque guild chapel of *Sv. Marija od Lakuća* has well preserved 15C frescoes and the smaller chapel of *Sv. Antun* has more frescoes by the same hand.—27 km. *Brajkovići* and thence to (40 km.) Rovinj, see Rte 4.

FROM PAZIN TO PLOMIN, 28 km. A gravel road runs S.E. passing (3 km.) a turning (l.) for the village of *Lindar* (view of the Učka massif). The N. wall of the Gothic parish church of *Sv. Katarina* is decorated with well-preserved rustic frescoes (1409) depicting the rare motif of a Living Cross.—Continuing E. we climb to a mountain ridge (views) on which stands (9 km.) **Gračišće** (1500 ft) a small fortified town that flourished in the 15–18C. The walls are partially preserved and a Venetian loggia

(1549) stands just inside the gate. In the main square are the chapel of *Sv. Marija* (1425), the 15C Gothic 'Bishop's Chapel' and the slightly later *Palača Salomon*. Beyond the square the Baroque parish church (1769) has carved stalls, while *Sv. Eufemija* contains a 13C wooden crucifixion. The steep, picturesque street running s. of this church preserves almost intact its 15C aspect. The town commands views of the Raša Valley, Čepičko polje (Čepić Plain) and Učka Massif.

11 km. *Pićan*, another small hilltop town with well-preserved fortifications. Known as *Petin* in Roman times, the town was a bishopric from the 5C to 1788. Up to the 16C it was a stronghold of the old Slavonic rite and Glagolitic texts. The former *Cathedral* was totally reconstructed in the Baroque style during the 18C (view from the Campanile). The painting over the main altar is by V. Metzinger (1738); the treasury preserves a 15C silver cross and a 16C monstrance. In the cemetery the small Romanesque church of *Sv. Mihovil* has good 15C frescoes on the N. wall: Mount of Olives, Kiss of Judas, and Christ before Pilate.

From Pićan the road descends in steep turns to the floor of the Raša valley. Crossing the Raša and and the Kozjak–Raša railway line we climb again to (23 km.) *Kršan*, where a narrow gravel road leads left to Čepic and its fertile plain, or right to Labin (see Rte 6). We reach the main Pula–Rijeka highway at (26 km.) Vozilići, whence to (28 km.) *Plomin*, see Rte 6.

Continuing E. from Pazin we cross the Divača–Pula railway line twice and run beside it to (41 km.) *Cerovlje*, where a poor gravel road forks left to Draguć (9 km.) and Buzet (22 km.; p. 19).

Draguć was once fortified and still has a ruined castle, but its main interest lies in its two frescoed churches. The older of the two, the Romanesque cemetery chapel of *Sv. Elizej*, contains poorly preserved rustic frescoes from the 13C. The early 15C church of *Sv. Rok*, erected as a votive offering to combat the plague, is covered with paintings by Anton of Padova (i.e. Kaščerga, a village c. 10 km. s.w. of Draguć), who was also responsible for frescoes at Hum (p. 20) and Oprtalj (p. 19). The side walls and roof were painted in 1520 and that behind the high altar (SS Fabian, Roch, and Sebastian) in 1537. Note particularly the large Adoration of the Magi on the lower N. wall and the three square panels above, representing (l. to r.) Baptism of Christ, Temptation in the Wilderness, and St Margaret (?). On the s. wall (top left) Votive Offering Against the Plague and (bottom left and centre) the Birth of Christ and Flight into Egypt; and the large Imago Pietatis over the w. door.

Bearing right we cross the river Fojba and follow one of its tributaries E.—At 44 km. a gravel track leads (r.) to the hamlet of *Gologorica*, where the church of Sv. Marija contains the remains of 14C frescoes in rustic Gothic.

51 km. *Paz*, with the ruined castle of the Walterstein. In the parish church is a late Gothic custodial (1496) with an inscription by Walter Walterstein, while the cemetery church of Sv. Vid contains Venetian-style frescoes by Master Albert (1461).—The road now winds down towards the valley of the river Boljunščica, a tributary of the Raša, where it meets the minor gravel road that runs s. through the Čepić Plain and the heart of the Ćić country (see p. 20) to Kršan and Labin (see Rte 6).

On this road, beyond Šušnjevica (6 km.), the church of Sv. Duh (Holy Spirit) at *Nova Vas* has good 16C frescoes by Blaž of Dubrovnik, while those in the church of Sv. Kvirin at *Jasenovik*, the next hamlet s., were painted by Master Albert (15C; restored 1965).

Climbing once more we pass beneath the Divača–Pula railway line and pass below (54 km.) *Boljun*, another small walled town in decay. The ruined fortress dates from the 15–17C and the parish church (note the high altar) and town hall are also of the 17C.

58 km. *Vranja* has late Gothic frescoes (1470) in its parish church. The left branch here runs through Ćićarija to Buzet (p. 19), but we fork

right to climb by spectacular hairpin bends to the pass of *Poklon* (3145 ft) in the centre of the Učka Massif. The scenery changes from barren karst to Alpine meadows and woods, which in turn give way to thick forest. A good gravel road runs through the forest (r.) in c. 10 min to the comfortable *Hotel Učka* (32 R, showers, rest.). A mile farther on is the more modest Hotel Poklon (10 R). From either of these it is possible to reach the summit of Učka (4580 ft; comp. p. 45) on foot in c. 1½ hrs. Alternatively the gravel road may be followed by car for a further 7 km. to within a few hundred yards of the summit. Both hostels are centres for hunting in the season (especially wild boar) and skiing in winter.

Beyond the pass the road broadens and improves as it drops rapidly through oak, beech, and pine woods, with views over the Kvarner to Rijeka and the offshore islands.—73 km. *Veprinac* (1700 ft) clings to the side of the mountain. A Baroque loggia by the main gate gives excellent views over Opatija and the Kvarner. The parish church (Sv. Marko) has carved choir stalls and pews. Frequent buses during the season link Veprinac with Opatija and Rijeka.

We continue along the E. slope of the Učka Massif and parallel with the coast, with Opatija directly below. Soon the gravel surface gives way to asphalt. At (81 km.) *Matulji*, whose railway station serves Opatija, we join the main Trieste–Rijeka highway (see Rte 1) to (91 km.) **Rijeka.**

6 FROM PULA TO RIJEKA

ROAD, 102 km. 28 km. **Barban.**—43 km. **Labin.**—57 km. *Plomin.*—77 km. *Mošćenička Draga.*—84 km. **Lovran.**—90 km. **Opatija.**—102 km. **Rijeka.**
BUSES every other hour in 2½ hrs.
STEAMER once a week (Wednesday) from Pula to Rijeka in 2½ hrs.

Leaving Pula by the Trg Avnoja and Ul. 43 Istarske divizije, we drive N.E. parallel with the coast. At 6 km. a narrow gravel road leads off right to Valtura and Nesactium (comp. Rte 3).

A flat, straight asphalted road continues to (28 km.) **Barban,** overlooking the Raša valley. Originally attached to the margraviate of Pazin, Barban passed to the Habsburgs in 1374 and during the 16C to Venice as the patrimony of the Loredan family. Parts of the medieval fortifications still stand, but the extensive *Kaštel* has been incorporated in later buildings, including the *Palača Loredan* (1606). The campanile of the parish church rests on one of the castle towers. The *Church* itself contains Venetian pictures of the 16–18C and a late-Gothic stone custodial. Of the two surviving gates the *Vela Vrata* dates from 1718 and the *Mala Vrata* from 1720. Near the latter is a Venetian *Vijećnica* of 1555, with loggia and clock tower. Gothic frescoes have been preserved in the two guild churches of *Sv. Antun Opat* and *Sv. Jakov,* both 15C.

The road descends by hairpin bends into the Raša valley with views s. to the fjord-like Bay of Raša and N. to the Učka Massif. The Raša was for centuries an important frontier line, marking first the boundary between the Roman provinces of Istria and Liburnia and later the limits of the kingdom of Croatia under King Peter Krešimir IV. It was regarded by many, including Dante, as the E. boundary of Italy. Crossing the river and railway line we pass through the coal-mining villages of *Raša* and *Krapan*, whence galleries extend 600 ft under the sea.

43 km. Labin, a town of 6000 inhab., is sharply divided into its ancient and modern components. At the bottom of the hill lies the modern mining community of *Podlabin*. The old town crowded on its narrow hilltop is one of the prettiest in Istria, but the hill on which it stands has been so extensively undermined by galleries and tunnels that it is subsiding almost daily. Many of its buildings have been declared dangerous, the population is being evacuated to the newer part and there is a possibility that it may one day collapse in ruins.

Known to have been inhabited in prehistoric times, probably by the Celts, the town was called *Albona* by the Romans and Pliny attests its status as a municipium. In the 7C it was sacked by the Slavs, who began to settle the area at this time, but it passed to Charlemagne and the Franks. For a short time during the 10C Labin represented the westernmost town of the kingdom of Croatia under King Peter Krešimir IV, but later passed to the Patriarchate of Aquileia and in the 15C to Venice. In 1921, under Italy, a miners' strike turned into an armed uprising that led to the proclamation of a short-lived 'Republic of Labin' before order was restored. Labin was the birthplace of Mathias Flacius Illyricus (Matija Vlačić–Franković; 1520–75), theologian of the Reformation.

The focal point of the town is the spacious main square where the local bus deposits visitors. The once celebrated 17C loggia was dismantled in 1965 owing to subsidence, and plans for its reconstruction elsewhere have not yet been completed. Beyond the round fortress tower on the N. side of the square the *Town Gate* (1587) leads into a maze of twisting streets. The *Palača Scampicchio* (1570; r.), with courtyard and colonnaded balcony, adjoins the parish church of *Sv. Marija*, originally 14C Gothic, but reconstructed in the Renaissance style (1582) on Scampicchio's initiative. His portrait is built into the w. front over a bricked-up Gothic window. The church also is suffering from subsidence. The former *Pretorska palača* (Captain's Residence), opposite, is occupied by nuns of the Paulician order, while the somewhat overblown Baroque *Palača Battiala–Lazzarini* (1717), just beyond, houses the small Town Museum (daily, 10–4). Here is a claustrophobic reconstruction of one of the mining galleries, which visitors can negotiate complete with helmet and lamp. A little farther on we emerge on the battlements of the medieval fortifications, whence there is a superb panorama of the Kvarner Bay, the islands of Cres and Lošinj and, on a clear day, of Krk, the Velebit Mountains and the North Croatian coast. Returning viâ Ul. Martinuzzi we pass the 17C Baroque mansions of the Vlačić–Franković, Manzin, and Negri families and the dilapidated church of *Sv. Marija od Zdravlja* (keys from nunnery), with some Baroque wooden statuary.

Buses ply hourly to the small harbour and resort of **Rabac** (*Sant Andrea, Primorka, Mediteran, Marina, Primorje;* autocamp for 100 cars; P.O.: Tourist information; pebble beach), 5 km. S.E. of Labin. A car ferry runs thrice daily in the season from Rabac to Porozine on the island of Cres (Rte 12).

The main road continues N.E. and at (55 km.) *Voziliči* joins a road from Pazin (see Rte 5), turning S.E. to skirt the narrow Plomin Bay.—**57 km. Plomin,** now a deserted backwater, retains its medieval system of fortifications (13–17C) in fair preservation.

First Illyrian and then a Roman castrum, known as *Flanona*, Plomin was sacked by the Avars in the 6C and resuscitated only after 1012, when it came under the

Patriarch of Aquileia. After joining Venice (1410) it was sacked on repeated occasions in the 16C by the Uskoks of Senj.

At the s. edge of the town (view over the Kvarner Bay) is the tiny 11C Romanesque church of *Sv. Jurje* (St George), built to a cruciform plan with a small bell tower. In the s. wall are fragments of a primitive relief together with the oldest Glagolitic inscription in Istria (11C or 12C). In the centre of the town is a later and larger church of *Sv. Jurje* (1474) with Renaissance altar and stalls.

The road runs beside the strangely green waters of Plomin Bay before twisting N. again high above the shore. On our right between the mainland and the island of Cres is the *Vela Vrata*, one of the two main navigation channels leading into the bay and harbour of Rijeka. Passing through (70 km.) *Brseč*, a compact little township and birthplace of Eugen Kumičić (1850–1904), the Croatian novelist, we descend to the shore and enter the region of the Kvarner or Quarnero (see p. 47). Although geographically a part of Istria, the coast between here and Opatija, sometimes known as the OPATIJA RIVIERA, is linked administratively and economically with Rijeka.

77 km. *Mošćenička Draga* (Miramar, with annexes; Autocamp; P.O.; Information), a popular small resort with a pebble beach. An obelisk on the shore commemorates the landing here in 1945 of Yugoslav forces to begin the liberation of Istria. High up on the hill above the town is the old settlement of **Mošćenice** (535 ft), which is reached by 760 steps from the s. end of the beach or by gravel road (3 km.). The quaint old town is entered by a gate surmounted by the arms of the Habsburg family and the date of its repair, 1634. The plain 17C loggia in front is known as the 'stražarnica' (look-out) from its traditional use for keeping watch on the sea. The Baroque parish church of *Sv. Andrija*, situated in the main square, contains 17C choir stalls and, over the high altar, sculptures by I. Contieri, an 18C Paduan. Just inside the main gate, in a private house, are preserved an ancient olive press, a horse-operated mill, and other primitive equipment, still used in November and December.

Following the coast road N., with attractive pebble beaches to our right and the Učka Massif towering on our left, we pass through the resort villages of *Kraj*, birthplace in 1870 of Viktor Car Emin, the Croatian novelist, and *Medveja* (autocamp).

84 km. **Lovran**, an attractive resort (2700 inhab.) still has an Austrian *fin de siècle* flavour. The surroundings are noted for their luxuriant vegetation and wide variety of flora, the cause in 1845 of a botanical expedition to the town by King Frederick Augustus II of Saxony. Lovran came to prominence as a seaside resort at the turn of the century after the railway had been constructed from Vienna to Trieste and Rijeka.

Hotels. Beograd, with annexe, 100 R; **Belveder,** with annexes, 100 R; **Primorka,** with annexe; **Park, Miramar, Udarnik.** AUTOCAMP.
Buses (local) from the front to *Mošćenička Draga* and to *Opatija* and *Rijeka*. Long-distance services to *Labin*, *Pula*, and the rest of Istria.

Named *Lauriana* after the laurel that grows in great profusion in these parts, the town existed in Roman times, though its name first receives mention only in the 7C. In 799, Eric of Strasbourg, nephew of Charlemagne, was killed here in a battle with the Avars and Slavs. Later Lovran formed part of the kingdom of Croatia, then passed to the Patriarchate of Aquileia and in 1374 to the Habsburgs, when it was ruled first by the noble family of Walsee and then by the counts of Pazin. During the 16C Lovran was sacked repeatedly by the Venetians and the Uskoks and in the 17C the population was decimated by plague.

The MODERN QUARTER is centred on the front and the excellent beaches (shingle and pebble), where most of the hotels are situated. It is joined to Opatija by an attractive promenade (comp. p. 46), at the s. end of which is the tiny Romanesque chapel of *Sv. Trojstvo* (Holy Trinity), later reconstructed, with ornamented doorway and traces of 15C frescoes within. The MEDIEVAL QUARTER, formerly fortified, lies above the main street on the lower slopes of Učka. The *South Gate* is all that remains of the walls. In the main square the parish church of *Sv. Jurje* (St George), basically 14–15C Gothic, was later twice enlarged. The choir walls and the triumphal arch are decorated with 15C frescoes (discovered 1952) showing Alpine influence (Crucifixion and Last Judgement). Also in the square are a Romanesque bell tower and fortress tower, probably 12C; among Baroque town houses, note especially St George's House, named for the equestrian statue that adorns the tympanum, opposite the church, and (w. side) the house with a Turk's head in relief and the town arms.

Above the town marked paths offer pleasant walks on the lower slopes of **Mt. Učka** amid groves of cherry, chestnut, laurel, beech, and pine. Places that can be visited include the hamlets of *Oraj* (900 ft) reached in about 1½ hrs; *Liganj* (¾ hr); *Lovranska Draga* (1300 ft), 1½ hrs; *Dobreč*, ¾ hr; and *Poljane*, 1½ hrs. Marked paths also lead higher to some of the peaks of the Učka Massif. *Mali Knezgrad* (2000 ft) can be reached in c. 2 hrs viâ Liganj, and *Veliki Knezgrad* (2000 ft) viâ Liganj and Ivulići. The name Knezgrad ('princetown') is said to commemorate the death here (but comp. Rte 7) of Charlemagne's nephew, Eric of Strasbourg, in 799. The summit (4580 ft) can be reached on foot in about 4½ hrs viâ Liganj and Ivulići or 3½ hrs viâ Dobreč.

Continuing N. along the coast, the main road passes through the villages of *Ika* and *Ičići* (motel), now virtually suburbs of Lovran and Opatija.

90 km. **OPATIJA,** a prosperous, well laid-out holiday town (8000 inhab.) with a strong Central European flavour, is Yugoslavia's leading tourist resort. Its geographical situation gives it a particularly benign climate, since it is cooled in summer by the proximity of the Učka Massif, while in winter the mountain acts as a barrier to the cold winds from the North. The sea here is also exceptionally rich in minerals and the air in iodine, which makes Opatija an important convalescent centre, particularly for rheumatism and heart diseases. A clinic has been recently established for sea-water cures. Visually Opatija remains Austrian in character. Its architecture, symbolized by the Hotel Kvarner, is in a rich variety of eclectic, imitative and florid styles which give the town an air of 19C opulence.

Railway Station at *Matulji* (5 km. from town centre, frequent buses), on the Ljubljana–Rijeka line.

Hotels. Ambasador, 200 R, all with bath, swimming pool, kavana, dancing, beach; **Slavija,** 220 R, kavana, dancing; **Kvarner,** 90 R, kavana, dancing, beach; **Adriatic,** 145 R, swimming pool; **Belveder,** 140 R, beach; **Imperial** (formerly *Central*), 110 R, dancing; **Residenz,** 100 R; **Zagreb,** 105 R; **Kristal,** 100 R, kavana, swimming pool, dancing, beach; **Dubrovnik,** 105 R; **Brioni,** 78 R. beach; **Kontinental; Atlantik; Istra,** 95 R, beach; **Palme,** 93 R; **Jadran; Avala.**

Restaurants. *Vasanska, Riblji restoran* (fish), *Zelengaj, Lovor,* and *Liburnija,* all in Ul. Maršala Tita; *Jedro* on the quay; *Mali raj* in Ičići.

Kavanas in most of the big hotels. Also *Bellevue, Jadran, Central,* and *Continental* in Ul. Maršala Tita.

Post Office, Kumičićeva ul. 2, and opposite bus station.

Information. TURISTICKI BIRO on the promenade behind Hotel Amalija.— TOURIST OFFICES. Kvarner Express, Autotrans, Kompas, Generalturist and Putnik, all on Ul. Maršala Tita.

Buses run through the town to *Rijeka* and *Lovran* every 15 min. Bus station for all local and long-distance buses at Slatina at the s. end of the main street (Ul. Maršala Tita); connections with all parts of Yugoslavia and with *Trieste, Venice,* and *Vienna.*

Motor boats to Rijeka every hour.

Theatre. *Ljetna Pozornica* (open-air) in the Park 1 maj, for stage shows or films. —OPERA FESTIVAL annually in July and Aug.—FESTIVAL OF POPULAR MUSIC annually in Oct.—CASINO at the Hotel Rosalia.

Beach artificially made of sand and cement.—SPORT. Tennis, sailing, water-skiing, rowing, water polo.

Opatija (Ital. *Abbazia*) takes its name from the Benedictine Abbey of St James founded here in the 15C. Its existence as a resort dates from 1844 when Iginio Scarpa, a Rijeka businessman, built the Villa Angiolina. Opatija's popularity was given a tremendous fillip by the construction of the railway from Vienna to Trieste (1857) and its extension to Rijeka (1873). It became a favourite resort of Viennese high society and the ex-Empress Maria Anna of Savoy, consort of Emp. Ferdinand, holidayed here repeatedly during the 1860s. Later the Emp. Francis Joseph kept it in the fashion by purchasing a villa for Katarina Schratt, his mistress, in near-by Volosko.

Of the ancient Abbey, only the small chapel of *Sv. Jakov* (St James) survives near the promenade. After reconstruction in 1774 and enlargement in 1937, little of the original structure of 1506 remains. Adjoining is Scarpa's *Villa Angiolina* (open to the public); its beautiful park (now called **Park 1 maja**) is maintained as a botanical garden. The fine selection of exotic flora includes giant evergreen sequoias, giant magnolia, Japanese orange and banana, grape myrtle, wild cinnamon, Chinese forsythia, gingo, tropical lilies, and eucalyptus. There are also Lebanon, Deodara and Mount Atlas cedars, tamarisk, agave, balsam, japonica, bougainvillea, and palm trees. The excellent PROMENADE extends for 12 km. from Lovran in the s. to Volosko in the N., while marked paths lead up to Vrutka Park (view), Veprinac (see p. 42), and the Učka summit (see p. 45).

Beyond Opatija the main coast road continues N. through *Volosko*, formerly a fishing village but now a picturesque suburb of Opatija, and *Preluk* (autocamp, beach, speedway track) where tall tunny ladders jut out over the sea. Designed as lookout posts from which to spot the tunny shoals as they came close inshore (comp. p. 55), the Preluk ladders are now rarely, if ever, used. We enter the w. suburbs of (102 km.) **Rijeka** (see Rte 7).

II THE KVARNER

7 RIJEKA AND ITS ENVIRONS

RIJEKA, thanks to its protected harbour, strategic position, and excellent communications with the interior, is the largest port of Yugoslavia, second city (120,000 inhab.) of Croatia, and a major industrial, commercial, and cultural centre. Ringed on the landward side by high mountains, it stands at the mouth of the small river Rječina at the head of Rijeka Bay, which in turn forms part of the Kvarner Gulf. Relatively few of its ancient monuments survived an earthquake in 1750 and the town suffered heavy air raids in the Second World War. As the headquarters of Yugoslavia's passenger fleet, it has become for many visitors the gateway to the eastern Adriatic.

Railway Station, Ul. Borisa Kidriča, for services to Ljubljana and Zagreb, with through coaches to Belgrade and in summer to many European cities.

Hotels. In the centre: **Bonavia** (a), 170 R with bath or shower, Dolac; **Zagreb** (b), Ul. Narodne Revolucije. In *Sušak*, **Neboder** (c), Ul. proleterskih brigada; **Kontinental** (d), Titov trg. In *Vežica*: **Jadran, Park,** both Šetalište XIII divizije, both on beach. On the road to Bakar: **Motel Lucija,** 80 R.

Restaurants. *Triglav,* Ul. Fiorello la Guardia; *Torpedo,* Ul. B. Kidriča; *Zlatna Školjka* (fish), Kružna ul.; *Žabica,* Ul. Rade Končara; *Tri palme,* Ul. Ivana Zajca; *Feral* (fish), Ul. Mateja Gupca; *Gradina,* at Trsat.

Kavanas. Gradska kavana, Trg republike; Zora, Narodni trg; and in hotels Bonavia and Neboder.

Post Offices. General, Korzo 13; branches next to railway station, Ul. Borisa Kidriča and at Sušak, Ul. proleterskih brigada 8.

Information Office. *Turistički informativni centar,* Obala Jugoslavenske mornarice. TOURIST OFFICE. *Kvarner-Express,* Narodni trg. MEDICAL AID. *Turistička ambulanta,* Trg republike 2.

Trolleybuses. *Kantrida*—Bulevar Marksa i Engelsa—Ul. Borisa Kidriča—Beogradski trg—Kumičićeva ul.—*Trsat. Zamet*—Istarska ul.—Bulevar Marksa i Engelsa—Ul. Žrtava fašizma—Šetalište XIII divizije—*Pećine.* Also *Krnjevo* viâ same central route to *Vežica.* TOWN BUSES. 4. Splitska ul. to *Kozala.* 5. Beogradski trg to *Škurinje.* 6. Beogradski trg to *Podmurvic.* 9. Beogradski trg to Podmarči and *Draga.* 10. Beogradski trg to *Kostrena.*

COUNTRY BUSES depart from Beogradski trg for *Kastav, Matulji, Opatija, Lovran, Mošćenička draga;* for *Martinšćica, Bakar,* and *Kraljevica;* and for villages of the Gorski Kotar.

Long-distance Buses from Trg Žabica for all parts of Istria and the Adriatic coast and major cities of Yugoslavia. Also for Trieste, Venice, Graz, and Vienna.

Steamer quay, Obala Jugoslavenske mornarice, for all services. Steamers to every major city in Dalmatia and Istria, including frequent express services to the islands of Krk, Cres, Lošinj, Rab, Pag, Hvar, and Korčula; and to Venice, Greece, Turkey, Lebanon, Israel, and Egypt.

Amusements. THEATRES. *Narodno kazalište* 'Ivan Zajc', Sarajevska ul; *Lutkarsko kazalište* (Puppets), Ul. Blaža Polića.—CINEMAS. *Car-Emin,* Račkoga ul; *Beograd,* Ul. Borisa Kidriča 2; *Garibaldi,* Ul. Josipa Kraša; *Jadran,* Ul. Braće Šupak; *Neboder,* Ul. proleterskih brigada 1; *Partizan,* Dolac; *Viševica,* Ul. Borisa Kidriča 16; *Sloga,* Zamet.

Swimming at Delta beach, by the mouth of the river Rječina in Sušak; Kantrida beach; and Sablićevo and Glavanovo beaches at Pećine. SAILING at Sailing Club 'Galeb', Martinšćica. FOOTBALL stadium at Kantrida. SKIING in winter at Platak in the Gorski Kotar.

History. The town of *Rijeka* is first mentioned in the 13C as Terra fluminis sancti Viti (later *St Veit am Pflaum, Fiume,* like Rijeka all meaning 'river') although it grew up on the site of the much older Roman settlement of *Tarsatica* (comp. the suburb of Trsat) which seems to have been destroyed by Charlemagne in 800. From the possession of the lords of Duino, it passed by marriage (1399) to the lords of Walsee and in 1471 to the Habsburgs, who retained it for three centuries. During this time, together with Trieste, Rijeka flourished as an Austrian port and became a commercial threat to Venice, provoking Venetian attacks (1508, 1599, 1612) as well as attention from the Uskok pirates of Senj. In 1527 Rijeka was granted its own statute and in 1719 (with Trieste) was declared a free port by Charles VI. In 1776 the Empress Maria Theresa united Rijeka with Croatia under the Austrian monarchy but in 1779 the city was declared autonomous, with responsibility for its external affairs transferred to the crown of Hungary, and its history becomes turbulent and complex. The Hungarians, seeing an opportunity to establish an outlet to the sea, built new roads to the interior and favoured the Italian minority at the expense of the Croats. This was interrupted by Napoleon's occupation of the area in 1809–14 (the English bombarded Rijeka in 1813), after which Rijeka with the legacy of a road to Karlovac reverted to Vienna. During the Hungarian Revolution of 1848, the Croats under Ban Jelačić sided with the Habsburgs and afterwasrd regained the port, with Jelačić as governor. The 'Settlement' between Croatia and Hungary in 1868, however, awarded Rijeka once more to the central government in Budapest and Hungarian domination persisted until the First World War. During the war many Fiumani joined the Italian forces. In 1919 Rijeka became a focus of world attention when Italian irredentists, led by d'Annunzio, occupied the town and attempted to set up a regency. Under the Treaty of Rapallo (1920) Fiume became a free state and in 1924, as a result of the Rome Agreement, part of Italy; Sušak was incorporated into the new state of Yugoslavia. The border ran down the Mrtvi kanal with the Yugoslav Baross harbour separated from the port of Fiume only by a wall. The two parts of the town were reunited after the Second World War.

Rijeka was the birthplace of Vinko Jelić, the 17C musician, and of Ivan Zajc (1832–1914), who was instrumental in establishing a Croatian national musical tradition, particularly in opera.

The busiest part of Rijeka for most of the day is the **Harbour,** where the arrival and departure of steamers attract almost as many onlookers as passengers. The Obala Jugoslavenske mornarice leads N.W. past the shipping offices of Jadrolinija to Trg Žabica with the long-distance bus station and, on the E. side, the ostentatious unfinished *Kapucinska crkva* (church of the Capuchins, 1906) in wedding-cake Gothic.

Farther on, the broad busy Ul. Borisa Kidriča passes the railway station (l.), the principal hospital (r.), and the attractive town park, *Djardin*, at Mlaka, before giving way to the Bul. Marksa i Engelsa, which leads to Kantrida and the road for Preluk, Volosko, and Opatija.

Just before Kantrida, to seaward of the railway, are the diesel engine works that began as the *Stabilmento Tecnico Fiumano* in 1856. Here their founder (and later owner), Robert Whitehead (1823–1905), a native of Lancashire, invented the modern torpedo in 1866 for the Austrian navy. The paper-mill farther on was another English foundation (1893), and beyond once stood a hostel for 3000 people, constructed by the Hungarians to accommodate emigrants in transit from central Europe to America.

On the other side of the harbour Ul. Ivana Zajca, following the railway line, leads past the Baroque church of *Sv. Nikola* (Orthodox) and the main *Tržnica* (market place) to the so-called *Mrtvi kanal* or dead channel, a sealed off arm of the Rječina that marked the frontier between Italy and Yugoslavia between the two world wars. At the junction of Sarajevska and Titogradska ul. is the neo-classical *Narodno Kazalište 'Ivana Zajca'* (People's Theatre), designed by H. Helmer and F. Fellner (1886).

Just behind the harbour lies the main square, the uninspired Narodni trg, where the Kvarner Express offices and the Seamen's Club are located. The KORZO NARODNE REVOLUCIJE (or simply *Korzo*), Rijeka's most attractive street and the main shopping centre, brings us to the General Post Office opposite the entrance to the old quarter.

We enter what is left of **Stari grad,** the badly bombed old city, by an ornamental gateway known variously as the *Gradski toranj* (City

Tower) or Južna or Morska vrata (South or sea gate). The gateway itself was probably built in the 13C, when the sea came up to this point; the Baroque tower was added in 1654 (inscription); and the cupola dates from 1801 when the whole structure was renewed. The arms over the arch are of imperial Austria while a niche above enshrines busts of Leopold I (l.), who granted Rijeka new arms in 1659, and Charles VI (r.; face damaged). Inside extends the Trg Ivana Koblera, a square still torn by gaps from the bombing. A stone column represents the base of a former flagstaff, erected according to the inscription by Captain Tivan Tozich in 1565. A relief shows St Vitus, Rijeka's patron, holding a model of the city. Behind stands the 16C *Palac komunaričkoga*, the town hall from 1532 to 1835, which became a music school (plaque) under the direction of Ivan Zajc.

From the square, Užarska ul. leads s.e. through the heart of the old quarter to the parish church of *Sv. Marija*, an old foundation completely rebuilt in the Baroque manner in 1695–1726. The detached *Campanile* (1377) in transitional Romanesque-Gothic leans considerably to the e. In the square of Grivica at the far end of Ul. Jurja Šporera the Baroque Jesuit church of *Sv. Vid* (1638–1742), has an octagonal groundplan and large cupola modelled on Santa Maria della Salute in Venice. A cannonball embedded in the wall to the left of the main entrance is said to be a memento of the English bombardment in 1813. Inside, in the chapel of Čudotvorno raspelo (Miraculous Cross), is a 13C Gothic crucifixion in wood. The relics displayed are of St Victor. Next door is a small *Diocesan Museum* (open 8–12, 4–6). Farther w., in the decayed Ul. Marka Marulića, is the Renaissance church of *Sv. Sebastijan* (1562). Passing through a battered *Roman Arch* of the 1C A.D., we may regain Trg Ivan Koblera by the narrow Ul. Stara Vrata.

From Trg Ivana Koblera we pass behind the *Narodni Odbor Kotara* (Regional Council Chamber) to the small Trg Riječke rezolucije and the 18C Baroque church of **Sv. Jeronim** (Jerome), practically all that remains of an extensive Augustinian monastery founded in 1315 and abolished in 1788 by the Emp. Joseph II. In 1835 its main buildings were altered to serve as municipal offices and now house the town archives. Within the church a chapel to the left of the sanctuary admits to the vaulted sacristy, from which we enter the Baroque monastic *Cloister*. Here have been collected many inscribed tomb slabs of Rijeka's noble families removed from the church floor. Off the cloister is the attractive Gothic *Rauber Chapel*, built in 1482 by Nikola Rauber, a Rijeka Captain. Its proportions have been spoiled by additional chapels and an over-sized Baroque altar, but it preserves its painted vault.

At the corner of the long narrow Trg republike and Dolac stands the excellent *Reference and Lending Library* (c. 200,000 vols.), based on a former Jesuit College collection begun in 1627. Above is a small *Museum of Modern Yugoslav Art* (Moderna Galerija; open 9–12, 5–7) with an imaginative policy that enables much foreign work to be exhibited.

Ul. Frana Supila, following the line of the former w. wall of the old town, mounts by steps to the neo-classical **Guvernerova palača**, built in 1896 to the design of Alajos Hauszmann, architect of the Palace of Justice in Budapest. The seat of the Hungarian governor until 1914, it was occupied by d'Annunzio during his brief rule and from its balcony in 1924 the Italian annexation of Fiume was proclaimed in the presence of Victor Emmanuel III. The Italian governors occupied it until 1943 when it became temporarily the headquarters of the regional People's Council;

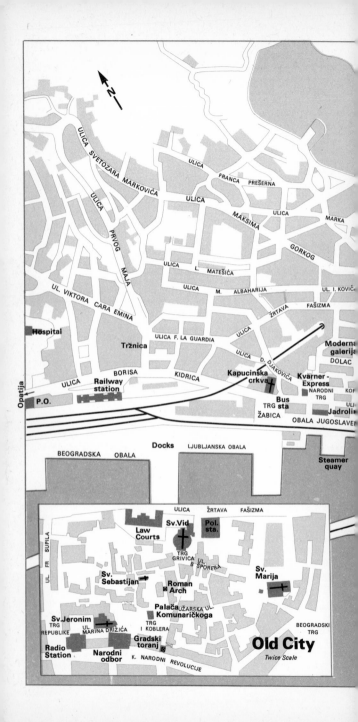

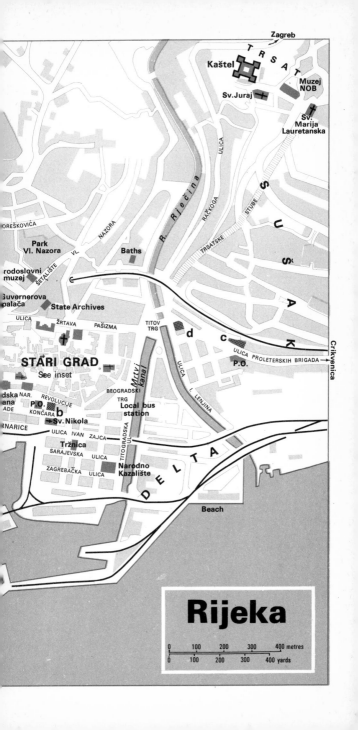

Rijeka

Zagreb

T R S A T

Kaštel

Muzej NOB

Sv. Juraj

Sv. Marija Lauretanska

R. Riečina

RAČKOGA

STUBE

ULICA

NAZORA

OREŠKOVIĆA

Park Vl. Nazora

Baths

TRSATSKE

S U Š

rodoslovni muzej

ŠETALIŠTE

VL

Guvernerova palača

State Archives

ULICA

ŽRTAVA

PAŠIZMA

TITOV TRG

d

c

ULICA PROLETERSKIH BRIGADA

Crikvenica

STARI GRAD
See inset

Mrtvi kanal

ULICA

P.O.

ČKAS

Crikvenica

dska ana
ADE

NAR. REVOLUCIJE

P.O.
KONČARA

b

BEOGRADSKI TRG

Local bus station

ULICA

I. LENJINA

Sv. Nikola

RNARICE

ULICA IVAN ZAJCA

TITOGRADSKA UL.

Tržnica

SARAJEVSKA ULICA

Narodno Kazalište

D E L T A

ZAGREBAČKA ULICA

Beach

| 0 | 100 | 200 | 300 | 400 metres |
| 0 | 100 | 200 | 300 | 400 yards |

it is now a scheduled national monument, and also houses the *Pomorski i Povijesni Muzej* (Maritime and Historical Museum; open 9–12, 5–7).

The public rooms have been restored as far as possible and arranged as they were when the governors were in residence. The sumptuous furniture, made specially for the mansion, has suffered from its multiplicity of masters; pieces bearing the arms of Austria were systematically defaced by order of d'Annunzio. Violins in the Crvena sala (Crimson Room) are the work of Franjo Kresnik, a local maker, who after studying the methods of Stradivarius claimed that the master's secret lay in the lacquer he used. The piano of Ivan Zajc is exhibited. On the second floor the *Maritime Collection* displays ship models, documents, and portraits.

The Šetalište Vladimira Nazora leads uphill to a small park in which stands the building containing the *State Archives* of Rijeka and the archives of Istria and the Kvarner. Adjoining it is the *Prirodoslovni muzej* (Natural History Museum) with an aquarium and small zoo. A little behind the park, on the hill called *Kalvarija* (Calvary), can be seen remains of the so-called Liburnian Wall, erected by the Romans (? 2C A.D.) against the Illyrian Iapidae. The hill gives a fine view of the town and harbour.

We descend to the broad Ul. Žrtava fašizma, which follows the line of the demolished town wall S.E. past the *Law Courts.* The extensive suburb of **Sušak** lies to the E. of the Rječina and is joined to the city by the spacious TITOV TRG, straddling the river. On the s. side of the square stands the *Liberation Monument* (1955) in bronze and stone, by Vinko Matković, a native of Rijeka.

Ul. proleterskih brigada leads S.E. from here past the Hotel Kontinental to the suburbs of Kostrena and Pećine and the highway to Dalmatia, while Račkoga ul. runs N. through the Rječina gorge (view) to the main road for Karlovac and Zagreb.

The castle and quarter of **Trsat** are reached from the N.E. side of Titov trg, where a Baroque archway (1745) bearing a relief of the Madonna marks the beginning of the TRSATSKE STUBE, a flight of 538 steps. These were designed to provide a suitable approach for pilgrims to the church of St Mary Laureta.

The lower flights were built in 1531 under a bequest from Petar Kružić, Captain of the fortress of Klis in Dalmatia and a Croatian warrior noted for his exploits against the Turks, while the steps were completed (1725) by Gabriel Eichelburg, who was also responsible for the archway at their foot. A Gothic votive chapel (1531) stands at their head.

According to legend the Santa Casa, or house of the Virgin, was transported here from Nazareth in 1291, and remained three years before being carried across the Adriatic to Loreto. The arrival is said to have been witnessed by an old lady named Laureta, whence the name of the church.

The church of **Sv. Marija Lauretanska,** built by Count Nikola Frankopan of Krk in 1453, was enlarged in 1644 and almost completely reconstructed in 1824. The Gothic triumphal arch remains from the earlier building. A good wrought-iron screen (1705) separates the sanctuary from the nave. On the Baroque high altar (1692) is a painting of the Mother of God, presented by Urban V in 1367. In the N. aisle are the tombs of the founder and his wife Elisabeth (d. 1513). Ex-votos adorn the walls.

Adjoining the s. side of the church is a FRANCISCAN MONASTERY, founded from a bequest by Count Martin Frankopan, also in 1453, and enlarged in the 17C. The *Refectory*, off the pleasant cloister, is elaborately decorated. The far wall, by the Swiss painter Fra Serafin Schön, depicts a mystical supper; the side walls (Miracle of the Loaves and Fishes, Manna in the desert) and ceiling (Assumption) are by the Venetian artist Cristoforo Tascha (1705). The *Treasury* (on view only by special request), on the second floor, contains incunabula, vestments (chasuble donated by Maria Theresa), a silver reliquary donated by Barbara Frankopan, and two 15C Gothic chalices.

Ul. Petra Zrinskog from the church (or a trolley-bus from Narodni trg) brings us to the **Kaštel** of Trsat (432 ft) on the site of an encampment of the Iapidae and a Roman observation post. By 1288 it was in the possession of the Frankopan family, who retained it until 1487. It then passed to the Habsburgs and in 1779 to the town of Bakar. Marshal Laval Nugent of Austria purchased the castle in 1826 and restored it in the romantically eclectic style it has today.

The quadrangular keep has circular towers at three corners and the entrance-tower at the fourth. The well-preserved N. tower affords fine views over the town and bay of Rijeka and into the Rječina canyon. Arcades (added by Nugent) surmounted by a loggia cross to the E. tower, now a café-restaurant. The small Doric temple, incorporating Roman columns from Pula, was erected by Nugent as a family mausoleum. The striking bronze chimaera, in front, bearing a banner inscribed 'DECREVI' and the arms of the Nugents and the related Sforza, is one of a pair by the Viennese sculptor, Anton Fernkorn (1813–78).

Adjoining the castle are the 13C church of *Sv. Juraj* and a *Museum* of the National Liberation Struggle. About ¼ m. to the E., between Ul. Slavka Krantzeka and Ul. Zeljka Marča, the extensive *Park narodnog heroja*, with a monument to the Unknown Warrior by Z. Kolacio and Z. Sila, commands excellent views over the town.

A PLEASANT EXCURSION may easily be accomplished in a day to Platak (regular bus service and excursion buses) in the Gorski Kotar. We take the road for Karlovac, passing through the Rječina canyon and rising rapidly by a series of hairpin bends to the karst plateau of Grobničko polje.—At (7 km.) *Čavle* a minor road forks left for **Grobnik** (1465 ft), at the far N.W. end of the Vinodol Valley (see p. 54), a fortified settlement in medieval times and one of the seats of the Frankopan counts. Their castle (good well head) and much of the old town walls (15–17C) survive. The parish church of Sv. Filip, half Gothic, half Baroque, has inscriptions in Glagolitic. The belfry was erected in 1572. The bare plateau, near by, was used by the Germans as a military airfield; a memorial stone commemorates the battle by which the Partisans destroyed it in Sept 1944.

Climbing further from Čavle, at 17 km., we diverge left from the main road on to a steep and narrow by-road and climb to *Platak* (Sporthotel with rest.), a small winter and summer resort (3670 ft) frequented for walking, skiing, and hunting. On foot the neighbouring peaks of Mt. Snježnik (4950 ft; refuge hut) and Mt. Veliki Risnjak (5025 ft; refuge hut) maybe reached respectively in c. 1 hr and 2½ hrs.

8 FROM RIJEKA TO ZADAR

ROAD, 244 km. (151½ m.), the Adriatic Highway (Jadranska Magistrala), well engineered but poorly surfaced to Senj. 17 km. *Bakar.*—23 km. *Kraljevica.*—37 km. *Crikvenica.*—40 km. *Selce.*—46 km. *Novi Vinodolski.*—69 km. *Senj.*—109 km. *Jablanac.*—133 km. *Karlobag.*—178 km. *Starigrad–Paklenica.*—199 km. *Posedarje.* —244 km. **Zadar.**

STEAMER, daily in c. 7½ hrs; twice daily in summer.

Rijeka (see Rte 7). We leave the town by Ul. proleterskih brigada and Šetalište XIII divizije, passing through the residential suburb of Pećine and reaching the shore at the mouth of the small bay of *Martinšćica* (autocamp). Skirting the bay with its growing shipyard (Viktor Lenac) we pass the motel and restaurant Žurkovo on our right and continue S.E. on the JADRANSKA MAGISTRALA (Adriatic Highway) with the high range of the Velebit Mts. on our left and views out to sea of Cres and Krk.

The road swings left in a broad curve, crossing the branch railway linking Bakar with the Rijeka–Zagreb line at Škrljevo, and affords superb views into the elliptical, almost landlocked *Bakarski zaljev*. The Bay of Bakar (c. 3 m. long) owes its steep sides and fjord-like appearance to its formation by subsidence, and is the largest such bay in the Kvarner. We circle the bay under the steep slopes of the Velebit (leaving on the left an asphalt road for Škrljevo and Trsat), passing terraced vineyards that produce an excellent sparkling wine called Bakarska vodica, and at 16 km. double back and descend to the sea.

17 km. **Bakar** (*Jadran*) an old maritime town (2000 inhab.) has declined like so many places along this coast into a sleepy backwater, although a modern oil refinery stands just outside.

Bakar may be the Volcera of Ptolemy. Part of the Frankopan county, it was unsuccessfully besieged by the Turks in 1527 and by the Venetians in 1616. After a period of union with Fiume it was united to Croatia. Bakar was blockaded by the British in 1812–13. From its shipyards was launched the first steamship of the Austrian navy. In his story, 'La Beffa di Buccari', D'Annunzio describes an exploit in which three Italian torpedo boats crept into the harbour in 1918 and fired torpedos at Austrian ships at anchor.

The old quarter, reached by steps, preserves its medieval character with narrow twisted streets and closely packed houses. *Sv. Andrija*, dominating this quarter, has an altar painting of the Holy Trinity by Girol. da Santa Croce (also a 14C Romanesque cross, a 16C reliquary of St Ursula, and Baroque chalices in the treasury). Higher up the hill is the crumbling *Castle* (1405?) of the Frankopans (see p. 68), who held Bakar from 1225 to the 15C and later of the Counts Zrinski (see below), who held it in 1557–1671. The ruined interior (key from house opposite) affords excellent views over the town and Bay of Bakar. Between the church and the castle lie the *Hospicij* (Hospice) of 1526, renovated 1716; the *Plovanija* (Vicarage) of 1514; the so-called *Turska kuća* (Turkish house), an uninspired copy of Moslem architecture built by a local sea captain; the *Biskupija*, a former palace of the bishops of Modruš (escutcheon dated 1494); the 18C Petazzi Mansion; and the so-called *Rimska kuća* (Roman house), the 18C Baroque residence of the Bakar Captains. *Sv. Kriz* (17C) half-way down the hill, has a late Gothic crucifixion on the main altar. The Baroque church of *Sv. Margareta* (1668), was endowed by the Zrinski family and contains pictures by V. Metzinger (1757). In the house of the former town magistrate is the cell in which Tito was confined before being sent to prison at Ogulin.

Returning to the Adriatic Highway we pass on our right Bakar's lampblack factory and small railway station.

A minor road (gravel) forks left here to (6 km.) *Hreljin*, a former fortified settlement of the Frankopans and later the Zrinskis. Remains of the medieval castle, town walls and houses can still be seen, though the population migrated outside the walls in the 18C.

The treasure of the ancient parish church of Sv. Juraj (modernized in the 16–17C) has now been transferred to the large new parish church by the main road (15C Gothic monstrance and some Baroque reliquaries).

Hreljin lies in the **Vinodol** ('wine valley'), a long fertile valley running roughly parallel with the coast and located amid the lower slopes of the Velebit Mts. In the Middle Ages the name also came to signify a political region stretching from Grobnik (see p. 53) in the N.W. to Novi Vinodolski (see p. 57) in the S.E. and including the coastal region as well. In 1225 this region came into the hands of the Counts Frankopan of Krk who made it their main centre after being driven from Krk in

1480. The main towns at this time were Grobnik, Trsat, Bakar, Hreljin, Drivenik, Grižane, Bribir, Ledenice, and Novi Vinodolski, all of which signed the famous Vinodol Statute (see p. 57) in 1288. In the 16C when Dalmatia and the Kvarner islands were subject to Venice, the coast between Zadar and Karlobag under the Turks and Senj, Rijeka, and Istria under the Habsburgs, this small region represented the only access to the sea left to Croatia and it has always been noted for its Croatian national sentiment. Nowadays the Vinodol, as a geographical term, embraces only the southern part of the valley from Hreljin to Novi Vinodolski and does not include the coast.

From Hreljin the so-called Caroline Road (asphalt), built by the Emperor Charles in 1728, leads N.W. through Škrljevo, Kukuljanovo, and Čavle to Rijeka, and S.E. (asphalt and gravel) to Grižane, Bribir, and Novi Vinodolski, while a tortuous mountain road (gravel) winds through the Velebits to Gornje Jelenje on the main Rijeka–Zagreb road.

22 km. *Bakarac* (autocamp, small beach), once the port for Hreljin but now a sleepy village. The two tall *tunere* projecting over the sea are the only working tunny ladders left on the mainland.

These tunny ladders were once characteristic of every bay of the Kvarner. The local fishermen kept a 24-hour watch in two-hour shifts from ladders 20-30 ft high for shoals of tunny; once a shoal was within the bay, the entrance would be closed with nets and the tunny hauled in; the dramatic final stages attracted many sightseers, but Bakarac and the island of Krk are now the only places where the custom survives.

23 km. **Kraljevica** (*Uvala Scott*, 300 R ; *Carovo, Almis, Praha*, autocamp; all at *Oštro* w. of the town) lies on a small inlet near the mouth of the Bay of Bakar, an untidy little town that was once an important Frankopan centre. Its Italian name was *Porto Re*. Charles VI initiated the harbour as an Austrian military base. In the 19C it enjoyed some prosperity when its main shipyard was run by Pritchard Brothers of England. It was again under English management between the two world wars. President Tito worked here as a young man (1925–26) shortly before his arrest for illegal agitation (plaques in yard and on the house where he lived). The shipyard, named after him (Titovo brodogradilište) now does mainly repair work.

Conspicuous are the twin castles of the Zrinski family (see p. 54). *Stàri grad*, near the harbour, has three storjes built round two courtyards with simple Baroque arcading. In the near one a well head bears the Zrinski arms, the inscription C.P.A.Z. (Comes Petrus a Zrinio), and the date 1651. A Baroque belfry (1790) is built on to the façade. The adjoining church of *Sv. Nikola* (patron saint of the Zrinski family) is part Gothic and part Baroque, with a rib-vaulted ceiling. The interior of the castle is in popular occupation and one courtyard serves as a cinema in summer. The more interesting *Novi grad*, begun in 1650 by Petar Zrinski, stands on a small promontory near the water's edge. Modelled on the late-Renaissance palaces of Italy it is rectangular in plan with cylindrical towers at the corners and an imposing double-arcaded courtyard inside. A well head in the courtyard bears the arms of the Frankopan and Zrinski families. The revolt of these two families against the Habsburgs was supposedly plotted in this castle beneath the rose window of the great hall (hence the expression 'sub rosa'). After the smashing of the revolt and the execution of Krsto Frankopan and his brother-in-law, Petar Zrinski, at Wiener Neustadt (1671), both castles were slighted. In the mid-19C the castle was bought by the Jesuits who added a floor and modernized it, and it now serves as a hostel for workers from the shipyard. The war memorial in the main square is by Zvonko Car (1952).

A by-road runs down from Kraljevica to the shore at (4 km.) *Crišnjevo*, whence a car ferry plies in 15 min approximately every two hours to *Voz* on the island of Krk (see Rte 9).

The Adriatic Highway continues s.e. high above the shore between the strait of Mala vrata, here only ¼ m. wide, and the Velebit Mts. Here the island of Krk is closest to the mainland, and clearly displays its bare and rugged n.e. shores. The small island at the n. end of the strait is *Sv. Marko*, with the ruins of a Venetian fortress erected to guard against the Uskoks of Senj (see p. 58). Its striking triangular shape is a well-known landmark to Adriatic sailors.

At about 2 and 6 km. out of Kraljevica gravel roads fork left to *Križišče* whence a mountain road leads up viâ *Fužine* to *Lokve* and *Delnice* on the main Rijeka–Zagreb road (trains from Rijeka and Bakar). With an Alpine climate and terrain, these three small resorts (each with mountain chalets) are attracting visitors for skiing, hunting, fishing, walking, and mountain climbing. At Delnice in particular there are many ski-runs as well as a ski-lift and two ski-jumps, with picturesque lakes at Lokve (Omladinsko jezero) and Fužine (Jezero Bajer).

37 km. **CRIKVENICA** is a pleasant thriving seaside town (3700 inhab.) nestling on a well-protected slope between the Adriatic Highway and the sea. It is a modern and, by Yugoslav standards, relatively sophisticated holiday resort, with good hotels (including one specializing in sea-water cures), a modicum of entertainment and an excellent and well equipped sandy beach. There are also good natural beaches extending to the Kačjak Peninsula to the n. and to Selce (see p. 57) to the s.

Hotels. In the centre: **Therapia**, 130 R, hydropathic, with swimming pool, beach and tennis courts; **Miramare**, with beach; **Mediteran**, with beach; **Esplanade**, with tennis courts and beach; **International**, with cabaret and beach; **Marina**; **Crikvenica**, with beach; **Praha**; **Zagreb**, with beach: **Slavija**, with tennis courts and beach. At *Dramalj*: **Villa Danica**, with tennis courts and beach. At *Kačjak* (3 km. out of town): **Kačjak**, 225 R, all w. bath, in main building and chalets, with beach.

Autocamp near the centre in pine woods, with beach.

Restaurants. *Petak*; *Riblji restaurant* (fish); *Marina*; *Primorac*; *Galeb;* all on the front.

Bus station behind the Hotel International for buses to *Rijeka*, *Pula*, and *Istria*; to *Ljubljana; Zagreb;* and *Belgrade;* to *Senj*, *Zadar*, *Split*, and *Dubrovnik*.

Steamers. Car ferry eight times daily to Šilo on the island of Krk (see Rte 9). Passenger steamers daily to Rijeka, Novi Vinodolski, Senj, Baška (Krk), Lopar (Rab), Rab and Novalja (Pag); four times weekly to Lun (Pag), and Novalja (Pag); Mondays and Thursdays to Mandre (Pag), Povljana (Pag), Vir and Zadar.

Amusements. Cabaret at Hotel International; Motor racing every May day; water-skiing club; sailing club; bowling club; tennis; water polo; underwater fishing.

Near Crikvenica is the birthplace of Julija Klović (Julius Clovius, 1498–1578), Croatia's most famous miniature painter, who was educated at the monastery here. Nikola Car, a hero of the national liberation struggle, was born in the town.

Although Crikvenica seems to have been inhabited more or less continuously since Roman times, its sole relic of the past is the so-called *Kaštel* or Frankopan Castle (1412), in reality a fortified Pauline monastery of a single story erected by Nikola Frankopan (d. 1439) on the bank of the small river Dubračina. A second story was added in the 19C and the Kaštel now stands at the entrance to the park.

Regular excursions are run from Crikvenica to the islands of Krk (see p. Rte 9) and Rab (see Rte 10); and to Opatija (see p. 45), the Postojna Caves (see p. 9), Plitvice Lakes (see p. 63), and Vinodol Valley on the mainland.

An asphalt road runs due N. from Crikvenica along the valley of the river Dubračina to join the highland road from Križišće (see p. 56) to Bribir (see p. 58) in the Vinodol (Hydro-electric station 'Vinodol' at the junction). At the hamlet of (2 km.) *Badanj*, left of the road, are the ruins of one of the medieval castles of the Frankopans, while in (9 km.) *Drivenik*, lying about 1 km. off the main road at the end of a rough track, is a much better preserved example dating from the 13C (added to in the 16C), with four horseshoe-shaped corner turrets and a rectangular entrance tower. Adjoining it is the medieval church of Sv. Dujam (badly restored in the 19C) and at a little distance the Gothic church of Sv. Stjepan.—At Badanj a poor and tortuous gravel road forks right to join the Križišće–Bribir road (gravel at this end) 5 km. from Bribir.

40 km. *Selce* (Marin; Jadranka; Slaven; Esperanto; autocamp) is a small resort on the lines of Crikvenica of which it forms virtually a suburb. It can also be reached by a local asphalted road (3 km.) along the shore. Just outside Selce a gravel road runs N. to Bribir (p. 58) in the Vinodol.

46 km. **Novi Vinodolski** (*Povile, Lišanj, Horizont, Villa Palma, Zagori, San Marino*, autocamp), also known as *Novi*, is the chief town (2075 inhab.) of the Vinodol region and an ancient centre of Croatian national consciousness. It is noted for its rich folklore, national costumes and individual folk dances, most of which can be seen during the colourful carnival known as the Mesopust (three days ending with Ash Wednesday). The town has developed into a successful small holiday resort.

Here was signed (1288) the famous Vinodolski zakon (Vinodol Statute), the oldest complete Croatian historical document, in which the overlordship of the Frankopans was formally recognized and the rights of the Vinodol citizens set out. In 1614, during the Uskok Wars, the town was ferociously sacked by Admiral Marcantonio Venier for aiding the Uskoks of Senj.—Ivan Mažuranić (1814–90), former Ban of Croatia and author of a classic narrative poem ('Smrt Smail-age Cengijića') was a native; his brother Antun (1805–88) was a pioneer in the scientific study of the Croatian language.

The older part of the town on the high hill overlooking the Adriatic Highway has suffered from indiscriminate demolition and rebuilding in the 19C. The 13C Frankopan *Castle* in the main square, where the Vinodol Statute is thought to have been signed, has been much reduced in size and renovated; Kvadrac, one of its towers, affords views over the town and Velebit channel. The 18C parish church of *Sv. Filip and Jakov* has a Gothic sanctuary (1520) dating from an earlier building (Tomb of Christophorus, Bishop of Modruš, 1499, before the main altar; 15C Gothic relief of Madonna in wood on side altar), while opposite it, in the former residence of the bishops of Senj and Modruš, is the *Narodni muzej* (Town Museum; open Mon and Thurs 9–11).

The museum combines local history, ethnography, and art and is as noteworthy for the loving care with which it has been assembled as for its contents (voluminous catalogues available in half a dozen languages, including English). Exhibits include a photocopy of the Vinodol Statute (see above), mementoes of the Mažuranić family, an early Baroque altar frontal and the folk costumes of Novi Vinodolski.— The neighbouring Mažuranić birthplace is marked with a plaque.

Below the Adriatic Highway and to the s. lies the modern part of Novi Vinodolski with its enormous promenade (bust of Ivan Mažuranić), beach and hotels. At the edge of the park are the ruins of Lopar, a Roman fortress. On a hill above the harbour are the extensive ruins of a 15C Pauline monastery and church.

Excursions can be made from Novi Vinodolski to the islands of Krk and Rab and to Senj (see below), and the Plitvice Lakes (see p. 63).

A winding asphalt road runs N. from Novi Vinodolski to (5 km.) *Bribir* in the Vinodol valley (see p. 54), with the remains of medieval town walls and a square tower from the former Frankopan Castle (1302). The tower (key from the town hall) affords views over the Vinodol valley and down to Novi Vinodolski and the sea. The Baroque parish church (1740) has a picture of the Washing of Christ's Feet by Palma Giovane and the treasury contains a gold Romanesque cross (c. 1200), the work of the goldsmith Milonigus. Beside the church is a monument to Josip Pančić, first president of the Serbian Academy of Sciences, a native of Bribir. Also born in Bribir was the Croatian literary scholar and critic Mihovil Kombol.

South of Novi Vinodolski the Adriatic Highway hugs the coast at the foot of the Velebit Mts., which here descend abruptly into the sea. Off-shore is the barren coastline of Krk (see Rte 9), and the intervening channel widens to form the beginning of the VELEBITSKI KANAL, or *Podgorski Kanal*, that extends for nearly 100 miles to Maslenica Bridge near Zadar.

At 47 km., just S. of Novi Vinodolski, a gravel road (l.) ascends in zigzags into the Velebits and across the Velika Kapela Mts. to Ogulin in the interior. Called the *Rudolf Road*, it was built in the 18C to link inland Croatia with the coast. At 9 km., perched at a dizzy height on the mountainside is the ruined medieval castle of *Ledenice* (visible also from the coast), an important stronghold until sacked by Venice in 1614 during the Uskok Wars.

69 km. **SENJ,** the largest and oldest town (4000 inhab.) beneath the Velebit Mts., with a colourful and turbulent past, owed its prominence in earlier times to good communications with the interior and strategic command of the Velebitski kanal and the sea. It was for long the home of the Uskok corsairs (see below). Unlike most towns on the coast, it was never occupied by Venice and in consequence has a strongly conti-nental flavour. It was badly damaged by allied air raids during the Second World War. Senj is the nearest town on the coast to the National Park of Plitvice and its famous Lakes.

Hotels. On the front: **Nehaj**, with kavana (a). In the old town: **Velebit**, with kavana (b).

Autocamps. *Bunica*, 4 km. N. of town; *Spasovac*, 3 km. S. of town; both small and with beach.

Restaurants. On the front: *Zagreb*. In the old town: *Lipa*, Trg Marka Balena.

Post Office and **INFORMATION OFFICE** on the front.

Bus Station in front of restaurant Zagreb; services to all parts of Istria, the Kvarner and Dalmatia, to *Karlovac* and *Zagreb* and to the *Plitvice Lakes*.

Steamers, daily in the season to Novi Vinodolski, Crikvenica, and Rijeka; to Baška (Krk), Lopar and Rab (Rab), and Novalja (Pag). Four times weekly all the year round to Crikvenica and Rijeka; to Baška and Stara Baška (Krk), Lopar and Rab (Rab); to Lun, Novalja, Mandre, and Povljana (Pag); and to Vir and Zadar.

History. *Senj* is thought to have been founded in 432 B.C. by the Celtic tribe of Senones who came from the region round Modruš, 25 m. inland. As *Senia* it was a Roman trading port of some importance and is mentioned by Pliny. In the 9C Senj passed from the Franks to Croatia; in 1154 it was made a bishopric; in 1271 the Frankopans became hereditary captains; and in 1388 the town received its own statute. Later (1469) it was attached directly to the throne of Matthias Coₗvinus, king of Hungary and Croatia, but in 1526, as a result of the battle of Mohač, passed to the Habsburgs. An era of notoriety ensued. The Turks had overrun Greece, Bulgaria, Serbia, Bosnia, and parts of Croatia. Large numbers of Slavonic refu-gees from these lands gathered in Senj and soon became known under the collective name of Uskoks (Ital. *Uscocchi*), the Serbocroatian word for runaway or refugee. At first, under the aegis of Austria, they constituted virtually an élite and autono-mous frontier force against the Turks, but soon turned to the sea, and throughout the 16C and early 17C operated as freebooters, the scourge of Venice and the Vene-tian fleet. Their legendary exploits and superhuman courage earned them a Euro-pean reputation. Austria, as a natural rival to Venice, turned a blind eye, particularly in view of the Uskoks' role against the Turks, but in 1615 Uskok depredations finally led to the so-called Uskok War between Venice and Austria. By the Peace of Madrid (1617), the Uskoks were disbanded by Austria and resettled inland. To the Venetians they were lawless brigands; to Austria turbulent but useful irregulars; but in Croatia and Serbia they were and are regarded as Slav patriots, hostile to Turkey and Venice alike and tolerant of Austria only as their titular overlord. After their dispersal Senj, with an Austrian garrison, went into a long decline, which was aggravated by the growth of Trieste and Rijeka.

Senj, always a centre of Croatian culture, had the earliest known Croatian printing press (in Glagolitic) in 1493–1508. The town was the birthplace of many prominent writers, including Pavao Ritter-Vitezović (1652–1723), S. S. Kranjčević (1865–1908), Vjenceslav Novak (1859–1905), Milan Ogrizović (1877–1923), and Milutin Cihlar Nehajev (1880–1931). The folk ballads relating the heroic deeds of the Uskoks are among the most beautiful in Yugoslav literature.

Senj is also noted for the Senjska bura, a N. wind that blows down from the Velebit Mts. and out to sea with such ferocity that it inspires universal dread. The Uskoks, the only sailors ever to have mastered it, used it as a cover for their raids. It gives Senj the lowest average temperature on the Adriatic seaboard.

The focal point of Senj has moved from the old city to the *Harbour* and sea front, which lie directly on the Adriatic Highway. Opening from the harbour a busy little square adjoins the Hotel Nehaj. The War Memorial ('On Guard') is by I. Vukušić; on the far side the dilapidated 16C *Palača Posedarić* preserves the family arms in its badly altered façade. Two houses adjoin it at the rear, the first Renaissance in style and the other (1541) with a Gothic doorway. POTOK, the old main street of the town, passes the Hotel Velebit and, immediately opposite, the house (plaque) in which was born Vjenceslav Novak.

The pleasant TRG MARKA BALENA, the main square or *Velika placa*, is mainly Baroque in character with an early-19C drinking fountain known as *Cilnica*. On the E. side rises the massive **Kaštel**, a Frankopan castle erected in 1340. After 1469 the building became the residence of the Senj captains and housed the city's garrison. In 1896 it was given a new façade and became a school. The entrance corridor is adorned by an elaborate 15C escutcheon of Matthias Corvinus, king of Hungary and Croatia. The **Velika vrata**, or *Great Gate* (1779), adjoining the castle, was erected to mark the completion of the Josephine Road from Senj to Karlovac under the Emp. Joseph II of Austria (as the inscription above records). The distances marked on the left gatepost are in German miles.

Outside the gate a path continues (r.) past the town wall and over the Kolan kanal to Nehaj Fortress (see below); while to the left a road follows the line of the walls past the ruined Gulden tower (l.) and the Neda textile works (r.) to the E. end of Stara cesta (comp. below).

Ul. Vl. Gregovića, running at right angles to Potok behind the three Baroque houses that close the w. side of the square, has several ancient houses. Carved on the lintel of No. 2 is a pair of rustic heads, male and female, a typical feature of Senj; No. 3 has a Gothic doorway with an escutcheon; and the corner of the end house bears a carved cross as a spiritual protection against damage by wheeled traffic. In the corner of the main square adjoining Ul. Vl. Gregovića is the **Narodni odbor** (Town Hall) and former *Franciscan Monastery* (1558), built round a Renaissance cloister by Captain Ivan Lenković. The second story was added in 1698 and the monastery restored in 1816 (after fire) and adapted to its present use in 1896.

The modest Baroque campanile on the corner of Ul. P. Preradovića, is all that remains of the monastery church (bombed 1943), which was the traditional burial church of the Uskoks. The house to the E, on the corner of Ul. Vl. Pavelića, has a well-preserved lion of St Mark in the entrance way and is thought to have been the home in the 13–14 C of the Venetian ambassador. On the other side, a few steps down, is the 15C *Palača Hajduković–Petrovski*, with the excellent Lavlje dvorište or Lion Courtyard, so named from the corbels that support the balcony. A carved well head in the courtyard bears the arms of (?) the Duke of Zweibrücken. The *Music School* (Niža muzička schola) immediately opposite the bell tower, occupies the former 14C church of Sv. Ivan Krstitelj (John the Baptist), of which Gothic details can still be seen on the façade; inside are 15C frescoes. Behind the school is *Uskoč-ka ulica*, a picturesque narrow cul-de-sac, with a double-arcaded courtyard, the best remaining example of a local style of architecture.

From Ul. P. Vitezovića we may shortly reach Kaptolski or Stari trg. Dominating this small square is the **Cathedral of Sv. Marija**, a Romanesque single-nave church of the 12C with aisles added in the 18C, when the building was remodelled in Baroque. Bombing during the Second World War revealed part of the original façade with blind arcading in brick, which has been restored. The interior, also restored after bombing, is Baroque, except for a Gothic triumphal arch and sacristy of 1497. Above the sacristy half obscured in a niche is the fine Gothic sarcophagus of Bishops Ivan and Leonardo de Cardinalibus de Pensauro (1392–1401). In the s. aisle is a 15C stone custodial and by the door a good Baroque font.

The quarter to the N.W. of the cathedral, behind the modern bell tower (1900), is GORICA, the oldest section of the city with a maze of narrow streets and houses dating back to the 15C. Here, in a narrow street beside the cathedral, the birth-place of the poet, S. S. Kranjčević is marked by a plaque. House No. 24 has a Glagolitic inscription on the lintel (1477) and No. 25, adjoining, with an arcaded courtyard, is thought to have housed the first Glagolitic printing press (1493, see above). Beyond Gorica are the surviving town walls (see below). Opposite the w. front of the cathedral is the *Palača Živković* (1487), with a handsome Renaissance doorway and a small statue in a niche. The Živković escutcheon is just inside the door. The street beside the palača descends to a small square just within the *Mala Vrata* (Little Gate), though the actual gateway has been destroyed. In the square is the house (plaque) in which Milutin Cihlar Nehajev, was born. Beyond the gate-way is a large 18C Baroque edifice known as the *Verein* (or Ferajna) in which, in 1835, was opened one of the earliest Croatian reading rooms.

Steps descend to the left towards the harbour. Stara cesta, the broad street to the right, skirts the remaining section of the CITY WALLS (12–15C) with three circular towers. The *Leonova* or *Papina Kula* is named after Pope Leo X (1513–21) who financed its erection. *Rondel* has been badly modernized. Beyond *Lipica* or Salapan we may regain the Velika vrata (comp. above).

The 16C *Palača Vukasović*, to the s.w. of the cathedral, houses the **Gradski Muzej** or Town Museum (open daily 9–12 and 4–7 in summer; at other seasons on Thurs and Sun, 10–12), which is in the course of formation (lapidary and archaeological section, Partisan relics, and a collection devoted to the history of literature in Glagolitic and Senj's literary past). A little farther down Ul. M. Ogrizovića, on the opposite side, the 18C *Palača Carina* with a typical Uskok head sculpted over the doorway, is now the palace of the bishops of Senj-Modruš. The ground floor houses the **Dijecezanski Muzej** or Diocesan Museum in which are displayed the Gothic Kaptolski križ in silver and wood, a similar but larger Gothic cross in beaten silver, a set of silver votive tablets, church plate and vestments, a small lapidary collection, and the Diocesan Library with a number of early codices and incunabula. In the spacious Trg žrtava fašizma or Mala Placa, which owes its irregular shape to wartime bombing, the 15C *Palača Dančić* has a good Venetian Gothic three-light

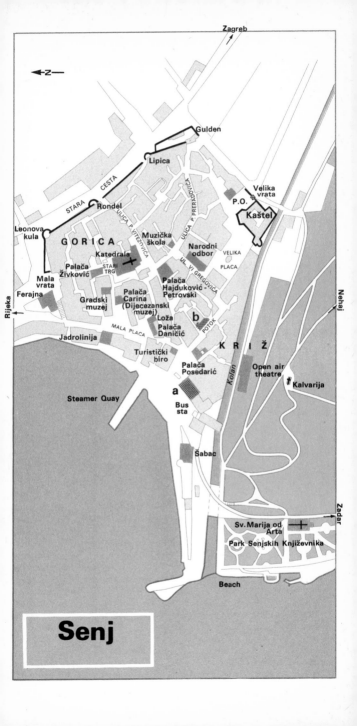

window on the third floor. The adjoining *Town Loggia* (16C) has been transformed as a dwelling but is to be restored. In the narrow Ul. I. Vlatkovića, behind these two houses, is the 14C Gothic chapel of *Sv. Marija Mandaljena*; the tiny cul-de-sac opposite is hemmed in with old houses, one with a relief of the Madonna.

Regaining the front we follow the shore, where the Restaurant Zagreb gains atmosphere from the vaulted basements of former warehouses it occupies. The former s.w. limit of the city walls is marked by *Šabac*, a round fortress tower, near the water's edge, now the harbourmaster's office. Beyond the canal, between the Magistrala and the sea, extends the pleasant green *Park Senjskih književnika* (Senj Writers' Park) with busts of native literary figures. The church of *Sv. Marija od Arta* (key from diocesan museum) inside the park (1489, restyled in Baroque), known as the Sailors' Church, contains a large number of 18–19C ship models. Beyond the church a path leads to the town beach, equipped with cabins, showers, and a cemented foreshore. Traces are visible of the artillery battery that once covered the shipping channel and commanded the islands of Krk and Prvić.

Opposite the park a footpath winds uphill, past a handball court and a rustic Calvary of 1740, to the imposing **Castle Nehaj** (open 9–12, 5–8 in the season).

Nehaj (Fear Not) was built by Ivan Lenković, most famous of Senj city captains, between 1538 and 1558, when the Turks were at the height of their power in the Balkans and had repeatedly attacked Senj. Lenković had all buildings outside the city walls destroyed and incorporated much of the masonry into his castle. Fragments and inscriptions from the 13C monastery of St Peter and the Benedictine Abbey of St George, can still be traced. The square keep built to face the cardinal points of the compass, with corbelled turrets at each corner, has an additional machicolated turret above the entrance.

The interior has recently been restored. A well head in the courtyard bears the arms of Lenković (1558) and of the town of Graz, under whose jurisdiction Senj was placed by the Austrian court. The ground floor housed the men's quarters; when restoration is complete it and the courtyard will be used for small concerts and refreshments. The first floor, formerly officer's quarters and the site of the powder magazine, is to be adapted as an Uskok Museum. The second floor, which constituted the firing platform, is to be restored to its former condition, with its heavy cannon (some of which have done duty as bollards on the quayside). The roof affords superb views of the entire Kvarner, extending as far as Istria on a clear day, and inland of the peaks of the Velebit Mts. and the pass of Senjska draga.

FROM SENJ TO PLITVICE AND THE PLITVICE LAKES, road, 89 km.(55 m.), buses daily in c. 3 hrs; numerous excursions in summer. The Josephine Road leads inland from the Velika vrata towards the Velebit Mts. After 2 km. asphalt gives way to gravel and we climb by a series of hairpin bends through typical karst scenery to the passes of Senjska draga and Vratnik (2300 ft), with superb views back to the coast and islands. The prominent memorial at Vratnik is the tomb of Kajetan Knežić (d. 1848), builder of the road. At (23 km.) *Žuta Lokva* a road diverges left for Karlovac and Zagreb, but we continue on good asphalt through the green and fertile valley of Lika viâ (42 km.) *Otočac*, and (58 km.) *Vrhovine*, on the Zagreb–Split railway line.

89 km. **Plitvice National Park** (*Plitvice*, with cabaret; *Bellevue*, 110 R, open all year round; *Labudovac*; autocamp; fishing, swimming, boating, skiing), an area of outstanding natural beauty covering 75 sq. m., com-

prises woodlands, meadows, lakes, waterfalls, rivers, and caves (entrance fee; guided tours twice a day in season). While visitors are given every facility for access, the park is strictly administered as a nature reserve, all flora and fauna being alike protected. Particular attention is paid also to the protection of the abundant travertine (a crystalline calcium carbonate formed by the deposits of the lake and river waters) in the park, which is essential to the balance of natural forces. Delightful walks may be taken through the woods, particularly at the w. end of the park where in virgin forest trees reach heights of 150 ft and more. Excursions can also be made to some of the hilltops, caves and smaller river valleys in the park.

The *Plitvice Lakes (*Plitvička jezera*), a continuous chain of sixteen lakes and innumerable waterfalls, form a system c. 4 m. long of unrivalled natural beauty. They are best visited in the spring, when the water-level is high; in the autumn, when the colouring of the foliage is particularly brilliant; and in the middle months of winter when many of the falls freeze over to form gigantic icicles and ice barriers.

Running from s. to N., the lakes take their source from two small streams, the Crna (Black) and Bijela (White) Rijeka (river), which join in the hamlet of Plitvički Ljeskovac to form the river MATICA. This feeds PROŠĆANSKO JEZERO (*Lake Prošće*), the highest lake (2087 ft), 170 acres in area. A road running along its entire E. bank and a footpath on the w. bank afford excellent views of many inlets and coves, of which *Limunska draga* (Limun cove), at the extreme s. end, is the most striking. Prošćansko jezero then falls by a series of small lakes and waterfalls, notably the *Labudovac Fall*, to *Galovac jezero* and this cascades in turn into *Gradinsko jezero* and JEZERO KOZJAK, largest of all the lakes (205 acres) with a depth of 150 ft. The *Galovac* and *Kozjak Falls* are particularly beautiful; a closer view is obtained from the footpaths that cross at these points. The road from Lake Prošće closely follows the lakeside as far as Lake Kozjak, then bends away to the village of Plitvička jezera, below which are the main bathing beach and facilities for hiring boats. Beyond the village a lower road keeps close to Lake Kozjak as far as the *Milanovac Falls* where it crosses to the other shore and continues for Zagreb, while the upper road remains at a distance from the shore until it reaches Lake Gavanovac. The footpath on the w. side, however, follows the water's edge right round the lake. At the N. end of Lake Kozjak we come to the lower group of lakes *Milanovac, Gavanovac,* and *Kaludjerovac,* which feed one another in a series of superb cascades tumbling in quick succession down a rapidly deepening gorge lined with limestone caves. Most spectacular are the waterfall of the Plitvice river (228 ft) which here flows into the lakes and the magnificent plunge of the *Sastavci* (250 ft) into the canyon of the river Korana, with which the series ends. Numerous footpaths and observation points give ample opportunity to observe the falls from various angles and the wild Korana canyon can also be explored on foot.

Other excursions can be made from Senj to the islands of Krk (Rte 9), Rab (Rte 10), and Pag (Rte 11); to Zavratnica fjord (see p. 64); and to the Velebits for mountain walking (information about marked tracks and mountain huts from the Planinarsko društvo 'Zavižan').

The rugged grandeur of the coast takes on a forbidding air in all but the finest weather as the Velebits fall straight into the sea. The road, with a vastly improved surface, winds and twists at their foot all the way to the end of the Velebitski kanal and we have excellent views out to sea of the impressively barren N.E. shores of the Kvarner islands.

79 km. *Jurjevo* (Istra, modest; beach; P.O.), a small village at the water's edge, is the starting-point for excursions to Oltari and *Mt. Vučjak* (5346 ft) in ZAVIŽAN NATIONAL PARK (mountain hut) in the Velebit Mts. A twisting gravel mountain road gives access to the park (on foot c. 3 hrs).

From Zavižan another footpath leads through beautiful wooded uplands (c. 1½ hrs) to the mountain hut Rosijeva koliba, just below the summit of *Mt. Gromovača* (5443 ft), the highest peak in this section of the Velebits. Footpaths descend from here to the village of Gornja klada (c. 2 hrs) on the Adriatic Highway and to Jablanački Alan and the road to Stirovača National Park (see below). At Oltari a left fork in the road leads to Otočac (pass of 3410 ft) and inland Croatia.

Just s. of Jurjevo are autocamps (81 km.) *Rača*, with room for about 70 cars, and (83 km.) *Žrnovnica*, for 250 cars, both with shingle beach. The road swings inland slightly and climbs away from the shore to a height reaching 1000 ft, with views to the islands of *Prvić*, *Grgur*, and *Goli*, and the northern shores of Rab. Threading hamlets, many of them with twin-named settlements down on the sea-shore, we pass under a cable railway at (103 km.) *Stinica*. The railway ascends to 4300 ft in the Velebits and is used to bring down timber from the vast forests of Jablanački Alan. The intended addition of passenger cars to the railway would provide convenient access to the Velebit mountain region.

109 km. **Jablanac** (*Jablanac; Alan; Zavratnica;* P.O.; bathing station; boats to Senj and Rab), with a history dating from the 12C, is reached by a winding asphalt by-road. Set in a quiet, deeply indented little bay, it has a car ferry to the island of Rab (see Rte 10), here at its closest to the mainland. On the headland just s. of the harbour are the scanty ruins of a castle (1251) built by Ban Stjepan Šubić, and 2 km s. of the village is the fjord-like inlet of *Zavratnica* (20 min on foot, or by boat), with steep rocky sides and exceptionally clear water.

Jablanac is the starting point for excursions to Jablanački (5239 ft) and Stirovača National Park (mountain hut) in the Velebits and for longer trips to Rosijeva koliba and Zavižan (see above). Beyond Stirovača the road divides for Otočac (l.) and Karlobag (r.)

We continue s. To seaward, Rab disappears behind us, and is replaced by the bleak outlines of Pag (Rte 11), which after about 10 km. comes close inshore.—At (128 km.) *Cesarica* the road descends to the sea again to run along the shore of the Velebitski kanal.

133 km. **Karlobag** (*Jadran*) is the largest of the villages along the Velebitski kanal, a regular halt for long distance buses and the terminal of a car ferry to Pag. The settlement grew up around the *Fortica*, a massive 14C castle rebuilt in 1579 after being sacked by the Turks; its extensive remains are visible on a hill overlooking the town. The Baroque Capucin monastery dates from the 18C when Austria attempted to build up Karlobag as a port for the inland district of Lika. From Karlobag a fair asphalt road climbs steeply (gradient 1 in 5 in places) to *Gospić* (40 km.), the main town of the Lika region.

Just s. of Karlobag we pass the ruins (r.) of Vidovac, an old lookout tower and a ruined Gothic church. Successive small fishing villages lead on to (178 km.) *Starigrad-Paklenica* (Alan, 200 R.; Motel Paklenica, with beach), an unprepossessing village with no visible centre and a mushroom growth of summer bungalows, simple restaurants, and pensions. Starigrad's main interest is its position at the entrance to *Velika Paklenica Canyon* and *Paklenica National Park*.

A narrow gravel road leads 4 km. into the mouth of the canyon, whence we must continue on foot. A reasonably easy ascent follows the course of the river Velika Paklenica and brings us in c. 2 hrs to a mountain hut with beds and facilities for simple meals (the local honey is recommended). A number of caves may also be visited on the way up, of which *Manita Peć* (165 yds long, torch needed) is the best known. From the mountain hut excursions may be made through the Velebit uplands to the neighbouring peaks of *Stirovača* (4199 ft), with refuge hut (open in the summer only), *Badanj* (5326 ft), *Babin Vrh* (5658 ft), *Sveto Brdo* (5697 ft) and *Vaganjski Vrh* (5713 ft), the highest peak of the Velebit range.

Beside the lower course of the Velika Paklenica and to the left of the Adriatic highway is the small pre-Romanesque church of *Sv. Petar* with an irregular number of lesenes on its outer walls and a single semi-circular apse. The unusual Romanesque campanile has an open ground story and four Romanesque windows at the top, while the graveyard contains a curious roofed structure that once served as a baptistery and Bogomil gravestones with primitive carvings. Where the watercourse meets the sea stands the ruined tower of *Večka kula* built by the Venetians as a defence against the Turks.

Beyond Starigrad-Paklenica is the adjoining village of Seline and the entrance to *Mala Paklenica*, a smaller canyon also accessible by footpath.—At (189 km.) *Rovanjska* where the unusually shaped pre-Romanesque chapel of Sv. Juraj (10–11C) at the water's edge has a charnel house and cupola, we reach the head of the Velebitski kanal and bear right in the direction of Zadar. A gravel road (l.) goes to Obrovac (see Rte 14B). The new suspension bridge over *Masleničko ždrilo*, the narrow cleft joining the landlocked Novigradsko more (Sea of Novigrad) to the Velebitski kanal, affords excellent views in both directions.

199 km. *Posedarje* (Luna), on the shores of the Novigradsko more, is a pleasant seaside village with a shingle beach. In the village is the medieval Romanesque chapel of Uzašašće Marijino (The Assumption) and on an islet close inshore the Gothic church of Sv. Duh. Posedarje is the starting point for daily boats to Novigrad (see Rte 14B) from mid-June to September.

From Posedarje a good asphalt road runs N.E. towards the island of Pag (see Rte 11). At (4 km.) crossroads, a gravel road (r.) leads to *Vinjerac* on the shores of the Velebitski kanal, with the small ruined fortress and medieval church of Sv. Marko, remnants of a former Pauline monastery. The roads continues through barren karst, passing (13 km.) just inland of *Ražanac*, a rundown village with the remains (walls and tower) of a 16C Venetian fortress built to resist the Uskok pirates and the Turks. Here a road runs s.w. to *Krneza* (6 km.), a hamlet whence a track leads to *Ljubač* on the seashore, where the modern church preserves a 14C Gothic monstrance from *Rt Ljubljana*. This picturesque cape, 3 km. walk beyond the village, was the site of a medieval Croatian town destroyed by the Turks in the 17C. The considerable ruins include remains of the 13C Romanesque basilica of Sv. Marija.—Continuing by the main road we arrive at (21 km.) the suspension bridge (under construction) linking the mainland with the island of Pag (see Rte 11). A car ferry will continue to run from *Miletići*, near by, until the bridge is opened.

We cross the fertile plain of Ravni Kotari, where the road is frequently encumbered by peasant carts, to (244 km.) **Zadar** (see Rte 13).

9   THE ISLAND OF KRK

STEAMERS, once a week in the season to Omišalj, Njivice, and Malinska from Rijeka; daily in the season to Baška from Rijeka, Crikvenica, Novi Vinodolski, Senj, Lopar (Rab), Rab, and Novalja (Pag); and twice weekly all the year round to Baška and Stara Baška from the above ports and also Zadar, Vir, Povljana (Pag), Mandre (Pag) and Lun (Pag).—CAR FERRY to Voz from Crišnjevo (frequent in the season); daily to Šilo from Crikvenica (frequent in the season).
BUSES connect Rijeka, etc, with Krk viâ the car ferries.

KRK is the largest and most populous island (15,000 inhab.) in the Adriatic, 38 miles long, up to 18 miles wide and with an area of 158 sq. miles. It is the only island having a river (the Ričina, flowing into Baška) in addition to seasonal streams, and it has two small lakes, Omišaljsko jezero, near Njivice, and Ponikve jezero between Malinska and Krk. Agriculture and fishing are the principal occupations and tourism, though growing, has not yet spoiled the character of the island. Six of the seven major centres (Dobrinj is the exception) are on the coast. The island is famed for its traditional adherence to Croatian culture, retention of the Glagolitic liturgy until well into the 19C, a vigorous folklore, and colourful folk costumes. The city of Krk, however, retained until recently a Romano-Venetian dialect, called Vegliot, carried over from an earlier era. Krk has an excellent network of good signposted gravel roads.

History. The first known inhabitants of Krk, the Liburnians, gave way about the end of the 2C B.C. to the Romans. Strabo refers to the island as *Cyractica* and Pliny as *Curicta*, while Ptolemy also mentions the city of Curicum (presumably today's Krk), from which the modern Croatian name is derived. Caesar is thought to have had a base on Krk and he was defeated by Pompey in a naval battle (49 B.C.) just off the island. With the arrival of the Slavs in the 7C the Roman population withdrew into the city of Curicum which in the 8–10C became the *Vecla* of Byzantium (whence Venetian and Italian *Veglia*). So strong was this Roman element that its language survived in a dialect form until the 19C. For a century or more Krk oscillated between Venice and Croatia until 1133, when Count Duymus, having defeated a large force of pirates with Venetian assistance, achieved insular autonomy under token Venetian protection. Duymus reputedly founded the Frankopan (Frangipane) dynasty (see p. 68). Under the Counts of Krk the island preserved a fluctuating state of independence and prosperity until 1480, when, whether owing to Frankopan misrule or Venetian perfidy, Count Ivan was driven out and replaced by direct Venetian rule. The severe economic decline that followed was aggravated by plague in 1499 and by the depredations of the Uskoks during the 16C and 17C and not halted until the fall of Venice in 1797. Austrian rule was kinder to Krk than the Napoleonic interregnum (1805–13), and ended only with the First World War. In 1918 D'Annunzio tried unsuccessfully to occupy the island before it passed to Yugoslavia. During the Second World War it was again occupied by Italy and then Germany (from 1943) until freed by Partisan forces in March 1945.
As a centre of the Glagolitic movement Krk for centuries played an important role in the preservation of Croatian national identity and was a major influence on the early development of Glagolitic printing.

The city of **Krk** has for centuries been the cultural, administrative, and political centre (1300 inhab.) of the island but is now much reduced in population and importance. Its great antiquity, however, and good state of preservation makes it the most interesting town on the island.

Hotels. Dražica, Beograd, Dubrava, Ljubljana, Jugoslavija (a).
Restaurants. *Riblji restoran*, Obala 17 og. aprila.—KAVANA. *Gradska Kavana*, Titov trg.—GOSTIONA. *Zagreb*, Ul. Ive Lole Ribara.
Post Office, Titov trg.—INFORMATION OFFICE. 'Turist', Obala 17 og. aprila.

Bus Station, behind the Gradska kavana. Services to all parts of Krk and (viâ car ferries) to the mainland.

Amusements. *Kino Kvarner,* Ul. Jug. Armije.—KRK FESTIVAL OF FOLKLORE, annually in August.

Beaches. *Dražica* and *Porta Pisana,* 1 km. E. of town: rock, shingle and sand.

The spacious TITOV TRG opens between the harbour and a well-preserved section of the *Town Walls* (15–16C). In front of the walls is a small market place. The *Glavna Straža* (1493) a rectangular watch tower at the far end, was erected by the Venetians as the town's main gate and now houses the Gradska kavana. A sundial and the escutcheons of four doges adorn the wall, and a lion of St Mark embellishes the central boss of the vaulted interior. Following the walls towards the sea we quickly reach a 15C hexagonal bastion into which is built a Roman gravestone bearing the old arms (see p. 68) of Nikola Frankopan carved on its upper part and the date 1407.

We turn left along the waterfront, still following the line of the walls into which have been built the Narodna banka, fish restaurant and information office. Ahead is the main steamer quay but we turn left through the *Mala vrata* (Little Gate) into the fascinating labyrinth of the old town. In Ul. Jugoslavenske armije, to the right, only the ugly cinema mars a typical medieval street as we approach the unusual architectural complex of Krk cathedral.

Beyond the triple apses of Sv. Kvirin (see below), a narrow vaulted passage leads to the w. door (r.) of the **Cathedral of Uznesenje Marijino** (The Assumption) erected by Bp. John in 1186–88. The early-12C NAVE, nine bays in length, is divided from the aisles by Romanesque arches of uneven height supported on reused columns, some Roman, some from the 5C basilica that preceded the present building. The majority of the *Capitals, however, were specially carved for the cathedral and are fine examples of the Byzantine type, being mainly variations on the Corinthian order. A significant exception is the second from the w. end in the N. arcade, an outstanding Romanesque example carved with birds and beasts. The w. end earlier terminated in a narthex which was demolished in the 13C when the present w. wall and two responds were added.

The CHOIR, an addition of the 16C remodelled in 1743 after a fire, is closed by an excellent Renaissance Balustrade of red breccia flanked by contemporary octagonal ambones of the same material. The next bay to the E. on the N. side is occupied by a 17C Baroque Pulpit of wood carved in relief. In the floor an elaborate 14C memorial to 'Bishop John', the founder, shows the prelate in low relief; there is also a memorial to Ludovicus Cicuta, commander of a galley that Krk sent to Lepanto. The four paintings in the choir are by Cristoforo Tasca (1706). Off the N. AISLE the 14C Gothic *Chapel of Sv. Vid* (St Vitus) has elaborate rib-vaulting with the Frankopan arms, both old and new, emblazoned on the bosses. The N.W. chapel is built over a Roman bath whose mosaic floor can be seen beneath a trap door. The picture of the Entombment on the wall (sometimes attributed erroneously to Titian) is by Giov. Ant. Pordenone.—In the first chapel of the S. AISLE opposite is a celebrated Gothic *Reredos in silver by P. Colero (1477) depicting the Madonna in Glory, a gift of the Frankopans. Above is a large 15C crucifix in wood.

Immediately opposite the w. entrance of the cathedral across the vaulted passageway·is the LOWER CHURCH (formerly *Sv. Margareta*) of the unusual 10–11C Romanesque basilica of *Sv. **Kvirin** (St Quirinus), built on two levels and oriented from N. to S. The simple interior with massive square-ribbed vaulting supported by rectangular piers was restored in 1963 after long use as a wine vault. An expressive wooden crucifixion stands in the central apse. The *Campanile* (open 9–12 or key from bishop's palace), Romanesque below with a hideous Baroque superstructure and onion dome added in 1776, provides access to the beautiful UPPER CHURCH, a model of harmony and simplicity. The arcades are supported by plain columns with cushion capitals. On the altar stands a wooden figure of St Quirinus (a 4C bishop of Siscia, now Sisak) flanked by two panels of a Gothic polyptych depicting St Quirinus and St John. Traces of frescoes have been uncovered in the apse to the right.

In 1960 an early-Christian baptistery was discovered beneath the courtyard on the N. side of the cathedral with a polygonal immersion font and mosaics. Restoration is in progress.

Ul. Petra Franolića, beyond the covered passage, follows the course of the Roman cardo maximus through the centre of the town (comp. below).

The long low building between the cathedral and the sea, is the *Bishop's palace*, in which an ecclesiastical museum is being prepared (inquire locally for details). The main exhibit will be the large *Polyptych on wood (1333–45 ?) by Paolo Veneziano, brought here from Jurandvor. Adjoining the Bishop's palace and forming one side of the small square known as Kamplin (Poljana XXVI udarne divizije) is the large **Kaštel** of the counts Frankopan of Krk.

The origins of the family are obscure. Duymus (Dujam, Doimo), the first to receive historical mention, defeated a force of pirates off Krk in 1133 and achieved local autonomy for Krk under the nominal suzerainty of Venice. The title of *count* was first assigned to his two sons, Bartholomaeus (Bartolommeo) and Guidonis (Vid, Guido). In 1193 the counts of Krk were granted the fief of Modruš (Modrussa) by King Bela III of Hungary–Croatia, and their growing influence on the mainland was immensely increased when the grateful Bela IV, who had taken refuge on Krk in 1242 in his flight from the Tartars, granted them the fief of Senj. These honours earned them the disfavour of Venice and a period of exile from Krk but after 1260 the Frankopans played the role of peacemakers between Venice and Hungary–Croatia from a unique position as simultaneous feudatories of both powers. In 1358 by the Treaty of Zadar, Krk was ceded by Venice to Hungary-Croatia. Count Ioannis (Ivan, Giovanni) maintained his former rights and in addition was appointed Ban (viceroy) of Dalmatia, Croatia and Slavonia. Although all their possessions were now in Hungaro-Croatian hands the Frankopans retained their seat in the Gran Consiglio of Venice. Count Nicolaus (Nikola, Nicolò), the son of Ioannis, was temporarily ejected from Krk when he and the population took opposite sides in Hungary's dynastic struggles of 1387–1400. Informed by Pope Martin V in 1425 (so the story went) that his family was descended from the famous line of Roman Frangipani, Nicolaus exchanged the old arms of the counts of Krk, gold stars on a white ground, for the twin lions of the Frangipani a device which henceforth was used exclusively by the whole family. (The Slavonic name may be derived from Franko and 'ban' or viceroy.) After Nicolaus' death, the elder son, Ioannis (Ivan, Giovanni), who inherited Krk, began to quarrel with his brothers on the mainland and placed the island under the protection of Venice, abrogating his title to it completely in 1480. The mainland Frankopans continued active in Senj, Modruš and the Vinodol valley throughout the 16C and early-17C. With the rise of Austria the Frankopans became identified with Croatian nationalism and the last of the line, Fran Krsto Frankopan (b. 1643), was executed at Vienna in 1671 for raising a rebellion against the central government.

The castle is roofless and empty. The oldest part, the plain square

№ 002722

CROATIA hotel de luxe

KONGRES HALL

FOLKLOR

★★★★★

DIN. 200.000 —

CROATIA hotel de luxe

KONGRES HALL

FOLKLOR

№ 002723 DIN. 200.000.—

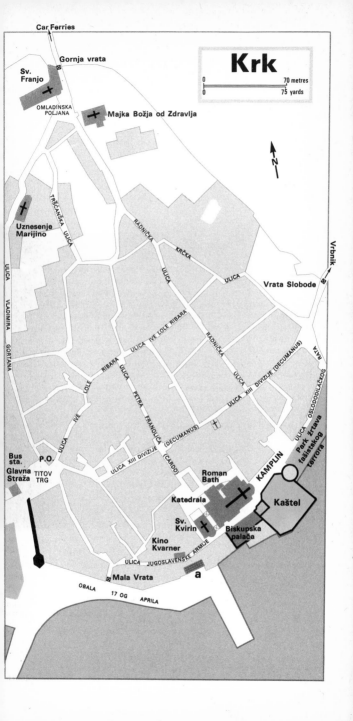

tower opposite the cathedral, dated 1191, was once the tribunal and prison of the commune of Krk. A wall of later and cruder construction connects this with a well-preserved circular tower of the 16C in the s.e. corner. The seaward flank consists of a curtain wall topped by forked battlements, constructed in 1407 by Count Nikola. The interior forms a garden to the Bishop's palace, but the round tower and battlements afford excellent views of Krk and across the bay to Punat and the island of Košljun.

Ul. žrtava oslobodilačkog rata continues beside a small park extending above the shore. The road bends sharply left to join the decumanus. On the right is the *Vrata slobode*, or Porta Pisana, one of the three main entrances to the old walled town, though the gateway has disappeared. Beyond, it is a short walk to the town beach on the small bay of Dražica (shingle with sandy bottom).

The picturesque Ul. XIII divizije follows the line of the Roman decumanus through the middle of the town, crossing Ul. Petra Franolića (the former cardo), in the main shopping area. Any of the ancient streets to the right lead to Omladinska Poljana, an irregular open space at the n. end of the town. The 12C Romanesque basilica of *Majka Božja od zdravlja* (Our Lady of Health), with a Liburnian cippus standing in front, is entered through the Campanile, essentially Romanesque but as with Sv. Kvirin, deformed by the addition of an unsuitable spire. The interior was restyled in Baroque in 1730, when the columns were stuccoed and varnished and the apse painted, but it is hoped to restore the church to its Romanesque appearance. As in the cathedral the columns are reused and of irregular height, but the capitals are good; a fine example, depicting an eagle devouring a lizard on each of its four sides, may be noted on the n. side. The Gothic church of *Sv. Franjo*, opposite, was erected in the 14C and extended in 1626, when the present roof and an organ loft were added. The tall trifoliated windows are filled with 19C Viennese stained glass. At the e. end a vaulted chapel with corbels carved in the shape of human heads shows traces of Gothic frescoes. The high altar bears a painting of the Madonna and Saints by Bern. Licinio (1531). The 19C pulpit is of inlaid wood. Gravestones in the floor include the carved slab of Iohannes Bernardini captain of another Krk galley at the Battle of Lepanto. The Renaissance cloister on the n. of the church has a pleasant well head. The tower dates from the rebuilding of the monastery in 1626 with additions of 1743.

Just n. of Omladinska poljana is the third of the original landward gates in the town walls, *Gornja vrata*, or Porta di Su, again without its gateway.

We may return to Titov trg by Ul. Vladimira Gortana, passing (l.) the Benedictine nunnery of Uznesenje Marijino (The Assumption). Among the picturesque Romanesque and Gothic houses in this street are the Kotter house, with lion-head corbels, and an excellent example of 'na koljeno' door and counter (comp. Rte 22).

EXCURSIONS FROM KRK

A. FROM KRK TO PUNAT, 7 km. (4¼ m.). A good gravel road leads e. passing the town beaches of Porta Pisana and Dražica and skirting the Bay of Krk. Just to the right of the road (3 km.) is the tiny pre-

Romanesque church of *Sv. Dunat*, cruciform in plan with a primitive dome of Byzantine type. It was badly damaged in the war.—At (4 km.) *Kornić* we branch right from the main road (comp. below), continuing round the bay.

7 km. **Punat** (*Park*, with annexes; autocamp; 'Acapulca' naturist beach) a neat attractive village (1700 inhab.) and the most populous settlement on the island, stands on the small shallow Puntarska draga, an almost landlocked inner bay linked with the larger Bay of Krk by Usta, a narrow strait (490 ft wide). A bridge that once spanned this strait gave its name to the town (Villa di Ponte). Francesco Orlich president of Costa Rica (1962–66), was born in Punat. The Baroque parish church (1773) of *Sv. Trojstvo* (Holy Trinity) has a Baroque high altar from Sv. Nikola in Senj (1787) with a Baptism of Christ by Maggiotto (1713–94). In the s. aisle is a 15C polychrome statue of St Anne. The 18C houses on the hillside facing the bay are typical of the domestic architecture of the Kvarner islands, with characteristic vaulted staircases (balature) leading up to small terraces on the first floor. An 18C olive press (Toš) stands in the centre of the town.

On the second Saturday in Aug each year is held an elaborate carnival and regatta called Puntarska noć.

The small wooded islet of **Košljun** in the bay is reached by boat in 5 min. Here an abandoned 12C Benedictine abbey was granted to the Franciscans by Ivan Frankopan, last count of Krk, in 1447. The present buildings of the **Franciscan Monastery** (open daily, 9–12 and 4–6), erected at the beginning of the 16C, incorporate parts of the earlier structure. The monastic church of *Navještenje* (Annunciation) consists of an aisleless nave with an open tiebeam roof and a vaulted Gothic choir. The triumphal arch is covered by a huge canvas of the Last Judgement by E. Ughetto (1653), more notable for size than for quality. Over the high altar is a polyptych of 5 panels by Girol. da Santa Croce (1535); behind the altar the friars' choir is adorned with a Christ in the Manger (school of Raphael). Just inside the main entrance on the left is the gravestone of the church's benefactress, Katarina Frankopan, daughter of Ivan and the wife successively of Doges Francesco Dandolo and Andrea Foscolo, who was formerly buried in the chapel of Sv. Bernardin. The Stations of the Cross were painted by Ivan Dulčić (1961).

The 12C Gothic chapel of *Sv. Bernadin*, reached from the Renaissance cloister (well-head, Roman child's sarcophagus and gravestones) houses the monastic Museum. Notable among the paintings (16–17C Venetian) are works by Franjo Juričić (1671–1718), a local artist. There is a good collection of Krk folk costumes. In the *Library* (opened on request) are an early copy of Ptolemy's atlas (1511), the Papal bull granting Košljun to the Franciscans, a fragment of one of the earliest printed books in Croatian (1483), Katerina Frankopan's will (1520), and c. 100 incunabula; a large collection of manuscripts in Glagolitic and Latin dates back to the 11C. Beside the door stands a primitive local boat called a *ladva*, hollowed out of a tree, and said to have been in use up to the end of the 19C.

B. From Krk to Baška, 18 km. (11¼ m.). To Kornić, see above.

We quickly come to (5½ m.) *Kuka* and branch right on the narrower road, which climbs steeply by zigzags to 1000 ft. The barren plateau of Treskavac and *Mt. Obzova* (1849 ft), the highest point on the island, rise on the right. The road gradually descends the fertile valley of *Suha ričina*, where the river Ričina almost dries up in summer, to the coast.

17 km. *Jurandvor*, an attractive village with typical vaulted terraces and wide courtyards. Just s.e. of the village stands Sv. Lucija, the 11C pre-Romanesque church of a former Benedictine abbey. Built into its Romanesque Campanile, which has lost its top story, are four sculptures depicting the symbols of the evangelists. The bell dates from the early 14C. The church is entered through the vaulted base of the tower; its plain nave contains architectural fragments. Off the s. side is the Gothic chapel of *Bogorodica od ruzarije* (Our Lady of the Rosaries), built in 1498 by the Juranić family. On the wall is a cast of the Bašćanska ploča (Baška Tablet; original in the Yugoslav Academy at Zagreb). The slab, decorated with early Romanesque relief carvings of vine leaves, bears an inscription in Glagolitic recording the gift of land for the abbey by King Zvonimir of Croatia (1076–89). Excavations around the church in 1955–62 revealed remains of a Roman villa and traces of a 6–7C church.

18 km. **Baška** (*Adria; Velebit; Baška*), the most southerly village on the island, is strung out along a sheltered bay at the mouth of the river Ričina. Beside its long sand and pebble beach, one of the finest in the Kvarner, extend small hotels and villas. The main street runs along the shore to the picturesque old quarter with curious houses (note the unusual chimneys), some of the 16C. Those on the seaward side were originally raised on piles above the water. The Baroque parish church of the *Sv. Trojstvo* (Holy Trinity; 1722), contains a Last Supper by Palma Giovane and the Virgin with Saints and Angels by M. Marziale (c. 1495). On the Baroque high altar from Senj, the Coronation of the Virgin is by Franjo Juričić (18C). In the main square is the small Renaissance church of *Sv. Antun* (1482) with a painting by Celestin Medović (1859–1920); and behind the Hotel Velebit the small Romanesque chapel of *Sv. Marko*. In the fields behind the beach the small 16C church of *Sv. Mihovil* (key from parish priest) contains a tryptych by Paolo Campsa (1514).

Baška has excellent steamer connections with Senj on the mainland and with the island of Rab, whither excursions are easily made in a day. More locally, the cave of Škuljica, accessible only by boat, opens in the cliff just opposite Prvić. The narrow *Senjska vrata* between the islands of Krk and Prvić, notoriously the most dangerous strait in the Adriatic, has been the scene of countless shipwrecks. The lighthouse on the barren Prvić affords excellent views.

C. From Krk to Vrbnik, 11½ km. (7¼ m.). Beyond (5½ km.) *Kuka*, the main road passes through the fertile plain of Vrbničko polje, known for grapes and tomatoes.—11½ km. **Vrbnik** (*Galeb; Vrbniče nad morem; Jadranka*), situated on a steep cliff overlooking the Velebitski kanal, is the only major settlement on the e. side of the island. In the 14–15C it was a stronghold of the Counts Frankopan (castle ruins in Vrbničko polje, fragmentary town walls) but declined in importance with the rise of Krk. The parish church of Uznesenje Marijino (The Assumption), erected in the 15–16C on an E.–W. axis but rebuilt in Baroque to face N. and S., preserves Gothic elements in the choir. The Last Supper in the predella of the altarpiece was painted by Marin Cvitković (1599), a native of Kotor. In *Ružarija*, a vaulted side chapel, is the fine 15C Renaissance altar of Sv. Marija Ružarica (Mary of the Rosaries) depicting the Virgin and Child with fifteen rosettes illustrating the life of Christ.

Beside the detached Renaissance tower (1527), now disfigured by an ugly spire, the tiny chapel of Sv. Marija (key from the parish priest) has a 15C polyptych depicting St Anne, a pietà carved in relief, and a Madonna, all in wood and Gothic in feeling.

In the nearby Zadružni dom the *Dinko Vitezić Library* (c. 15,000 vols.) preserves a number of Glagolitic manuscripts, incunabula, and rare books. The most outstanding book on display is one of two copies extant (the other in Cambridge) of the beautifully illustrated *Atlas of Johann David Kochler, printed in Nuremburg in 1612. There are also photo-copies of the Glagolitic Vrbnički statut (Vrbnik Statute) of 1388 and Petrisov zbornik (Petris Miscellany) of 1468. In the temporary charge of the parish priest are the First Vrbnik Missal (1456) in Glagolitic with illuminations; the Second Vrbnik Missal (1463) also in Glagolitic with outstanding miniatures and curious initials in Latin; a rare copy of Transitus Sancti Hieronymi, printed (prob, in Senj) in 1508; and four 15C breviaries thought to have been composed also in Vrbnik. It is hoped eventually to house these works with an ethnographical collection in a single museum.

Vrbnik produces a white wine called Zlahtina. The plant where it is pressed and bottled may be visited on request.

THE N. AND N.E. SHORES of the island, are served by roads which divide at 2 km. N. of Krk.

D. FROM KRK TO ŠILO (Crikvenica), 20 km. (12¼ m.). The right branch passes just E. of (14 km.) Dobrinj, one of the four early fortified villages on the island and the only settlement of importance not on the coast. The unusual defensive system consists of a ring of linked houses built with thick outer walls specially strengthened. The parish church of *Sv. Stjepan*, rebuilt in the 18C, preserves fragments from the 12C and a rectangular Gothic choir with a rib-vault (1602). The treasury contains a 14C altar frontal embroidered with gold and silver thread, depicting the Coronation of the Virgin; 15C silvered crosses; a 16C ciborium; and a gold reliquary of St Ursula. Beyond Dobrinj lies the bay of Soline where the Frankopans had extensive salt works and which is now occupied by oyster beds. *Sv. Vid*, by the Dobrinj fork, is the pre-Romanesque church whose foundation in 1100 is described in the 'Dobrinjska listina', one of the earliest documents in Croatian.—Beyond Sv. Vid the road continues to (20 km.) *Šilo*, a small resort linked by car ferry to Crikvenica (Rte 8) on the mainland by which it is administered.

E. FROM KRK to OMIŠALJ (Kraljevica), 26 km. (16 m.). The left branch of the road from Krk runs N.W. to (13 km.) *Malinska* (Adriatic; Marina; Malin; Slavija; Haludovo; Jadran) also a resort with a pleasant promenade, three pebble beaches, and an open air theatre. During the first week in August it is the principal venue of the Krčki Festival, a concert of local folk songs and dances with visiting groups from other parts of the country. In *Porat*, a hamlet across the bay (15 min by boat), is a 15C Franciscan monastery. A favourite excursion from Malinska is by boat to Glavotok (see p. 74)—17 km. *Njivice* (Domus; Jadran; autocamp) stands peacefully on a bay in pretty wooded surroundings.

26 km. **Omišalj** (*Adriatic*, on the beach, night club, dancing; *Bodulka; Jadran; Ruža; Marija*) comprises a picturesque but dilapidated old quarter on a lofty hill overlooking the sea, and the new tourist quarter

known as *Zagradi*, on the shore. The town was once a centre of the Frankopan family.

In the spacious main square stands the parish church of Sv. Marija. The plain Romanesque w. front with a good relief carving in the tympanum is embellished with a fine rose window inserted in 1405 by the mason Sinoga. The cupola and rectangular choir were added in the 16C and numerous side chapels at the same time or a little earlier. The interior is surprisingly harmonious and the cupola imposing from within, but the effect is spoiled by indiscriminate painting of the walls in 1925. In the s. apse is a 15C polyptych of St John by Jacobello del Fiore. A stone carved with pre-Romanesque basketwork is built into the interior of the pulpit. The detached Renaissance *Campanile* erected in 1533–36 is disfigured by an inappropriate spire. The small Gothic church of *Sv. Ivan* (1442) beside it serves as the sacristy. On the e. side of the square is the Gothic church of Sv. Jelena (1470).

A narrow street runs down to the left of the parish church to the small square of Dubac perched just inside the remnants of the town walls. On one side is the Romanesque church of *Sv. Antun* with a loggia. The square commands superb views over the deeply indented Omišaljski zaljev (Bay of Omišalj) and out over the Kvarner to Rijeka, Opatija, and the Učka mountains of Istria. Clearly visible also is the neighbouring bay of *Sepen* (or Sapan) to the s.w. (reached by boat or on foot) with the massive overgrown ruins of a 5C early Christian basilica and remains of an extensive Roman settlement (? *Fulfinium*).

The Stomorina, Omišalj's annual harvest festival (15 Aug) is the biggest and most colourful of the Krk festivals. Folk costumes are worn and the many indigenous Krk songs and dances performed, including one famous song Turne moj lipi (My beautiful tower) said to have been sung by Ivan, last Count Frankopan of Krk, when he was exiled by Venice.

Beyond Omišalj the road continues through a flat plain covered with scrub and climbs to the rocky n.e. tip of the island. From the summit of the ridge glimpses may be had of the typical Kvarner tunny ladders (see p. 55) in Peškera bay before the road serpentines down to the quiet sheltered cove of *Voj* (café) whence the principal car ferry to the mainland departs for Crišnjevo (p. 56; crossing c. 10 min; bus connection to Rijeka, etc.).

F. From Krk to Glavotok, 14 km. (8¾ m.). A narrow gravel road runs n.w. to (14 km.) *Glavotok* on the westernmost tip of the island. About 300 yds from a pleasant shaded beach, with a café set among the trees, is the Franciscan Monastery endowed by Ivan Frankopan in 1473. The church in Franciscan Gothic erected in 1507 was extended to the e. in the 17C and the façade remodelled in 1879. The bare interior consists of a single nave with an open tie-beam roof and barrel-vaulted choir. On the high altar, SS Francis and Bonaventura by Girolamo da Santa Croce.

In the neighbouring bay of *Čavlena*, accessible only by boat, the pre-Romanesque church of Sv. Krševan has a cupola and triple apses.

10 THE ISLAND OF RAB

STEAMERS. Rab is served by the *Express Service* daily from Rijeka, Zadar, Šibenik, Hvar, Korčula, Dubrovnik, Hercegnovi, and Bar; weekly from Venice. *Local service* to Rab and Lopar daily from Rijeka, Crikvenica, Novi Vinodolski, Senj, Baška (Krk) and Novalja (Pag); thrice weekly from Mali Lošinj to Rab; twice weekly to Rab and Lopar from Vir, ports on Pag and Stara Baška.—CAR FERRY daily to Rab from Jablanac in the season.

RAB (8500 inhab.) 14 m. long and 2–6 m. wide, and of very irregular shape, consists of three parallel ranges of limestone hills, which result in great variations in vegetation and climate. On the N.W. side, *Kamenjak* (Tinjarosa), the longest and highest range, runs the length of the island, rising in the centre to 1350 ft. This bleak rocky barrier protects the island from the cold N. and E. winds giving it a mild climate. In the centre the parallel *Mundanija* is much shorter and lower, and to the S. and W. is the smaller ridge of Kalifront. Between these ridges are two long fertile valleys (Supetarska draga and Kamporska draga), watered by over three hundred natural springs—a rare phenomenon on an Adriatic island—the presence of which has turned the people towards the land rather than the sea. In addition to olives and grapes they grow grain and vegetables, and silk culture is by local tradition supposed to have been introduced to Europe by a native of Rab. The N.E. side of the island is almost bare of vegetation but the peninsula of Kalifront in the W. is noted for its luxuriant woods. Juniper, fig, cypress, jasmine and agave are also found in abundance.

History. The first known inhabitants of Rab were the Liburnians who, with a few Greek settlers, were conquered by the Romans in early Imperial times. With variant names on the root *Arba*, the town is mentioned by both Ptolemy and Pliny the Elder and early became a bishopric. Under Byzantium about the 8C Rab came into conflict with Croatia and was eventually absorbed into the Croatian kingdom of King Tomislav (910–28). In the year 1000 Doge Pietro Orseolo subjugated the islands of Dalmatia and the Kvarner to safeguard the communications of the Venetian merchant fleet. During the three centuries struggle that followed between Croatia and Venice, Rab passed repeatedly from one side to the other. Like the other cities on the seaboard she developed a complex system of self-government by a bishop and a city captain, called a prior and later knez (prince). Throughout this period the city's autonomy was recognized by its overlords and Rab prospered. But in 1409, when King Ladislaus of Naples sold Zadar and Dalmatia to Venice, Rab quickly followed. Power remained nominally in the hands of the nobles, but Venice exercised effective control. In the 15C the island population was decimated by plague and has never since recovered its numbers. Rab passed to Austria (1797) and in 1805 to Napoleon's France. From 1815 to 1918 it was again administered by Austria and then joined to Yugoslavia. During the Second World War Italy and Germany occupied the island which was liberated in April 1945 by the Ninth Division of Tito's partisan army. Rab had begun to develop tourist facilities before 1900 and is now one of the best organized and prosperous of the Adriatic islands with a growing population.

Rab was the birthplace of the Jesuit theologian and natural scientist, Mark Antun Dominis (Marcantonio De Dominis, 1560–1624), bishop of Senj, archbishop of Split and later, during his apostacy, dean of Windsor. His pioneer work on the spectrum was acknowledged by Newton, and he was the first to prove the influence of the moon on tides. Also born in Rab were Ivan Krstitelj Rabljanin (Giovanni Battista di Arbe) the 16C bell-founder, and the painters Stjepan Crnota (Stefano Cernotto, 16C), a pupil of Titian, and Matej Pončun (Matteo Ponzoni, 17C), a follower of Palma Giovane.

Rab, the sole town (1500 inhab.) on the island, perched on a sloping peninsula at the mouth of the deeply indented Bay of Sv. Fumija with four graceful belfries pointing slender fingers to the sky, is the most beautiful town of the Kvarner, especially striking from the s.w. seaward approach. In spite of its great popularity with holidaymakers it retains an unspoiled medieval atmosphere of great authenticity and charm. At the s. end of the peninsula lies the oldest quarter, called *Kaldanac*, with crooked, narrow streets winding uphill to the cathedral. To the N. lies *Novi grad* (the 'New Town'), dating mainly from the 14–17C and still the social centre; and beyond this again the *Varoš*, the newest section where most of the hotels are located.

Hotels. Imperial, 170 R., kavana, dancing, tennis; **Istra**, 100 R. kavana; **Beograd** (a); **Kontinental**; **Park** (c); **Slavija** (b); **Miramar** (d); **Slovenija** (e); **Jadran**. —TOURIST COLONY, **Suha Punta**, 400 R. with bath in chalets, own beach, kavana, dancing (c. 2 m. s.w.; regular bus or boat). AUTOCAMP at Treća Padova, c. 1 m. s.E. of town.

Restaurants. *Grand*, on the quayside; and at the Imperial, Beograd and Slovenija hotels.

Kavanas. *Grand*, Obala 12 oga aprila; *Sutjeska*, Trg Maršala Tita; and at Slovenija and Imperial hotels.

Post Office. Ul. Ive Lole Ribara (opp. loggia).—INFORMATION. *Turističko društvo*, Trg Maršala Tita.

Buses to *Kampor*, *Supetarska draga*, and *Lopar* daily.

Beaches. *Gradsko kupalište* (cabins, showers), at far end of Komrčar Park (shingle); *Prva*, *Druga*, and *Treća padova* about 1½ m. s.E. of town, beyond the autocamp (pebble and sand); Nudist beach (Nudistička plaža) on Rt Frkanj (rock, shingle and sand), entrance 1 din.

Amusements. Open air cinema (ljetno kino); tennis (at Imperial Hotel); sailing; underwater fishing.

Opening from the Nova obala (or Nova riva), the steamer quay, the popular TRG MARŠALA TITA, gay with café tables, is a favourite vantage-point opposite the entrance to the inner harbour. On the N. side is the **Knežev dvor** (Prince's Palace), former residence of the Rab town governors, now the offices of the Turističko društvo. The handsome rectangular Romanesque tower (13C), that forms its main part, preserves its original entrance and a window on the second floor. A two-light window on the first floor and two windows above present contrasting additions in Renaissance and Venetian Gothic styles, and the w. side has Renaissance details. A vaulted courtyard contains a small lapidary collection.

The quay, known from here on as Obala 12 oga aprila, continues to Trg palih boraca and the hotel quarter of Rab. At right angles to it Ul. Stjepana Radića mounting from Trg Maršala Tita to Trg slobode (comp. below), divides Kaldanac from Novi grad.

Behind Knežev dvor is Ul. Marka Oreškovića or Donja ul. (Lower Street), the lowest and quietest of three that run the length of Novi grad. We turn N. and come immediately to the Galzigna-Marčić mansion, the Renaissance doorway of which bears the family motto. Along the street numerous architectural details (doorways, windows, escutcheons) may be noted. At the far end on the right the ornate late-Venetian Gothic doorway of the *Mala Palača Nimir*, with the Nimir arms in the tympanum and a good Renaissance balustrade above, admits to an arcaded courtyard containing architectural fragments; the remainder of the mansion has been demolished and the basement houses a night club. The adjoining garden, partially enclosed by remnants of the town walls, now forms part of the restaurant and kavana Grand.

The wide TRG PALIH BORACA, open to the harbour on the E., marks the boundary between Novi grad and Varoš. On the N. side are hotels; on the rising w. side paths and steps lead into the pleasant town park of Komrčar (comp. below) from the small informal market (fruit and vegetables; occasionally lace and other handicrafts). A bronze war memorial, by Vinko Matković, marks the site of the land gate to the town. Most of the fortifications have been destroyed, but steps behind the market lead up to *Turjon*, a 14C bastion, now occupied as a dwelling.

Leaving the square again on the s. side we follow UL. IVE LOLE RIBARA or *Srednja ul.* (Middle Street), the busy main shopping street of the town. Immediately on our right is the imposing Renaissance *Velika Palača Nimir-Dominis* (mainly 15C) with well-proportioned windows (one Gothic) and doorway, bearing on the lintel and upper façade respectively escutcheons of the Dominis and Nimir families. On the N. wall, facing the square, is a Roman head of Jupiter. This palace, the largest in Rab, was the birthplace of Marcantonio De Dominis (comp. above). It now has the town pharmacy on the ground floor and a hotel school above. Ul. Ive Lole Ribera, with numerous souvenir shops, is crowded morning and evening; attractive narrow residential streets rise (r.) in steps to Ul. Rade Končara, from which water descends in cascades after rain. Halfway along, two vaulted houses span the street on broad arches, the first bearing the Benedetti escutcheon. Beyond them (l.) the *Palača Tudorin* has a handsome Renaissance window on the N. side with lion-head corbels supporting the sill. The intersection with Ul. Stjepana Radića just above Trg Maršala Tita, marks the centre of Rab. On the corner stands the Renaissance *Palača Crnota* (Cernotta) with a richly ornamented main door in Ul. Stjepana Radića. The finely executed arms in the tympanum are an outstanding example of the transitional Gothic-Renaissance style of the E. Adriatic. On the other side of Ul. Stjepana Radića the *Palača Kašić* (Cassio), for a time the residence of Rab's bishops, has a simpler doorway in similar style. Adjacent, on the corner of the main street is the *Loža* (1509), a plain Renaissance structure with a wooden roof supported on six columns (in bad repair). The 14C *Clock Tower* facing the Loggia was renovated in 1831.

Here the main street changes its name to Radnički prelaz as it enters Kaldanac. Passing (r.) the tiny Gothic church of Sv. Nikola, now abandoned, the street narrows and darkens beneath vaulted houses on single arches before joining Ul. Vladimira Gortana. Many of the ruined houses in this quarter were built before the terrible plague of the mid-15C and have never been reoccupied. At its lower end Ul. Vladimira Gortana joins Radnička ul., which runs from Trg Maršala Tita past the Renaissance courthouse to *Dorka* a small park enclosed in a section of town wall. We turn uphill, passing the extensive ruins of the *Episcopal Palace* (since 1828 when the bishopric was merged with Krk, the residence of the parish priest). Steps mount to the ridge on which stand the churches of Rab.

The former *Cathedral of Sveta Marija Velika, consecrated in 1177, is an excellent example of a small Romanesque basilica. The w. front (well seen from the campanile), built of local stone and breccia in alternate courses of pink and white, is decorated at the base with two stories of blind arcading. The marble Renaissance doorway, pierced in 1490, has a simple Pietà by Petar Trogiranin (1514) in the tympanum. In the dignified INTERIOR the nave arcades are borne on columns with undistinguished capitals of Byzantine type. The spacious choir raised on six steps has sumptuous Gothic *Stalls (1445) carved in walnut; on the front ends the angel of the Annunciation (l.), with the arms of the Nimir family, and the figure of the Virgin Mary (r.), with the Crnota arms. Further steps lead to the Sanctuary. The high altar has a 17C Baroque frontal of inlaid marble depicting St Christopher (patron saint of Rab). The remarkable *Ciborium*, hexagonal in plan, rests on six marble columns with Byzantine capitals. The three sides of the canopy towards the front are uninteresting Renaissance work but the three at the rear are outstanding examples of early Croatian decorative carving probably 9C or 10C from an earlier church. The low pyramid roof has an elaborately carved finial.

In the N. AISLE, the apsidal chapel of *Sv. Križ* has a Baroque crucifix on the altar and late Gothic altar rails attributed to Andrija Aleši of Durazzo. A polyptych by Paolo Veneziano adorns the first altar in this aisle and a curious wooden figurine of St Christopher hangs over the second.—S. AISLE. At the square E. end the altar of Gospa žalostna (Our Lady of Sorrows), is surmounted by a Madonna showing Byzantine influence (Italo-Cretan; ?15C). A gravestone built into the wall (r.) bears a carved head of Bp. Ivan Skafa of Rab (1456). The altar rails bearing the Skafa arms are also attributed to him. In the chapel of the *Sv. Sakrament*, a Byzantine marble icon (13C) shows Christ Enthroned. The simple Gothic chapel of *Sv. Petar*, contains a hexagonal font (1497) by Petar Trogiranin and more altar rails attributed to Aleši. Two pilasters inside the W. door, showing angels with candelabra, are also Aleši's work. These separated fragments were probably once part of a destroyed Skafa chapel. The stucco work on the ceilings (1798) is in course of removal in order to reveal the open Gothic roof.

The magnificent *Campanile, standing apart from the cathedral, is a masterpiece of 12–13C Romanesque architecture "that may challenge comparison with any of its kind elsewhere". Jackson took this tower as his model when completing the cathedral campanile at Zadar. The tower rises c. 90 ft from a base 20 ft square. An effect of increasing lightness is obtained by the disposition of the windows. The ground story is pierced by a single light in each face, above which in succession are two single lights, two double lights, a triple light, and at the top a four-light aperture. The additional tracery is given correspondingly richer decorative ornament. The top two stories are finished with a delicate cornice of acanthus leaves and the tower is surmounted by a Romanesque balustrade and a pyramidal spire (rebuilt in 1495). The summit affords magnificent views.

In the *Treasury* (rarely open), is preserved a *Reliquary of silver parcel-gilt with a gabled lid containing the head of St Christopher, by which in the 11C Rab was miraculously saved from a besieging army of Sicilian Normans. The casket, attributed to the 12C is of very fine workmanship; the skull inside wears a crown said to have been the gift of Queen Elisabeth the Younger of Hungary. Here also are four copper plates bearing champlevé enamels of Saints, executed probably in Limoges in the 12–13C, perhaps part of another reliquary.

Immediately behind the cathedral, above the tip of the promontory, is the nunnery of *Sv. Antun*, founded in 1493. Except for the original choir the present church is of the 16C with rustic Baroque altars and a picture showing Rab in earlier times. There is a bas-relief of St Antony over the entrance to the nunnery.

Ul. Rade Končara or Gornja ul. (Upper Street) leads back along the ridge. Almost immediately we come on our left to the Benedictine

Rab

Hotel Kontinental

OBALA 12 OG APRILA

TRG PALIH BORACA

Tržnica

VAROŠ

Komrčar Park

Mala Pal. Nimir

Velika Pal. Nimir-Dominis

Turjon

Pal. Tudorin

UL. M. OREŠKOVIĆA (DONJA UL.)

IVE LOLE RIBARA

NOVI GRAD

UL. RADE KONČARA

Knežev dvor

TRG MARŠALA TITA

NOVA

OBALA

Dorka

RADNICA

UL. VL. GORTANA

Sv. Antun

Katedrala

Sv. Andrija

K A L D A N A C

P.O.

(SREDNJA UL.)

UL. STEFANA RADIĆA

Loža

Pal. Crnota

Pal. Dominis

(GORNJA UL.)

TRG SLOBODE

Sv. Justina

Sv. Križ

Sv. Ivan

Uvala Sv. Fumija

nunnery and church of Sv. ANDRIJA, entered through a small courtyard paved with carved gravestones. The nunnery was founded in the 11C and an aisled basilica was probably erected a century later, though it received its present Renaissance form mainly in the 15C. The polyptych in the N. aisle is a poor copy of a Vivarini, the original of which has been removed to Boston. Adjoining is a Venetian ambry in Florid Gothic. The Campanile is the oldest of Rab's celebrated towers, a smallish Romanesque structure erected in 1181. In the small Trg slobode a tree planted in 1921 commemorates the Treaty of Rapallo. The 16C Baroque church of *Sv. Justina* is adjoined by Rab's third bell tower. The Death of St Joseph, inside, long attributed to Titian, is a good example of 17C Venetian painting. The *Palača Dominis*, opposite, with good Gothic windows, bears escutcheons of the Dominis and Nimir families.

The w. side of the square commands excellent views over Frkanj peninsula and the Bay of Sv. Fumija; steps descend to a path along the shore that leads to the town beach.

The street narrows between picturesque old houses. The small 16C Baroque church of *Sv. Križ* on the left is in a poor state of repair but has a stuccoed ceiling by the Sommazzi (1798). Adjoining in a pleasant garden, the foundations of the Romanesque church of *Sv. Ivan* include fragmentary mosaics. Its simple Romanesque Campanile still stands. At the town hall, the street divides. To the right a slope and steps descend to Trg palih boraca (see p. 77); other steps mount to the ruins of the former castle (and the ruined church of St Christopher within the walls), where one of the towers offers an excellent view of the bay. On the far side a gate leads into the beautiful **Komrčar park** laid out with pleasant walks. A path runs along the ridge to *Sv. Franjo* (1491), once the church of a vanished Franciscan monastery and now the chapel of the town cemetery, with a decorated façade and emblazoned memorials.

EXCURSION FROM RAB

A pleasant walk may be taken through Komrčar Park and past the town beach to the head of the Bay of Sv. Fumija (also reached by boat). Here, on the shore, stands the Franciscan monastery of **Sv. Fumija** (Euphemia), built in 1446 by Juraj Dimitrov of Zadar, that gave the bay its name. In the pretty cloister, surmounted on two sides by an upper story, are displayed a fine 15C Gothic sarcophagus, said to be of Manda Budrišić, a Bosnian noblewoman who founded the convent of Sv. Antun in Rab; the memorial slab of Petar Car (de Zara), founder of Sv. Fumija; and, among Roman and medieval fragments, a 7C crux gemmata. The simple Franciscan Gothic church of *Sv. Bernardin Sijenski* (St Bernardin of Siena; 1456) was restyled in Baroque in the 16C and the ceiling paintings executed in 1669. There is a good 13C Byzantine icon on the main altar flanked by two paintings of saints (15C). One of the altar rails incorporates a stone slab decorated with pre-Romanesque knotwork carving. In the chapel of Sv. Križ (Gothic windows from the original nave), s. of the choir, is a late Gothic crucifixion (wood; 15C); the tasteless chapel opposite is relieved by a polyptych of the Madonna and Saints by Ant. and Bart. Vivarini (1458). The *Library* (open 9–12, 4–7 daily, except Sun) contains 14–15C illuminated codices and two dozen incunabula. Also exhibited are a small Roman statue of Diana and a Gothic figure of St Francis in wood.

Beyond the monastery a pleasant footpath through the shallow valley of Kamporska draga leads in c. 20 min to the *Slovensko groblje* (Slavonic Cemetery), a memorial to 5000 victims of an Italian concentration camp established here in 1942. The project was designed by Edo Ravnikar (1955) and the central mosaic is by Marijan Pregelj. To the w. extend the cool, shady *Dundo Woods*, of Italian oak, cypress and pine with a scattering of cork oaks. Footpaths serve the small bays along the w. shore of Kalifront peninsula. Due w., a further 20 min walk brings us to the shallow, deeply indented Bay of Kampor with its broad almost deserted sandy beach (no rfmts. at the near-by hamlet).

To SUPETARSKA DRAGA AND LOPAR (daily boat to Lopar). A good asphalt road (local bus) winds round Rab harbour to *Mundanija* at the foot of Mt. Kamenjak, whence it continues through the valley of Banjol. —8 km. The former Benedictine monastery and church of Sv. **Petar** (200 yds r. by track), founded in 1059, was confirmed in its possessions in 1071 by King Petar Krešimir of Croatia, but abandoned by the 16C. The conventual buildings form a residence for the parish priest. The church is a Romanesque basilica with three apses, although the purity of its design has been spoiled by heightening the aisles in 1761 and enlarging the windows. The handsome stone canopy over the w. door rests on brackets carved with animal heads, but the tympanum is now empty. In the pleasant interior the five pairs of columns dividing the nave from the aisles exhibit five kinds of capitals representing variations on acanthus leaf and other vegetation motifs. The Romanesque Campanile was truncated in 1906 because it was unsafe. The two bells date from 1299 and 1593.

At 9 km. we come to the upper part of *Supertarska draga*, with a view across the sandy bay of the lower village (café) by the water. The road then hugs the N. shore of the bay before swinging right to wind over the barren Kamenjak plateau to (14 km.) **Lopar** (*Pensions Mira, Jadran*; autocamp; P.O.), the second largest settlement on the island. It is connected with Rab by daily steamers. Legend states that the stone carver, Marin Biza (St Marinus), who with his workmen founded the Republic of San Marino, was born in Lopar. In the bay of *Crnika*, on the other side of the narrow isthmus joining Lopar Peninsula to the main island, is the so-called Rajska plaža (Paradise Beach), a magnificent crescent of golden sand extending for over a mile. One of the finest beaches on the entire coast, it is now attracting tourist development (*San Marino*, 300 R. all with bath; autocamp). Elsewhere around the Lopar Peninsula there are similar but smaller beaches accessible only by boat.

Other excursions from Rab may be made by boat to numerous attractive bays on Kalifront: *Gavranišće*, with its naturist beach and restaurant; *Matovica; Suha punta*, with tourist colony nearby; *Krištofor; Planka;* and *Sv. Mara.* The quiet village of *Barbat* (Pens. Barbat, restaurant) lies in the opposite direction. Organised excursions are run to Jablanac and Zavratnica Bay (see p. 64) and to *Lun*, a hamlet on the N. tip of Pag which is traditionally administered by Rab. A walk to the summit of Mt. Kamenjak takes c. 2 hrs from the town of Rab.

11 THE ISLAND OF PAG

STEAMERS daily to *Novalja* from Rijeka, Crikvenica, Novi Vinodolski, Senj, Baška (Krk), Lopar (Rab), and Rab; thrice weekly to *Lun* from Rijeka, Crikvenica, Baška (Krk), and Rab; thrice weekly to *Metajna* from Karlobag; twice weekly to Povljana, Mandre, Novalja, and Lun from Zadar, Vir, Rab, Lopar (Rab), Stara Baška (Krk), Baška (Krk), Senj, Crikvenica, and Rijeka; once weekly to *Pag* from Rijeka, Crikvenica, Novi Vinodolski, Baška (Krk), and Rab.

CAR FERRY daily to Pag from Karlobag throughout the year.

Pag is now connected with the mainland by a new suspension bridge (p. 84) from Rt Fortica at its s.w. tip to Rt Ošljak just N. of Zadar.

PAG (8500 inhab.), the third largest island of the Kvarner, consists of one long ridge extending for 36 m. which exceeds 3 m. in width only across parallel peninsular ridges. Its deeply indented coastline extends for 162 miles. Like most of the Kvarner Islands Pag rises abrupt and barren on the mainland side, reaching 1130 ft in Mt. Sv. Vid in the centre, and is flatter and more fertile in the west. There are extensive olive groves on Lun Peninsula in the N. and large quantities of white wine, called žutica, are produced in the district around the town of Pag. The two most famous products are a hard, piquant ewe's milk cheese, known simply as Paški sir, and hand-made lace (čipka), of great delicacy and beauty. Salt beds, in use since Roman times, were once in almost every bay; now they are concentrated in Solana Bay immediately to the s. of Pag town. A good road runs the full length of the island, asphalted from the bridge in the s.E. to Pag and then gravel from Pag to Lun. The tranquillity of the island, hitherto relatively untouched by tourism, is not likely long to survive the road link.

History. The chief Roman settlement of the island was *Cissa*, a fortified castrum on the site of present-day Caska. A Roman port was also founded at *Novalia* and among other settlements was *Pagus*, which subsequently gave the island its name. With the coming of the Croats (7C) Novalja became the new centre of the island, but in 1071 King Petar Krešimir divided the island administratively between Rab in the N. and Nin in the s., and in the 12 C the centre was moved to 'old' Pag, then located 2 km. s. of present-day Pag. Dispute over control of the island between Rab and Nin and later Rab and Zadar, was temporarily resolved by the interven-tion of Venice in 1192 and more satisfactorily in 1244, when Bela IV of Hungary and Croatia proclaimed Pag an autonomous city with privileges similar to the other ancient cities of the seaboard. This autonomy was short-lived, however, for Pag, Rab, and Zadar almost immediately passed under the sway of Venice and Pag was divided once more, a situation in which it remained, under Venice and Hun-gary-Croatia alternately, for another 150 years. In 1393 Pag was sacked by an ex-pedition from Zadar and although the city was awarded compensation by Sigis-mund in 1396, it was not until 1409, when Dalmatia passed to Venice that Pag at last gained effective local autonomy free of Rab and Zadar. In 1443 'new' Pag was laid out and old Pag abandoned. In 1538 Lun, Novalja, and Caska were regained from Rab and thenceforward the island became a political and administrative entity under Venice. In 1602 the Uskoks here surprised the galley of Crist. Veniero, carrying off the admiral and his men to execution in Senj. After 1797, with a short Napoleonic interval, she passed to Austria for 120 years. The First World War was followed by three years of occupation by Italy, then under the Treaty of Rapallo, union with Yugoslavia. During the Second World War Pag was occupied first by Italy (1941–43) and then Germany.

From the early Middle Ages Pag has always had a pronounced Croatian character and like Krk has preserved a vigorous folklore. Bartul Kašić (1575–1650), author of the first Croatian grammar (Rome, 1604), was born on Pag.

The main settlement is **Pag** (*Dalmacija; Jadran*), a small town with 2400 inhab. lying at the s.E. end of the bay of the same name and at the neck of the inlet in which the famous saltpans are situated. Laid out in 1443 with a regular street plan, Pag is a rare and relatively pure example of early Renaissance town planning. Its inhabitants have a reputation for seriousness and hard work.

In 1443 the citizens of old Pag (Terravecchia) asked permission from Venice to reconstruct their capital on a better site. On 2 March Doge Fr. Foscari gave consent and on 18 May Count Pietro Faliero laid foundation stones of the walls and church. Juraj Dalmatinac may have been the overall planner but if his hand is possibly to be seen in some of the public buildings, most of the detail was left to his pupils with mediocre results.

Two straight main streets at right angles meet at NARODNI TRG, the spacious central square, dividing the town into four. The large parish church of **Uznesenje Marijino** (The Assumption), 1443–88, modelled to a large extent on its predecessor in Old Pag, presents a curious mixture of Gothic, Renaissance and even Romanesque elements. The plan is basilican but without apses, and the w. front Romanesque in feeling. The w. portal, Renaissance in style and embellished by egg and dart mouldings, is enclosed by an ogee arch. The high relief in the tympanium depicts the Virgin shielding the townspeople under her cloak and is an accurate portrayal of 15C local costume, particularly the women's head-dresses. Above the w. door a finely carved wheel-window is flanked by Gothic figures of Mary and the Archangel Gabriel (representing the Annunciation); beneath them are SS Michael (l.) and George (r.). The last three are unfinished. The tower was begun in 1562 but discontinued before the final story had been raised.

The church is entered from Vela ul. by one of two Renaissance doors pierced in a wall decorated with blind arcading. The Renaissance arcades spring from capitals carved with ingenious variations of traditional acanthus leaf, scroll, and animal motifs. There are twin hexagonal pupits. In the Baroque stuccoed ceiling three medallions portray St George and the Dragon, the Assumption, and the Martyrdom of St Sebastian. Each of the aisles terminates in a simple Gothic chapel (Gothic crucifixion in the s. chapel).

The 15C **Kneževa palača** (Prince's Palace) has a fine side entrance (from Vela ul.) in Venetian Gothic. The carving on the lintel is worthy of attention and the tympanum carries the escutcheon of Toma Zorzi, prince in 1467. The well head in the courtyard is also finely carved. Adjoining the Kneževa palača are fragments of a similar gateway of the unfinished *Biskupska palača* (Bishop's Palace). The palace was intended for Antun Palčić, Bishop of Osor (p. 88), a native of Pag, who is known to have commissioned Juraj Dalmatinac for the work. The Prince's palace has also been attributed to him on stylistic grounds.

At the far end of Vela ul. can be seen remnants of the town walls and the small Renaissance church of *Sv. Juraj*. In Štrosmajerova ul. the cruciform 15C church of *Sv. Margarita*, with a triple bellcot, adjoins the nunnery. In the treasury are a 14C silver cross, a silver-gilt reliquary and a silver hand reliquary of St Margaret fashioned in florid Gothic. Round the corner, in Samostanska ul., a pleasant doorway bears another ornate Zorzi escutcheon (1468).

About 3 km. s. of Pag on the w. side of the salt lagoon are the ruins of **Old Pag**, known as *Stari Grad*. The Romanesque-Gothic church of *Uznesenje Marijino* (completed 1392), whose w. front was the model for the later church in new Pag, is fairly well preserved. In the tympanum of the Gothic doorway we find an equivalent figure of Mary protecting the citizens of Pag. Higher up there is a similar wheel-window and statues; here, however, two angels flank the window, with SS Peter, George, and Martin below. The altar is 17C Baroque. Near by are the cloister of the former *Franciscan Monastery* (founded 1589), and a ruined bastion.

The road N. from Pag (gravel after 1 km.) leads over the bridge, passing numerous salt warehouses (some from Venetian times) and the town beach, and follows the shore of Pag Bay. To the left the abrupt ridge rises to 1140 ft in Sv. Vid while a narrow strip of fertile fields divides the road from the landlocked bay. After 15 km. the road swings away from the bay on to the flattening ridge, affording views towards Cres and Lošinj.—27 km. *Novalja* (Liburnia) is a sprawling village with a sandy beach and steamer connections with Rijeka and Zadar. Its early history as the port (navalia) for the Roman town of Cissa is obvious from scattered fragments of Roman masonry in the cemetery; remains of a large basilica have been discovered (not yet excavated). Parts of a Roman wall have been built into the Palčić Mansion in the main square and an Imperial aqueduct, known locally as the *Talijanova buža*, runs for part of the way between Novalja and Stara Novalja to the north. On *Rt Gaj*, N.W. of the village, a mosaic floor and walls belong to a 5C basilica.

In nearby *Caska* (3 km.), which can be reached only on foot, are the remains of an aqueduct, a Roman acropolis, and the ruined medieval church of Sv. Juraj, but much of the former Roman town of *Cissa* now lies underwater. The round tower at the water's edge is a modern structure used for tunny spotting (comp. p. 55).

North of Novalja, *Stara Novalja* stands on the small bay of the same name. *Lun*, remote at the far end of a narrow tongue of rock (20 km.), is more usually visited as an excursion from Rab.

An asphalt road runs s. past the Pag salt flats, continuing to (23 km.) *Rt Fortica* and the bridge that links Pag to the mainland (see p. 82).—At (7 km.) *Gorica*, a rough gravel road diverges (r.) to *Povljana* (7 km. more), an untidy village with a shingle beach and steamer links with Zadar and Rijeka. Just s. of the village beside the sea stands the small pre-Romanesque church of *Sv. Nikola* (?9–11C).

The island of *Vir* (600 inhab.) just s.w. of Povljana can be reached twice weekly by steamer from Zadar or from ports between Povljana and Rijeka. The Romanesque church of Sv. Ivan (12–13C) stands in the graveyard and a ruined 17C Venetian fortress on the shore nearby.

The island of *Maun* to the N.W. is inhabited only seasonally by Pag shepherds pasturing their sheep.

12 THE ISLAND OF CRES

STEAMERS daily to Cres, Martinšćica and Osor from Rijeka, Unije, Susak and Mali Lošinj.—CAR FERRIES daily to *Porozine* from Rijeka and Rabac.

BUSES direct to Cres, Martinšćica, and Osor from the mainland viâ the car ferries; also from the island of Lošinj.

CRES although sparsely populated (4000 inhab.), is the second largest island (156 sq. m.) in the Adriatic, exceeded in size only by neighbouring Krk. It is 42 miles long, and together with Losinj, to which (across an artificial strait) it is joined by a bridge, forms the beginning of the outer chain of islands that end in the Kornat archipelago. The E. side consists mainly of bare rock exposed to the fury of the N. wind (bura) and descending steeply to the sea, and the highest point of the generally mountainous island, is Gorice (2100 ft) in the N. between the town of Cres and Porozine. All the settlements are on the w. side where the land slopes gently to the sea and the climate is milder, though even here soil is sparse and the ground infertile. The main crops are olives, vegetables, and grapes, though most of the vineyards were wiped out by phylloxera at the turn of the century. Fishing plays an important part in the island economy, the catch being canned at Cres and Martinšćica. While there are no springs or rivers on the island, Vransko jezero (Lake Vrana) is the largest freshwater lake in the Adriatic and supplies both Cres and the island of Lošinj.

History. Extensive remains show that Cres has been occupied since Neolithic times. With Lošinj, it bore the Greek name of *Apsyrtides*, said to preserve the memory of Absyrtus, brother of Medea, who was murdered during the flight of the Argonauts and his dismembered body flung into the sea. In Classical times two settlements are mentioned, *Crepsa* (now Cres) and *Apsoros* (Osor), the larger of the two. Although sacked by Attila in the 5C and by the Saracens under Sahib Kalfun in 841, Apsoros, later *Ossero*, continued to grow in size and importance, having meanwhile under Byzantium become a bishopric before 530. In 924 the island became part of the Croatian kingdom under Tomislav but between 998 and 1018 the two principal cities, constantly troubled by piratical raids, sought the protection of Venice, under whose rule they remained until 1358. For much of this time Ossero was ruled by hereditary counts, notably the Morosini (1180–1304), instead of the more usual elective ones. For half a century Cres again belonged to Hungary-Croatia, but with the sale of Dalmatia (1409) returned to Venice until the republic's fall in 1797.

Osor meanwhile began to decline. Its prosperity had largely depended on command of the artificial strait between Cres and Lošinj, the main route for shipping from the north Adriatic until the 15C. With its unhealthy climate, which led to the spread of malaria and the plague, Osor could not survive the growing preference for open-sea sailing and was eclipsed. In 1459 the centre of Venetian rule was moved to Cres which grew rapidly, while Osor, repeatedly pillaged by the Uskoks in the 16C and 17C and also by Genoa, sank to a village. In 1797 the island passed to Austria, then briefly to France (1805–14) and back to Austria (the bishopric was suppressed in 1818) until the end of the First World War. Under the Treaty of Rapallo (1921) Cres was awarded to Italy until the Second World War. It was the scene of fierce fighting because of its strategic importance and was attacked by British naval units in Sept 1944. In 1945 it was joined to Yugoslavia for the first time.

Cres, the main settlement on the island, is a delightful small fishing town (1850 inhab.) not much visited by foreigners. Situated on a magnificent natural harbour on the w. side of the island, it packs a deceptively large number of streets into a small area; and although built by Venice, its main interest lies less in monumental or patrician architecture than in domestic dwellings with details typical of the Kvarner. Almost all the inhabitants are bilingual in Croatian and Italian in which the town is called *Cherso*.

Hotels. Kimen, 100 R. most with bath; Bristol, on the harbour front (a).— AUTOCAMP for about 200 cars.

Post Office on the front.—INFORMATION: Turističko društvo, on the front.

NARODNI TRG opens on the picturesque double harbour with its numerous fishing boats. Here a large *Loža* (Loggia; 15–16C), is used as a market, and a 16C *Clock Tower* surmounts the main gate into the old town. Ul. 29 og. novembra, the main street, curves N. and E. past the *Mjesni ured* or Town Hall, which incorporates a Venetian Gothic window from its predecessor on the site. The ground floor is arranged as a historical collection, with inscriptions, medieval wooden figures of SS Jerome and Isidore, and coins. The street ends at the *Porta Marcella*, a fine Renaissance gateway, decorated with the escutcheons of Doge Pasquale Cicogna (1585–95) and the Marcello family and a defaced lion of St Mark. A broad avenue follows a long section of the town *Walls*, erected by the Venetians between 1509 and 1610, to the *Porta Bragadina*, a similar gate also with a lion of St Mark.

We may complete the circuit of the old town, rejoining the quay near the harbour mouth. The Hotel Bristol occupies the former Venetian *Fontico* (15C) or grain warehouse. The handsome 15C *Palača Petris* on the corner of Pionirska ul., is to house the town museum. Farther along Pionirska ul., which leads into the oldest quarter of the town, are two other mansions in Venetian Gothic in a neglected state. A narrow street leads left to the church of *Sv. Sidar* (St Isidore), with a Gothic w. front and a Romanesque apse decorated with blind arcading. Inside are a polyptych and a wooden effigy of St Isidore (both 15C).

About 50 yds to the N. stands MAJKA BOŽJA SNIJEŽNA (Mary of the Snows) another 15C church with a detached campanile that is prominent from the harbour. The handsome Renaissance West Doorway has a good Madonna in the tympanum with an Annunciation above. In the plain interior are a 15C Gothic pietà in wood and a picture of Cres in the 17C. In the parish offices behind the church (opened on request) are a polyptych by Alvise Vivarini (1486?) showing St Sebastian with Saints, a wooden Renaissance crucifixion, Venetian pictures of the 16–18C, reliquaries and a Baroque chalice (1617).

Just s. of the town is a 14–15C FRANCISCAN MONASTERY with two cloisters; the smaller one with Gothic arcades, is particularly attractive. The *Church*, in essence Franciscan Gothic, has a Renaissance w. doorway. Behind the high altar are good Gothic stalls (15C). Entered through a Renaissance arcade from the s. side of the choir is a large rib-vaulted chapel. A gothic wooden crucifixion adorns its altar, while a slab bearing an effigy of Antun Marcello, a 16C bishop of Novigrad, is built into the wall behind. The *Library* (open to men only), in addition to 15 incunabula and manuscripts from the 14–18C, possesses a good Madonna in low relief by Andrea da Murano (1470?). The Benedictine nunnery farther along the shore is not open to visitors.

Excursions by boat from Cres may be made to the neighbouring coast of Istria (see Rte 6) and to Martinšćica and Osor down the w. coast (see below). Across Valun Bay (c. 1 hr by boat) is *Valun* (Inns) a tiny hamlet favoured with good shingle beaches. The Valunska ploča (Valun Tablet), built into the sacristy wall of the parish church, bears an 11C inscription in Glagolitic and Carolingian Latin. The white wine from Lubenice, close by, is the best known of Cres wines.

A good gravel road connects Cres with (24 km.) *Porozina* in the north, and car ferries to Rabac and Rijeka.

To OSOR, 33 km. (20 m.). The road runs s. with good retrospective views.—8 km. Turning right (narrow gravel road) for Valun (see above). —15 km. *Vrana* affords views (r.) to *Vransko jezero* (Lake Vrana), 2 sq. m. in area and 273 ft deep. The lake offers excellent freshwater fishing (pike, eels, and carp).

17 km. *Martinšćica* (rest.) a scattered little village with excellent shingle beaches, lies 6 km. to the w. The Franciscan Monastery, frequently rebuilt, was founded in the 15C. On the high altar is a painting of

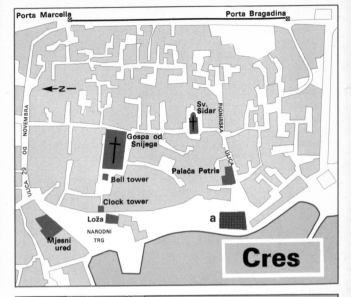

Porta Marcella — Porta Bragadina

Sv. Sidar

Gospa od Snijega

Palača Petris

Bell tower

Clock tower

Loža

Mjesni ured

NARODNI TRG

a

Cres

ULICA 29 OG NOVEMBRA

PIONIRSKA ULICA

Slatina

Luka Mali Lošinj

PT. PRIVLAKA

Mali Losinj

0	500	1000	1500 metres
0	500	1000	1500 yards

Srebrna uvala

Spomenik

Čikat Lighthouse

ANUNCIJATA

Veli žal

Telegraph

MALI LOSINJ

PT. KIJAC

Sv. Martin

Valdarke

Mali žal

PT. VILA

Vela Draga

VELI LOSINJ

Rovenska

ARAT.

Sv. Nikola

St Jerome by Baldassare d'Anna (1636) and in the refectory six paintings representing the twelve apostles (17C Venetian school). The adjoining 17C Sforza Palace (rebuilt as dwellings) retains only a well head with
the Sforza arms.

33 km. **Osor** (autocamp), once a Roman city of 20,000 inhabitants,
now a sleepy village with less than 100, commands the narrow strait,
Cavanella, that divides Cres from Lošinj. In the main square is the
early Renaissance *Cathedral* (1465–98), begun by Bp. Antun Palčić,
with a handsome Lombardesque w. front. The w. door closely
resembles that at Cres. The interior (apply at parish offices, see below)
suffered from bombardment by British naval units. On the high altar
is a Madonna enthroned with SS Gaudentius and Nicholas (School of
Palma Giovane); Gaudentius (d. 1044) was bishop of Ossero. The bell
tower built in 1675 by the mason Gallo of Krk, offers excellent views
of the islands of Krk and Lošinj. The *Museum* (open on request; ask
for Mr Sokolić, house No. 8) occupying the former Venetian town hall,
contains fragments of masonry, Roman busts, burial urns and pottery;
also Illyrian jewellery, pottery, and weapons, all excavated locally.
In the former *Bishop's Palace* opposite (escutcheon on wall) are the
parish offices where the cathedral treasury (seen on request), includes
vestments, plate and 15C Gothic sculpture. In the courtyard is a well
head with pre-Romanesque ornamentation.

The 15C Gothic church of *Sv. Gaudencije* has traces of frescoes in the choir and
a curious 15C statue of its patron bishop behind the high altar. Outside the city
gate, with a lion of St Mark built into the wall, the small Gothic church of *Sv.
Marija* (1414) has a Romanesque apse, beside which foundations were exposed in
1950–54, of a 6C double basilica with baptistery, thought to be Osor's first cathedral
(fragmentary mosaics). Near by a larger Roman mosaic floor has been uncovered
again. Beyond the church the cove of *Vijar* marks the outer limits of Apsoros.
Traces of the Roman walls can be seen, but little else remains above ground of the
city. Sir Richard Burton dug here in 1877 while British Consul in Trieste. Just beyond Vijar is Osor's harbour with a pleasant promenade, and, in the pine wood beyond, an autocamp. On the other side of the village stands the ruined Benedictine
monastery of Sv. Petar (11C).
From Osor a narrow gravel road runs S.E. to Punta Križa at the S. end of the
island.

13   THE ISLAND OF LOSINJ

HYDROPLANE daily (except Thurs) in the season to *Mali Lošinj* from Rijeka and
Opatija. Steamers to *Mali Lošinj* daily from Rijeka, Cres, Martinšćica (Cres), Osor
(Cres), Unije, Srakane Veli, Susak, and Ilovik; thrice weekly from Rab and Punta
Križa (Cres); twice weekly from Trieste, Koper, Rovinj, Pula, Silba, Zadar, Šibenik,
Split, Makarska, Orebić, Dubrovnik, Hercegnovi, Budva, and Bar.
CAR FERRY from the mainland to *Porozina* (Cres) and thence by road (see Rte
12).
BUSES to *Nerezine*, *Mali Lošinj*, and *Veli Lošinj* from all parts of Cres and, viâ
car ferries, from Rabac and Rijeka.

Lošinj (8500 inhab.) the smallest of the principal islands of the
Kvarner is 19 m. long. Two steep and rocky ends are joined by the
long narrow isthmus of Privlaka, which also encloses the deeply
indented bay of Mali Lošinj. In the N. the precipitous ridge of Osoršćica,
rising to a height of 1910 ft at Televrina peak, is separated from Cres
only by a narrow artificial canal. In the w. the Kurila peninsula is

continued, geologically, in the islands of Vele- and Male-Srakane and Unije. In the s., Grgošćak peak (790 ft) marks the highest point and Lošinj's rocky spine finds its continuation in a cluster of small islands at its southern tip, of which Ilovik is the most prominent. Susak, to the w., is geographically associated with Lošinj, but in geological terms is something of a curiosity (see below). Although poor for crops, Lošinj is noted for the luxuriance of its vegetation and the pine woods on its western shore. Fishing and ship-building continue to occupy the islanders and a merchant shipping line is based at Lošinj.

History. Lošinj was known in classical times as one of the components of the Apsyrtides (comp. p. 85) and until relatively recently had no history separate from that of Cres and Osor. The first record of its name (*Lussin*) is in 1384. With the decline of Osor in the 15C Lošinj became more independent, but did not develop its own trade links until the 17C. In the 18C Lošinj turned decisively to the sea for its living and by the end of the century, when Austria displaced Venice as master, had over 100 ships, a ship-yard and a nautical school. Napoleon's continental blockade and British reprisals harmed the industry but its fortunes were restored under Austria during the Russo-Turkish war of 1828 and the Crimean War, when numerous ships were chartered by Russia and later by Britain and France. Lošinj's apogee came in the 1870s when its fleet of 150 ships ranged the Mediterranean, and six shipyards employed over 600 men. The change from wood and sail to steel and steam was successfully made and Lošinj was home port for many large ships until the First World War. With the rise of Trieste and Rijeka its shipping industry declined. Chosen by leading Austrian physicians in 1886 for its dust-free air and even humidity, by the end of the century Lošinj was second only to Opatija as a health and holiday resort. Between the wars, under Italy, its development was retarded, but since 1945, as part of Yugoslavia, Lošinj has regained its place as one of the leading holiday islands of the northern Adriatic.

Mali Lošinj, long known as *Lussinpiccolo* but despite its name the principal town (4000 inhab.), rises in a natural amphitheatre at the head of its beautiful bay. Owing to its early rise as a tourist resort, it resembles Opatija rather than the other island towns in the E. Adriatic, having a strong Austrian flavour mingled with its Mediterranean elements.

Hotels. At Čikat: Helios, 200 R in main building and bungalows, all with bath; Alhambra; Beograd; Rijeka; Karolina; Dubrovnik; Sarajevo; Zadar; Čikat; Elora. In the town: Istra.
AUTOCAMP in Srebrna uvala, just beyond Hotel Helios, for 150 cars.
Restaurants. *K ribi* (fish), Trg Moše Pijade; *Tri palme*, Obala Maršala Tita; *K raskrsnici*, Ul. 20 og. aprila; *Riblji restoran* (fish), Ul. 20 og. aprila; *Skverić* (music), Obala Maršala Tita.—KAVANA. *Kvarner*, Obala Maršala Tita.
Post Office, Obala Maršala Tita.—INFORMATION. *Turist*, *Kvarner Express*, both on Obala Maršala Tita.
Beaches. Main beach (sand and shingle), with cabins, in Čikat Bay; also at Uvala Sv. Martin and Uvala Valdarke (rock and shingle); naturist beach at Mali Žal, c. 1 m. s.w. of town.
Amusements. Regatta on 10 Sept; international underwater fishing championships 'Kup nacija' on 1 Jan; sailing; tennis.

The deep basin of the excellent harbour is lined by two pleasant broad promenades, Obala Maršala Tita and Obala Jugoslavenske narodne armije, converging in Trg Moše Pijade, the main square. The memorial to the national liberation struggle on the front is by Dušan Džamonja (1956). Brdina ul., with a small museum, leads up to the older part of the town. Beyond the parish church, on the top of the hill, stand extensive ruins of a 15C Venetian fortress known locally as the *Kaštel* or Fortizza (views over Lošinj, Cres, and the Kvarner Bay).

A winding road and numerous paths lead through pleasant pine woods to the attractive bay of *Čikat*, the main recreation area and the peninsula of Annuncijata, with many good walks through the woods or along the indented shore.

An asphalt road winds over the hill to the sister community, reached alternatively on foot in ¾ hr by a pleasant shaded path along the shore.

Veli Lošinj (*Punta*), once the larger of the two settlements, as its name indicates (comp. *Lussingrande* in Ital.), is now a quiet fishing village (1000 inhab.) situated picturesquely on an almost landlocked little harbour. Just behind the harbour, the so-called *Uskok Tower* (1455) was built with forked battlements and machicolations by the Venetians against piratical Uskok depredations. On the other side of the harbour the large parish church of *Sv. Antun* (1774) contains a Madonna with Saints by Bart. Vivarini (1475), in poor condition and badly placed. On the adjoining altar is a Baroque Madonna and Child in marble (17C). The floor is paved with memorial slabs of local sea captains from the 17C to the present day. In the sacristy are a St Francis by Bern. Strozzi and a St Gregory by Fr. del Cossa.

Beside the church a seaside walk leads round to the tiny fishing hamlet of *Rovenska*, the oldest settlement at this end of the island with a picturesque harbour. On the hill above it, reached in about 30 min is the part-Gothic church of *Sv. Nikola*, a 15C foundation with 18C votive pictures showing local people in the folk costume of the period. In *Sv. Marija*, on the hill opposite, are two paintings by Fr. Fontebasso (18C). Above the church the former villa (1885) of an Austrian archduke has become a hospital for allergies, for the treatment of which Lošinj's climate is particularly suitable. At Rovenska and in the town there are similar hospitals for children. The former garden of the villa, planted with many Mediterranean species, is now a public park.

From Mali Lošinj, Obala Maršala Tita continues N. as an asphalt road along the narrow isthmus separating Mali Lošinj Bay from Lošinjski Kanal to serve the N. part of the island.—14 km. *Sv. Jakov* has two parish churches, of which the later (16C) contains a Gothic crucifixion and a 16C triptych.

16 km. *Nerezine* (autocamp; rest.; P.O.) stands on the site of the oldest settlement on the island. The Franciscan monastery (1509–15) has a pleasant cloister and Renaissance bell tower (1590) and its church (choir added in the 19C) contains a large St Francis with Saints by Girol. da Santa Croce (16C), and a 15C Venetian Madonna. Just outside the village is the 16C fortified tower of the Draža (de Drusa) family, who endowed the monastery. From Nerezine, *Televrina* (1910 ft), the highest point on the island, can be reached on foot in about 1½ hrs.—20 km. *Osor* (comp. Rte 12) lies across the swing bridge that connects Lošinj with the island of Cres.

The most interesting of the smaller islands encircling Lošinj is Susak (1500 inhab.). Alone of the Adriatic islands, it is composed entirely of clay and sand, not rock. It lies 6 m. w. and is reached by boat from Mali Lošinj. Susak is intensively cultivated with terraced vineyards producing good red wine (pleskunac). Sardine are fished in quantity. The isolation of the inhabitants has produced a distinct local dialect and traditional customs, seen to best effect at weddings, vintage, and carnival time. The folk costumes of the women are characterized by brightly coloured tights, and short flared skirts. An 11C cross from a vanished Benedictine monastery adorns the parish church; inside there is a 12C Romanesque crucifixion.

To the s. of Lošinj is Ilovik where the fishing village (350 inhab.) is reached from Veli Lošinj. On the adjoining islet of *Sv. Petar*, which protects the harbour, are the remains of Roman summer villas and the ruins of an 11C Benedictine monastery enclose a cemetery. A ruined Venetian tower (1597) recalls the depredations of the Uskoks. Unije (300 inhab.), largest of the lesser islands, off Kurila peninsula to the w. of Lošinj, has boat connections with Osor and Mali Lošinj. The village on the w. side of the island has an inn and seasonal restaurants.

III NORTHERN DALMATIA

14 ZADAR AND ITS ENVIRONS

A Zadar

ZADAR, the largest and most important town (26,000 inhab.) of northern Dalmatia, stands on a narrow peninsula at the western edge of the Ravni Kotari, a broad flat plain unique on the E. Adriatic seaboard. For centuries the chief town of Dalmatia, Zadar was displaced at the turn of the present century by Split and lost further ground by becoming a remote outpost of Italy between the two world wars. Though the town suffered heavily from allied bombing, many of its most precious monuments were unharmed and rebuilding is being accomplished with taste.

Airport (opened 1969), 10 km. N.; services twice weekly from Zagreb.

Railway Station, S. of the town; services to Knin on the Zagreb–Split line. Change at Knin for Zagreb and Šibenik; one through train daily to Belgrade.

Steamer Quay. *Radnička obala* for all services: long distance steamers arrive and depart in front of the Hotel Beograd, local steamers between Lančana vrata and Mornarska vrata.—CAR FERRY to Ancona from *Istarska obala.*

Hotels. In town: **Zagreb** (b), 100 R. with bath, kavana, Ul. Borisa Kidriča; **Beograd** (a), kavana, dancing, Radnička obala; **Forum** (c), U. Ive Lole Ribara. At *Borik* (Puntamika): **Slavija,** 127 R. with bath; **Park; Zadar; Donat;** all close to beach, tennis, sailing and dancing.

Autocamp at *Borik* for 350 cars.

Restaurants. *Riblji restoran* (fish) at Foša; *Zadar,* Sarajevska ul. *Primorac,* Ul. Natka Nodila.

Kavanas. *Central,* Ul. Ive Lole Ribara; *Hotel Zagreb,* Ul. Borisa Kidriča. CAFÉS also in Ul. Ive Lole Ribara, Poljana Vl. Gortana and Narodni trg.

Post Office (General) in Ul. Rade Končara; branch in Poljana Vl. Gortana.— INFORMATION OFFICE. Turist biro, Ul. Božidara Petranovića.—TOURIST OFFICES: *Turisthotel,* Poljana Petra Zoranića 1; *Kvarner Express,* Narodni trg.

Bus Station, *Radnička obala.* TOWN BUSES, to Borik; to Arbanasi. LOCAL BUSES to all parts of the Ravni Kotari. LONG DISTANCE BUSES to all parts of the coast and the main towns inland.

Amusements. THEATRE: *Gradsko kazalište.* Ul. Ive Lole Ribara.—CINEMAS: *Pobjeda,* behind Narodni trg; *Zadar,* Ljetno kino (open-air), Ul. Narodne milicije. —CONCERTS in the church of Sv. Donat.

Beaches. *Kolovare,* Ul. J. N. A.; *Borik*; both with cabins and showers.

History. *Zadar* entered recorded history in the 4C B.C. as *Idassa,* when Greeks from Pharos (present-day Hvar), according to a contemporary inscription, repelled invaders there. From the 9C B.C., however, Zadar had been a stronghold of the Illyrian tribe of the Liburnians who, sometime around the 1C B.C., threw in their lot with the Romans. In 69 B.C. Roman *Jadera* became a municipium and eleven years later received a Roman colony. With the fall of the Western Roman Empire the city passed to Byzantium and in 752 became the chief town of the theme of Dalmatia and seat of the Byzantine duke. Byzantine sovereignty, although only nominal in later centuries, continued until 1105. Constantine Porphyrogenitus listed the city under the name of *Diadora.* Zadar began paying tribute to the Franks in 803, but returned to Byzantium as a result of the treaty of Aachen in 810. Later in the 9C and throughout the 10C the city was forced to pay tribute to the Croats. As the most important and populous city of Dalmatia, Zadar became the chief object of the struggle between Venice and first Croatia and then the dual kingdom of Hungary-Croatia. Zadar (Italian *Zara*) first swore allegiance to Venice in 998, after the triumphant Dalmatian campaign of Doge Pietro Orseolo, but quickly reverted to Croatia again. In 1084 the Venetians tried to reassert their claim, but in 1105, Zadar acknowledged king Koloman of Hungary-Croatia. After his death in 1116 Venice prevailed until 1178, when she was again rejected by the Zadrians with the aid of Hungary–Croatia. The most significant battle occurred in 1202 when Venice tricked the members of the Fourth Crusade into storming Zadar as a precondition for assisting the Crusaders with transport to Constantinople. Despite several uprisings, Zadar remained in Venetian hands until 1358, when the Hungarians compelled Venice to renounce all claims to the city and to Dalmatia. In 1409 both city and province were sold to Venice by King Ladislaus of Naples and ceased independent existence. As the administrative centre of Venetian Dalmatia, Zadar had an uneventful history, apart from occasional Turkish forays to her walls. Zadar passed to Austria in 1797 and in 1808 to Napoleonic France. In 1813 the port was blockaded by the British navy while the Austrians attacked and recaptured the city from the land, and it remained in Austrian hands until 1918. By the Treaty of Rapallo in 1921 Zadar was attached to Italy as a solitary enclave on the Dalmatian mainland. Later, as a centre of Italian operations during the Second World War, Zadar was heavily bombed by the British and American air forces. Liberated by Partisan units in Oct 1944, it has since been a part of Yugoslavia.

Among famous natives of Zadar are Juraj Matejević Dalmatinac (d. 1473), also known as Georgius Dalmaticus and (erroneously) Giorgio Orsini, the Dalmatian sculptor and architect, and Andrea Meldola lo Schiavone (Andrija Medulić; 1500?–63), the painter. Two other prominent sculptor-architects, Lucijan (1420?–1502) and Franjo (1420?–79) Laurana (Luciano and Francesco de Laurana), although born outside the city, both received their early education at Zadar. Zadar was also the birthplace and home of a group of 16C writers, Petar Zoranić (b. 1508), Brno Krnarutić (1515?–72), Juraj Baraković and Sime Budinić, who were among the founding fathers of Croatian literature.

The broad long RADNIČKA OBALA, where the steamers moor and buses terminate, is a convenient starting place for touring the town. At its N.W. end the Hotel Beograd adjoins a massive *Bastion* (late 16C), erected on the site of a medieval fortress when the fortifications were rebuilt by Venice. The interior (steps by hotel) is laid out as a small park (café in summer). Beyond the bastion the pre-Venetian town walls extend the length of Radnička obala, to the seaward end of which the former Venetian *Custom House* (rebuilt 1791) was moved in 1920.

The *Lončana vrata* (Chain Gate), from which in medieval times a massive chain barring the harbour was stretched across to the Porporella opposite, admits to the town. Immediately inside the gate on the left is the *Veliki Arsenal* (1752), with a double staircase rising to a classically simple façade. Opposite, a hexagonal corner tower and part of the outer wall of a 14C fortress (18C Turkish cannon in the embrasures) were uncovered by bombing, which also created the large open square beyond. The three wells (well heads 1761), which have given it the name of TRG TRI BUNARA, are fed by the former fortress moat, while the medieval house just behind the third well (popularly but erroneously called the *Mali Arsenal*) incorporates the former main entrance to the fortress. The façade bears four defaced escutcheons and a 15C lion of St Mark. On the far side of the square, a small Rotunda (1582) alone remains of the church of *Gospa od Kastela*, or Gospa od zdravlja (Our Lady of Health). The wrought iron gates bear the arms of Abp. V. Zmajević (1718–45), who is buried here, and in the tasteful Baroque interior is a Gothic ambry (1413).

Leaving the square by Ul. Borisa Kidriča we pass on our right the marine headquarters of Jugotanker, with parts of the city wall behind. Beyond, Istarska obala provides the embarkation point for the car ferry to Ancona. At the far end of the street (l.) the former church and monastery of *Sv. Nikola* (1760), with a good courtyard and Romanesque bell tower, is to be restored after long use as barracks. The Army Club opposite occupies the former seat of the Austrian governor of Dalmatia, with just behind, the bastion of Sv. Nikola (view out to sea).

Entered from the tiny and almost concealed Trg Vranjanina is the **Franciscan Church and Monastery**, supposedly founded by St Francis himself while on his way to Syria in 1213. Although the first Gothic church to be built in Dalmatia (1283), it preserves of the original style only a restored two-light window in the rebuilt w. front (1780), the choir, and the partly Gothic Detrico chapel. Within, a lavishly decorated Romanesque column supports the stoup to the left. In the N. aisle the *Detrico Chapel* (1480) bears the elaborately carved Detrico escutcheon, attributed to Nikola Firentinac, over the entrance, and on the N. wall a large allegorical painting by Lazzaro Bastiani (late 15C). In the s. aisle, above the centre altar: Palma Giovane, St Francis. In the choir behind the altar are outstanding Gothic *Stalls (1394) by Giovanni da Borgo Sansepolcro, with carving of great purity. On the returned stalls are depicted St Chrysogonus (Patron of the city) on a horse, with Fra Benedict, who ordered the stalls (below), and on the other side St Francis receiving the stigmata, with a bust of Louis of Anjou.

From the choir opens the *Sacristy* where the Treaty of Zadar (comp. above) was concluded in 1358 (memorial plaque 1958). On the wall (r.) the fine polyptych (15C), attributed to Dujam Vušković of Split, came from the Franciscan monastery at Ugljan. The two enormous chests are of oak (1724). Over the door to the choir hangs a small bronze crucifix by Ivan Meštrović.

In the adjoining monastic *Treasury*, the large wooden Crucifixion (?13C) is unusually carved in low relief and painted. Also displayed are the Dead Christ with Angels, a painting from the Bassano workshop; a Madonna (15C), tempera on wood: SS Jerome, John the Baptist, and Simeon, three figures from a polyptych by Pietro de Riboldis (1433); two additional screens from the choir stalls; and, in cases, three illuminated codices (13C, 14C, and 15C). Notable among the church plate are a 14C silver processional cross decorated with miniatures and three 15C silver-gilt chalices.—A door in the w. wall of the treasury admits to the small Renaissance chapel of *Sv. Ante* (Anthony), the former chapter house, and thence into the graceful cloister (1556),built by local masons Ivan Trifunić and Ivan Stijović. In the centre stands a late 15C well head and into the walls have been built gravestones of the 15–17C.

Continuing round the monastery we reach the excavated N.W. end of the Roman forum (see below) and turn left along Ul. J. Sundečića. Immediately on our left is the Orthodox (Serbian) church of *Sv. Ilija* (Elijah), erected 1773, with a small collection of late icons (16–18C) and, adjoining it, the *Palača Janković*, with a Baroque façade. In the small Trg 27 marta stand the *Teologija*, an Austrian-built seminary of 1867, and, enclosing the s. side of the square, the **Slavensko** (or Ilirsko) **sjemenište** (Slavonic Seminary), founded by Abp. V. Zmajević. A plain Baroque building dating from 1748, with a pleasant cloister (well head with Zmajević arms; view of s. side of cathedral), the Seminary has since the war housed the joint *Treasury of the Cathedral and of the Benedictine Nunnery of Sv. Marija*, one of the most important collections of church treasure in Yugoslavia (not yet open to view).

Special permission to view the treasury may sometimes be obtained either from the Conservationists' Department (Zavod za Zaštitu spomenika) in Zeleni trg or the Archbishopric in the same building. Plans have been made to put the collection on permanent exhibition in the Benedictine nunnery of Sv. Marija when it is rebuilt, but no date has been set.

Among the contents are a pre-Romanesque cross of gilded copper, thought to have belonged to the abbess Čika, step-sister of King Krešimir of Croatia and foundress of Sv. Marija in 1066, and a 12C processional cross with miniatures. The remarkable 14–15C *Reliquary of the Holy Cross and Sponge, consists of four silver gilt dragons whose tails support a crystal cube and the carved figure of St Chrysogonus, patron saint of Zadar, on horseback. The silver-gilt Gothic *Pastoral Staff (1460) of Abp. Maffeo Valaresso is a superb example of the silversmith's art with tabernacle work and many statuettes. Both of the 11C are the silver *Reliquary of St Jacob*, a round casket, carved with saints, having a domed lid, the gift of Božna, wife of Kaža (Chaseus), one time prior of Zadar, and the *Reliquary of St Orontius*, an oblong casket covered on three sides with silver plates. The saints depicted are named in a mixture of Greek and Latin letters. Later treasures include a silver-gilt monstrance; the silver-gilt *Reliquary of St Chrysogonus (1326), a casket richly decorated with embossed vine leaves, and enamel medallions; the 12–13C silver-gilt *Reliquary of Pope Gregory*, a casket with a pyramidal lid; and the 15C silver-gilt and enamelled *Reliquary of St Euphemia*. The 12C *Reliquary of St Isidore* has the form of an arm, richly decorated with delicate silver filigree work and set with semi-precious stones and patterns in cloisonné enamel. Also in the form of an arm are the *Reliquary of St Chrysogonus*, on which Zadar notables used to swear the oath in the 14C, and another 14C silver-gilt *Reliquary purporting to contain a finger of St John the Baptist, gift of Katarina, wife of Duke Sandalj Hranić of Bosnia. The 13C *Reliquary of St Nicholas takes the form of a bust of the saint, as does the *Reliquary of St Sylvester (1367), an outstanding work by Kotor goldsmiths Melsa and Radoslav. There are also silver-gilt busts of Mary Magdalene (1332), and of Martha (14C). The *Mitre of St Sylvester, in silver-gilt ornamented with fleurs-de-lys and scrolled vine leaves, is set with semi-precious stones and decorated with four silver medallions. The treasury contains also a 12C silver-gilt Pax of Pope Gregory; a 13C miniature Crucifixion on parchment in a silver frame; and outstanding collections of church *Embroideries and vestments (14–17C), including much Dalmatian lace.

The *Cathedral of Sv. Stošija (Anastasia), the largest and finest Romanesque church in Dalmatia, is less ancient than its appearance would suggest, owing to stylistic conservatism. It was restored and given a new roof in 1924–28.

Constantine Porphyrogenitus refers to a cathedral on this site in the 10C and Pope Alexander III visited it in 1177. In 1202 the city was sacked by the Crusaders when many churches are said to have been destroyed, though it is not certain that the cathedral was among them. In 1285, however, the cathedral was rededicated by Abp. Lorenzo Periandro. The main apse probably remains from the older church while the remainder, reconstructed in the 12C, may have undergone extensive repairs in the 13C after the visit of the Crusaders. At this time the building was also lengthened, and the w. front, completed in 1324, ranks among the latest Romanesque work in Europe.

EXTERIOR. The WEST FRONT, the finest single feature of the cathedral, has affinities with the better-known Tuscan churches of Pisa and Lucca, with the difference that the lower part is completely unadorned, except for the three portals. The upper part is decorated with four stories of blind arcades, the middle two flanking a great wheel window (restored), a device that gives it extraordinary harmony, though the gable story is, unusually, broken by a second and later rose window. The device is continued along the N. wall by an arcaded gallery beneath the eaves. The large centre *Portal* consists of five recessed orders; in the tympanum, the Virgin and Child are flanked by SS Anastasia and Chrysogonus. The statues of the four apostles that flank the portal are earlier than the rest of the work. The fine N. portal has a sculptured agnus dei in the richly ornamented tympanum and figures of the Virgin Mary (restored) and the angel Gabriel on either side. The two similar figures flanking the s. portal are replacements made in the late 19C by T. G. Jackson, the English architect.

The spacious INTERIOR (162 by 58 ft) is basilican in plan. The nave, three times wider than the aisles, is divided from them by arcades having round arches, supported alternatively by piers and marble columns. The two columns nearest the w. door have spiral fluting and capitals of pre-Romanesque design. The next two are rectangular and have Corinthian capitals. The four columns at the E. end are Roman with good Corinthian capitals. Above the arcades is an ornamental string-course. The triforium has six small arches in each bay with arcaded balustrades.

The raised CHOIR, lined on both sides by elaborate late Gothic *Stalls (1418–50), is the work of the Venetian artist Matteo Moronzoni (restored 1883). The more sumptuous seats were for the bishop and the town governor. The Gothic *Ciborium* (1332) over the high altar is loftier than that of St Mark's in Venice, and rests on four marble *Columns individually decorated with fluting and diaper work, while one of the capitals has little figures worked into the foliage. The rib-vaulted canopy is finished with a horizontal cornice of acanthus leaves and bears an inscription with the date and name of Abp. Ivan Butovan, during whose tenure the w. front was also completed. Behind the high altar the spacious apse (?10C) retains its Byzantine *Synthronon* with the Cathedra (bishop's throne) raised on five steps, while slabs from an old altar rail have been built into the high altar.

The CRYPT, beneath the choir, is probably contemporary with it. Fragments of 9C ornament have been built into one column. On the spot beneath the high altar a stone sarcophagus contains relics of SS Agape, Chionia and Irene, martyred in Salonika under Diocletian. The simple altar is formed of a damaged slab with a 13C relief of St Anastasia at the stake.

In the N. Aisle there is a 17C altar frontal of St Dominic and a painting by Palma Giovane. The apse has poorly restored 13C frescoes depicting Christ and St Thomas Becket. The altar here contains a 9C sarcophagus, presented by Bp. Donat, with the relics of St Anastasia, while its frontal has a 15C Gothic relief of the saint in marble.—In the S. AISLE is the Rococo altar of the Holy Sacrament (1719) by A. Viviani and on the next altar to the w. a Madonna by Blaž Zadranin (Blaise of Zadar, 1447), thought to be the same as Blaž Jurjev Trogiranin (of Trogir); this came from the rotunda in Trg tri bunara, which retains a copy. The wooden crucifixion on the wall between these altars formed part of a great rood, now lost, by Matteo Moronzoni (1426). Six apostles, also from this screen, will be returned to the cathedral after restoration. Two doors, one Gothic, one in Renaissance style with the arms of Abp. Valaresso, formerly led into the baptistery, a rare 6C building consisting of a central dome with six apses, which was shattered by a bomb. It will be reconstructed when funds are available. In the s. apses are more 13C frescoes and a door leading to the Gothic SACRISTY (1398), formerly the chapel of *Sv. Barbara*. Here are a polyptych showing six saints by Vitt. Carpaccio (1480) and a late 13C icon of the Madonna. Between the sacristy and the main apse, a barrel vault remains from an earlier church.

The **Campanile** towers above Ul. Ive Lole Ribara at the E. end of the cathedral. Begun in 1480 by Abp. Valaresso and interrupted after only one story had been built, it was completed in 1892 according to plans by T. G. Jackson, who took the tower at Rab as his model.

Beyond the hotel Forum we turn right along Ul. Božidara Petra-novića which crosses a large, irregular open space created by bombing in the Second World War. This is the site of the **Roman Forum**.

Excavations (most recently in 1963–64) have established that the forum measured 309 ft long by 146 ft wide, while the capitol at the N.W. end was almost as long again. Restoration of the somewhat scanty remains is in progress.

Ul. Božidara Petranovića and Stomorica represent the decumanus and cardo maximus of the Roman town. Looking N.W. from their intersection we see the low walls of a row of taverns and parts of the cloaca or drainage system. Steps descend to the level of the porticus, with its Roman paving, and a further step marks the level of the original pavement of the forum. Low walls to our left define the E. end of a large *Basilica*, with a semicircular apse; the w. end has been destroyed to make way for a well. The floor of the forum is strewn with fragments of Roman masonry from the lapidary collection formerly housed in Sv. Donat. The remains of a Roman triumphal arch are from Podgradje (Roman Asseria) near Benkovac (see p. 107), and there are large numbers of the characteristic Liburnian gravestones (cippi) with their foliated tapering tops. More spolia can be seen built into the base of Sv, Donat, which stands on the floor of the forum. Beside the bishop's palace in what is now Zeleni trg a lofty Roman column (34 ft high by 4 ft in diameter) stands in its original position. Originally a votive column, it served as a pillory in the Middle Ages when the small pre-Romanesque plaque (9C) near its base and the gryphon on top were added. Beyond the column where the forum is crossed by Ul. J. Sundečić steps lead up to the former capitol, now partly occupied by the complex of buildings joined to the church of Sv. Ilija (see p. 93). Immediately behind these buildings are the excavated foundations of a massive *Temple* to Augustus, Juno, and Minerva. Extensive remains of the surrounding peribolus may be seen s.w. of here behind the new block of flats. Further foundations of the peribolus can also be seen N.E. of the Palača Janković.

The monumental round church of ***Sv. Donat** (St Donatus) on the N.E. side of the forum is one of the most curious and original buildings in Dalmatia. The church, circular in plan and 88 ft tall, consists of a plain drum with narrow lesenes spaced at regular intervals and with three apses on the E. side, decorated with shallow blind arcades that rise from ground level to just under the eaves. In the centre rises a smaller concentric drum topped with a gently sloping conical roof. The foundations consist of fragments of Roman masonry laid directly on the floor of the forum.

The exact date of its construction and the origins of its style are uncertain, but it was probably built in the 9C (Constantine Porphyrogenitus provides the first mention of it in 949), although not necessarily by Bp. Donat, whose name became popularly linked with the church only in the 15C; the original dedication was to the Holy Trinity. Its style links it with Charlemagne's chapel at Aachen, St Vitale at Ravenna, and the church of SS Sergius and Bachus at Istanbul; but differences, notably in the matter of the apses, seem to point to the local Croatian architecture of the period. A number of minor changes have been made to the church in recent centuries (in 1798–1870 it served the Austrians as a military magazine and under the Italians it became a museum), but its form remains substantially unaltered. It is used for occasional concerts and for art exhibitions.

An irregularly shaped narthex on the w. side admits to the main doorway, composed of antique fragments. The lofty INTERIOR gives an impression of massive strength. Within the circular outer wall a concentric arcade rises in two stories to form an ambulatory with a gallery above, leaving the central space open to the full height of the inner drum. The round arches are supported on huge rectangular stone piers set directly upon the forum pavement; similar piers support the roof, while the arches opening towards the apses are borne by two

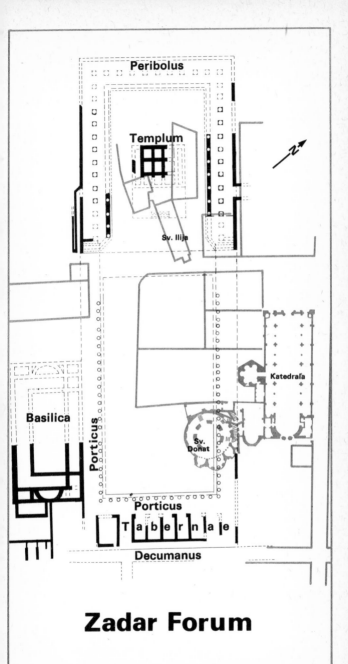

Zadar Forum

Roman columns with composite capitals from the colonnade of the forum. Two similar columns in the gallery above have been truncated to make them fit; here one capital is Corinthian. Among the many Roman fragments built into the structure the most interesting are two Roman altars dedicated to Juno and Jupiter on the pier next to the main entrance. Two flights of stairs give access to the upper gallery. Those on the right are thought to be original, although reconstructed in 1733, while those on the left were added at the same time. The access doors both bear the Zmajević escutcheon. The upper gallery is entered from a vestibule of 1752, with an entrance also composed of Roman fragments, and is identical in plan with the ground floor below.

The *Bishop's Palace* (1830), attached to the w. side of Sv. Donat, incorporates the episcopal offices and Institute for the Conservation of Ancient Monuments.

On the E. side of the forum the badly damaged church and former Benedictine nunnery of **Sv. Marija** was founded in 1066 by Čika, a Zadar noblewoman said to have been the stepsister of King Petar Krešimir IV of Croatia, who granted the new foundation many privileges. In 1091 the present church, an aisled basilica, was consecrated and King Koloman commemorated his entry into Zadar in 1105 by endowing the construction of a bell tower and chapter house. In 1529–36 the church was enlarged and given a graceful Lombardesque façade with a Renaissance doorway and a wheel-window. The E. end was rebuilt and a cupola added in 1762.

The bare INTERIOR (open 9–12, 5–7) has been re-roofed since the war. The Romanesque arcades acquired a Rococo facing of stucco in 1744. The spacious triforium, also richly stuccoed, served the nuns as their matroneum; the arches are closed by wrought-iron lattices. On the N. wall is a Baroque memorial with a bust of Simon Comfanfogna (1707). The Benedictine device and a Latin inscription commemorating the foundation of the nunnery surmount a closed aperture through which deceased nuns were passed from the nunnery into the church. On an altar in the s. aisle is a Gothic pietà (15C).

A Romanesque gateway by the N. wall of the church gives access to the nunnery. The handsome Romanesque *Campanile (1105), the oldest of such dimensions in Dalmatia (restored 1438–53), has well-proportioned groups of windows culminating in fine four-light windows at the top. An inscription records its endowment by King Koloman.

Behind the campanile is the badly damaged *Chapter House* (1105–11), with a barrel-vaulted roof reinforced by cross ribs, an early example of a method of construction that became a Dalmatian idée fixe, surviving as a glorious anachronism in Šibenik cathedral. In the s.e. corner stands the Romanesque *Tomb of Vekenega* (d. 1111), daughter of Čika and abbess when the campanile and chapel were built (as the inscriptions attest). A narrow flight of stairs mounts to *Vekenega's Chapel* on the first floor of the campanile. Detached columns in the corners support two massive diagonal ribs carrying the roof, one of the earliest examples of rib vaulting in Europe. On the faces of the cushion capitals are carved the letters of Koloman's name: R.CO/LLO/MAN/NVS. Contemporary frescoes on the walls, difficult to see, show Christ Triumphant and the Deposition. A door in the s. wall, whose lintel is a fragment of a

Roman frieze, leads to stairs to the top of the bell tower with views over
Zadar and out to sea.

When the nunnery is rebuilt, one wing will form a museum for the combined
treasuries of Sv. Marija, Sv. Krševan and the cathedral (comp. above).

Walking N.E. along Ul. Božidara Petranovića we pass the Turist
biro and kavana Express and come to the small Trg Vladimira Gortana.
On the right side is the *Narodni muzej* with memorials of the Second
World War. The street terminates in the *Lučka vrata*, or Harbour Gate,
which incorporates fragments of a Roman triumphal arch, a plaque
commemorating the battle of Lepanto (1571), and an equestrian relief
of St Chrysogonus. The 16C lion of St Mark on the side facing the
quay was defaced after the Second World War during squabbles between
Croat and Italian nationalists. Turning back, we take Sarajevska ul.

The Romanesque church of **Sv. Krševan** (Chrysogonus), dedicated to
Zadar's patron saint, is second only to the cathedral in interest and
beauty. Built in the 10C on the site of an earlier church and reconstructed in its present form in 1175, it was attached to a Benedictine
monastery until its dissolution in 1807. The monastic buildings disappeared in the bombing. The W. front is plain with the mere stump of a
tower, begun in 1546 and never completed, but the S. wall is beautifully
decorated with shallow blind arcades resting on spirally fluted columns.
Particularly striking is the central **Apse* where arcades resting on
slender columns with cushion capitals form a high open gallery, with
blind arcading beneath. Just N. of the apses a two-light Romanesque
window from the former monastery has been built into the wall.

The S. door admits to the plain but well-proportioned INTERIOR, basilican in plan,
with arcades supported alternately on piers and columns. The wooden apostles
above four of the piers are from the cathedral rood (comp. p. 95), the work of
Moronzoni (1426). In the N. apse and on the wall adjoining Romanesque frescoes
(restored) depict the Birth of Christ, the Last Judgement, the Annunciation, and
Saints. The incongruous Baroque high altar (1632) bears marble statues of Zadar's
patron saints (1717); built into the reverse side is an early 15C Gothic relief of St
Anne. In the S. aisle an altar dedicated to St Zoilus has a painting attributed to
G. B. Piazzetta. Over the S. door is a memorial with marble bust to Marino Zorzi
(d. 1675), a Venetian provveditore.

Continuing by Sarajevska ul. we pass the *Palača Gverini* and, on the
next corner, the *Palača Fanfogna*, with interesting details. On the
opposite corner are *Sv. Andrija* (Andrew) and an adjoining Renaissance
façade, all that remains of the church of *Sv. Marcela* (1540).

In Sv. Andrija (key from Inst. Conserv. Monts.) the apse and S. wall are decorated with poorly-preserved 11C frescoes in Byzantine style. A door in the apse
leads into the curious pre-Romanesque church of *Sv. Petar Stari* (?9C) with nave
and single aisle divided by a simple arcade. Many Roman fragments went into its
construction and traces of 11–12C frescoes remain.

The colourful **Tržnica**, one of the biggest markets in Dalmatia,
occupies a small square and several adjoining ruins adapted since
the war for the purpose. In the E. corner are the vine-clad remains of
one wall of the church of *Sv. Marija Velika*, which held the sarcophagus
of St Simeon until it was demolished to make way for the new fortifications in 1543; its roofless chapel of *Sv. Rok* now serves as a meat
market. Beside them stands the uncompleted W. front of what was

intended to become the church of St Simeon, bearing the date (1600) and the escutcheons of benefactors. On the N.E. side of the square the 16C *Gate of Sv. Rok* through the Venetian walls, later blocked up, was reopened in 1847 to Radnička obala and the quays. Immediately on the left here is the *Bastion of Sv. Rok* and farther to the right, where the quayside ends, the *Bastion Moro*, now built over. Between the two, opposite the footbridge to Voštarnica (see p. 104) a 19C opening, by a newsagent's kiosk, leads back through the walls. Immediately inside the gateway steps mount (l.) to a pleasant walk along the top of the town walls.

Taking Ul. 1 novembar we recross Ljubljanska ul. passing, at the corner, the remains of the *Palača Cedulini*, with a good doorway in Venetian Gothic. On the opposite side the Romanesque *Palača Ghirardini*, adjoining the pharmacy, has a typical Dalmatian 15C balconied window from the workshop of Nikola Firentinac.

We reach NARODNI TRG, the Platea Magna of the middle ages and main square and gathering place of Zadar, crossed on the far side by Ul. Ive Lole Ribara, the Corso and main shopping street of Zadar, that runs from the cathedral (p. 94) to Sv. Šimun (see below). The N. and W. sides of the square are dominated by the pompous *Vijećnica* (Town Hall) in neo-classical style, with reliefs showing scenes from Zadar, erected by the Italians in 1936. It also houses the *Naučna biblioteka*, an important library founded by Pier Aless. Paravia in 1855.

A wing of the town hall encloses the small 11C church of *Sv. Lovro* (Lawrence), now partly ruined (key from the Institute for the Conservation of Monuments). It takes the form of a miniature basilica with aisles divided from the nave by four columns; two with Roman capitals also have reversed Roman capitals as bases, while the other two have pre-Romanesque capitals of which one represents a man with outspread arms. The nave is barrel-vaulted with transverse ribs, but the aisles are covered with semi domes resting on squinches.

The former **Loža gradske straže** (Guardhouse), an elegant loggia, erected in 1562, has been attributed to Gian Girolamo Sammicheli, nephew of Michele. The *Clock Tower* was added by the Austrians in 1798. The Guardhouse now contains the *Etnografski muzej* (open daily except Monday 8–11, 6–8) founded in 1945 and notable for an excellent collection of folk costumes. On the S.E. corner of the square stands the **Gradska loža** (Town Loggia), designed by Gian Girolamo Sammicheli and built in 1565. The inscription over the door refers to a restoration in 1792. The building, originally open on all four sides, has been adapted for mounting art exhibitions, but still contains the stone magistrates' bench ornamented with reliefs and escutcheons.

The picturesque narrow Klaićeva ul. leads into one of the few old quarters of the town which escaped bombing. A number of houses with attractive façades include the Palača Papafava (No. 1), with courtyard, and the Palača Civalelli. At the end on the left is the Franciscan Gothic church of **Sv. Mihovil**, with an excellent original w. portal (1389), probably the work of Paolo (Vanuzzi) da Sulmona. In the tympanum is a relief of St Michael, with SS Anastasia and Chrysogonus on either side. Above this is a Madonna and Child, while on the gable is a Roman relief of three heads on which haloes have been carved at a later date. The choir, the work of Andrija Desina, a local architect, bears traces of Gothic frescoes in various states of preservation, and a large painted Crucifixion (13C) in low relief on wood, the pair of which is in the Franciscan monastery (see p. 93). By the entrance is a stone font (15C) supported by four angels.

In Varoška ul. straight ahead and Ul. Sima Matavulja beyond are the oldest houses in Zadar, some of the 12–13C with Romanesque doors and windows. There are also good later houses in Ul. Dimitrija Tucovića (16C), notably the Baroque Palača Fozze (18C).

Turning left along Ul. Žrtava fašizma, the E. continuation of Stomorica, we pass on our left the Venetian *Palača Nassis*, the main portal of which has the Nassis escutcheon in the tympanum. Ahead the Land Gate leads out to the old harbour (see below), but we make a detour left along Ul. Andrije Medulića to the *Moderna Galerija* (open daily 8–12) housing a small collection of late icons and works by modern Yugoslav painters; here an international photographic exhibition is held biennially entitled 'Man and the Sea'. Above the gallery is the *Prirodoslovni muzej* (Natural History Museum), with a collection of Mediterranean fish and birds. The street ends in the irregularly shaped Trg Oslobodjenja where a tall *Roman Column* incorporates drums from two temple columns brought here from the forum in 1729. A railed pit encloses the excavated foundations of the Roman triumphal arch which marked the E. limit of the ancient town.

The square opens into the Poljana Petra Zoranića, which is lined on one side by the *Providurska palača* (1607), the former residence of the Venetian Provveditore generale (Governor-General) of Dalmatia. The upper story was added by the Austrians in the 19C, and the ground floor is now occupied by Zadar's largest travel agency, Turisthotel. A well head in the courtyard bears the Austrian imperial arms.

Adjoining is the former *Knežev dvor* (13C) or residence of the town governor, also reconstructed by the Austrians (1804), with a Venetian well head in the arcaded courtyard, while a little farther on, in Omladinska ul., the 18C Venetian *Kamerlengo* has a Baroque façade. No. 7 in this street has a Romanesque façade and a Renaissance courtyard.

The Baroque church of **Sv. Šimun** (Simeon) is a 17C reconstruction of the older church of St Stephen, whose name was changed when the sarcophagus of St Simeon was transferred here from the church of Sv. Marija Velika (1632). The Campanile, on the N. side, is crowned by four busts of prophets removed from the unfinished church of St Simeon in the market square. The INTERIOR is mainly Renaissance in feeling with a nave and two aisles divided by arcades with fluted columns and rich Corinthian capitals. An unusual feature is that it has two triumphal arches, one (added in 1705) marking the choir, the other the sanctuary. On the high altar stands the sumptuous *Sarcophagus of St Simeon*, a superb example of the silversmith's art.

According to legend a ship was driven ashore at Zadar either in 1213 or 1273 from which landed a nobleman bearing apparently the body of his brother, which he deposited at the cemetery. Shortly afterwards he died and from his papers it appeared that the body was that of Simeon the Just, who had held Christ in his arms in the Temple. The body was taken to the church of Sv. Marija Velika (comp. p. 99) and accredited with miracles. At the request of Elisabeth the Younger, daughter of Ban Stjepan Kotromanić of Bosnia, who visited Zadar with her husband Lewis the Great of Hungary in 1371, five nobles of Zadar commissioned the goldsmith Francesco di Antonio da Sesto of Milan to build a silver sarcophagus for the relic. With the assistance of Andrija Markov of Zagreb, Peter son of Blaž of Rača, Stipan Pribčev, and Mihovil Damjanov, the work was begun in 1377 and completed in 1381.

An oblong coffer with a pitched roof and gable-ends rests on two bronze angels (1678), cast from cannon captured from the Turks, which replaced four original angels in silver. The sarcophagus is covered with silver panels embossed with religious and historical scenes. On the front, Presentation of Christ in the Temple (after Giotto), flanked by the finding of the body of St Simeon (l.) and the triumphal entry of Lewis the Great into Zadar (r.). On the lid, a full length effigy of St Simeon. The ends are notable, both for their workmanship and the detailed picture of contemporary life. On the left, the storm-tossed boat that brought St Simeon's body to Zadar; on the right (supposedly) the wife of Ban Pavle Šubić taking the oath after being accused of adultery. The arms of King Lewis appear in the gable at both ends. Panels on the reverse depict (l.) the handing of a casket to St Simeon by Queen Elisabeth; (r.) the death of Ban Stjepan Kotromanić, Elisabeth's father; and (centre) an inscription giving the date and name of the maker. On the lid, amid scenes depicting the miracles wrought by the saint, the artist has included a self-portrait. The sarchophagus is opened annually on 8 October. Inside, further panels depict miracles done by the saint while, enclosed in glass, the mummified body wears a silver crown and an embroidered apron, the gift of Djordje Branković, despot of Serbia.

An earlier sarcophagus of St Simeon in stone (13C), also with a lifesize effigy, stands against the s. wall of the choir. On the N. side are a 17C Venetian chair and a memorial bust (1764) of Rossini, the engineer who restored Zadar's fortifications. The sacristy, entered from behind the altar, contains a number of 17C paintings. In the TREASURY (apply to sacristan) an outstanding Gothic chalice, the gift of Elisabeth the Younger of Hungary, is decorated with the Angevin arms. There is also a 17C silver dish.

Of some interest in the NAVE are a gilt stucco relief of the Madonna and Child (18C) at the E. end of the N. aisle; an ornate silver frame, in the s. aisle opposite, by Matej and Luka Boričević (1564); a 13C Romanesque relief of the Birth of Christ built into the wall next to the s. door.

In Zagrebačka ul. on the N. side of the church, houses with interesting details include the 15C *Palača Petrizio* and the *Palača Grisogono*, a rare example of a secular Romanesque building, with an upper story added in the 15C.

Returning to Trg oslobodjenja we see in front of us the *Bablja kula*, a tall pentagonal tower, from the fortifications of the 13C (altered inside in the 17C), the top of which commands a view of the town (open 8–12 5–7). Behind the tower we may pass between a remnant of the 13C wall and an earlier wall, while some remains of the Roman city wall in the courtyard of a Children's Clinic (Dječji dispanzer) recall a still earlier stage of fortification. The large raised space on the far side of the square with a line of five well heads (Trg pet bunara) is in fact the roof of an enormous cistern constructed in 1574 over the former moat. It provides access to the contemporary *Grimani Bastion*, the massive pentagonal key-point of the city's eastern defences. Filled up in 1829, the bastion now forms a children's playground, around which are scattered fragments of masonry from various vanished buildings.

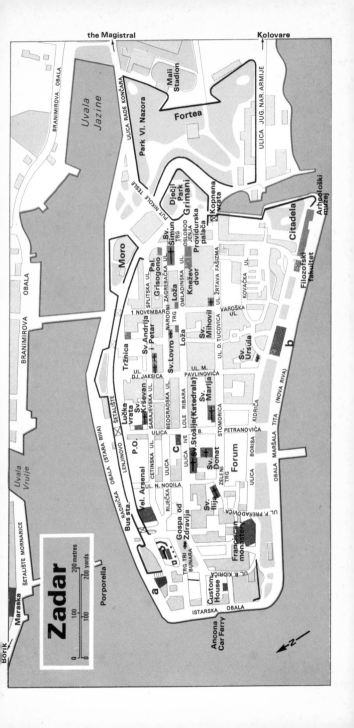

The main road leaves the town on the N. side of the bastion, but on foot it is more convenient to descend by steps on the s. side to the **Kopnena vrata**, or *Land Gate*, constructed in 1543 to a design by Mich. Sammicheli. The imposing façade in rusticated Doric is embellished with inscriptions and the escutcheons of its Venetian builders. The keystone of the centre arch bears the arms of Zadar (St Chrysogonus on horseback) while a large lion of St Mark fills the niche above.

At the seaward end of the former moat, and enclosed by the city bastions, is the pretty little harbour of **Foša**, crowded with small fishing and pleasure craft. A former guardhouse (1786) on a small mole has been transformed into a fish restaurant.

Beyond the broad road that separates it from the Grimani Bastion rises the **Velika utvrda**, or *Fortea*, erected in the late-16C as an advance post for defence. This great bastion is laid out as the pleasant *Park Vladimira Nazora* in which a former barracks (1789) is now the grammar school. The main entrance to the Fortea, on the E. side, displays the arms of Sforza Pallavicino, its builder, comprising a seven-headed hydra crowned with laurel leaves.

The tree-lined avenue to the s. leads shortly to *Kolovare*, Zadar's nearest beach (rfmts.), much patronized by the locals. Farther on, beyond a large polygonal well, the *Carev Bunar*, built in 1546 to supply water to ships, the rocky shore offers opportunities for bathing, but access is steep and only for experienced swimmers only. The large suburb of *Arbanasi* was settled by Albanians from the Lake Skadar region in the early 18C and a form of Albanian is still spoken.

To the left of the Land Gate a stone parapet skirts the Foša at the foot of the walls. At the harbour mouth stands a large corner bastion known as *Citadela*, flaunting the usual lion of St Mark high up on the wall and the date, 1574. The broad acacia-lined OBALA MARŠALA TITA, also known as the *Nova obala* or *Nova riva*, runs the length of the town on the seaward side. Constructed in 1874 when the s. walls were demolished, the promenade is a favourite resort of Zadrians especially for the evening corso, when the sunsets are often spectacular. The large neo-classical building on the right, erected by the Austrians in 1905 as a girls' college, houses the *Filozofski fakultet* (Faculty of Arts), a constituent college of the University of Zagreb; also a teachers' training college and the **Arheološki muzej** (Archaeological Museum). The museum possesses prehistoric jewellery, pottery and utensils, mosaics and sculpture from Roman times, and medieval Croatian items, but the collections are scattered throughout the building and only partially on view. Farther along we reach the hotel and kavana Zagreb, opposite the entrance to which (on the landward side) are excavated foundations of the small pre-Romanesque church of *Stomorica* (or Sv. Ursula), with an unusual plan consisting of a rectangular entrance hall and five apses.

The mainly residential suburb of *Voštarnica* beyond the main harbour, can be reached either by footbridge or by passenger ferry from the bus station to the breakwater opposite. Along the shore are a small shipyard, yacht marina, and the *Maraska Distillery* where, among other liqueurs, is made the famous maraschino (visit by application to the Turistbiro). Beyond the distillery is a small bathing-place and in c.4 km. we come to the main beach of *Borik*, with hotels, restaurant, autocamp and all modern facilities. On the other side of Voštarnica, in Ul. Ivana Gundulića, the church of Sv. Ivan incorporates fragments from earlier churches, including a Romanesque relief of the agnus dei, a 15C relief of St

Francis receiving the Stigmata, and a medieval altar rail, while in the parish office is a marble relief of St Jerome attributed to Andrija Aleši.

B Excursions from Zadar

FROM ZADAR TO NIN, 18 km. Buses several times daily throughout the year. Beyond Borik (see above), asphalt gives place to gravel, with views out to sea on the left. At 10 km. a by-road diverges to *Petrčane* (2 km.) a village with a sandy beach and restaurant.—Just beyond (15 km.) *Zaton*, on a tumulus (l.) stands the tiny 11C church of Sv. Nikola, a typical example of early Croatian architecture, with a nave and triple apses forming a cruciform plan; the crossing was surmounted with a fortified watch tower at the time of the Turkish invasion.—17 km. Crossroads. To the left *Privlaka* (6 km.; Rest.), occupies the site of Roman Brevilaqua, and preserves a pre-Romanesque church. Its sandy beaches mark it for tourist 'development'. Crossing a small stone bridge, with salt flats on our right, we come to the historic but devastated settlement of (18 km.) **Nin**, which stands on an artificially created island.

Nin, once the Roman municipium of *Aenona*, later Nona, became the chief town of Croatia in the 9–11C and preferred seat of Croatia's early peripatetic kings. Its prosperity continued under joint Croatian-Hungarian rule, but in 1328, as a result of deteriorating relations Nona sought the protection of Venice. In 1571 it was partly evacuated and slighted to avert Turkish invasions and in 1646 it was wholly abandoned and deliberately set on fire, from when it has steadily declined to its present sad condition. Nin was the seat of Bp. Gregory (Grgur Ninski), the leading champion of the Slavonic liturgy at the Council of Salona in 1059.

Ruins of the former town walls stand desolate on all sides amid a litter of Roman masonry. The rebuilt church of *Sv. Anzelm* is interesting only for the reliquaries from the former cathedral. In a case on the high altar, two silver caskets are believed to date from the 8–9C, and two more in front (14–15C) contain relics of SS Anselm and Marcella. A hand and two feet in silver gilt, the gift of Prince Pavao Šubić, were made in 1309. Behind the altar is a carved and gilded wooden sarcophagus on which a casket contains relics of St Ambrose.

A chapel remains on the s. side of the church from the earlier Gothic cathedral, hideously decorated but preserving on its altar a 15C statuette called Our Lady of Zečevo, the object of a local cult. Pilgrimages are made each May on the day of St Saviour (Spasov dan). A memorial stone to Bp. Divnić bears his effigy and the date 1530. Two Gothic heads representing SS Anselm and Ambrose have been set over the N. door.—Beside the church is a good Romanesque Campanile in undressed stone, with two-light windows set in the higher stories.

The *Museum* is opened on request (ask for the čuvar), and holds the keys to the other churches. There is a small collection of prehistoric and Roman ornaments and copies of some of the objects found at Nin but since removed. Close by is **Sv. Križ**, the church of the Holy Cross, erected in the 9C as the first cathedral of Nin. Cruciform in plan, with small apses between the chancel and the transepts and a central drum, Sv. Križ is a perfect specimen of the miniature rustic churches erected by the Croats during the period of their allegiance to Byzantium. Above the w. door a bevelled lintel richly ornamented with interlacing knots and scrolls in the Byzantine fashion, records the building of the church by the Croatian župan Godežav. The 13C church of *Sv. Ambroz*, formerly Benedictine and now a mere shell, has a good w. front incorporating an unusual window in the shape of a cross. Behind the church are part of the town walls and a gateway called *Rimska vrata*. The *Roman Remains*, on the N. side of the town, were partially excavated at the beginning of the present century. The existence of an amphitheatre, forum and temple, was established, but the best finds were removed and since the excavations were never finished the visible remains are fragmentary.

FROM ZADAR TO OBROVAC VIÂ THE ZRMANJA CANYON. By road and boat (frequent excursions organized from Zadar in summer); or by road (45 km.) and on foot (buses thrice daily, six times to Posedarje). A whole day should be devoted to the round trip. We take the Adriatic Highway (comp. Rte 8) to (25 km.) *Posedarje*, where boats can be hired. The boat crosses the almost landlocked Novigradsko more (Sea of Novigrad) and then pushes up the river Zrmanja through the impressive ZRMANJA CANYON, the bare rocky sides of which rise in places to over 600 ft. The ruined towers seen at intervals were erected by the Turks against the Venetians. The alternative is to continue along the main highway to the bridge over the Masleničko ždrilo. Here a right fork (gravel) joins the asphalt road from Starigrad (p. 65) just short of (36 km.) *Jasenice*. This runs below the Velebits (views, l.) and parallel with the Zrmanja canyon (r.) which may be reached on foot across scrubland. At the T-junction we turn right on gravel again and descend into the Zrmanja valley.

45 km. *Obrovac* (rest.; private rooms) is the usual terminal point for excursions. On a hill overlooking the town and the canyon is the 13C castle of the Gusić-Kurjaković family, now empty. The town is half Catholic and half Orthodox and since the town cemetery on a bank of the Zrmanja c. ½ m. downstream is accessible only by water, funeral processions of both faiths take place by boat. During the Turkish occupation of the interior, Obrovac marked the western limit of Turkish power in Dalmatia (1527–1685).

FROM ZADAR TO KARIN AND NOVIGRAD, 46 km., poor gravel road; buses twice daily. Leaving Zadar by Benkovačka cesta we follow the course of a Roman aqueduct, considerable remains of which front the town cemetery, with a memorial to the Borelli family by Ivan Rendić (1888).—Beyond (13 km.) *Donji Zemunik*, we branch left from the Benkovac road.—22 km. *Smilčić* is the site of one of the largest Neolithic settlements in the Balkans (1 m. w.; excavated in 1957–62). In the village itself rich finds have been made from the Illyrian, Roman, and early medieval periods. Most are now in Zadar museum. A number of villas of the 17C and 18C formerly belonged to noble families from Zadar.

From Smilčić a road (l.) leads directly in 10 km. to Novigrad (see below); or (turning left again after 2 km.) to *Islam Grčki* (7 km.), with the fortified 17C home of Serdar Stojan Janković, a prominent opponent of the Turks and hero of many epic folk songs.

We continue to Dubraja and (34 km.) **Karin** (Roman *Corinium*) at the S.E. end of the *Karinsko more*. This small 'sea' opens out of the Sea of Novigrad and like the latter is shallow, rich in fish, and almost landlocked. At the mouth of the small river Karišnica is the *Franciscan Monastery*, founded in 1429, but badly damaged by the Turks and rebuilt in 1736. The church retains a Gothic choir and the attractive Renaissance cloister has a decorated well head. Among architectural fragments from the medieval Croatian town of Karin, preserved in the monastery, is a pre-Romanesque Croatian cross with knot-work carving. Karin Fair (2 July) attracts residents from all over Ravni Kotari, many of whom wear national costume.

From Karin the road continues N.E. around the Karinsko more to Obrovac (see p. 106), but we return to Dubraja and (1 km. beyond) turn right for Novigrad. In (38 km.) *Pridraga* the 11C pre-Romanesque church of Sv. Martin has triple apses decorated with lesenes and shallow blind arcading, while about 100 yds away stand the foundations of an earlier Croatian church with six apses arranged in a circle.

43 km. **Novigrad** (*Mediteran*) a picturesque small town of Mediterranean type, stands on an attractive winding inlet above the s. shore of the Novigradsko more. It is well known for its oysters, mussels, and tuna fish. In the huge *Castle*, built in the 13C by the Gusić-Kurjaković family, Queen Elisabeth the Younger of Hungary, together with her daughter, Maria, were imprisoned in 1386–87 as a result of dynastic quarrels over the throne and here Elisabeth was murdered. Parts of the town walls can still be seen, and the pre-Romanesque church of *Sv. Kata* in the graveyard has stone fragments ornamented with interlacking knotwork, birds, and animals built into the w. front.

Excursions may be made by boat up the Zrmanja canyon to Obrovac (see p. 106) or to Posedarje (see p. 65).

FROM ZADAR TO BENKOVAC, 34 km., good gravel; buses 8 times a day. To *Donji Zemunik*, see above. We branch right for Benkovac.— At 30 km. a track (r.) passes under the railway line to *Raštević* (1 km.), a further km. beyond which the ruined medieval castle of Kličevica stands on a spur of rock overlooking a narrow canyon.—34 km. *Benkovac*, a bustling small town (1500 inhab.), with pleasant broad streets, was for the period between the two world wars, when Zadar was Italian, the cultural and administrative centre of the Croatian Ravni Kotari. There is a market every Monday and on the 10th of each month a colourful fair. High above the town stands the well preserved 14C castle of the Benković family.

A little beyond Benkovac, just left of the road to Knin, is the hill of Podgradje, site of the Roman city of *Asseria*. The extensive site has been well quarried and little remains except the lower courses of the Roman walls on the N. The gravestones round the primitive small church of Sv. Duh (Holy Spirit) consist of Roman fragments, some of them bearing ornament and inscriptions. The hilltop commands views of the surrounding plain and of the chain of beacon towers, used to give warning of the Turks, that extends over the hills on all sides.—To the N. of Benkovac, on the road to Smilčić, is the village of (3 km.) *Kula Atlagić*. Here the Catholic church (Sv. Petar) has Romanesque features and a pre-Romanesque s. wall with primitive blind arcading, while the Orthodox church of Sv. Nikola (1440), Gothic in style, contains a large 18C iconostasis displaying icons in both Byzantine and western styles.

C The Zadar Archipelago

The Zadar Archipelago consists of over 200 islands of greatly varying size and character, extending from Silba in the N.W. to Kurba Vela in the S.E. Many are exceedingly fertile, being specially rich in figs, olives, and grapes, and the fishing grounds around them are generally reckoned the richest in the Adriatic. They also represent an area of great natural beauty which, because of its relative inaccessibility, remains largely unspoiled. Accommodation is generally simple and informal and transport slow. While frequent steamers ply from Zadar to all the main islands and towns, many of the more interesting places have to be visited by small boats hired locally, of which, fortunately, there is no shortage. The islands are here described from N.W. to S.E.

Silba (400 inhab.). The most northerly island of the group, lying no more than 4 nautical miles from Ilovik (see p. 90) and $7\frac{1}{2}$ m. from Lošinj (see Rte. 13), covers an area of $5\frac{3}{4}$ sq. m. Olives, almonds, grapes and figs are grown, and goat's milk cheese produced. Silba has shingle and sandy bays and is a favourite haunt of artists and writers from Zagreb. There is no electricity on the island. The only settlement, dominating both shores from a ridge, is *Silba* (Pensions, Zalič and Kupalište; rest.; steamers every weekday from Zadar, three times a week from Rijeka and twice weekly from Koper, Rovinj, Pula, Mali Lošinj and and principal places s. of Zadar), a picturesque fishing village that prospered as a maritime centre in the 17–18C but subsequently fell into decline. Baroque paintings by Carlo Ridolfi adorn the parish church, the parish offices and the church of Gospa od Karmena, while his canvas in Sv. Marko (1637), dated 1640, includes a self-portrait. Gravestones of former sea captains are carved with reliefs of ships. Walls and one tower survive of the 16C fortress built to guard against pirates. A curious stone look-out tower, called Toreta, was erected in the last century.

Immediately E. of Silba is the larger but less visited island of **Olib** (580 inhab.), with an area of 11 sq. m. The main occupations of the islanders are fishing and, on the open E. side of the island, the growing of grapes and olives. On the wooded w. side lies the only village, *Olib* (Pension Vila Justina; steamers from Zadar every weekday, once a week from Mali Lošinj), with a low fortified tower. In the treasury of the parish church are a Gothic cross, monstrance and pyx, while the cemetery church has two Baroque altars and a 16C polyptych.

To the w. and s. of Silba is a group of four islands, all inhabited but with little to offer the casual visitor: *Premuda*, *Skarda*, *Ist*, and *Molat*. Molat is the largest, with three small villages and a memorial in Uvala Jazi to mark the site of a notorious Italian prison camp of 1941–43. The parish church has a Gothic chalice and Renaissance and Baroque crucifixes in its treasury and a Baroque painting of SS Simeon and Michael on the altar. The waters around these islands are particularly suitable for underwater fishing.

The largest island of the Zadar Archipelago is the well-named **Dugi Otok** (5500 inhab.), meaning 'Long Island', situated in the chain of islands farthest from the mainland. Nowhere exceeding 3 m. in width, and extending for 27 m., it has an area of 48 sq. m. The seaward shore consists of a high, barren ridge rising sheer from the sea to over 1000 ft, while the gentler shore facing the mainland is partly wooded. On this side all the villages are situated. The islanders, traditionally occupied with agriculture and fishing, are increasingly involved with tourism.

In the N. is *Božava* (Božava; steamer 4 times a week from Zadar), a picturesque fishing village with a good pebble and sand beach. The small church in the cemetery (1469) contains a 15C crucifixion in wood and two ornamented stone slabs from an earlier, pre-Romanesque building (9–11C). Pleasant excursions can be made to the deeply indented bay of Soliščica, with good beach at *Soline*; the long sandy beach at *Saharun*; and the smaller islands of *Zverinac* (18C Fanfogna villa in village), *Sestrunj* and *Rivanj*, all visited by regular steamers. Of the small villages s. of Božava (regular boat services from Zadar), the farthest, *Savar*, has a church incorporating a 9C pre-Romanesque chapel.

Except by boat there is no means of communication between the N. and S. halves of Dugi Otok, for the central part consists of trackless, barren rock, rising to a peak at *Vela Straža* (1110 ft), the highest point on the island. Offshore lies the small island of *Rava* (300 inhab.; steamer 4 times weekly from Zadar) with many coves for bathing and fishing, and beyond Rava the larger island of Iž (comp. below).

The southern line of villages on Dugi begins with *Luka* (rest.; steamer 4 times a week from Zadar), with a pleasant rock and sand beach. In the church is a 15C painting of the Dead Christ. Two of the local limestone caves, Strašna peć and Kozja peć, are rich in stalactites and stalagmites. *Zaglav*, to the s., beyond Žman, is picturesquely situated on a high cliff. The Franciscan Gothic church of Sv. Mihovil (1458), preserves two processional crosses and a rustic crucifixion, but the attached Glagolitic monastery was rebuilt in the 19C.

Sali (Pension Kornat; rest.; cinema; beach; steamers every weekday from Zadar), a thriving fishing centre (1200 inhab.) with a fine natural harbour, is the largest settlement on Dugi Otok, with a cannery and fish-meal factory. The parish church of *Uzašašće Marijino* (The Assumption) has a narrow 15C nave with recently uncovered wall paintings of galleys and a more spacious E. end added in 1584. The reredos incorporates an earlier painted panel of the Madonna. Among old houses round the harbour, are the Renaissance Gverini house on the N. side and the 17C Baroque Petriccioli house, now the Pension Kornat. A small festival with donkey races is held on the second Sunday in July.

Sali is the centre for excursions to the southern part of Dugi Otok and the Kornat Islands. The deeply indented bay of Telašćica (6 m. long) at the S.E. end of Dugi is entered by boat from Sali viâ the strait, Mala proversa, on the N. side of which stand the foundations of a Roman summer villa. A frequent halt is the tiny bay of Mir near the salt lake of Mir (rest.; camp site). The impressive cliffs on the w. can be seen from the far side of the lake, but are better viewed from the sea.

Immediately s. of Dugi Otok begins the large complex of 125 islands known collectively as the **Kornati** (Kornat Islands or Kornat Archipelago), named from the largest one among them, Kornat. Consisting almost entirely of barren rock, they are uninhabited except for a few seasonal settlements when the owners of the land, mainly from Sali and Murter, bring sheep to graze and cultivate the miniscule plantations of figs, olives and vines that the islands are able to support. *Kornat Island*, 15 m. long and 12¼ sq. m. in area, is the largest uninhabited island in the Adriatic, although a ruined medieval fortress on Tarac hill (opposite Levrnaka island) and the foundations of an early-Christian basilica below bear witness to past habitation. Other large islands in the group are Žut, Sit, Levrnaka, Jadra, Lavsa and Vela Kurba. The Kornati are particularly famous as rich fishing grounds and for their scenic beauty, the most interesting being the outer line of islands running from Levrnaka to Kurba Vela. Frequent excursions are organized in summer from Sali, Zadar, Biograd, and Šibenik.

Iž, a fertile and populous island (1800 inhab.), lies midway between Dugi Otok and Ugljan. It has celebrated olive groves and is the only island in the northern Adriatic to produce its own pottery. It won local fame during the Second World War as the first island to take arms against the Italian occupation. There are two main settlements (steamer to both from Zadar on weekdays). *Iž Veli* (Pension Slanac, beach) is an

attractive fishing village. Among its older houses are the former residence of the Canigietti family and the Fanfogna house, adapted as a
school. In the less compact *Iž Mali*, the small circular church of Sv.
Marija Iška (9–11C) above the harbour, was enlarged in the 17C. The
neighbouring Kaštel Begna is a fortified summer mansion.

Rather different in character from the rest of the archipelago are the
two large inshore islands of Ugljan and Pašman.

Ugljan is the most densely populated island (10,252 inhab.) in the
Adriatic. With a length of 13 m. and 17½ sq. m. in area, it is steep and
rocky on the N. and seaward side, but exceptionally rich and fertile in
the populous E. It lies under 5 m. from Zadar.

At the N. end is the scattered village of *Ugljan* (rest.; steamer daily
from Zadar), predominantly agricultural in character, with a Franciscan
Monastery (1430) attractively situated on the edge of the harbour (open
daily 10–11 & 5–6). The rustic cloister has excellent Romanesque
capitals brought from Zadar (four angels, three fishes with a single head,
eight heads intertwined with foliage, etc.), and preserves the gravestone
of Simun Begna, Bp. of Modruš and Senj (1537). The simple Gothic
church of Sv. Jeronim attached to the convent was dedicated in 1447.
In the sacristy is a Gothic trefoil stoup and there is a Gothic crucifixion
in the small chapel above. The parish church on a hill overlooking the
village has good plate, including a Gothic cross, pyx and chalice, all in
gold, and a later gold chalice dated 1515.

A pleasant excursion may be made by boat (1½ hr) or on foot (¾ hr) to the sandy
bay of *Muline*, where the foundations of an early-Christian basilica and mausoleum
have been excavated and extensive remains of a Roman villa show tiled and mosaic
floors.

At a midway point on the island and immediately opposite Zadar is
Preko (rest.; steamer daily from Zadar), the largest of the island villages
(2400 inhab.). The small 12C church of Sv. Ivan has part of a Roman
frieze built into the w. wall. About 60 yds offshore from Preko is the
beautiful small island of *Galovac* with a Franciscan Glagolitic Monastery (1443) noted for its luxuriant garden. Over the high altar of the
church (1596) is a Madonna and Child with Saints by Zorzi Ventura of
Zadar (17C). Preko is the starting point for the climb to the *Fortress
of Sv. Mihovil* (1–1½ hr), whose ruins dominate the island. Erected in
1203 by the Venetians after the sack of Zadar by the Fourth Crusade,
the fortress was restored by Hungarians in the mid-14C. Incorporated
into the fortress is the 10C church of a former Benedictine monastery.
Unsurpassed views from the fortress (850 ft) extend over the surrounding islands and to the mainland opposite.

Kali (rest.; steamer daily from Zadar) the second largest village (2250
inhab.) on Ugljan and the most picturesque, is crowded with the fishing
vessels of the prosperous local zadruga or co-operative. Visitors can
usually arrange to go out with the fleet (two nights and a day).

Kukljica (Pension Kukljica; steamer daily from Zadar), the southernmost village
has a good beach which is attracting visitors.

Divided from Ugljan only by a strait (11 yds wide) dug in 1883,
Pašman is similar in size and geological formation. Its 3760 inhab. are
occupied in farming and the island is as yet untouched by tourism.

The northern villages of Ždrelac, Dobropoljana, and Nevidjane, afford good beaches for excursions (daily steamer service from Zadar and Biograd). In *Pašman* (rest.; beach) half way down the E. coast the Baroque parish church has a medieval choir and two Gothic processional crosses in the treasury. In the village of *Kraj* (daily steamers from Zadar and Biograd) the Franciscan Monastery of Sv. Jeronim has a relief of St Jerome (1554; sch. of Andrija Aleši) above the w. door, an attractive Baroque cloister (1683), and 15–17C paintings in the refectory.

The largest village is **Tkon** (766 inhab.; rest.; daily steamers from Zadar and Biograd) at the s. end opposite Biograd. The parish church has a Madonna attributed to the 15C Zadar artist, Petar Jordanić. The walled monastery of *Čokovac* (open 9–11, 4–6) on a high hill overlooking Tkon can be reached in 40 min on foot, or with less effort in 15 min from Ugrenići, a coastal hamlet nearer Kraj (comp. above).

Founded by Benedictines from Biograd after their town was razed by Venice in 1125, the monastery was repeatedly attacked until after the peace of Zadar in 1358, when most of the present buildings were erected. It became a leading centre of the Slavonic rite and Glagolitic writing. The monastery was closed by the Napoleonic invaders and reopened only in 1956 as the sole Benedictine monastery in Yugoslavia. During the war it served as the secret H.Q. of British intelligence agents in this part of the Adriatic.

The monastic church, a plain Gothic edifice dedicated to Sv. Kuzma i Damjan, was begun in 1367. The w. doorway has a statue of the Madonna and Child in the tympanum with the date of the church's completion (1418) and the arms of Bp. Maripetro of Split. A contemporary statue of one of the dedicatees stands on the w. gable. In the interior hangs a large Gothic Crucifixion. The sacristy is a Romanesque fragment of the original foundation.

15 FROM ZADAR TO SPLIT

ROAD, 164 km. (102 m.). ADRIATIC HIGHWAY. 30 km. Biograd.—76 km. Šibenik.
—137 km. Trogir.—164 km. Split.
BUSES. Frequent express service between Zadar, Šibenik and Split; many slower services stopping at smaller places.—STEAMERS daily from Zadar to Šibenik and Split.

Leaving Zadar by Benkovačka cesta, we turn right at the crossroads to follow the coast road s. with views out to sea of Ugljan and Pašman. —11 km. *Sukošan* (rest.) a dilapidated village with a good sandy beach. The 17C parish church of Sv. Kasjan has a decorated pre-Romanesque altarpiece built into the wall over the side entrance, and similar pre-Romanesque decoration can be seen on the doorposts of the cemetery church nearby. Ruins of the summer palace of Abp. Valaresso of Zadar (15C) remains near the harbour. A gravel by-road leads inland from Sukošan to join (8 km.) the road from Zadar to Bankovac.

Continuing s. with the island of Pašman on our right we pass through (19 km.) *Krmčine* with remains of the Roman aqueduct from Vrana to Zadar. On the low peninsula of Tukljača just before the road forks right to Turanj is a well-preserved small pre-Romanesque church (11C). A Glagolitic inscription on the lintel mentions the Mogorovići, one of the twelve tribes of Croatia that concluded the treaty of union with

Hungary in 1102.—23 km. *Turanj* takes name from the large fortress erected in the 17C as a defence against the Turks. A corner tower and part of the battlemented walls still remain, and other parts have been incorporated into the houses along the front.—25 km. *Filipjakov* (Zadar; autocamp) a pleasant village, was once the harbour for the Benedictine abbey of Rogovo, c. 1 m. inland. Its small church (Sv. Rok; 12–14C), easily reached by a good gravel road, contains a fine painted Gothic crucifixion (key from parish priest at Filipjakov).

30 km. **Biograd** or *Biograd na moru*, just off the highway to the right (1 km.) is reviving, after centuries of neglect and stagnation, as a pleasant seaside resort (2400 inhab.) with a modern centre and a pine-shaded beach. So thorough were the two destructions of Biograd that all that remains of the historic small town is a few fragments in the modest town museum.

Hotels. Adriatic, 105 R. with bath; **Ilirija**, both near the beach. **Motel Slijeme** on the main road.—Two AUTOCAMPS on beach.
Restaurants. *Slovenija*, *Evropa*.
Buses several times daily to *Zadar*, *Šibenik*, etc.—STEAMER daily to Pašman island and Zadar.
Beach. Pine shaded, shingle and pebble entry, sandy bottom.

Biograd, meaning 'white city' (Alba Civitas in the early Middle ages) became one of the seats of the peripatetic kings of Croatia and in 1050 was made a bishopric by Petar Krešimir, who later installed his court here permanently. Koloman was crowned here in 1102 (Rex Hungariae, Croatiae et Dalmatiae) as a result of the union with Hungary, but in 1125 the town was razed by Doge Michieli. After the sack of Zadar by the Fourth Crusade (1202) a number of refugees here founded 'New Zadar' (Zara Nueva), which, when they returned home, became Zara Vecchia, still its name in Italian. Later fortified against the Turks, the town was abandoned and burnt in 1646 during the Candian War.
A good gravel road, lined with cypresses, leads inland through the former Borelli estates, now a state co-operative, in the fertile Vransko polje, reclaimed from marshland in 1897. At 6 km. we turn right, catching sight of Vransko jezero (Vrana Lake).—At 10 km. **Vrana** is the enormous ruin of the *Castle* of first the Knights Templar (1138–1311) and, after their suppression, of the Knights of St John (1311–92). The castle fell into disuse after the coming of the Turks (1538) and was dismantled during the Venetian occupation of 1647. Even more interesting is the *Turkish Han* or Caravanserai (1644) of the native vizier and Kapudanbaša (Admiral) Jusuf Mašković, one of very few Turkish buildings still standing on the Adriatic coast and one of the best examples of a caravanserai in Yugoslavia, although dilapidated and used as a farmyard. A triple archway with oriental arches gives access to a broad courtyard, with a Turkish well. A second courtyard is lined on three sides by travellers' rooms on two floors each with a chimney. A walk round the outside of the han gives an idea of its massive construction and a view of two Moorish windows in the w. wall.—The road continues to Benkovac (see p. 107) while s. and w. lies Vransko jezero (see below).

The Adriatic Highway now runs a little inland.—33 km. *Crvena Luka* a conspicuously signposted tourist settlement has excellent accommodation in hotels or individual chalets (220 R), its own boats, a night club, and facilities for water ski-ing and other sports.—35 km. *Pakoštane* (rest.) a village with a good sand and shingle beach, shaded by pine trees, where the Club Méditerranée maintains a permanent camp. Within 15 min walk is the semi-salt *Vransko jezero*, the largest lake in Dalmatia (11½ sq. m.) rich in mullet, mackerel and eels. It offers excellent duck shooting in the season. A poor gravel road runs past the lake to Vrana (see above).

After traversing the narrow neck of land dividing Vransko jezero from the sea we cross the cut between them to (52 km.) *Pirovac* (motel; autocamp) on the deeply indented bay of the same name, with a pleasant pebble and sand beach and remains of 16C defensive walls. In the chapel of the Draganić-Vrančić family in the cemetery is a rich Gothic sarcophagus (1447) by Andrija Budčić and Lorenzo Pincino.

About 4 km. beyond Pirovac an asphalt road branches right to **Murter** (7 sq. m.), a populous small island linked to the mainland by a bridge over the Murterski kanal. Crossing the bridge at (6 km.) *Tijesno* (Borovnik; cinema; beach), a pleasant village straddling the channel at its narrowest point, the road continues to (13 km.) *Betina* (rest., sandy beach) and (15 km.) *Murter* (Pension Slanica; three restaurants; sandy beach; cinema) the main settlement (2150 inhab.) on the island. The Baroque parish church (Sv. Mihovil) has a high altar by Pio and Vicko dell' Acqua (1770). Murter is a favourite starting point for excursions to the Kornat Islands (see p. 109).

64 km. *Vodice* (Punta, 300R; autocamp; steamer from Šibenik once a week) is an inexpensive small resort (2900 inhab.) very popular with Yugoslavs. The road swings inland to cross (71 km.) the handsome bridge across the Krka estuary.

76 km. **ŠIBENIK**, one of the leading cities of the Adriatic coast, with a fine cathedral, lies on a long, narrow and almost landlocked lagoon near the mouth of the river Krka. Electro-chemical and other industries N. and S. of the old centre have encouraged a rapid rise of population in recent years and the town (26,300 inhab.) is an important port exporting bauxite and a lively centre, though not well situated for sea-bathing. May and Oct tend to have the greatest rainfall.

Railway station, Ul. Ive Lole Ribara, for trains to *Perković* on the Zagreb–Split line.

Steamer quay. Molo (or Gat) Krka for all services. Express service daily to all major towns on the coast, local service to offshore islands and Skradin daily except Sundays.

Hotels. Jadran; Krka, kavana; both in town. **Jadrija** bungalows, beach, 3 km. from town at the main bathing establishment at the mouth of the river Krka.

Autocamp at *Martinska* across the bay, 150 tents.

Restaurants. *Rijeka*, Zagrebačka ul.; *Skradin*, Cesta bratstva jedinstva; *Turist*, Obala oslobodjenja; *Dubravka*, in the Šubićevac fortress; *Šibenik*, Ul. Jugoslavenske armije.

Kavanas. *Hotel Krka*, Obala Jugoslavenske mornarice; *Hotel Jadran*, Obala oslobodjenja; *Medulić*, Ul. 12 kolovoza, 1941.

Post Office. Ul. Vladimira Nazora.—INFORMATION OFFICE. Turističko društvo, Trg Sime Matavulja.

Bus Station, Obala Jugoslavenske mornarice. LONG DISTANCE BUSES to all the major towns on the coast and inland. LOCAL BUSES to Vodice, Skradin, Drniš and the surrounding villages.

Beaches. *Jadrija*, at the mouth of the Krka estuary, with cabins, showers, café; concrete foreshore, stony bottom. Boats every half hour.—*Martinska*, rock and pebble, restaurant, across the harbour (ferry every 15 min).—Open-air SWIMMING POOL at the N.W. end of the town.

Amusements. *Narodno kazalište* (theatre), Poljana Maršala Tita.—Children's festival every other year (odd years).

History. Šibenik, a Slav foundation, grew up round the fortified hill of Sv. Ana, and is first mentioned in 1066 when a special assembly was called here by Petar Krešimir IV. Despite two short periods of Venetian occupation during the 12C, its Slavonic character remained and was augmented after the destruction of Biograd (1125), when most of the inhabitants fled to Šibenik. In 1167 Stephen IV of Hungary–Croatia gave the city a charter, and in 1298 it was made a bishopric by Pope Boniface VIII. Like other Dalmatian cities, Šibenik became involved in the struggles between Hungary–Croatia and Venice and was ruled for a time by the Croatian feudal lords of Kačić and Šubić and later by King Stjepan Tvrtko of

Bosnia. In 1412 Venice gained the upper hand, fostering two centuries of prosperity and learning in Šibenik. At the same time it suffered heavily from the Turks; seven major attacks culminated in 1647 when the town was heavily besieged by Tekely Pasha of Bosnia and successfully defended by Baron C. M. Degenfeld. From 1797 to 1815 Šibenik formed part of Napoleon's Illyria before passing to Austria until the First World War. In 1918 it was briefly occupied by Italy but joined Yugoslavia in 1921 as a result of the Treaty of Rapallo. In Aug 1936 Edward VIII here embarked in the yacht 'Nahlin' for Istanbul, at a time when Anglo-Italian relations precluded departure from Venice. The town was occupied by Italy and Germany in 1941–44.

Among the best known natives of Šibenik are Juraj Šižgorić (1420–1509) the scholar and humanist; Antun Vrančić (Antonius Verancius, 1504–73), Abp. of Gran and Primate and Viceroy of Hungary–Croatia; his nephew, Faust Vrančić (1551–1617), philosopher and inventor; the engravers, Martin Kolunić-Rota (Martinus Rota Sibenicensis, ?1532–82/3) and Natale Bonifacio (1548–92); Ivan Tomko Mrnavić (1580–?1637), scholar and historian; the painter Nikola Vladanov (?1390–?1466); the short-story writer, Simo Matavulj (1852–1908); and the Italian writer, Nicolò Tommaseo (1802–74).

The principal coastal steamers moor at the mole opposite the Krka Hotel near the Bus Station and the railway. To the right colourful local craft bring in fish and agricultural produce. To the left a pleasant promenade, busy morning and afternoon with local steamers bringing children to and from school, and in the evening with the Corzo, faces the Kanal Sv. Ante across the landlocked bay. The church of *Sv Nikola* (1451), by Ivan Pribislavić, has a coffered wooden ceiling (1762) and ex-votos in the form of model ships.

Beyond the modern Town Hall and the Hotel Jadran, with a bronze fountain, pleasant gardens front a section of the old fortifications that extend from a large pentagonal *Tower* to the cathedral steps. A pair of 18C French cannon and a bell, cast in Ancona in 1266 and recently dredged from the sea, stand in front of the Gothic *Mliječna vrata*, while busts of local partisan heroes line the walks. The next rectangular tower that projects to seaward once held the Venetian law courts and dungeons. The Renaissance *Morska vrata* opens between the Governor's and the Bishop's palaces, affording the most picturesque approach to the cathedral. A better first impression of the exterior is, however, gained by continuing along the waterfront as far as *Sv. Dominik*, a church hideously rebuilt in 1906, but preserving old fragments behind and, inside, paintings by Palma Giovane and Matteo Ponzoni, from which we turn back to mount a broad flight of steps.

The ***Cathedral of Sv. Jakov,** a striking amalgam of Gothic and Renaissance styles with many individual features, stands in an enclosed square (Trg republike) just above the quay.

The building was begun in 1431 on the site of an older church after a design sometimes attributed to Ant. di Pier Paolo Dalle Masegne, by the Italian architects Franc. di Giacomo, Lor. Pincino, and Ant. Busato with the assistance of local masons. The side walls and w. front were erected to the height of the w. and N. portals (the decoration of which was completed by Bonino da Milano), when in 1441 local dissatisfaction was expressed with both the old-fashioned (Gothic) style and the cost. We may note in passing that this was the year of the foundation of King's College Chapel, Cambridge. Juraj Matejević Dalmatinac (Giorgio Orsini) was appointed master of the works and under his direction the side walls were completed and the choir added. The apses, baptistery (1462), and sacristy (1454) followed, after which Orsini retired to Italy leaving the work to assistants. After his death in 1475 had brought work to a halt, the building was resumed in 1477 under Nikola Firentinac, who completed the aisles and the w. front and placed the dome above the crossing. The nave roof was completed to his design by Bart. di Giac. da Mestre and his son Pietro, who virtually finished the building. The wheel-window in the w. front was carved by Ivan Mastičević (Giov. da Zara; 1536) and the church was consecrated in 1555. In 1850–60 the cupola and the nave vault were restored.

The WEST FRONT shows clearly the three stages of construction. Its unusual but successful resolution of Gothic and Renaissance elements became the model for the composite style that survived so long on the Adriatic coast. The richly ornamented *W. Portal* is by Bonino da Milano. On either side a fluted column carries a two-storied tabernacle. The jambs are carved with figures of the apostles culminating in a keystone depicting Christ blessing. The graceful upper part with semicircular gable and quadrants over the aisles in Lombardesque fashion is purely Renaissance in feeling, though the large wheel-window in the centre is Gothic in detail.

The N. or LION PORTAL (Lavlja vrata), in the centre of the Gothic N. wall, is partially composed of Romanesque elements from the earlier church. Octagonal columns on a pair of lions support on their spreading capitals Romanesque statues of Adam and Eve. Gothic tabernacles above hold figures of SS Peter and Paul, by Juraj Dalmatinac. Above the pointed windows a rich cornice of interlaced trefoils resting on corbelled heads is topped with a continuous horizontal cable moulding, another surprising blend of Romanesque, Gothic, and Renaissance motifs.

The Gothic elements appear less dominant from the far side of the square, whence we see also the singular barrel vaulted roofs of the nave, aisles, and transept, and the octagonal cupola. The system of tongued and grooved stone employed on such a scale is unique to Šibenik and an impressive feat of construction.

A narrow opening gives access to the EAST END, where the three *Apses*, rising from different levels, are given cohesion by a magnificent *Frieze of 74 portrait heads of contemporary figures. On the N.E. angle a lively scroll and inscription record the laying of the foundations of the choir and apses in 1443 by Juraj Dalmatinac.

In the beautiful **Interior,** seen to advantage in the early morning, the nave and aisles are divided by graceful Gothic arcades resting on six pairs of columns with modified Corinthian capitals. An unusual frieze is carved with acanthus leaves blowing in the wind, above which a low triforium in classical style rises to a plain clerestory. An undecorated barrel-vault binds together the disparate elements to produce a harmonious effect of proportion and spaciousness. The aisles are vaulted.

S. Aisle. Tomb of Juraj Šižgorić, executed by Andrija Aleši (1454) to a design by Juraj Dalmatinac; Crucifixion by Juraj Petrović (1455). In the *N. Aisle* are the tomb of Ivan Stafilić (16C), a painting of SS Fabian and Sebastian by Filippo Zanimberti (early 17C), and two angels in marble relief by Nikola Firentinac. The wooden pulpit is by Girolamo Mondella (1624).

The raised CHOIR, approached by concentric steps between a balustrade, has seats of carved marble. The delicate balustrading of the galleries is carried round two of the piers to form a pair of ingenious ambones. The altar rails are by Nikola Firentinac. The decorated apses are pierced by windows in a transitional style between Gothic and Renaissance.

From the s. apse stairs descend to the remarkable *BAPTISTERY, by Juraj Dalmatinac, a little gem of Italian late-Gothic design. It is square in plan but the walls are curved to form shallow apses. At the four corners low columns support the domed roof. Niches above the columns were intended for statuettes of prophets, but only two are filled (Simeon and David). Above, profusely decorated ribs taper to a central boss carved with the image of God the Father. The conches of the apses are carved and Gothic tracery fills the spandrels above. Angels with flowing draperies occupy the segments of the dome. The marble font, carried by a trio of putti, is the work of Aleši. The outer door leads into a graceful loggia at the foot of the steps to the Morska vrata.

The *Sacristy*, approached by a long flight of stairs, is ornamented in the manner of the apses and furnished with carved chests by Mondella.

On the N.E. side of the square stands the dignified **Loža** (Town Loggia; 1532–42), a long arcaded building of two stories in the style of Sammicheli, restored after bomb damage. The small church of *Sv. Barbara* (1447–51), opposite the E. end of the cathedral, was built by Ivan Pribislavić and has a relief of St Nicholas by Bonino da Milano on the N. wall. Adjoining the S.E. corner of the cathedral is the **Biskupska palača** (1439–41; comp. p. 114) with a late Gothic arcaded court and, in an inner court, an excellent traceried three-light window. The figure above represents St Michael, patron saint of the city. Two polyptychs by Nikola Vladanov (?1340–1466), a Šibenik painter are kept in the palace chapel. The former *Kneževa palača* (15C), next to the Bishop's Palace, bears a fine statue of Niccolò Marcello (1609–11) and the elaborate escutcheon of the Šubić family. It now houses the **Gradski muzej** (Town Museum, open 9–12, 5–7 daily except Mon), with archaeological collections and exhibits devoted to the history of Šibenik and the Partisan movement.

The *Statue of Juraj Dalmatinac*, at the w. end of the cathedral square is the last work of Ivan Meštrović (1961). The narrow Ul. Juraj Dalmatinca mounts in steps past two Venetian Gothic houses, and bears left above the *Velika čatrnja* (Great Well) built by (?) Giac. Correr (1446) and decorated with escutcheons and a Lion of St Mark. This, the oldest part of the city is embellished with a great number of interesting doorways, escutcheons, and inscriptions. The *Palača Orsini*, residence of Juraj Dalmatinac, was burnt down in the 16C, but the excellent doorway still stands, carved, presumably by Dalmatinac himself, with a bear, symbolizing the sculptor's assumed Italian name (Orsini), and with the tools of his trade. Turning back we diverge almost immediately left along Ul. Andrije Kačića and through an archway by a quaint artificial grotto of 1926 to the monastery church of *Sv. Lovro* (1677–97), with Baroque altars by Pio and Vicko dall'Acqua and (in the sacristy) an inscribed silver chalice presented by Marshal Marmont (1808). A staircase by the w. end of the church gives access to the monastery where a collection of paintings (15–18C) is poorly exhibited in the refectory. Among them are a 15C Madonna and Child (school of Bellini), the Assumption by (?) Dom. Robusti, and a portrait of Napoleon (the only one in Yugoslavia) by Andrea Appiani. The Codex

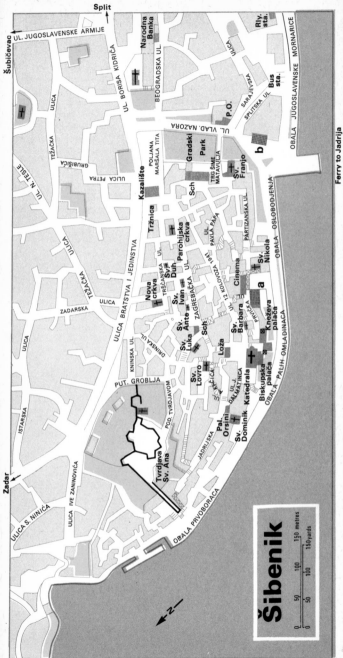

of Bp. Kosirić (16C) is illustrated with many fine drawings, although many more have been stolen.

Continuing farther we pass the nunnery of *Sv. Luca* and the fine Gothic *Palača Foscolo* and come to the small 15C church of *Sv. Ante* (undergoing restoration). Behind is the attractive little Trg pućkih kapetana with a well. Steps on the left lead up through a maze of narrow streets to the 12–13C Fortress of *Sv. Ana* (rebuilt 16–17C), now used as a signalling station. In picturesque Tršćanska ul. is the so-called *Nova Crkva* or church of *Sv. Marija Milosrdje* (Our Lady of Compassion) built (1516) in transitional Gothic–Renaissance style, with a richly decorated interior. The coffered ceiling (1623–32) is by Girol. Mondella, Ivan Bojković, and Andrija Sisanović, the wall paintings by Mihovil Parkić (1619) and Antun Moneghin (1628). A Venetian Gothic guildhall adjoins the church and in the wall of the courtyard between them is a good Pietà by Nikola Firentinac (1502). Another relief, showing the burial of Christ, by Ivan Pribislavić, adorns the bell tower (by Ivan Skoko, 1742–59).

ZAGREBAČKA UL., the medieval main street to the s., retains many churches and patrician houses. Midway, is the Renaissance church of **Sv. Ivan Krstitelj* (John the Baptist, 15–17C), with a graceful ornamented staircase and balcony on the s. side by Nikola Firentinac and Ivan Pribislavić (1460). A lintel by Pribislavić beneath the balcony, depicting St John, shows the city and cathedral of Šibenik in the background. The Baroque bell tower, erected to celebrate the withdrawal of the Turks from Dalmatia, incorporates a Turkish clock of 1648. Beyond the Renaissance *Palača Mišić* lies the small Krešimirov trg, with a local market and the *Palača Draganić*, behind which a narrow alley leads left to the church of *Sv. Duh* (Holy Spirit), a small gem of Dalmatian Renaissance architecture built by Vicko Piakarić in 1592–93. The Serbian orthodox church of USPENJE BOGORODICE (The Assumption), also known as *Parohijska crkva* (1390), originally belonged to the Benedictines but was presented to the orthodox church by Marshal Marmont during the rule of Napoleon (1805) and is now the seat of the orthodox bishop of Dalmatia. The w. front has a remarkable Baroque bellcot (late 16C) incorporated into the wall; within are a number of Italo-Cretan icons.

The limits of the old town are marked by the spacious POLJANA MARŠALA TITA, dominated by the *Narodno Kazalište* (theatre) and a modern civic centre incorporating a Venetian bastion with a large relief of St. Michael.

The open Tržnica (market) lies at a lower level along Ul. bratstva i jedinstva, which is the main exit to Knin and N. Dalmatia. Hence streets lead uphill to the residential quarter and the massive *Šubičevac Castle*, also known as the *Forte Barone* (in honour of Baron C. M. Degenfeld who in 1647 defended the city against attack by the Turks) and now a restaurant with excellent views over the town and harbour. Behind the castle a monument (K. Angeli Radovani) and memorial park mark the spot where Rade Končar and 25 partisans were executed by the Italians in 1942, and a path ascends to *Sv. Ivan*, the highest of Šibenik's three forts.

To the s.w. of Poljana Maršala Tita the *Town Park* and quayside enclose a picturesque section of the old town in which many ancient houses display interesting doors, windows and balconies. The 14C Gothic *Franciscan Church* adjoining the park, has been remodelled inside, with a richly painted coffered ceiling by Marco Capogrosso (1674), and Baroque wooden altars made in Venice by Iseppo Ridolfi (1635) to designs by Girol. Mondella. The bell tower was erected by Ivan Skoko in the 18C and the monastery library possesses a good collection of codices and incunabula. The silver on display includes several reliquaries.

Immediately opposite the old town the narrow *Kanal Sv. Ante* gives access to the Bay of Šibenik from the sea. On the N.E. side of the strait is the bathing beach *Jadrija* (ferries every half hour in the season) while to the s.w. is the Fort of *Sv. Nikola* (1540–47) built by Gian Girol. Sammicheli. This operates together with Sv. Ana (comp. above) as a signal station controlling navigation in the strait.

Steamers ply thrice daily from Šibenik to the islands of Zlarin and Prvić. **Zlarin** (*Koralj*; sandy beach), the largest and best known of the small group of islands off the coast at Šibenik, is situated immediately opposite the entrance to Šibenik harbour. *Zlarin*, the only village (920 inhab.), is noted for the beauty of the local costume, now seen only on feast days, and its coral fishery, the only one in Dalmatia. The local co-operative also sells coral jewellery. The Baroque parish church was built by Ivan Skoko (1735–49), though the bell tower is older. In the church of Gospa od Rašelja (15C, restored 1714) is an alterpiece by the Dall' Acqua brothers (1767). Of the Baroque summer villas the Palača Žuliani (early 17C) is the most interesting.

Prvić lies just to the N. of Zlarin and slightly closer inshore. *Prvić luka* (rest.), the larger and more attractive of its two villages, has a 15C parish church where Faust Vrančić (comp. p. 114) is buried. His summer home (15 min walk), containing his portrait (1605) and a Madonna (school of Titian), lies half way between Prvić and *Šepurine*, the other village.

EXCURSION FROM ŠIBENIK.

To SKRADIN, THE RIVER KRKA, DRNIŠ, AND KNIN (77 km.). The journey may be made entirely by road (distances given cumulatively including diversions) or by a combination of road and boat. There are steamers twice daily to Skradin and numerous excursions are run by boat from Šibenik to Skradin and the Slapovi Krke (Krka Falls) at Skradinski buk.

We quit Šibenik by Ul. bratstva i jedinstva and Stara cesta and at 1½ km. across the Adriatic Highway. The asphalt road now climbs through karst country with views left over the Prukljansko jezero and Krka estuary.—At 11 km. *Tromilja* the road divides; for Drniš, see below. Keeping left we come almost immediately (12 km.) to a second fork where the road divides for Skradin and Skradinski buk.

A good gravel road (l.) descends by hairpin bends to a bridge over the River Krka and (19 km.) **Skradin** (*Skradinski buk*) a sleepy small town. Known to the Romans as *Scardona* and a city of some consequence under the Croatian Šubići, the Venetians, and the Turks (1522–1684), Skradin declined after the 17C and in the 19C was notoriously malarial. Juraj Ćulinović (Giorgio Schiavone, c. 1436–1505) was born here. The modern Serbian orthodox church of *Sv. Spiridon* has a good 16C Venetian iconostasis with three life-size figures; and, among the icons of the Italo-Cretan school around the walls, a Last Judgement by Gregory Margazinis (1647). The earlier Sv. Spiridon (1347) is to be restored. Leading N.W. from Skradin is the road for Zadar by which we shall return from Knin (see below).

The Krka Falls may be reached in ½ hr by boat hired at Skradin, or by car we may return to the second fork and continue (asphalt road) to (27 km.) *Skradinski buk* (pension, rest.; autocamp). The volume of water is greatest in spring and early summer. The falls comprise 17 steps dropping 155 ft in four stages over a distance of about 500 yds. Outcrops of rock and clumps of vegetation spread across the river allowing close access to individual rapids. At the top end, near the main observation platform (café), is a cluster of old water mills. One is still used to pound the woollen blankets of the local peasants; the water-powered oak hammers can be seen in action (gratuity).

A further excursion may be made up river by boat (hired at the falls). From the broad lagoon above the falls, where the Krka is joined by its tributary the Čikola, the river narrows between water meadows enclosed by steep limestone cliffs. After ½ hr it widens again to reveal the beautiful island of Visovac, thickly planted with cypress and poplar. The *Franciscan Monastery* and Seminary (sometimes shown on request) includes in a small collection of pictures (mostly 17–18C) a Madonna (1576) and an Annunciation (17C) in mother-of-pearl inlay. The library has one of three known copies (others in the British Museum and the Bodleian) of an illustrated translation of Aesop's fables, published by Boninus de Boninis (Dobrić Dobričević) of Dubrovnik in 1487 and a collection of Turkish documents (signed decree of Sultan Mehmed IV). Visovac and its surroundings provided the setting for Simo Matavulj's celebrated novel, 'Bakonja fra Brne' (1892). Upstream there is good fishing for brown trout and eels.

Continuing upriver we pass the mouth of the Voša tributary on our left and high on the cliffs to the S.W. the ruined circular *Uzdah-kula* (tower of sighs), a Turkish stronghold during the 16–17C. We then enter the deep narrow *Visovački kanjon* with the ruins of *Kamičak Castle* on the right, said to be the birthplace of Petar Svačić (1090–97), the last Croatian king, and come in c. 15 min to **Roški slap** (Roški Falls; rfmts. on w. bank). The falls resemble those at Skradinski but have a smaller fall of 84 ft spread over 430 yds. A bridge carries the road from Drniš to Djevrske.

Above Roški slap the river is again navigable as far as the monastery of Arhand-jelovac (see p. 121), but in general it is difficult to find a boat and the upper reaches are best visited by road (see below).

By car the next objective is Drniš. We return to (32 km.) Tromilja and take the gravel road that follows the river Čikola, with views into the canyon and across to the ruined castle of Ključ.

54 km. Drniš (*Danica*), a small country town beside the river Čikola on the edge of the fertile plain of Petrovo polje, has a colourful market on the 5th day of the month. The place was the main bridgehead of the Turkish advance into N. Dalmatia early in the 16C, and grew to a population of over 20,000 during the two centuries of Turkish rule, when it was known as 'little Sarajevo'. Few monuments remain. A ruined castle on the hill overlooks the town (view) and a roofless minaret. The only mosque remaining in Dalmatia has been converted into a church (*Sv. Ante*) but preserves Turkish honeycomb decoration. A *Town Museum* (open daily 8–12, 4–6) has been opened in the house of Božidar Adžija, a communist intellectual shot during the Second World War. Here is a collection of sculptures presented to the town in 1960 by Ivan Meštrović. Other works by Meštrović can be seen at the Dom kulture, the local hospital, and in the town park.

Meštrović was born at *Otavice*, a pretty village in an idyllic pastoral setting beside the river Čikola, 10 km. E. of Drniš off the Knin main road. On a hill, to the s., stands the **Meštrović Mausoleum** (ask for the house of Ante Meštrović to obtain key and a guide). Designed by the sculptor for himself and his family, the mauso-leum was built in 1929–36 of stone with cast bronze doors, on which the heads of the members of the family are depicted. Within, niches are decorated with religious scenes carved in low relief, while a single low altar is surmounted by an unusual crucifixion, in which a youthful Christ is enfolded in the arms of a guardian angel who forms the cross.

Continuing N. from Drniš on fair gravel, the road passes between Mt. Promina (l.; 3800 ft) and Mt Svilaja (r.; 4904 ft) keeping parallel with the Drniš–Knin railway line.—65 km. *Biskupija*, a hamlet just off the road (r.), preserves considerable remains of five medieval churches and a monastery (9–11C). The site is associated with the reign of King Zvonimir of Croatia who died here in 1089. Its excavation (1886) marked the beginning of autonomous Croatian archaeology and the rich finds of medieval jewellery, pottery, sculpture, and architectural frag-ments, formerly displayed at Knin, are now to be seen in Split (see p. 144). In 1938 a memorial church was erected with sculptures by Ivan Meštrović and mural paintings by J. Kljaković.

77 km. **Knin** (*Dinara*), a railway junction and market town, is pictur-esquely sited on the upper reaches of the Krka river. It was the seat of the last Croatian king, Petar Svačić (1090–97), and here on 4 Dec 1944 the Partisans won a decisive victory over the Germans. The town is dominated from the hill of Sv. Spas by a huge *Fortress*, one of the largest in Yugoslavia, comprising three sections, Romanesque, Gothic, and 18C Venetian. The Gothic portion was reconstructed and height-ened by the Turks in the mid-16C and the Venetians restored the whole in the early 18C. The Baroque entrance gate with the lion of St Mark dates from 1711.

A pleasant excursion from Knin is to the *Topoljski Slap* (Topolje Falls) on the the river Krčić, 1½ m. s.w. of the town.—Knin is linked by bus with Zadar.

From Knin we cross the river Krka and follow the Obrovac road for 7 km. before turning N. along the Krka. In the hamlet of (98 km.) *Ivoševac* stand two enormous arches known popularly as Šuplja crkva, the remains of the Roman praetorium of the castrum *Burnum*. A narrow track leads s. to the falls of Brljan and Manojlovac, the second par-ticularly fine, with a width of 650 ft and a drop of 195 ft. About a mile downstream are the Rošnjak (or Sondovjel) and Miljacka falls, of which the latter has a drop of 78 ft.

105 km. *Kistanje* is the starting point for a short excursion to the orthodox monastery of Sv. Arhandjel, known as Arhandjelovac. A gravel road runs left in 4 km. to the brow of the Krka valley, with views of the river and monastery and s.e. to Mt. Promina. To the N.E. are visible the round tower and ruins of the medieval Čučevo Castle, built by the Šubić family, and opposite it, on the far side of the river, the 15C castle of the Nelepić family. A path leads down to **Arhandjelovac** which stands in delightful surroundings beside the river. The mona-stery was founded in 1345 from a bequest by Princess Jelena Šubić, sister of Stefan Dušan of Serbia, and altered in 1402 and 1683. The church is in Byzantine style, cruciform in plan with a large green cupola over the crossing. The iconostasis is Greek 17C work with 18C Russian gates. The best icons however, St Jerome (1562) and Three Hermits in

the Wilderness (16C), are in the library. Here also is the illuminated 14C Mokropoljsko evandjelije (Mokropolje Gospel), discovered locally in 1954, a Russian gospel of 1689 with MS. illustrations, and a Bulgarian paterikon of 1346. A collection of embroidery includes a fine epitrachelion (stole) embroidered in gold with figures of 32 saints.

From Kistanje a good gravel road continues w. through more fertile country to (112 km.) *Djevrske*, where a side road leads left to Roški slap (see p. 120). A little beyond Djevrske another road leads left to the village of **Bribir** (5 km.). The hill of Glavice is the site of Roman *Varvaria* and medieval *Bribir*, seat of the Šubić family, the most powerful Croatian nobles of Dalmatia in the 13–14C. Bribir was partially explored in 1912–13, but renewed excavations are still continuing. The Roman walls stand in places to a height of 15 ft and the Forum and several villas are being excavated. Among Croatian buildings, the most interesting are the 13C church of Sv. Marija, beneath which one of the Šubić graves has been found, and a large Franciscan monastery. The round tower at the summit is a relic of Turkish occupation and the adjoining fortifications were erected by the Venetians in the 17C.

Returning to the main road at Djevrske we continue to (118 km.) crossroads on the main Zadar–Skradin road, where a left turn brings us once more to (135 km.) Skradin (see p. 119) and thence to (154 km.) Šibenik.

————————

The Adriatic highway curves round the Krka estuary to return to the shore at Ražine.—84 km. *Brodarica*. Across a strait (400 yds wide) from the hamlet lies the village and island of *Krapanj* (boat every hour) with an attractive waterfront. There is a sponge fishery and factory in the village, founded in 1700 by a Greek Franciscan monk on the model of Greek fisheries. The Franciscan monastery, founded in the 15C has a contemporary Madonna in the church and a Renaissance cloister. In the refectory an extensive collection of sponges, shells, and coral, with Greek and Roman pottery brought up from the seabed, is arranged below a Last Supper by Francesco da Santacroce.

Hugging the coast the road continues in a series of serpentine bends with views out to sea of the Šibenik archipelago.—101 km. **Primošten** (*Adriatic*, 400 R) is an attractive old place picturesquely situated on an island once joined to the mainland by a bridge, now by a causeway. The church was excellently restored in 1967 and given a beautiful modern sanctuary. There are numerous pebble and shingle beaches around the village and the Esperantists have a permanent international camp in one of the bays.—108 km. *Rogoznica* is similar to Primošten, but quieter and set on a deep inlet just off the main highway (2 km.).

134 km. **TROGIR** occupies a compact island, joined to the mainland by a bridge over an artificial channel and to the larger island of Čiovo by a bascule bridge across a narrow strait, a situation similar to that of Taranto in Italy. One of the most attractive and interesting towns (5000 inhab.) on the Adriatic, Trogir preserves almost intact its medieval entity. Many Romanesque and early Gothic houses are still lived in and, though individual buildings have been deprived of symmetry and

beauty by decay and inept repair, the general aspect of an early medieval town survives to a degree that makes the more saddening its continuing neglect.

Hotels. Radovan(a), modest, in old town; **Motel Trogir**, with rest. and kavana.—At *Seget* (1¼ m. from town): Jadran, 109 R, on shore.

Autocamps. *Lokvice*, 70 cars, on beach. *Soline* (1 m. from town), 200 cars, on beach.

Gostionas. *Tri volte*, Gradska ul.; *Saldun*, Narodni trg.

Post Office, Ul. Rade Končara.—INFORMATION OFFICE in Palača Cipiko on main square.

Buses daily to all major places on the coast; LOCAL BUSES every half hour to Split.

Steamer once daily to Drivenik, Šolta and Split.

History. *Tragurion* was founded in the 3C by Syracusan Greeks and as Tragurium was developed by the Romans into a major port. The rise of Salona overshadowed the city for a while, but with the latter's destruction by the Slavs and Avars (614) it rose to prominence again, particularly under the aegis of Byzantium. In the 9C a prosperous Trogir began to pay tribute to the Croatians, but in 998 was captured by Doge Pietro Orseolo II of Venice, and from then on shared the vicissitudes of the cities of Dalmatia. In the 12C Trogir recognized Hungary-Croatia, Venice, and Byzantium in turn, seeking always to preserve a degree of autonomy, which did not save it from sack in 1123 by the Saracens or in 1171 by Venice. In 1242 King Bela IV of Hungary took refuge in the city from the Tartars, whose leader, Caydan, brought his troops to the very gates. Periods of submission followed: to Bosnia, the counts Šubić of Bribir, Venice, Hungary, and even a brief period of independence. In 1398 the Genoese fleet took refuge here after their defeat at Chioggia, but in 1420 Trogir was besieged and taken by Admiral Loredano of Venice, and thereafter, as *Traù*, led a peaceful existence under the Republic. In 1797, with the fall of Venice, Trogir passed to Austria, then to France (1806–14) and then back to Austria until the end of the First World War, when Yugoslavia came into being.

Famous natives include Blaž Trogiranin (15C), the painter; Ivan Duknović (Giovanni Dalmata da Traù, ?1440–?1509), the sculptor; Koriolan Cipiko (Coriolanus Cipicus, 1425–93), the humanist; Petar Berislavić (1450–1520), soldier-bishop and Ban of Croatia; Trankvil Andreis (Tranquillus Andronicus, 1490–1571), diplomat and friend of Erasmus; and Ivan Lučić (Ioannis Lucius, Giovanni Lucio, 1604–79), author of the first analytical history of Dalmatia, 'De Regno Dalmatiae et Croatia' (1666).

Trogir is separated from the mainland by a dike cut in the Middle Ages to strengthen the city's defences against the Turks. From the main highway and bus station we cross a stone bridge and pass between the pleasant gardens that occupy the site of the ring of walls demolished during French rule. Opposite the bridge we pass through the late-Renaissance *Kopnena vrata* (Porta terrae firmae), adorned above the keystone with the escutcheon of Antonio Bernardi (1656–60), the Venetian governor who built it. The figure on top of the gate is St John Orsini, the city's patron; the empty niche formerly held a Venetian lion. At the first junction we turn left along Ul. gradskih vrata and come to Ul. Rade Končara. In the pleasant small square on our left, the Post Office faces a 13C Romanesque house. The Baroque *Palača Garagnin-Fanfogna* houses the **Gradski muzej** (open 8–12, 5–7). The collections (in course of arrangement 1968) illustrate the history of Trogir and include a number of the city's more valuable paintings

Ul. Rade Končara broadens in front of the cathedral before entering *NARODNI TRG, the spacious main square round which many of Trogir's most important buildings are harmoniously grouped. On the N. side stands the *Cathedral of Sv. Lovrijenac (St Lawrence), a Romanesque basilica, begun c. 1180 on the foundations of an earlier church ruined by the Saracens, and completed towards 1250. The s. wall, decorated with blind arcading, terminates in an unusual dwarf loggia added when the pitch of the aisle roofs was altered. The interior division into five bays is marked externally by pilaster strips. The plain central Romanesque s. Portal, or *Kneževa vrata*, approached by steps, bears an inscription dated 1213. The e. end, with three apses ornamented with slender columns (spirally fluted on the main apse) and blind arcading, and pierced with well-proportioned round-headed windows, is a model of its kind.

Enclosing the full width of the w. end is a **Narthex, or Galilee, consisting of three large rib-vaulted bays rising to the height of the aisles. The walls are embellished with slender, rounded shafts and more blind arcading finished with a frieze of acanthus leaves, while a graceful balustrade encloses the flat roof. Above the s.w. bay soars the **Campanile**; an intended companion on the N. side was never built.

The first story above the balustrade was built before 1422. The second, added by Matej Gojković, is a splendid example of traceried Venetian Gothic, and the third, completed by Trifun Bokanić in 1598 combines Gothic detail with Renaissance feeling well enough for the four evangelists by Aless. Vittoria at the corners of the tall crowning pyramid to harmonize successfully.

A high Romanesque arch gives access to the vaulted interior which conceals the magnificent ****West Portal**, "a work which in simplicity of conception combined with richness of detail, and marvellous finish of execution, has never been surpassed in Romanesque or Gothic art" (Jackson). Basically the work of an otherwise unknown local master, Radovan (Raduanus), whose name and the date (1240) are inscribed on the lintel, the portal is Romanesque in conception and design, but with Gothic elements where the work was continued by pupils. The portal rises from a low marble step decorated with blind arcading. Flanking the doorway, classic consoles support a lion and lioness, above which stand life size figures of Adam and Eve. A gabled moulding, added in the 14C, to enclose a niche containing a statue of St Lawrence and frame the whole, springs rather clumsily from the outer capitals.

Two richly carved orders within are supported at the bottom by figures in eastern dress apparently imitated from some lost Roman triumphal arch. The outer jamb has three apostles to either side framed in vine-leaf medallions, while its inner sides are decorated with a profusion of beasts. On the inner jamb the months are depicted in scenes from rural life, and the inner faces are decorated with exquisite scroll-work. Two delicately sculptured limestone shafts at the inner edge are carved with lively hunting scenes. The winged cherubs in the impost blocks were added by Nikola Firentinac. The lunette and the inner arch tell the story of the Nativity: in the centre the Virgin with the infant Saviour in the manger with below, the washing of the child by Joseph; to the right the three kings approach on horseback, to the left the shepherds tend their flocks. On the arch the Annunciation at the bottom (l. and r.) and the Adoration of the Magi at the top, with flying angels between. The outer arch shows ten scenes from the life of Christ, beginning with the Baptism (bottom r.) and rising in alternate left and right panels to the Crucifixion. Two small Romanesque transennae on the w. wall depict a sinner being devoured by snakes, and a griffin devoured by lions.

The **Interior**, sombre and mystical, is basilican in plan, the narrowness of the aisles accentuated by their great height and the weight of the piers supporting the Romanesque arcades. The nave was vaulted in 1427–40. Paintings on the piers of the nave include a representation of the 14C Bp. Augustin Kažotić (Cazotti) by Palma Giovane (1599) and Mary Magdalen and a Pietà by Padovanino. The octagonal *Pulpit* (13C) is supported on marble columns with good Romanesque capitals. The carved walnut *Choir Stalls, worked in Venetian Gothic style by Ivan Budinić, a local artist, show invention of design and exuberance in execution. Set into the end pillar on the N. side, beside the high altar, is a Venetian Gothic tabernacle (15C), having doors carved with a Crucifixion scene. The altar is covered by a striking 13C *Ciborium*, supported on four marble columns with fine capitals and having an octagonal cupola rising in two stories with open colonnades to a pyramidal roof. The figures of the Annunciation above the columns are signed Mauro (14C). The main apse retains a synthronon, ornamented with blind arcading, but the bishop's cathedra in the centre is missing.

A majestic triumphal arch opens from the N. Aisle into the *CHAPEL OF IVAN ORSINI, one of the outstanding creations of the Renaissance in Dalmatia, built by Nikola Firentinac (1468–97; otherwise Nic. di Giov. da Firenze, a pupil of Donatello). The Annunciation figures added above the cornices came from some earlier monument. The chapel is rectangular with a coffered barrel vault, richly decorated by Nikola himself and Andrija Aleši. A central tondo is filled with a half-length figure of Christ, while each panel bears a cherub's head and wings. Above the altar rests the Gothic marble sarcophagus (1348) of John Orsini, first Bp. of Trogir (d. 1111), patron saint of the city. The lower part of the walls is divided into seventeen high relief panels representing half-open double doors from which emerge cherubs bearing torches. Above, elaborate niches, separated by engaged columns surmounted by putti, contains statues of saints and, on the rear wall, Our Lord flanked by Mary and John the Baptist. SS Thomas and John the Evangelist (l.) are the work of Ivan Duknović (a local sculptor who later made his name in Rome as Giov. Dalmata). The lunette above the windows is filled with a Coronation of the Virgin.

Farther E. opens the Sacristy, constructed in 1446–50, with an elaborately carved and inlaid Wardrobe by Grgur Vidov (1458). Here are displayed items from the *Treasury* (apply to the Sacristan). Among the paintings are a polyptych in a Gothic frame and a Madonna of the Rosary by Blaž Trogiranin (15C); two painted doors from an organ case by Gentile Bellini, depicting SS Jerome and John the Baptist; and a St Martin by Salvator Rosa. The plate includes a 14C silver-gilt ewer with a lid in the shape of the crown of Hungary, a gift of Elisabeth of Hungary, who was born in Trogir; a delicately worked monstrance of rock-crystal and gold (14–15C); two arm reliquaries, also the gift of the queen; a 15C ivory triptych; a silver cross with figures of St John and the Virgin on the arms; and a 14C Gothic cross from Avignon. A jewelled mitre is said to be that of Bp. Kažotić (14C), and a hood embroidered with a figure of St Martin came from the robes of its donor, Bela IV.

The Gothic chapel of *Sv. Jeronim* (Jerome), built in 1438, opens from the W. end of the N. aisle.

From the Galilee opens the BAPTISTERY (apply to sacristan), the principal known work of Andrija Aleši (1467). Over the door a relief shows the Baptism of Christ. The small chamber has a coffered vault, similar to that of Sv. Ivan Orsini, but slightly pointed, with fluted niches and a frieze of putti bearing garlands, in the manner of Juraj Dalmatinac. In the lunette, St Jerome (relief). The sacristan will also admit to a spiral stair leading to the flat roof and thence to the top of the Campanile (view).

Opposite the cathedral porch is the 15C **Nova Palača Cipiko** in Venetian Gothic (attributed to Nikola Firentinac and Andrija Aleši), with two notable three-light windows and a handsome doorway in Ul. Matije Gupca. In the vestibule are the Cipiko arms and a large wooden figure-head in the shape of a cock, captured from the Turks by the Trogir galley at the battle of Lepanto. It houses the *Turistički biro*, through which we may pass to the courtyard, with Renaissance arcading, an open gallery and a well-head decorated with the Cipiko arms. In this palace a previously unknown chapter of the Satyricon by Petronius, called Trimalchio's Feast, was discovered in 1650. Formerly an arch spanned Ul. Matije Gupca joining this palace to the **Stara Palača Cipiko** (Old Palace), now part of the Gostiona Saldun. Its façade has two three-light windows in Venetian Gothic, of which that on the left is a modern copy. A doorway in Gradska ul. gives access to the neglected courtyard with a doorway at the top of a flight of stairs by Nikola Firentinac and a laurel-wreathed head by Ivan Duknović, said to be of King Matthias Corvinus of Hungary. Hanibal Lučić, the 15C poet from Hvar, often stayed here.

On the s. side of the square is the fine city **Loža** (Loggia) erected in the 15C and restored in 1890. Some of the columns supporting the roof are antique, while of the capitals one is Roman, three Byzantine and two of Renaissance work. On the rear wall a relief by Ivan Meštrović (1936) depicts Ban Berislavić on horseback, and on the E. wall a large Relief by Nikola Firentinac (1471) showing Justice with St John Orsini, holding a model of the city, and St Lawrence. The composition was ruined in 1932 when the central lion of St Mark was dynamited (it bore the equivocal text 'Iniusti punientur et semen impiorum peribit'). The incident provoked a minor international crisis between Italy and Yugoslavia. The judge's bench and table date from 1606. The near wall of the loggia is formed by the small church of *Sv. Barbara* (or Sv. Martin), which is entered from Gradska ul. (key from Turistički biro). Built in the 9–10C it is a good example of an early Croatian church of Byzantine influence, narrow and lofty, with a semidome over the chancel and utilizing Roman spolia (probably from Salona) for its columns and capitals. The altar rail has pre-Romanesque plaited decoration and an inscription records a gift to found the church by a certain Croatian lady, Dobrica.

The **Clock Tower,** which forms the E. wall of the loggia, was once the Romanesque chapel of Sv. Sebastijan, remodelled in the Renaissance manner by Nikola Firentinac (1447) with figures of Christ and St Sebastian over the doorway. In the interior, now used as a souvenir shop, survive the Romanesque apse and a lintel with pre-Romanesque ornamentation. The windows of the shop look on to the foundations of the pre-Romanesque church of *Sv. Marija*, dating from the 8C, with a curious plan having six apses. The large **Vijećnica** (Town Hall), formerly the Venetian governor's residence, closing the E. end of the square, was erected in the 15C but remodelled in 1890. It bears the city escutcheon in the centre, with those of St John Ursini and an unknown

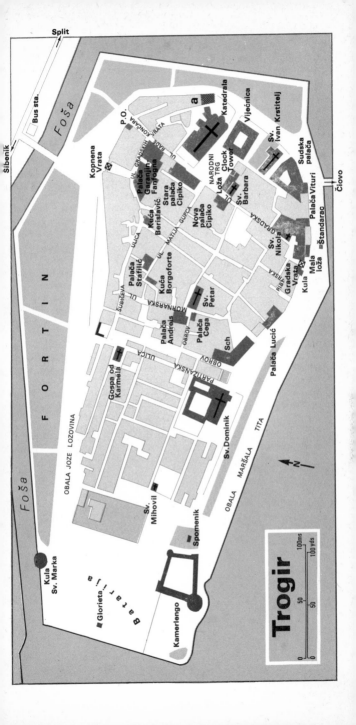

noble over the two side doors. In the courtyard (good well-head) is a handsome 15C staircase by Matej Gojković, who may be portrayed in the stone head beneath the stairs. Numerous escutcheons adorn the walls, and the only lion of St Mark remaining in Trogir.

Part of the s. side of the Vijećnica is now used as the Kavana Radovan, beyond whose garden is the 13C Romanesque church of *Sv. Ivan Krstitelj* (John the Baptist). Contemporary with the cathedral, which it resembles in many constructional details, the church was once attached to a Benedictine abbey. The exterior, decorated with blind arcading under the eaves, has a Romanesque agnus dei above the w. door and an unusually placed triple bell-cot added in the 14C. The neglected interior (key from sacristan of cathedral) contains a Pietà by Nikola Firentinac (1470), carved for the tomb of Korijolan Cipiko, a large painted Crucifixion (15C) and a cast of Meštrović's John the Baptist (original in the baptistery at Split). Traces of frescoes have been found on the walls.

A promenade follows the line of the shore. We pass the neo-Gothic *Sudska palača* (Courthouse), erected by the Austrians, on our right and come to a complex of buildings marking the line of the town walls. Beyond an attractive row of gabled fishermen's cottages, the former *Palača Vituri* (15–16C) incorporates in its tall balconied tower a medieval watch tower. It is now part of the Benedictine nunnery, the belfry of which (comp. below) rises behind. The beautiful **Mala Loža** (small loggia), erected by governor Alessandro Lipoman (1524–7) for the shelter of strangers awaiting admission to the city, serves as a fish market. Between the loggia and a tower remaining from the medieval fortifications, opens the *Gradska vrata* (Porta civitatis, or Porta marina) with an inscription recording its erection in 1593 by governor Delfin Delfino and the original wooden gates still in place.

Just inside the gate is the entrance to *Sv. Nikola* (open 8–12) erected in the 15–16C on the site of the Romanesque church of Sv. Dujam, traces of which can be seen behind the altar. The bell tower (1593) by the Bokanić family has unusual stone lattices in the upper story to screen bell-ringing nuns from prying eyes. Immediately behind the church a door admits to a court in various Gothic styles. Two inscriptions are built into the walls, one in Greek of the 3C B.C., the other concerning Ban Berislavić. The nunnery *Treasury* (8.30–11.30, 3.30–5.30) is notable for a rare marble *Relief of Kairos, the Greek god of luck (? 1C B.C.; shown on request). This figure became the symbol of the 1936 Olympic Games. Among icons and paintings are exhibited a painted wooden polyptych (c. 1400) and a Gothic crucifixion.

Continuing along the shore we pass the stone *Štandarac* (1605) or flagpole, and the *Palača Lučić*, home of Ivan Lučić the historian; the façade has been modernized, but there is a good Renaissance courtyard and doorway. Trogir's principal school occupies a not unpleasing neo-Gothic edifice on the corner of Partizanska ul., a broad straight street following the course of an old moat, which divided the original town from Pašike, a later medieval extension. On the opposite corner rises the conspicuous Campanile of the **Dominican Church**, built in the 14C by Bitcula, sister of Bl. Augustine Gazotich (Augustin Kažotić, Bp. of

Zagreb; d. 1323), a native of Trogir. Brother and sister figure as the supporters of the Virgin and Child in the lunette sculpture by Niccolò Dente (1372). Within, the nave has a flat ceiling and the short chancel a pointed barrel vault. On the s. wall the Subota tomb is by Nikola Firentinac (1469). There is a Circumcision (1607) by Palma Giovane, and a 15C polyptych of six panels. The Renaissance *Cloister* (apply to sacristan), bombed in the last war and now restored, houses a lapidary collection.

The imposing **Kaštel-Kamerlengo** in the s.w. corner of the town, a large Venetian fortress, complete with battlements and machicolated towers, was erected in 1424–37 to guard the harbour. The nine-sided principal tower (66 ft), called *Donjon*, is a reconstruction of a Genoese fort (1380) on the same spot. The interior is open (7–7) and in summer becomes a cinema. At the side is a bronze war memorial by I. Mirković (1951). Across the *Batarija*, now used for football and gymnastics, stands the graceful classical *Glorietta* of Marshal Marmont, Napoleon's governor of Illyria. The bell tower (r.) of the former church of *Sv. Mihovil*, destroyed during the Second World War, was built by Jerko Bokanić (1595). The landward end of Batarija is marked by the 15C round tower of Sv. Marko with conspicuous batter and machicolations. Here we turn right along Fortin. On the corner of Partizanska ul. (comp. above) is a fragment of a former bastion and a few steps down on the right is the small Baroque church of *Gospa od Karmena* (Our Lady of Mt Carmel; 1618), with a 14C Gothic relief over the door and a Gothic crucifixion inside.

The whole quarter E. of here, in an area roughly bounded by Fortin, Obrov, and the main square, repays exploration, though its winding alleys are dilapidated and the medieval houses imperfectly documented.

The small 16C church of *Sv. Petar*, in Ul. Obrov, has a statue of St Peter in the tympanum. In the Renaissance interior (coffered and painted ceiling) are paintings (16–18C), two Gothic crucifixes, a rustic wooden figure of Christ (15C) and a 17C Baroque organ case. On the opposite side of the street are two Venetian Gothic mansions, the *Palača Cega* (l.) and the *Palača Andreis*. Mornarska ul. and Šubićeva ul. are lined with houses exhibiting Romanesque, Gothic and Renaissance features. We may regain the Land Gate by the latter street passing Berislavić's house on the corner of the street bearing his name; or return to the main square by Ul. Matije Gupca, in which stand the Venetian Gothic *Palača Stafilić* and the *Borgoforte Mansion*.

A bascule bridge crosses the strait to the island of *Čiovo*, linking Trogir with its suburb, also called *Čiovo*. The churches of Sv. Jakov and Gospa kraj mora (Our Lady by the Sea) contain late-Gothic polyptychs (15C), and Sv. Ante na Dridu (1432) a painting of SS Antony and Paul in the Desert by Palma Giovane. A bad gravel road serves the village of Arbanasi. At 4 km. stands the 15C Dominican Monastery of *Sv. Križ* (Holy Cross), built by Ivan Drakanović and Nikola Mladinov, where the beautiful late Gothic cloister has an upper story on the s. side, and (E. side) the chapel of Sv. Jerolim (Jerome) in Venetian Gothic with a remarkable painted ceiling. The plain Gothic church has a fine crucifixion (15C) over the main altar; the rustic 15C choir stalls have carved bench-ends (Cipiko escutcheon). The two paintings on the N. altars are by Matej Pončun (Ponzoni) of Rab.

Continuing s. on the Adriatic Highway we pass the *Mlinice Restaurant* in a picturesque 16C mill.—At 140 km. the road forks, the highway continuing (1.) directly to Solin while the old road (poor surface) runs nearer the sea along the so-called **Kaštelanska Rivijera** with its eight Kaštela (fortresses).

The **Kaštela**, fortified mansions rather than castles, were built by the nobility of Trogir and, to a lesser extent, of Split between 1476 and 1556 as a defence against Turkish invasions. As a refuge for the local peasantry, they attracted the formation of villages. Only 8 of the original 14 remain. The belt of land enclosing the villages is exceptionally fertile and the traditional vineyards are giving way to orchards and market gardens. The kaštela are becoming increasingly popular tourist resorts, particularly with Yugoslavs. A frequent bus service runs between Split and Trogir and steamers call at Kaštel Stari.

We pass the village of *Divulje* on our right, whence a gravel track leads up the mountainside to Bijaći (or Bihać), a residence of Croatian princes in the 9C (pre-Romanesque church of Sv. Marta, extensively restored) destroyed by the Turks. We skirt the *Airport* of Split and beyond *Resnik* (Resnik, 220 R; autocamp; beach) continue to (144 km.) **Kaštel Stafilić** (*Nehaj*) where the westermost fortress of *Nehaj* projects into the sea. Begun by the Lodi brothers of Trogir (1548) and continued by the Papalić family of Split, it was never completed. *Kaštel Stafilić* itself was built by Stjepan Stafileo in 1508, as the escutcheon and inscription indicate. The Baroque parish church with its prominent bell tower (18C) was built by I. Macanović. A continuous promenade extends for 4 km. along the shore to Kaštel Lukšić.

The two villages of (145 km.) **Kaštel Novi** and Kaštel Stari are now continuous with Kaštel Stafilić. Both kaštels were erected by the Cipiko family of Trogir: Kaštel Stari, the oldest of all the fortresses by Koriolan Cipiko (1476–81) after his return from the Turkish wars in Asia Minor, and Kaštel Novi by his nephew, Pavao Cipiko, in 1512. *Kaštel Novi*, a plain tower in poor condition (Cipiko escutcheon), was the birthplace of the sculptor Marin Studin (1895–1960), whose war memorial, Herald of Victory, stands between Kaštel Novi and Stari. In Kaštel Novi village is an 18C town loggia and the Renaissance church of Sv. Rok (1586). **Kaštel Stari** (*Palace*, 120 R; rest. Plavi Jadran; tennis; water skiing; turistički biro; cinema) is a larger and more attractive village served by a railway station (2 m. N.). The *Kaštel* has a pleasant Renaissance courtyard and handsome façade facing the sea, and in the village is the Renaissance church of Sv. Josip.

A pleasant excursion is to *Biranj* (2050 ft), one of the peaks of the Kozjak Massif, c. 1½ hrs distant, on the road passing the railway station.

148 km. **Kaštel Lukšić** (*Slavija*) stands on the border between the former lands of Trogir and Split. The *Kaštel*, built by the brothers Jeronim and Nikola Venturi of Trogir (1487), with a Renaissance courtyard, is the largest still standing (now a school). The old parish church, a modest Renaissance structure by Ivan Rudičić (1515), has rustic Baroque altars. The new parish church houses the Altar of Abp. Arnerius (Bl. Arnir) by Juraj Dalmatinac (1444–45), from the Benedictine nunnery in Split. Beneath the recumbent figure of the archbishop, a relief depicts the stoning of Arnerius by the people of Poljica. West of the village, beside the promenade that links it with Kaštel Stari, are the ruins of *Kaštel Rušinac* (built 1482 by Mihovil Rosani of Trogir) and a small church with the grave (1681) of the lovers Miljenko and Dobrila, popular subjects of folk myth.

About an hour's walk from Kaštel Lukšić, on the lower slopes of the Kozjak Massif, lies the village of *Ostrog* with the pre-Romanesque church of Sv. Juraj (9C) and the 12C Romanesque church of Sv. Lovro.

149 km. **Kaštel Kambelovac** (rest.; turist biro), is an attractive fishing village with a handsome round tower (the Kaštel) erected by the Cambi family of Split in 1566 and rebuilt a century later (escutcheon and inscriptions); a Renaissance villa of the Cambi (1589) adjoins it. At the w. end of the beach a villa (1911), in its own park, once a favourite resort of King Petar II and his mother Queen Marija, was later used by President Tito before becoming the Ana Roja Ballet School.—150 km. **Kaštel Gomilica,** the most striking of the fortresses, occupies a tiny island joined to the mainland by a drawbridge. The entrance is guarded by an impressive square machicolated tower erected by the Benedictine nuns of Split in the early part of the 16C. Within, a conglomeration of small houses and narrow streets constitutes the village (rest.; autocamp; turist biro; sandy beach). The parish church of *Sv. Jerolim,* has a Baroque Crucifix by F. Bakotić (18C). The tiny Romanesque church of *Sv. Kuzma i Damjan* may be 12C.—153 km. **Kaštel Sućurac** (rest.; turist biro; cinema; dancing; beach), the most easterly of the Kaštela, despite its attractions as a holiday spot is in danger of being engulfed by Split's industrial expansion. The fortress built by Archbishop Gualdo of Split in 1392 was the earliest of the kaštela, but this was destroyed and rebuilt in 1489–1503, and only fragments remain. The present episcopal palace is a late reconstruction incorporating Venetian Gothic (good two-light windows) and Baroque portions. In the parish offices is an inscribed 7C lintel from the hamlet of *Putalj,* 3 km. to the N.

Putalj also figures in two charters issued by Princes Trpimir and Mutimir of Croatia in 852 and 892, the originals of which are preserved in the village archives. A small museum is devoted to the liberation struggle and Second World War, with a bronze relief on the wall by Joka Knežević. A strenuous excursion can be made to the summit of *Mt. Kozjak* (2400 ft) preferably with an overnight stay in a mountain hut near the top (inquire at turist biro).

Across the water the long wooded peninsula of Marjan gives way to the industrial suburbs and shipyards of Split. Rejoining the main road at (158 km.) *Solin* (see Rte 15) we continue through dreary suburbs to (164 km.) **Split.**

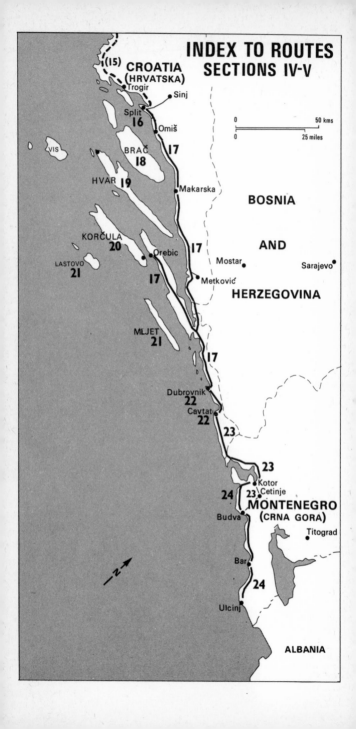

IV SOUTHERN DALMATIA

16 SPLIT AND ITS ENVIRONS

SPLIT, the largest and fastest growing city (100,000 inhab.) of Dalmatia and Yugoslavia's second port, stands on a broad peninsula at the E. end of the Kaštelanski zaljev. Bursting from the confines of the great Roman palace of Diocletian, the city spreads fanwise round a broad semicircular harbour and extends eastwards behind three attractive bays. Seen from the S. approach, it is attractively bounded by the wooded Marjan peninsula and backed by a fine range of mountains. Stark skyscrapers on the periphery are a reminder of the industrial quarters and commercial port that lie, largely hidden behind a ridge, on the N. shore. The centre, teeming with a lively and good-humoured populace, presents a fascinating palimpsest of sixteen centuries' organic growth. In the old town, though motor traffic is absent, Split rivals Naples for noise, with the shortest gap between the last evening revellers and the grind of iron-bound wheels on marble pavements as the first vendors come to market.

Airport, at *Kaštel Stafilić*, 22 km. N.; services to Zagreb and Belgrade, also in summer to principal cities in Europe (usually at weekends). Connecting bus terminates at J.A.T. office, Titova obala 8.

Railway Station (*Kolodvor*), Obala bratstva i jedinstva, for *Zagreb* (through coaches to Vienna, Munich, etc.; also Ostend in summer); connections at Zagreb for main cities of Yugoslavia.

Steamers moor at Obala bratstva i jedinstva (booking office) and Obala lazareta. Spring and summer connections to *Venice, Trieste, Corfù, Piraeus, Istanbul, Beirut, Haifa, Alexandria*, etc. Express service (Jadrolinija) to major coastal towns and islands of Yugoslavia. Local services to the islands of Drivenik, Šolta, Brač, Hvar, Vis, and Lastovo.—CAR FERRY to *Supetar* (Brač) and *Starigrad* (Hvar). Also in summer to *Pescara* (Italy).

Hotels. *Marjan* (a), 220 R with bath or shower, indoor swimming pool, kavana, dancing, Ul. J. N. A.; *Bellevue* (b), kavana, Trg republike; *Central* (c), Narodni trg, unpretending.—At *Bačvice:* *Park* (d), *Mosor* (e), *Bačvice* (f). At *Trstenik:* *Split*, 330 R with bath or shower, own beach; *Motel Inex*, 200 R with bath or shower.

Pensions. *Srebrna vrata* (g), Poljana Kraljice Jelene 3; *Dalmacija* (h), Prilaz XXVI dalmatinske divizije, dancing; *Slavija* (i), Adamova ul. 5; *Ljubljana* (j), Širina Filipa Grabovca 3.

Autocamp at *Trstenik* (Put Znjana 36) and at Inex (Duilovo).

Restaurants. *Zagreb*, Ul. Ivana Lučića-Lavčevića; *Marjan*, Marmontova ul. 7; *Sarajevo*, Ilegalaca ul. 6; *Gradski restaurant*, Dobrić; *Zvončac*, Obala J. N. A. 29; *Kula* (evenings only) on corner of Titova obala and Hrvojeva ulica; *Željezničar*, Radovanova ul. 2.—KAVANAS. *Luxor*, Peristil; *Zdravljak*, Titova obala; *Bellevue*, Ante Jonića 2; *Slavica*, Trg republike.

Post Office. *General*, Ul. Ivana Lučića-Lavčevića; branch offices at Obala bratstva i jedinstva, Ul. prvoboraca, Solinska ulica, and Ul. Vladimira Nazora.—INFORMATION OFFICE. Turistički biro, Titova obala 12.—TOURIST OFFICES. *Dalmacijaturist*, Titova obala 5; also at Obala bratstva i jedinstva and in the Peristil (guide service); *Generalturist*, Titova obala 22; *Kompas*, Titova obala 2; *Atlas*, Trg republike 7; *Putnik*, Adamova ul. 3.

British Consulate, Titova obala 7.

Bus Station, Obala bratstva i jedinstva. Frequent buses to all coastal towns and to main cities inland. Local buses to *Trogir* (every ¼ hr), the *Kaštela, Solin, Klis, Sinj*, and *Omiš*, from Ul. Ive Lole Ribara.

Amusements. THEATRES. *Narodno kazalište*, Kazališni trg; *Pionir* (puppet theatre), Omladinska ul. 3.—CINEMAS. *Split* (outdoor and indoor), Ul. Graničara;

Tesla (outdoor and indoor), Ul. Ivana Lučića-Lavčevića 6; *Bačvice* (outdoor only), at Bačvice; *Balkan*, Marmontova ul. 6; *Jadran*, Savéznička obala; *Marjan*, Trg republike; *Central*, Kazališni trg; *Zlatna vrata*, Dioklecijanova ul.

Summer Festival, annually (15 July–15 Aug), of music, opera, drama, ballet, and folklore (mainly al fresco).

Beaches. *Bačvice* (cabins, showers, café, games), with a concrete foreshore and sand. *Firule*, *Zenta*, and *Trstenik* to the E., and *Zvončac* and *Kašjuni*, both w. of the town, have similar establishments. There are also small beaches at *Bene*, on Marjan, and *Spinut* in Poljudska luka.—SWIMMING POOLS (open air) at the Jadran Club, Zvončac; Pošk Club, Zenta; and Mornar Club in Spinut; indoor pool at Hotel Marjan.

Sport. SAILING is offered to visitors by the Mornar and Labud clubs, both at Rt Sustjepan.—TENNIS at the Split Tennis Club, Šetaliste 1 maja 30.—FOOTBALL STADIUMS, Zrinsko-Frankopanska ul. 7 (*Hajduk*) and Lička ul. 26 (*Split*), both 1st division teams.

History. The city is said to derive its name from the Greco-Illyrian settlement of *Aspalathos*, but the recorded history of Split begins with the building of Diocletian's palace in A.D. 305. After the Slav destruction of Salona (c. 614) the inhabitants sought refuge within the palace walls and never went back; continuity was established by transferring the bishopric and the relics of St Domnius. By the 9C Aspalathos was one of the leading cities of the Byzantine theme of Dalmatia, and as Byzantine power waned evolved into a free city with its own statutes and charter. In 998 Venice appeared on the scene briefly and in 1069 Croatia, while from 1105 the city acknowledged the nominal suzerainty of Hungary–Croatia. The next three centuries were a time of economic and cultural flowering during which most of the present old town took shape, while in external affairs the city played off the Croats and Hungarians against Venice and periodically went to war with its nearest rival, Trogir. In 1241 the Tartars appeared before the walls in pursuit of King Bela IV of Hungary, but followed him to Trogir without attacking. By the 14C the rivalry of Hungary and Venice for possession of Dalmatia had grown intense and *Spálato* as it now came to be called, placed itself under the protection of Venice (1420). For a while the city continued to prosper and the arts in particular flourished under the influence of the Renaissance, but the increasing threat from the Turks, who had taken the fortress of Klis in 1537, and the slow decline of Venice led to stagnation and impoverishment. In 1797 Split passed with the rest of Dalmatia to Austria, under whose power it remained, except for the French interregnum (1805–13), until the end of the First World War.

Split was the birthplace of Thomas Archidiaconus (1200–68), author of 'Historia Salonitana'; of Marko Marulić (1450–1524), historian and author of the poem 'Judita'; of Jeronim Kavanjin (1641–1714), the poet; and of Ivan Lukačić (1574–1648), the composer. Marcantonio De Dominis (comp. p. 75) was Abp. of Split in 1602–15. In 1757 the city was visited by Robert Adam, whose observations and drawings of the palace became the basis of the celebrated Adam style of architecture. Ugo Foscolo studied at the seminary here. Franz von Suppé (1819–95), whose overtures have outlived their operas, was a native. Ivan Meštrović began his career in Split and his fellow sculptor and friend, Toma Rosandić (1878–1958), was born and died here.

I THE OLD TOWN

The **Old Town** comprises the original settlement (Stari grad) inside Diocletian's Palace and a quarter of almost equal extent (Novi grad) immediately to the w., which together form a fascinating complex of narrow streets, the product of an urban tradition of sixteen centuries. The ****Palace of Diocletian** (*Dioclecijanova palača*) determined the shape and development of the centre and remains the most important single element of the city. It is the largest and most perfect example of Roman palatial architecture extant and its frequent departures from classical rules give it a special place in the evolution of European building from trabeated to arched construction.

Built for Diocletian (Emp., 284–305), who had been born near Salona (p. 149), the palace was begun in 285 and completed during his reign. To it he retired on his

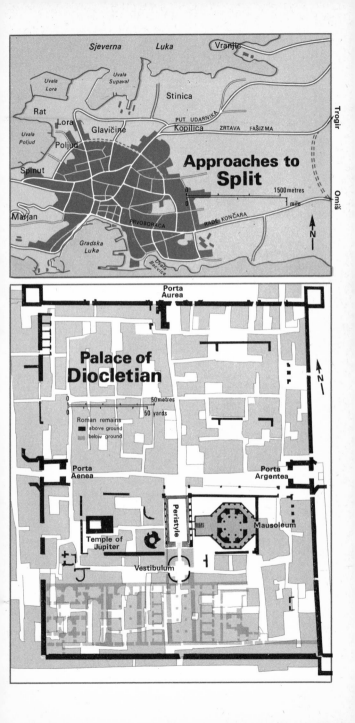

Approaches to Split

Sjeverna Luka

Vranjic

Uvala Lora

Uvala Supaval

Stinica

Rat

Lora

Glavičine

PUT UDARNIKA

Kopilica

ZRTAVA FAŠIZMA

Trogir

Poljud

Uvala Poljud

Spinut

Marjan

PRVOBORACA

RADE KONČARA

Omiš

Gradska Luka

Uvala Bačvice

0   1500 metres
0   1 mile

N

Palace of Diocletian

Porta Aurea

Porta Aenea

Porta Argentea

0   50 metres
0   50 yards

Roman remains
above ground
below ground

Peristyle

Mausoleum

Temple of Jupiter

Vestibulum

N

abdication and here in 313 he died. The palace passed to the State and a textile factory for the army was established here. Galla Placidia, daughter of Theodosius the Great, found sanctuary here, and Julius Nepos was probably assassinated in the palace in 480. In the 7C the palace was wrecked by the Avars when they sacked Salona but afforded refuge to the Salonitans, becoming the nucleus of a new walled town, with houses constantly rebuilt from the ruins left by barbarian raids. In the 13–14C its walls were further fortified. Many of the accretions were destroyed by allied bombing during the Second World War, and the opportunity has since been taken to effect further restorations (begun in the last century). More recently the palace vaults have been excavated and restored.

The palace, constructed of white limestone from Brač, covers a sloping site of c. 7 acres, being very similar in extent to the Escorial. It is almost rectangular in plan, the E. and W. sides measuring 718 ft; the s. wall 582 ft; and the N. wall 574 ft. The s. wall rises to 70 ft, whereas the N. wall, based on higher ground, is only 48 ft high. Originally the walls were reinforced with sixteen towers, rectangular except for the three pairs guarding the land gates which were octagonal. Three of the corner towers alone stand today; that at the s.w. was washed away in 1550 by the sea, which originally lapped the entire s. side. The general layout of the interior was a combination of fortified castrum and villa rustica, with a *decumanus* running E. and W. and a *cardo* meeting it at right angles from the N. gate. The quarters of the slaves, servants, and garrison occupied the N. half, while the Imperial apartments and offices of state filled the seaward half s. of the decumanus.

Although visitors arriving by sea generally gain their first impression of the palace from the s. façade on the waterfront, a better appreciation of its disposition and extent is gained by starting the tour proper from the N. side. The NORTH WALL, exposed for the greater part of its length, is bordered by gardens. The *N.W. Tower* is to be a restaurant. The imposing **North Gate**, known since the 16C as the *Porta Aurea* or Golden Gate (Zlatna vrata), was the main entrance; to it led the main highway from Salona. Only traces remain of its flanking octagonal towers. The doorway lacks its ornamental casing. The corbelled blind arcading above, with unequal arches, is surprisingly bold for its period, but has lost its ornamental columns. The niches probably held statues. Within, grooves for a portcullis are still visible. The inner entrance was equipped with hinged gates, leaving a rectangular *propugnaculum* into which strangers were admitted for identification before being allowed to proceed. The gallery at the top, designed to accommodate the guard, now forms the tiny church of Sv. Martin (comp. p. 142).

Facing the gateway is a colossal bronze statue (1929), by Ivan Meštrović, of Grgur Ninski (Gregory of Nin), the 10C Croatian bishop who defied the Pope in defence of the Croat liturgy. The statue stood in the Peristyle until the occupying Italians removed it; it was placed in its present position in 1954. To the w. rises the elegant Baroque *Campanile* of a Benedictine nunnery burnt down in 1877. The foundations of the 11C basilica of *Sv. Eufemija*, its church, have been cleared; of this the small Gothic chapel of Sv. Arnir (Arnerius), by Juraj Dalmatinac (1445), remains intact. Across the road is the small pleasantly shaded *Gradski Park*.

We pass round the N.E. Tower and descend Hrvojeva ul. as far as the **East Gate** (*Porta Argentea*, or Srebrna vrata), a simpler version of the N. gate. It was restored to its present condition in 1946 after bombs had destroyed the Venetian fortifications and church that had hidden it from view since the 17C. Its protecting octagonal towers are impressive in their ruin. Opposite the gate the 13C church of *Sv. Dominik* (rebuilt in 1682 and enlarged in 1932–34) contains a Gothic crucifixion, a Baroque altarpiece by Palma Giovane, and a Christ in the Temple, by one of his pupils. We now pass (l.) the colourful **Tržnica,** an extensive open market, gay with fruit stalls and frequented by itinerant souvenir vendors from the south. The S.E. Tower of the palace, now the *Kula* café-restaurant (summer evenings only), commands a panorama of the harbour.

We turn right along the busy TITOVA OBALA, a spacious palm-lined promenade along the waterfront. The seaward side affords an excellent view of the **South Façade** of the palace, once washed by the sea. The plain lower courses are now concealed by a row of houses and shops (18C and later). Higher up an open gallery, often misnamed *Cryptoporticus*, ran the full length of the façade. The detached columns, of which 38 survive of the original 52, rest on carved corbels and carry an entablature effectively interrupted by three tripartite loggias. The arched openings between the columns are mostly filled by the walls and windows of houses.

The *South Gate* (*Porta Aenea*, or Mjedena vrata), functional in design, served purely for convenient access from the sea. Within, we enter a vaulted hall connecting the waterfront directly with the Peristyle (see below). To the left is the entrance to the so-called ***Podrumi** (Underground Halls) of the palace (open 8–12, 4–8; guide available). These halls, impressive in scale, represent one of the largest vaulted structures in existence. Their main function was to raise the floor of the southern quarter of the palace to the level of the remainder. The pillars of cut and dressed stone and the brick vaults are of excellent workmanship. During the Middle Ages the basements were filled with rubble and refuse and though their existence was rediscovered around 1900, their restoration first by the Konzervatorski zavod and latterly by the Urbanistički biro has been carried out since 1946. The halls reproduce in their layout the disposition of the imperial apartments above (no longer extant). A long narrow cross-vaulted *Gallery*, corresponding to the 'Cryptoporticus' above (wooden beams on display from the original Roman scaffolding), gives access (r.) to a series of small rooms and, farther on, to a huge *Hall* of basilican plan with an apse. A smaller apsidal hall, beyond, forms part of a complex of chambers, circular, rectangular, cruciform, and quadrifoliate, all with massive stone walls supporting barrel or groin vaults or domes.—The E. side of the underground halls is still being excavated.

A flight of steps (lower half original) mounts from the central hall to the ***Peristil**, the main forecourt of the palace, which opens from the interrupted cardo just s. of its intersection with the decumanus. This attractive piazza, three steps lower than the surrounding streets, with a frequented open-air café, is still a social centre of the city, affording today's citizens access on the E. side to their cathedral, as it did their Roman forbears when the same building was the emperor's mausoleum. The peristyle (116 ft by 44 ft) comprises parallel open arcades made up of granite columns with fine Corinthian capitals, from which spring semicircular arches. The s. end is closed by a magnificent *Prothyron*, tetrastyle in antis, tied to the colonnades by a continuous entablature.

The entablature surmounts the arches of the lateral arcades, becomes conventional over the side doors of the prothyron and, below the apex of the pediment, springs in an arch over the two centre columns, an effect seemingly derived from the Temple of Hadrian at Ephesus. It makes a fine backdrop for operatic performances in summer.

The w. side of the colonnade has been incorporated into the façades of a row of patrician houses, resulting in a fascinating and unexpectedly felicitous blend of Roman and Renaissance architecture. In a bay of the open E. colonnade rests an Egyptian sphinx of black granite (c. 15 B.C.), one of two that originally flanked the entrance to the mausoleum.

Steps lead up between a pair of votive chapels, *Gospa od Pojasa* (1544) and *Gospa od Začeća* (1650), to the former **Vestibulum** of the palace, a rotunda once domed and lined with marble and mosaics, now a favourite venue of young footballers and (because of its acoustics) amateur singing groups. In the space behind the rotunda, now devoid of Roman remains, stands an 11C Romanesque house, beautifully restored and occupied by the *Urbanistički biro*. Farther to the right an open arch of the palace façade looks on to the harbour. The opening to the E. from the rotunda leads to the tiny space in which three Roman mosaic floors have recently been discovered; a similar opening to the w. leads to the maze of narrow streets immediately above the palace vaults.

On the E. side of the Peristyle 22 steps mount through the Campanile, which supersedes the mausoleum forecourt once guarded by sphinxes (comp. above). The Romanesque **Campanile** (171 ft), a landmark so characteristic that it has been incorporated into the city's badge, remains one of the most striking on the coast, though its patina was lost and many of the original details replaced in the reconstruction of 1882–1908. It is guarded by two (restored) Byzantine *Lions*, though the sculptured groups they bear are copies (originals in the museum, p. 142). Beneath the arched lower story are three Romanesque reliefs attributed to a pupil of Radovan. They depict the Annunciation, the Nativity, and (below) SS Peter, Domnius, and Anastasius, the last signed Otto, who is also thought to have carved the reliefs on the arch of the vault. The summit (gratuity) commands a fine view of town and harbour.

The reconstruction, effected under Alois Hauser by Dalmatian and Italian masons, faithfully copied the old lines, except that the crowning octagon was altered, not very happily. The original lower story was of the 13C; the second was consolidated and the next two added in 1501–25 (possibly by Bart. di Giac. da Mestre). The tower was struck by lightning in 1719. Replaced and similarly damaged in 1789, it was restored the following year to the form on which the rebuilding was modelled.

The *MAUSOLEUM OF DIOCLETIAN, converted in 652 by John of Ravenna, first Bp. of Split, into the **Cathedral of the Blessed Virgin Mary,** is known popularly as *Sv. Dujam* after its subordinate dedication to St Domnius, the Salonitan martyr. The building, octagonal in plan and well-preserved, is raised on a podium within a dignified Corinthian colonnade. Two or three panelled ceiling slabs remain in situ and holes in the wall above show that the walk had a pentise roof. The intercolumniations are filled with Christian sarcophagi, notably the ornate tomb of Prior Peter (9C). On the s. side is the entrance (apply to sacristan) to the crypt chapel of *Sv. Lucija*.

The rich Roman *Portal* is decorated with animals and vine leaves. The magnificent double *Doors of walnut backed with oak display some of the finest Romanesque woodcarving in Europe, executed in 1214 by Andrija Buvina, a local master. On either door 14 recessed panels, individually framed in intricate scroll or knot work, are separated by a continous vine motif, in which dogs, birds, and people pluck bunches of grapes. Many of the human figures are naked, an unusual feature for the time of their composition. The panels illustrate the life of Christ.

On the *Left Door*, Christ's birth and early life: Annunciation (top left); Nativity; Journey of the Magi; Adoration of the Magi; Massacre of the Innocents; Flight into Egypt; Presentation in the Temple; Baptism; Wedding at Cana; Temptation in the Wilderness; Miracle of the Gadarene swine; Christ and the Woman of Samaria; Healing the Blind; Raising of Lazarus.

Right Door. The scenes read upwards and show Christ's Passion: Mission of the Disciples; Christ weeping over Jerusalem; Entry into Jerusalem; Last Supper; Washing the Disciples' Feet; Agony in the Garden; The Betrayal; Christ before Pilate; Scourging; Crucifixion; Deposition; Entombment; Descent into Hell; Ascension.

The circular *INTERIOR, structurally unaltered and somewhat cramped and gloomy for its present use, is divided into eight bays by a double tier of ornamential columns standing forward of the wall. The lower tier has Corinthian capitals (restored) with a splendidly ornamental cornice, while the composite order above, standing forward of pilasters, carries another elaborately carved entablature, which returns over each column. A fine *Frieze*, below the entablature, depicts scenes from the chase with medallion portraits of Diocletian and his consort Prisca. The intact domical vault is remarkable for the fan-like pattern of its bricks. Between the columns open eight niches, alternately rounded and square. The entrance is flanked by two stoups. The exquisite Romanesque *Pulpit*, to the left, stands on six marble columns having capitals deeply carved with winged beasts twined in foliage. The hexagonal upper part is decorated with blind arcading resting on paired columns with rich capitals; each arch contains a sculpture. The lower cornice supports a crouching lion grasping a winged serpent, from which rises a spirally fluted column bearing a lectern in the form of an eagle grasping a pair of birds. The w. niche has been opened into the exterior colonnade to accommodate a Baroque altar dedicated to St Domnius.

The niches on either side of the high altar are filled with Gothic canopied shrines. On the N., *Sv. Staš*, by Juraj Dalmatinac (1448), contains the sarcophagus of St Anastasius, carved with a Scourging of Christ, of realistic violence. On the s., *Sv. Dujam*, by Bonino da Milano (1427), has frescoes beneath the canopy by a local painter, Dujam Vušković (1429); these were discovered in 1958 when a Baroque surface was removed. The altar, an early-Christian sarcophagus with a relief of Christ as the Good Shepherd, bears a reclining marble figure of St Domnius. A reredos of five panels portrays the Virgin and Child with saints.

A Y-shaped Gothic crucifixion (14C) hangs above the high altar. Behind extends the rectangular CHOIR added in the 17C by Abp. Marcantonio De Dominis. The magnificent *Stalls* are composite. Their Romanesque *Screens (the oldest in Dalmatia; c. 1200), attributed to

Buvina, show a variety of interlacing patterns and lattice-work surpass-ing that of the doors; certain motifs have an oriental look. The bench-ends carved with rampant lions are 15C Venetian work (the seats and cornices were added later). The paintings above include a Madonna and saints, by Palma Giovane, six scenes from the life of St Domnius, by Pietro Ferrari (1685), and works by Matteo Ponzoni.

From the s. side of the choir opens the TREASURY (open June to mid-Sept, 9–12, 4–7). A notable collection of codices, exhibited upstairs, includes the Evangeliarum Spalatense, a rare 8C copy of the Gospels; the Supetarski Kartular (11C); a missal and an evangelistary, both illuminated in the 12C and bound in engraved silver covers; the 12C illuminated Homilies of Origenes; and Archdeacon Toma's cele-brated Historia Salonitana (13C). On the lower floor the plate includes a silver monstrance (1532) in the shape of a ciborium; a Gothic morse, or brooch; a gilt cross (12C); two 15C ampullae; and several fine 15C chalices. Among the vest-ments are two embroidered chasubles of red velvet and a collection of lace.
By the small s. door of the cathedral is the 16C tomb of Janko Alberti, above which hangs a 15C crucifixion.

From the opposite side of the peristyle the narrow Kraj sv. Ivan leads to the *Temple of Jupiter (Jupiterov hram), later adapted as the cathe-dral *Baptistery* (Krstionica, open 9–12, 3–6). A small prostyle building on a raised podium, it has lost its portico but the cella (16 ft by 27 ft) is in an excellent state of preservation. The steps are guarded by a head-less sphinx of black granite, one of the pair from the mausoleum (comp. above). Outside the temple stands a Renaissance sarcophagus (1533). The 5C column attached to the house opposite is not from this temple. The engaged corner pilasters at the rear have good capitals. The finely carved portal is surmounted by an elaborate cornice borne on voluted consoles. Within, plain walls rise to another elaborate cornice and are roofed with a fine coffered barrel-vault, each panel decorated with flowers or fantastic heads in high relief. Both this roof and the doorway exercised a profound influence on the architecture of Dalmatia. The *Font* is constructed of 11C marble plutei decorated with pre-Romanesque carvings, the front slab bearing a low relief scene depicting an early Croatian ruler (as Christ?) on a throne. Behind are the sculptured sarcophagi of Abps. John of Ravenna (650–80) and Lovro (1059–99). The gilded bronze of John the Baptist is by Meštrović.

Inside the complex of 13–15C houses that form the *Radničko sveučilište*, or Workers' University (on our left as we return to the peristyle), can be seen the circular foundations of another of several temples that stood in this area.

The northern half of the area enclosed by Diocletian's palace is more purely medieval than the south, with hardly any Roman buildings remaining, and consists of a mass of tiny twisting streets of great fascin-ation and charm. At the N.E. corner of the Peristyle, an office of Dal-macijaturist occupies the converted Renaissance chapel of *Sv. Rok* (1516). To the E. the wide Poljana kralja Tomislava still preserves the paving and dimensions of the Roman decumanus with the column bases of a Roman stoa along the s. side. This is now a favourite pitch of flower, postcard and souvenir sellers whose bright parasols make a splendid show here and around the East Gate. On the N. side of the street (entered from Poljana Grgura Ninskoga) stands the Baroque church of *Sv. Filip Neri* (1735, key from cathedral), while Ul. Julija Nepota just beyond it preserves a number of early Gothic houses and is lined to the E. by Roman arches of the palace wall.

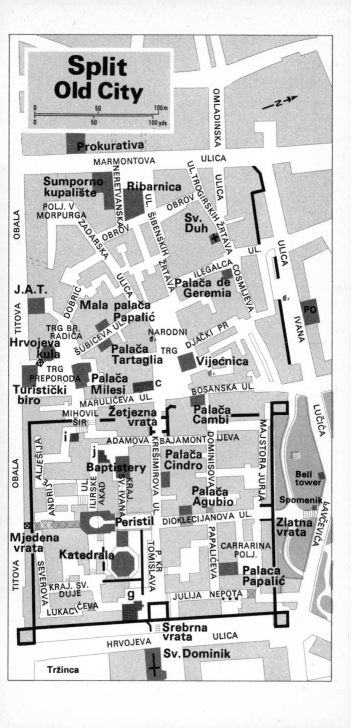

Running from the peristyle to the North Gate is the narrow DIOKLECIJANOVA UL. (the former cardo), one of the most picturesque streets in Split. Beyond the *Palača de Agubio* (15–16; l.), with Venetian Gothic doorway and Renaissance courtyard, we pass beneath a Gothic vault and turn right. Papalićeva ul. was recently renamed after the lovely Venetian Gothic *Palača Papalić* (15C) by Juraj Dalmatinac, with its flamboyant gateway, four-light traceried window and intimate courtyard with loggia and well-head. The palača now houses the **Gradski muzej** (open 8–12). On the ground floor the Armoury displays 15–18C weapons. Beside the entrance is a statue of Leonardo Foscolo, the Venetian general who defeated the Turks at Klis in 1648, while the collection includes both Turkish and European small arms and two rare examples of guns with wicks, the forerunners of flintlocks. On the walls are escutcheons of the city's nobility. The rooms upstairs illustrate the history of Split in the 12–16C with models, drawings and plans, etc. Exhibits include statutes of the city, original sculptures from the cathedral campanile with other Romanesque fragments, a Gothic crucifixion and a Gothic madonna.

Continuing along Dioklecijanova ul. we pass the entrance to Cararina poljana, where performances are held during the Split summer festival, and come almost at once to the North Gate (comp. p. 136). Here a vaulted passageway leads left to Ul. Majstora Jurja in which steps (r.) give access to *Sv. Martin* (No. 19; ring for admission), a tiny pre-Romanesque church (9C), 35 ft by 5½ ft, inserted into the gallery above the North Gate. The pre-Romanesque reredos (?11C) is carved in stone.

The entrance steps give an excellent view across Ul. Majstora Jurja of a recently discovered palača attributed to Juraj Dalmatinac. The unusual N. façade is pierced by three Venetian Gothic windows on the first floor with a loggia below, and the interior has been restored and modernized to house a branch of the Workers' University. It also contains the cinema, Zlatna vrata (entrance in Dioklecijanova ul.).

From the peristyle KREŠIMIROVA UL. the constricted, congested alley that forms the main shopping street, runs w. past the handsome Baroque *Palača Cindro* (17C) to the **West Gate** (*Porta Ferrea* or Željezna vrata), a bottleneck to pedestrian traffic and a favourite spot for barrow boys. The gallery of the propugnaculum is occupied by a medieval church, *Gospa od zvonika* (Our Lady of the Belfry), whose pre-Romanesque belfry (c. 1100) is the oldest in Dalmatia. The entrance is by steps in Bajamontijeva ul. (r.; key from house adjoining the church). The charming Baroque interior has murals by V. Meneghello and a marble relief of the Madonna protecting the townsfolk (1480).

We pass out of the Roman palace by a narrow cut (Ispod ure) into the spacious irregular NARODNI TRG, the social centre of medieval Split and still the city's busiest and most attractive square. It is thronged during the evening corzo, and the Kavana Central in the S.E. corner is particularly favoured by the local citizens. Looking back towards the East Gate we see the medieval *Clock Tower* with its 16C clock and in front of it a walled-up *Loggia* (15C) enclosing a pharmacy. The most striking building in the square is the old **Vijećnica** (Town Hall) with its triple-arched Gothic loggia on the ground floor. This retained its 15C form when the building was radically rebuilt under the Austrians (late 19C). The first government of the People's Republic of Croatia was constituted here in May 1945. The building now houses the **Etnografski muzej** (open 8–1, 6–8) with the finest collection of folk costumes and artefacts on the coast.

The costumes are exhibited on the *First Floor* in two sections according to regions. The Dinaric costumes of the interior are in general the more sumptuous and imaginative, especially those of the Ravni Kotari, Knin, Vrlika (especially blouses and aprons), Konavli and the Dalmatinska zagora. There are also Alka costumes from Sinj (see p. 153). The costumes of the Littoral tend to be more subdued and subject to foreign influences, but note especially the women's costumes of Split; the costumes (male and female) of Šibenik; and the lace of Pag, Primošten, and Novigrad. On the second floor are utensils, furniture, tools, weapons, interesting basketwork and an outstanding display of jewellery.

The Renaissance *Palača Karepić* (16C) is joined to the Vijećnica by a small Gothic bridge over the street.

From Narodni trg picturesque medieval streets radiate in all directions. Bosanska ul. follows the line of the vanished w. wall of the palace with the 15C Gothic *Palača Cambi* at its lower end and a number of old town houses near the top. Even more interesting is its continuation south, Marulićevica ul., lined with medieval houses and with a statue of St Anthony Abbot (1394) on the corner. From the w. end of the square Ilegalaca ul. passes (l.) the ornate Renaissance doorway (1583) of the former monastery of *Sv. Marija de Taurello* (relief of the Madonna in the tympanum). The damaged court within is bounded on one side by the small 14C Gothic church of *Sv. Duh*, the key to which is to be found in an adjoining courtyard reached through a door in the far corner (ring for sacristan). The roof and walls of the apse are decorated with frescoes, and over the high altar is a painting of the Descent of the Holy Ghost by Pietro Novelli. Here is buried Andrija Aleši, the sculptor. Over the main entrance to the church (in Ul. Trogirskih žrtava) is a Romanesque relief of Christ Enthroned. At the junction with Cosmijeva ul., the Renaissance *Palača de Geremia* preserves in the courtyard a Roman sarcophagus depicting the battle of the Lapiths and Centaurs.

To the w. and s.w. of Narodni trg a maze of narrow shopping streets leads out to Marmontova ul., forming the w. boundary of the old town, and to the Poljana V. Morpurga. Šubićeva ul., with (r.) the Venetian Gothic *Mala Palača Papalić* (15C), by Juraj Dalmatinac, and (l.) the Baroque *Palača Tartaglia* (17C), leads down to the busy TRG PREPORODA, adorned with a statue of Marko Marulić by Ivan Meštrović. The square is dominated by the striking Renaissance–Baroque *Palača Milesi*, where above an excellent bookshop is the POMORSKI MUZEJ (Maritime Museum, open daily except Mon, 9–12), with collections and models illustrating the maritime history of Dalmatia. Opposite stands the *Hrvojeva kula*, part of the 15C Venetian fortifications, through which a gateway leads out to Titova obala and the waterfront.

II Western Split

At the w. end of Titova obala opens the TRG REPUBLIKE, a somewhat incongruous arcaded square built by the Austrians, with the Kavana and Hotel Bellevue at its southern end. Split's principal taxi rank stands in front of the restored church of *Sv. Franja*, a miniature pantheon of Split notables, with the gravestones of Marko Marulić, Archdeacon Toma, Jeronim Kavanjin and Ivan Lukačić. The church contains a good Gothic crucifixion by Blaž Trogiranin and a 15C Gothic statue in wood of St Lucy. A charming Gothic cloister adjoins the s. side.

Behind the church the shady suburb of **Veli Varoš** occupies the lower slopes of Mt. Marjan. In Kozjačka ul. is the little pre-Romanesque church of *Sv. Nikola* (12C), domed and cruciform in shape; and a little to the N. the Baroque church of *Sv. Križ* (Holy Cross) has a Gothic painted crucifixion and Madonna. Lenjingradska ul. leads to the foot of Mt. Marjan and the *Marjanske stube*, a sequence of steps leading up through pleasant woods to the small **Zoološki vrt** and PRIRODO-SLOVNI MUZEJ (Natural History Museum, open 8–sunset). The zoo has a comprehensive collection of native animals and birds, and some Asian and African fauna; the museum has good collections of fossils, marine life, and particularly beetles (over 10,000 specimens). Its terrace commands fine views of the city and harbour. A winding road leads higher to an even better viewpoint at the summit of *Mt. Marjan* (553 ft). From the museum we may descend by more steps to the small 13C church of *Sv. Nikola*, and beyond to Saveznička obala (comp. below).

From Trg republike the broad Saveznička obala follows the shore. Passing (1.) the Gusar rowing club on its narrow jetty and (r.) *Botićevo Šetalište*, a long flight of steps ascending to Sv. Nikola (comp. above) and Mt. Marjan, we round the bend by the new Navy Club and continue along Obala J.N.A. A long, low single-story building temporarily houses the **Muzej hrvatskih arheoloških spomenika,** an attractive collection of Croatian archaeological finds. The exhibits are mainly pre-Romanesque from the period of early Croatian independence (9–12C) and include two excellent rectangular ciboria: one from Bijaći near Trogir and the other of white marble, with a beautifully carved canopy, from Biskupija near Knin. From Biskupija comes also a rare hexagonal ciborium and from the church of Sv. Križ at Nin, a hexagonal limestone font. Notable are a transenna carved witha Madonna and a 9C stone crucifix. The jewellery (esp. earrings and necklaces) and medieval weapons are worthy of notice, as is an 8C censer found at Stara Vrlika.

Beyond the *Hotel Marjan*, a striking modern building by L. Perković with an indoor swimming pool, the promenade continues to the delightful little peninsula of **Sustjepan**, with a fine yacht basin, park, and outdoor swimming pool. The church of *Sv. Stjepan* (1814) incorporates in its walls fragments of the pre-Romanesque cemetery church which it superseded. Inside is a 15C Gothic polyptych of the Nativity. The bathing beach and bay of *Zvončac* lie on the far side of Sustjepan.

The Šetalište Moše Pijade continues w. to the tip of the Marjan peninsula. About 2 km. from the old town (buses 7 and 12) is the **Galerija Meštrović,** the former villa of the sculptor Ivan Meštrović (1883–1962), which he designed for himself in 1937, and which since 1952 has contained a permanent exhibition of his works (open 10–7). The villa, a long low building of dazzlingly white Brač limestone, was designed as a combined mansion and gallery in an uneasy and ostentatious mixture of neo-classicism and modernism. The formal gardens were also intended as a setting for sculptures. The interior is arranged in chronological order to illustrate Meštrović's career and development.

The GROUND FLOOR shows his work from 1902 to the late twenties and the evolution from Viennese 'Secessionism' (note the bust of his mother in R 1) to a more individual and Romantic style inspired by patriotism and the cause of South Slav self-determination (Kosovo polje cycle in R 2). His best work includes various religious subjects carved in relief in walnut, especially two colossal unfinished figures of Adam and Eve, a fruit of his later work during the thirties and interrupted by the outbreak of war. On the FIRST FLOOR further rooms are devoted to the work of the thirties (bust of Vladimir Becić) and later, which show a gradual decline of the sculptor's powers into rhetoric and over-emphatic expressionism. His private apartments are also open to view and in the last hall is a miscellaneous collection of pieces too large for exhibition elsewhere (note the group in marble showing the Madonna with children).

In a pleasant pine grove a little farther on stands the **Kaštelet** (open 10–12, 4–7), the 17C summer villa of Jeronim Kavanjin, adapted and restored by Meštrović. The showpiece is the *Chapel*, designed and built by Meštrović and decorated by his great series of walnut panels carved in relief to illustrate the life of Christ. The panels, though carved over a long period (1914–54) and not in sequence, show extraordinary unity of style. They were designed to throw deep shadows by the natural lighting of the chapel (no artificial light being provided on the sculptor's insistence) and are best seen on a sunny morning.

Beyond the Kaštelet the road continues along the foot of Marjan to the bay of *Kašjuni* (pebble beach), with views out to sea of the islands of Brač, Šolta, and Čiovo. The pine-clad slopes are criss-crossed here with pleasant shady paths leading to the top of Marjan. At the w. end of the bay a by-road doubles back and climbs to the little 15C church of *Sv. Jere* (St Jerome), with a relief of the saint by Andrija Aleši. Cells cut into the rock beside the church were once inhabited by hermits. A little farther on, this road widens to form a platform below the 15C church of *Betlehem* (altar by Aleši) and then divides for (l.) the summit (comp. p. 144) and (r.) Sv Nikola (p. 144). Continuing round the foot of the hill we come to the very tip of the peninsula, Rt Marjana, and the **Institut za oceanografiju i ribarstvo** (Oceanographical Institute) with a small *Aquarium* (open 7–7) and restaurant. This is the terminus of bus No. 12. The road continues round the N. side of Marjan through more pinewoods to the beautiful little bay of *Bene* (bathing; bus No. 15 from the centre), with a rocky foreshore and sandy bottom, and thence to the residential suburb of *Spinut* with a pebbly beach and the yacht Marina of the Split sailing club.

III Northern and Eastern Split

The most direct road to the northern part of the city is Marmontova ul., passing the neo-Renaissance Prokurativa on our left and the Secessionist building of the Sumporno kupalište (Kamil Tončić) on our right. Adjoining the latter is the colourful *Ribarnica* (Fish market). At the top we emerge into Kazališni Trg with a bust of Luka Botić, the 19C poet, by Meštrović, in the centre. On the s. side stand two sections of bastion from the 17C Venetian walls, the E. part housing a small *Naval Museum*. To the w. stands the neo-classical *Narodno kazalište* (People's Theatre, 1893) and to the N. the church of *Gospa od zdravlja* (Our Lady of Health; 1937), with overpraised frescoes (1959) by Ivan Dulčić. The broad Zrinjsko-Frankopanska ul., one of the two main arteries leading N. from the centre to residential suburbs, passes the stadium of the Hajduk Football Club. In Ul. Maksima Gorkog, beyond the stadium, No. 19 is the former studio of Emanuel Vidović (1897–1953), the landscape painter, now a small gallery exhibiting his works. A bust by Frano Kršinić (b. 1897) stands on a pedestal in the small *Vidovića park*.

The far side of the park is bounded by Lovretska ul. in which No. 15 is the **Galerija Umjetnina** or Art Gallery (open 9–12, 4–6), founded in 1931. On the top floor a collection of 15–19C icons typifies the stereotyped techniques of the later Cretan and Venetian schools and illustrates the activities of the Boka Kotorska school, where the art was continued by certain families from generation to generation. Here also

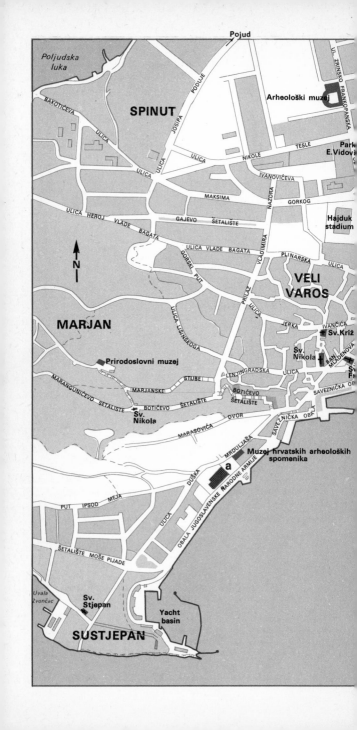

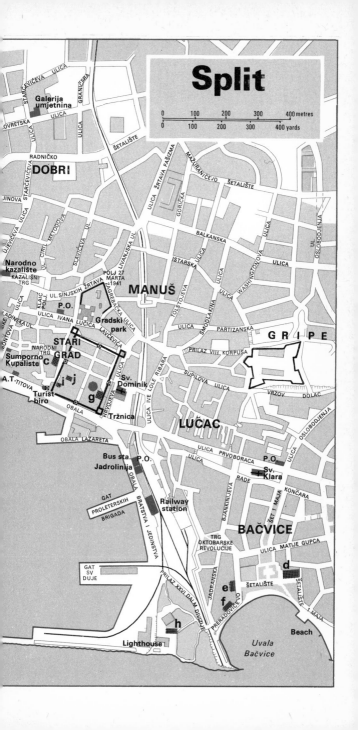

are two painted panels, Orpheus and Narcissus, from a chest by Andrea Meldola 'Schiavone' (Medulić); a relief of St Jerome by Aleši; two paintings, St Francis of Paola and the Holy Family with St Anthony of Padua, by Federiko Benković (Bencovich Schiavon); and a polyptych (school of Veneziano).

On the lower floors are paintings by local painters of the 19C and 20C (Medović Bukovac, Kraljević, Račić, Vidović, Job), and sculpture by Meštrović, Rendić, Rosandić, Kršinić and others. The museum also possesses drawings by Kokoschka and George Grosz.

Continuing up Zrinjsko-Frankopanska ul. we come on the left to the **Arheološki muzej** (Archaeological Museum, open daily except Mon 8–1). Founded in 1820, and moved here in 1914, the museum owes its expansion to Don Frane Bulić, the native archaeologist, and its interest to the fine Roman collection from Salona (see p. 149).

The greater part of the exhibits are housed under open verandas round the garden in roughly chronological order. From the entrance we turn left. A few Greek stelai from Vis lead on to ROMAN ANTIQUITIES, notably the enormous tomb of Pomponia Vera (in park to the right) from Salona and a relief from Tilurium (Trilj, near Split) believed to illustrate the victory of the Romans over the Illyrians. The headless statue of Tiberius is a copy. Of many Roman sarcophagi, two of the finest in the far left corner, show *Meleager Hunting the Calydonian Boar (somewhat weathered) and the Legend of Phaedra and Hippolytus. A portrait of a seaman (Gaius Utius) adorns the sarcophagus at the entrance to the following gallery. Here (far left) are a double relief of Mercury, a spherical sundial, a relief of Hercules and the Nemean lion, and reliefs connected with the cult of Mithras. Part of the main gate of Salona stands at the end of this section, with a relief of a goddess detached from it. Crossing the garden in front of the museum we come to the EARLY-CHRISTIAN ANTIQUITIES, which begin with burial urns and lead coffins. In the gallery (r.) are damaged mosaics from Salona and a marble mensa and altar rails from the Salona basilica. The original capitals from Diocletian's mausoleum are also on display. At the far end, in the corner, are two outstanding early-Christian sarcophagi, depicting the *Crossing of the Red Sea and Christ as the Good Shepherd, and four capitals from the baptistery at Salona. On the return to the main entrance we pass two mosaic floors from Salona, one a Triton medallion and the other portraying Orpheus.

In the main building are pottery, jewellery and artefacts from neolithic to Roman times. A headless Egyptian sphinx (? 14C B.C.) stands in the vestibule and a Greek frieze shows a group of seven dancing girls.

A short distance beyond the museum, Topuska cesta forks left from the main road and leads to the small bay of *Poljud* (bathing). On the N. side stands the Franciscan monastery of *Gospa od Poljuda* (Our Lady of Poljud), rebuilt in 1450 and fortified against the Turks a century later, when the existing towers were built. In the spacious cloister are two well-heads (one of the 15C bearing the rebus of the Delfini family) and fine memorials removed from the church, notably those of Bp. Thoma Nigris (1527) and Katarina Zuvetić (15C), both with full-length effigies. The church has as reredos a monumental *Polyptych by Girol. da Santa

Croce (1540), showing the Madonna and Child with saints, and another painting by the same artist of the Madonna; a Madonna with SS Peter and Clare is attributed to Girolamo's brother, Francesco. A picture in a side chapel, a poor copy of a lost original, depicts eminent writers who have praised the Virgin, including Mahomet holding a scroll with a quotation from the Koran; tradition holds that this painting helped to protect the monastery from attack by the surrounding Turks. The *Treasury* includes a portrait of Bp. Nigris by Lorenzo Lotto (1527) and two crosses, one Gothic (15C) and one Baroque by Fulgencija Bakotić, a local sculptor; also two codices illuminated by Fra Bone Razmilović (1675) and incunabula annotated by Marko Marulić.

Sutrojičin put, opposite the Museum, leads to the pre-Romanesque church of *Sv. Trojstvo* (The Holy Trinity), a rare surviving example of a round early Croatian church with six apses, though the dome has fallen. Roman fragments are apparent in the walls and four apses are decorated with shallow lesenes.

Immediately N. and E. of the old town extend the inner suburbs, many of whose streets and houses date back to the 17–18C. Between *Dobri* and *Manuš* a large wedge-shaped bastion remains from the Venetian fortifications, while *Gripe*, a massive star-shaped fortress of the same date stands on a hill on the edge of *Lučac*. The area N. of these suburbs is being developed as the new civic centre of Split in the modern manner. Ul. prvoboraca, the main road for Omiš and the coast, passes to the s. of Lučac; beyond it stands the Franciscan nunnery and church of *Sv. Klara*, with Byzantine icons and a painted Gothic crucifixion (13C) in its treasury. Still farther s. is the suburb of Bačvice.

Bačvice is usually reached by the OBALA BRATSTVA I JEDINSTVA along the waterfront. Passing the railway and bus stations on our left we leave the quay and follow Prilaz XXVI dalmatinske divizije. In the *Park Pomoraca* above the breakwater is the Hotel Dalmacija with a popular dance terrace and, on top of the cliff, the striking slender *Lighthouse* by B. Carić, erected in memory of sailors killed in action, with a monumental relief by Andrija Krstulović. A sharp bend in the road brings us to *Uvala Bačvice* a fine sandy beach (cabins, showers, café) above which extends a quarter of villas and hotels. In the Šetalište 1 Maja is the new home of the *Muzej narodne revolucije* with Partizan relics of the Second World War. Farther along the shore are the beaches of *Firule*, *Zenta*, and *Trstenik*, the last with a large autocamp.

EXCURSIONS FROM SPLIT

To SOLIN (Salona) 5 km.; local bus or trolleybus. We leave Split by the broad Ul. žrtava fašizma. At 1½ km. the road divides, the older road (l.) leading through industrial quarters to the new docks and the Kaštelanska rivijera. The main road (r.) runs beside a surviving part of Diocletian's Aqueduct. The roads rejoin to cross the Jadro just outside the village of *Solin*. The site of **Salona** lies on sloping ground between the modern highway to Trogir and the local road that diverges left to Kaštel Sućurac.

Salona is first mentioned in 119 B.C. as a centre of the Illyrian tribe of the Delmats, where the Roman consul Caecilius Metellus wintered. The place became a Roman colony after fighting for Julius Caesar against Pompey. Under Augustus it developed as the capital of the Roman province of Illyria, later Dalmatia, and reached the height of its prosperity as a seaport with c. 60,000 inhab. under Diocletian, who is generally supposed to have been born hereabouts. One of the finest provincial cities of the Roman Empire, Salona was noted for its cosmopolitan citizenship. During the Diocletian persecutions Domnius, a Syrian, and Anastasius from Aquileia were martyred, together with the priest Asterius and four soldiers of the Emperor's guard. Their graves became cult centres over which were later raised large basilicas. A century later the city suffered the first attacks of the Huns and the Goths and was torn internally by civil strife; after the fall of the western Roman empire it was occupied by the Ostrogoths under Theodoric. Byzantium later asserted her claim but c. 614 the city was attacked and totally destroyed by the Avars and Slavs, the population fleeing to Trogir and Split. The remains provide an important record of the development of Christianity under the Romans. They have been excavated over a long period notably in the late 19C by Don Frane Bulić (1846–1934).

The visible remains are dispersed over a wide unshaded area and are best visited on a cool day. *Tusculum*, an eccentric summer villa built by Prof. Bulić standing a short way from the car park (foot-path from the bus stop), forms the administrative office of the site (guide service), with a souvenir shop and a garden café. Roman and Romanesque fragments are incorporated in the villa and columns and capitals in the garden came from the cathedral campanile in Split.

Just N. of the Tusculum extends the Christian *Necropolis of Manastirine* overlying part of which are the well-preserved foundations of a 5C basilican church. The Basilica incorporates the burial place of St Domnius, Salona's patron saint and chief martyr. His tomb, a vaulted crypt entered from a square marble-paved chamber, can be seen in the sanctuary in front of the main apse. To the w. is the well-preserved sarcophagus of Bp. Primus, nephew of Domnius. Since the sanctuary was separated from the rest of the church c. 600 by a stout wall erected to protect it from barbarian incursions, it is necessary to walk round to view the narthex, nave and aisles, with their stylobates and broken off columns still in place. On the ground at the w. end is the original lintel bearing the inscription: DEVS NOSTER PROPITIVS ESTO REI PVBLICAE ROMANAE. The ground here is littered with about 100 sarcophagi plundered by the Avars; many of the best have been removed to the Archaeological Museum in Split (p. 148).—To the N. of the basilica are the remains of an early Roman *Wine Press*.

A similar complex to Manastirine but less well preserved is the necropolis of *Marusinac*, about 10 min walk on the other side of the car park. Here the grave of St Anastasius was enshrined in a mausoleum (foundations visible) beside which, in the 5C were built two linked basilicas, one hypaethral, the floor of which, a mosaic with geometrical designs is well preserved.

From the Tusculum a cypress avenue leads s. across a gravel road that follows the line of the northern *City Wall*, traces of which may still be seen at the side. Immediately inside the wall are the remains of the largest complex of Christian buildings so far discovered, which include two basilicas (basilicae geminae) joined by a common narthex. In the centre the spacious 4C *Basilica Urbana*, reconstructed in the 6C, has well-preserved stylobates and column bases and a prominent apse. From the narthex, steps lead up to auxiliary buildings, through which early initiates passed in sequence: a *Catachumeneum*, an octagonal *Baptistery*, with cruciform immersion font lined with marble and descending in steps, and a rectangular *Chrismatorium* for confirmation. Mosaics from these rooms and from the church are now in Split. To the s. is the *Basilica of Bp. Honorius* a rectangular structure erected in the 4C and

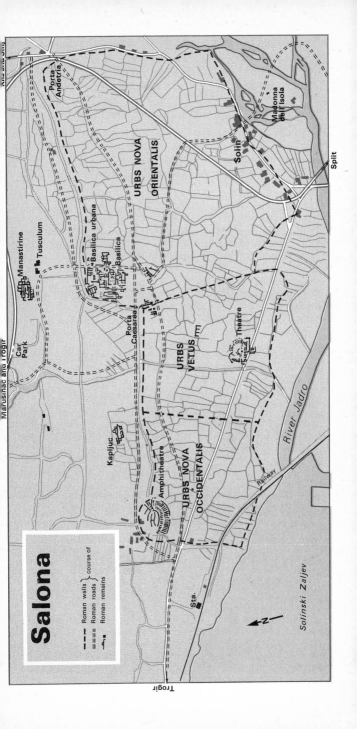

Salona

Roman walls } course of
Roman roads }
Roman remains

Marušinac and Trogir

Trogir

Split

N

Solinski Zaljev

River Jadro

Railway

Sta.

URBS NOVA
OCCIDENTALIS

Amphitheatre

Kapljuc

URBS VETUS

Theatre

Porta Caesarea

Basilica urbana

Basilica

Tusculum

Manastirine

Car Park

URBS NOVA
ORIENTALIS

Porta Andetria

Solin

Madonna
dell'Isola

later made cruciform under the influence of Byzantine models. It is thought that some of the well-known church assemblies of Salona were held in this building. Of the remaining buildings in this area, which include a bishop's palace and a well defined chapel, the most interesting consists of a gymnasium and *Thermae*, which have been excavated to show the hypocausts under the steam rooms. The floor of the frigidarium is still intact and in the N.E. chamber are traces of frescoes.

Continuing S. and then right along the gravel road we pass (down steps to the left) the former *Porta Caesarea*, marking the division between old and new Salona. The western and older half is the Greco-Illyrian quarter (Urbs occidentalis); that to the east (Urbs orientalis) the more purely Roman section. Ten minutes walk brings us to Kapljuč another Christian necroplis just N. of the Kaštela road, beside the stream of the same name. The remains of a 4C basilica stand beside the necropolis, dedicated to the Five Martyrs of Salona. At the W. end of the city are the scanty remains of the 2C *Amphitheatre* (undergoing restoration) with seating for 15–18,000 spectators. Only the foundations, the outline of the great eastern entrance, and the central arena remain.

Immediately beyond the amphitheatre we emerge on the road for Kaštel Sućurac, beside which, c. ¼ m w., is the *Hortus Metrodori*, Salona's largest necropolis, though little remains visible. In the opposite direction, towards Solin, we pass the ruins of a Roman *Theatre* on the very edge of the road, with the scanty remains of a temple opposite. The area between the theatre and the basilica urbana to the N. is the site of the forum. To the E. one of the city gates, *Porta Andetria*, opens on to the main road for Klis and Sinj; beyond the road, on the site of yet another necropolis, *Suplja crkva*, a pre-Romanesque basilica which may have been the coronation church of King Zvonimir of Croatia, has recently been excavated.

To KLIS AND SINJ, 34 km., asphalt road (bus). We take the Trogir road (comp. above) and at Solin bear right. The road rises in stages through the foothills, with magnificent views of *Kozjak* ridge to the left and of the jagged peaks of *Mosor* to the right, culminating in Debelo brdo (3390 ft) and, farther away, Ljubelj (4323 ft). Threading a tunnel, we turn sharp left before the summit of the pass on to a narrow asphalt road for (9 km.) **Klis**. Beyond the village and dominating the pass the castle occupies a romantic position (1300 ft) on the cliff.

Klis was occupied in Roman times and was later the estate of Prince Trpimir (?845–64) of Croatia. In the Middle Ages it was held by the Subić family and in 1242 King Bela IV sought refuge here from the Tartars. With the arrival of the Turks in Dalmatia its strategic position gave it added importance. The basic fortifications were erected by Marko Pavlović and Ivan Karlović in the 15C, but they were completed by the Turks after their capture of the castle in 1537. Petar Kružić, a celebrated Uskok captain from Senj, lost his life in the battle. Klis remained the keypoint of Turkish domination of inland Dalmatia until Leonardo Foscolo retook the castle for Venice in 1648, after which its importance declined.

The **Castle**, reached by footpath (ask for key in village), consists of a triple enceinte at different levels. The remaining buildings occupy the innermost ring, entered through a massive Baroque gateway. They include a small historical museum (mainly pictures and documents) and, a rarity in Dalmatia, a small Turkish mosque, later converted to Christian worship as Sv. Vid. From the top of the ramparts there are splendid views over the valley to Mosor and s. to Split and the islands.

Continuing on good asphalt, we cross a rocky karst plain to (30 km.) *Brnaze*, a village on the edge of the fertile Sinjsko polje, where we turn left. Sinj aerodrome (r.) formerly served charter flights for Split.

34 km. **Sinj**, a pleasant town of 4200 inhab. planted with trees, achieved its present appearance mainly in the 18C after the departure of the Turks. It is celebrated for the *Sinjska Alka*, an annual competition or tourney to celebrate a famous victory over the Turks on 15 August 1715. Fifteen mounted 'knights' or Alkari, dressed in 18C costume, tilt at a ring in the shape of a stirrup (the 'alka') to symbolize the capture of the Turkish general on horseback, a colourful and stirring ceremony that attracts huge crowds. The costumes used at the tourney can be seen at the *Alkarski muzej*, with the horses' harness and the riders' weapons. Also displayed are Turkish weapons and the saddle of Serašćer Mehmet Pasha, the defeated Turkish general. The conjoint *Town Museum* has a section devoted to the National Liberation Struggle. A small collection of *Persian furniture, put together by a former Yugoslav ambassador to Persia, includes a beautiful inlaid games table, a rich trellis screen, and a large bureau with a trellised front and inlaid with mother-of-pearl.

A *Franciscan Monastery*, not far away, houses a good collection of finds from the neighbouring Roman site of Aequum (now Čitluk). Outside are Roman gravestones, including a good mausoleum gate covered with reliefs (also a 14C font and a Bosnian cross dated 1703). A separate museum is devoted to sculpture, reliefs, and coins, with a notable marble head of Hercules, heads of Diana and Minerva, and a statue of Hecate. A good local Ethnograhic Collection includes folk costume, musical instruments, jewellery, and bygones.

17 FROM SPLIT TO DUBROVNIK

ROAD, 223 km. (138 m.), a fine stretch of the JADRANSKA MAGISTRALA close to the coast all the way. 26 km. *Omiš.*—63 km. **Makarska.** 114 km. *Ploče*, for (139 km.) *Metković.*—174 km. **Ston** for (237 km.) *Orebić.*—223 km. **Dubrovnik.** BUS every 2 hrs in c. 4 hrs.

STEAMERS to Omiš, Makarska and Dubrovnik; the express route between Split and Dubrovnik plies viâ Korčula.

Leaving Split by the Ul. proleterskih brigada and the suburb of Bačvice, we pass through vineyards to (3 km.) *Stobreč*, where the road regains the coast. Here was the site of Greek Epetion. Villages here are gradually being developed as quiet holiday resorts, with clean shingle beaches and accommodation in pensions or private rooms. In (20 km.) *Sumpetar* are two Gothic chapels, of which Sv. Stjepan in the cemetery has a pre-Romanesque altar rail and a Renaissance bust of St Stephen. Continuing s. with views offshore to the island of Brač we round the headland at Dugi rat, with its massive fertilizer factory, and come in sight of the Bay of Omiš and mouth of the river Cetina.

26 km. **Omiš** (*Brzet; Plaža;* P.O., rest., cinema, sandy beach) a somewhat shapeless small town (2200 inhab.) huddles at the foot of the towering Omiška dinara ridge on the left bank of the river Cetina. The Adriatic Highway divides the town into two, the newer part, with a

knitwear factory and a long sandy beach, lying on the broad delta s. of the road, and the old town clinging to the rock to the N. of it.

During the 12–14C Omiš was the lair of a band of gusari, or corsairs, first under the princes Kačić and subsequently the princes Šubić of Bribir. It passed to King Tvrtko of Bosnia and Matko Talovac of Dubrovnik, before surrendering to Venice in 1444. The town suffered considerably from Turkish incursions until 1684. Federiko Benković 'Schiavone' (1677–1753) is thought to have been born here and other natives include the poet, Jure Kaštelan (b. 1919).

A medieval gate gives access from the highway to the main street and crowded houses of the old quarter. The Baroque parish church of *Sv. Mihovil* (St Michael, 16–17C) in the main street has a fine w. door (1621) and detached campanile. Within are a good Baroque crucifixion and two paintings by Matteo Ingoli of Ravenna (? 1585–1631). Farther along a Renaissance house contains the modest *Gradski muzej* (open evenings 5–7), where the lapidary collection includes a Roman relief of Dionysus and the 13C memorial slab of Prince Miroslav Kačić. Among historical documents is preserved the Omiška dukala (1579), an illuminated parchment decree. Also displayed are folk costumes and relics of the Second World War. A little beyond the 18C chapel of *Sv. Rok* steps ascend to the clock tower and church of *Sv. Duh* (1585), with a painting by Palma Giovane of the Descent of the Holy Ghost; more steps mount from the clock tower to the ruined *Peovica-Mirabella Fortress*, affording excellent views of the town and coast and into the Cetina canyon. The *Starigrad Fortress*, perched on a rock pinnacle higher up to the E., can be reached in c. $\frac{1}{2}$ hr by a stiff climb. The main street continues to the pleasant main square on the bank of the river Cetina, with a Venetian štandarac (stone flagpole). A footbridge crosses the Cetina to the suburb of *Priko*, where the pre-Romanesque church of *Sv. Petar* stands beyond open ground. The 10C exterior is decorated with lesenes and blind arcading and has a curious gabled tower enclosing a small cupola. The s. wall is pierced by three stone transennae.

A pleasant excursion up the river Cetina to *Radmanove mlinice* may be made by road or, better, by boat through the impressive Cetina gorge. Beyond the dam of the Zakučac hydro-electric works stands the mill house and former summer villa of the Radman family, now a pension and restaurant (fishing and bathing in the park).

From Priko a gravel road leads to *Gata*, former capital of the tiny independent republic of Poljica, which extended to Žrnovnica in the N.W. and from the sea to the Cetina. Its independence, dating from the 11–12C, was ended by Napoleon in 1807.

Beyond Omiš the Adriatic Highway runs along the foot of the Omiška dinara (2835 ft) with the island of Brač visible offshore. At (45 km.) the bay of Vrulja begins the *MAKARSKA RIVIERA. For nearly 40 km. extend beaches of fine shingle and pebbles, bleached white by the sun. Pinewoods along the shore reach into the foothills of the *Biokovo Mts.*, the highest range of the Velebits, which rise in Sv. Jure to 5730 ft. The villages are especially popular with Yugoslav and central European visitors. The best known are *Donja Brela* (Maestral; Slavia; Tiha; Soline; Brela; Ruža; Primorka) and *Baška Voda* (Slavija; Dubravka; autocamp; night club).

Approaching Makarska we pass (l.) the caves of Veprić and the shrine of *Gospa od Veprić*, a modest emulation of Lourdes initiated by a local bishop in 1908. The road into town (Radnička cesta) leaves the highway by a small pyramid that originally honoured Marshal Marmont. In 1818 its inscription was replaced by another commemorating the visit of Francis Joseph I of Austria.

63 km. **MAKARSKA,** the only coastal town of size (3650 inhab.) between Split and Dubrovnik, is a delightful resort on a sheltered bay extending from the peninsula of Sv. Petar in the N.W. to the headland of Osejava in the S.E. at the foot of the awesome Biokovo Mts. A pleasant park occupies Sv. Petar, on the N. side of which extends the main beach of Donja luka; the town and harbour are farther south. Unlike most Dalmatian towns Makarska has a predominantly modern appearance, many of the oldest buildings (in a Baroque style dating from the 17C) having suffered from air attack.

Hotels. Riviera, 300 R with bath, c. 1 m. w. of town; **Park; Beograd; Makarska; Goran; Osejava.**—PENSIONS. *Vila Grle; Dubrava.*
Autocamp next to Hotel Park.
Restaurants. *Mali mulić,* Mala Obala; *Peškera,* Radnička cesta; *Ribar,* Partizanska ul.; *Plavi Jadran,* Put oslobodjenja; *Plaža,* at the beach; *Mare,* Titova obala.—KAVANA. *Central,* Titova obala.
Post Office, Titova obala.—INFORMATION OFFICE, Turistički biro, Ul. V. Nazora.—TOURIST OFFICES. *Dalmacijaturist,* Mala obala; *Putnik,* Titova obala.
Bus station, Omladinska ul. Frequent buses to all the main towns of the coast and interior. Local buses to *Baška Voda* and *Brela;* also to *Tučepi, Podgora,* and *Živogošće.*
Steamers from Mala obala. Services to most of the chief towns of the mainland and to Hvar; local services to Baška Voda and Split.
Beach. *Donja Luka,* just N.E. of Sv. Petar (fine shingle).

History. The Roman settlement of *Mucurum* was probably destroyed by Totila the Ostrogoth in 548. Makarska became a centre of the Slavonic Neretvans or Narentines, a widely feared nation of corsairs, sometimes known as Pagania, based on the river Neretva. They vanquished the Venetian fleet off Makarska in 887. In the 11–14C the city formed part of Croatia (later Hungary–Croatia), passed for a century to the Kotromanić princes of Bosnia and after a brief interval under Venice was occupied by the Turks (1499–1646), who made it their chief port on the Adriatic. Venice regained the city and in 1797 it passed to Austria. Makarska was demolished by the Turks and suffered from bombing during the Second World War; in 1962 it was damaged by an earthquake. Andrija Kačić-Miošić (1704–60), poet and scholar, was educated and lived in Makarska.

From the Mala obala, S.E. of the quay, steps lead up to KAČIĆEV TRG, the main square. In the centre stands a statue by Ivan Rendić (1890) of Andrija Kačić-Miošić, author in 1756 of a successful collection of patriotic verse, which had a marked influence on the development of Croatian literature. A large fountain (1770), bearing the city arms, stands in front of the Baroque parish church (cathedral until 1828) of *Sv. Marko* (1700–76), which has a good Venetian high altar of marble (18C) and a silver reredos (1818) portraying the Madonna of the Rosary. Paintings in the sacristy include portraits of former bishops and 16C icons. In a small square to the N. of the church is the market.

To the N. of the steamer quay Titova (Velika) obala, preserves a single Baroque mansion, and the church of *Sv. Filip Neri* (1769), built by Bp. Blašković. A number of Roman gravestones are kept in the courtyard.

From the S.E. end of Mala obala, Put žrtava fašizma runs past the *Sports Centre,* built in 1959 as a winter training centre for national and foreign teams, to the **Franciscan Monastery,** founded in 1400 and reconstructed in 1614. The Baroque bell tower was added in 1715. Within the precincts we pass a well-head decorated with the escutcheon of Bp.

Blašković and enter the charming rustic cloister, with an open loggia running round the top. The simple church (once used as a mosque by the Turks) will house the monastery's paintings. The *MALAKALOŠKI MUZEJ* (open 10–12, 5–7), off the cloister, displays an outstanding collection of seashells from all parts of the world.

Excursions may be made on foot from Makarska to the **Biokovo Mts.** A gravel road leads to the nearby village of *Makar*, whence footpaths lead to *Velo Brdo* (2066 ft), *Vožac* (4620 ft), with a mountain hut, and *Sv. Jure* (5730 ft) the highest point on the Dalmatian coast.

The Adriatic Highway continues a little inland while a minor road along the shore serves the narrow but attractive pebble beaches that comprise the southern half of the Makarska Riviera.—68 km. **Tučepi** stands back from the shore on the main road, but its name is commonly applied to the resort of *Kraj* that stands beside the sea (*Jadran*, 157 R with bath; *Maslinik; Kaštelet; Tamaris*, all on beach; rest.). The tiny 13C church of *Sv. Juraj* behind the Hotel Tamaris is an example of early-Croatian Romanesque and incorporates Roman capitals. The Hotel Kaštelet occupies the 18C *Palača Grubišić*.

70 km. **Podgora** (*Mediteran, Primordia, Lovor, Bambus, Podgorka, Borak;* autocamp) is a pleasant fishing village with an attractive harbour. During the war it was the first headquarters of the Partisan navy, founded here in September 1942, and was the object of 40 bombing raids. It also suffered damage from the earthquake of 1962. Above the harbour a striking monument, 100 ft high, takes the form of a symbolic seagull with wings outspread, designed by Rajko Radović in 1962 to mark the 20th anniversary of the new Yugoslav navy. An unusual church by Ante Rožič (1964) takes the shape of a tent.—81 km. *Igrane* with a long sand and pebble beach is overlooked by the roofless 17C fortress tower of Zale; lower down, beside the harbour stands the 18C Baroque Palača Simić-Ivanišević. Above the main road, amid olive groves, stands the early pre-Romanesque basilica of Sv. Mihovil (Michael; 11–12C). —84 km. *Živogošće* (Domus, 170 R with bath), the last village of the Makarska Riviera, is said to be the only place on the Adriatic where nightingales sing. To the S.E. of the village are the 17C Franciscan Monastery and the Baroque church of Uznesenje sv. Križa (Assumption of the Holy Cross, 1766), with a painted ceiling.

We continue along one of the most magnificent sections of the coast, where the Velebit Mts. descend directly into the sea. Offshore the island of Hvar comes its closest to the mainland off (88 km.) *Drvenik*, whence a car ferry plies to Sućuraj (see Rte 20). The long peninsula of Pelješac, previously glimpsed far off over Hvar, now fills the seaward view. We come to (92 km.) *Zaostrog* with a Franciscan Monastery of the 16–17C. The church contains good Baroque altars and choir stalls, an organ by Petar Nakić (1694–1770) and busts of Andrija Kačić Miošić and Ivan Despot by I. Rendić. There is a Roman mosaic floor in the garden.—104 km. *Brist*, birthplace of Kačić-Miošić (monument in the parish church by Meštrović), and (106 km.) *Gradac* (Laguna) with an excellent shingle beach ('Gornja Vala') and a ruined fortress tower (1661), are the last villages before the road veers inland to cross the estuary of the river Neretva.

Crossing the irregularly shaped *Baćinsko jezero* (Lake Baćin) by a bridge over its narrowest part we come to *Posrednica*, the broad Neretva delta, a feature unique to this coast. Just s. of the main road, (114 km.) **Ploče** (3220 inhab.) is being developed as a modern port to serve the hinterland of Bosnia and Hercegovina. A car ferry to Trpanj (see p. 159), on the Pelješac peninsula, affords the shortest route from Split to Korčula. The road now runs parallel to the electric railway (Ploče–Sarajevo) and one of the arms of the river Neretva. The marshy delta land is gradually being reclaimed for agriculture and, such is its fertility, produces two crops a year. The local reeds are extensively employed for basket-making. A unique design of boat, called a *trupica*, with a flat bottom and raised ends, is found locally on the Neretva river.—At (117 km.) *Rogotin* the road divides, one arm running along the right bank of the Neretva to Metković (22 km.) while the newer Adriatic Highway crosses it to follow the left bank (comp. below).

Metković is an untidy river port and the growing industrial centre (4500 inhab.) of the region. The town is a late successor to the Roman *Narona*, which was second to Salona in Roman Dalmatia and destroyed at the same time by the Avars (614). The village of *Vid*, 4 km. N.W. of Metković, occupies the site of the city and preserves numerous remains, including a large mosaic floor. There is also a small archaeological museum. The extensive marshes N.E. of Metković known as the *Hutovo blato*, are rich in bird life, particularly ducks (shooting in the season). The Ornithological Museum in Metković possesses over 300 species collected in this area.

From Metković excursions may be made up the Neretva valley to Bosnia–Hercegovina, whose border runs just N. of the town.—4 km. *Gabela*, once part of the Republic of Ragusa, has a good medieval square and 16C Turkish fortifications.—Near (15 km.) *Čapljin* at the hamlet of *Mogorjelo* are the extensive remains of a fortified Roman villa (4C) and two early-Christian basilicas (5C), with a lapidary collection.—17 km. *Počitelj* is a well-preserved example of a Turkish walled town, with a good Mosque (1563), clock tower, a small han and the house of the Gavran-Kapetanović family. A little beyond Počitelj a poor gravel road leads right to *Stolac* (41 km.), near which is the necropolis of Radimlje with a fascinating collection of ornamented Bogomil tombs.

The main road at Rogotin takes us across the river Neretva which it follows almost to (124 km.) *Opuzen*, once a possession of Ragusa and from 1685 the site of the Venetian Fort Opus (now ruined), that marked the s. limit of Venetian possessions in Dalmatia. The house of Stjepan-Steva Filipović, executed by the Germans at Valjevo in 1942, is marked by a plaque. *Podgradina*, with the castle of Brštanik (1373, rebuilt 1878), is visible on our left as we climb high above the Posrednica with a superb view of the marsh delta, before we return to the coast at the landlocked bay of Klek-Neum. The bay is named for two villages, Klek at the N.W. end of the bay and Neum in the S.E. The territory between them was ceded to the Turks by Ragusa under the Treaty of Passarowitz (now Požarevac) in 1718, providing the Turks with an outlet to the sea while placing a protective corridor between Venetian possessions in Dalmatia and the territory of Ragusa. After 1878 this strip of coast passed to Bosnia-Hercegovina and is still administered from Sarajevo as Bosnia's only outlet to the sea. In *Klek*, just off the main highway, is the ruined Monković tower and chapel from the 17C; the fortress Smrden-grad stands just outside the village, near a Bogomil cemetery (14–15C). Skirting *Neum* we continue s. along the barren shores of the Kanal Malog Stona, with views of the Pelješac peninsula across the narrowing channel. A bridge spans a wide inlet, affording views of a pretty inhabited islet; just beyond we get a fine glimpse of Mali Ston (see below).

At 166 km., by a petrol station, a good gravel road turns off right to the peninsula of Pelješac.

PELJEŠAC is all but an island; only since 1956 have all its settlements been linked by road. Traditionally it has looked to the sea for communications and a livelihood. With a width varying between 2 and 4 m. and 43 m. long, it is one of the most delightful and least explored territories left on the Adriatic coast, and has an abundance of reptilian life.

In ancient times the peninsula (Rhatanae Chersonesus) was settled by both the Greeks and the Romans and later was held by Byzantium. With the coming of the Slavs it was incorporated into the state of the Neretvans, then into the principality of Zahmulje and in 1333 passed to Ragusa, which held it until its fall in 1808. The peninsula reached the peak of its prosperity in the 18C and early 19C when its fleet based at Orebić, traded all over the world. When steam replaced sail, Pelješac declined into obscurity.

By Road to Orebić, 71 km., in course of improvement throughout, but still very rough going in 1968.—6½ km. **Mali Ston** together with Ston (see below) forms part of the most remarkable complex of fortifications on the Adriatic, designed to block off the neck of the peninsula from the ma inland. When complete it extended for a distance of just under 3½ m., and with a total of 41 towers and 7 larger bastions. The fortifications were begun by Ragusa in 1334, when they acquired Pelješac, and completed in 1506. Among the architects were Župan Bunić (1445), Michelozzo Michelozzi (1461–64), Juraj Dalmatinac (1465), Olivier Francuz (1472–78), and Paskoje Miličević (1488–1506).

Mali Ston was laid out as a square with a grid of streets running N.–S. and E.–W. and enclosed within walls (1336–58), most of which still stand. Entrance to the harbour (1490), which was modelled on the old harbour of Dubrovnik, is gained through the *Morska vrata* (1358), with a relief of St Blaise over the arch, while a large fortified salt warehouse, *Slanica* (1462–81), stands on the shore beside it. In the centre of the village is the 14C parish church (later rebuilt) with a bell cast in 1491. Mali Ston controls extensive oyster and mussel beds, situated in various parts of the Kanal Malog Stona and in the bay of Bistrina on the opposite shore.

On rising ground just s. of Mali Ston stands the massive fortress of *Koruna* with 5 towers facing the sea. Hence the main defence wall of the peninsula runs to the high hill of *Pozvizd* (812 ft; footpath), crowned by another fortress midway between Mali Ston and Ston. It affords an unparalleled view of the s.E. part of the peninsula and of the remaining fortifications. The road runs at the foot of the hill parallel with the wall to a third massive fortress, the Veliki kaštio in Ston.

8 km. **Ston** (*Prapratna*, turist biro, P.O., beach), an attractive but melancholy little town (650 inhab.), had suffered considerably from the improving efforts of earlier generations and lost all its walls and many of the public buildings erected under Ragusa, even before it was all but annihilated by 28 allied bombing raids during the last war.

The *Veliki kaštio* occupies one corner of the main square, in the centre of which the neo-Gothic church of *Sv. Vlaho* (St Blaise) replaces the former Gothic cathedral (destroyed by an earthquake in 1850). Relics from the previous building include an icon of the Virgin by

Andrea Riccio (1470–1532); wooden statues of SS Blaise, Peter, and Paul; and a Gothic font. On the far side of the square are the Venetian Gothic *Palača Sorkočević-Djorkić*, now the Hotel Prapratna; the Gothic *Chancery* of the Republic of Ragusa; and, a short way down the main street, the former *Biskupska palača* (1573), in which both Gothic and Renaissance elements are mixed. The loggia houses examples of pre-Romanesque stone carving and a number of statues of St Blaise. Farther down the main street, beyond a large open space, the *Franciscan Nunnery* (1347) has a beautiful cloister in South Italian Gothic and a late Romanesque church (*Sv. Nikola*). Both were damaged by bombing and are being restored. In the sacristy are a painted Crucifixion attributed to Blaž Trogiranin (15C), a Gothic silver censer, a silver-embossed missal and a Gothic figure in wood of St Nicholas. At the far end of the main street, beyond the limit of the former city walls, the 15C parish church of the *Navještenje* (Annunciation) has a loggia containing two bells cast by Ivan of Rab (1528).

On Starigrad and on Sv. Mihajlo, two hills overlooking the town, can be seen extensive remains of the two Roman castra of *Turris Stagni*, as it was then called, while Sv. Mihajlo was also the site of early medieval Ston. Near the top of the hill is the pre-Romanesque church of *Sv. Mihajlo* with Romanesque *Frescoes among the oldest in Yugoslavia; two other medieval churches survive intact.

To the s.e. of Ston are the extensive salt flats which for centuries have formed the basis of the town's economy. Beyond them a narrow gravel road runs to *Broce* on the Stonski kanal, with an abandoned Dominican monastery and church (1629), three other churches and the ruined villa (1539) of the bell and gun founder, Ivan of Rab.

The Pelješac road runs s.w. out of Ston, and leaving the bathing beach and autocamp of Prapratna on the left, turns N.W. along the peninsula's central spine of hills. Between the villages of Gornja and Donja Dubrava narrow gravel tracks lead off (left) to *Žuljana* on the open sea, with two Baroque churches and a good sandy beach, and (right) to *Brijesta*, on a deep protected inlet of the kanal, with a square fortress tower (1617) and the Baroque church of Sv. Liberan.—At (37 km.) *Drače* we touch the N. shore briefly and then cross to the s. shore, passing through *Janjina* (600 inhab.), the largest of the inland villages, and *Popova Luka* to *Trstenik*. A short distance away is the village of *Dingač*, which gives name to one of the best known red wines of Yugoslavia.—At (52 km.) *Potomje* a road forks right to Kuna and the fishing village of *Crkvice*. In *Kuna*, in the Zupa hills, is a Franciscan monastery (1705) with a Baroque church containing several works by Celestin Medović (1850–1920), whose birthplace this was. More paintings are displayed in his house, and there is a monument to the artist by Ivan Meštrović (1955). From Kuna a rough road continues to Trpanj, also reached by a by-road from Županje Selo, though it is better to continue to our junction with the main Trpanj–Orebić road, whence Trpanj is 3 km. down a steep descent.

The small port of **Trpanj** (780 inhab.) on the N.W. shore of Pelješac, opposite the estuary of the river Neretva, is reached by regular car ferry from Ploče (see p. 157) on the mainland, and has steamer services to Split, Makarska, and Korčula. The high altar of the church of *Gospa od Karmena* is decorated with the arms of the Gundulić family of Dubrovnik. The parish church has a richly ornamented window from an earlier 16C building. Beside the ruined medieval fortress overlooking the harbour are the remains of a Roman bath. A by-road leads to the hamlet of *Donja Vručica* with the summer villa of the Dubrovnik noble and poet, Dinko Ranjina (1536–1607).

Beyond Županje Selo the main road descends a long precipitous shelf of rock to the s. shore.

71 km. **Orebić** (*Rathaneum*, 120 R with bath; *Bon Repos; Bellevue;* Turist biro; P.O.) a delightful and peaceful village (560 inhab.) in surroundings of great natural beauty, faces the island of Korčula. An air of prosperity and even sophistication is imparted by the sea captains' houses that line its main street, although real wealth has long since departed. As a resort (with shingle beaches) it is noted for its benign climate, being well-protected by the mountains rising behind it, and its profusion of subtropical vegetation.

As the seat of a Dubrovnik knez (prince), the medieval village (comp. below) was known as *Trstenica*, but when the shore settlement became the centre of the Pelješac merchant fleet in the 16C it took the name of Orebić after a seafaring family from Bakar in the Kvarner.

In the centre of the village is the *Pormorski muzej* (Maritime Museum, open 8–11, 4–7), which illustrates the history of Orebić's merchant fleet, by models, paintings and documents. Two of the more interesting *Captains' Houses* (for adm. inquire locally) have been arranged as informal museums. The house of Mr Matko Zupa (curator of the Pomorski muzej), an 18C villa with painted walls and ceilings, contains an eclectic collection of furniture by Chippendale and Biedermeier, pottery by Wedgwood and the Russian court potter Kuznetsov, and excellent copper and pewter. The house of the Fisković family, now owned by the chief conservationist at Split, reproduces the conditions of life in the 18–19C and also includes interesting icons and 19C costume. The Baroque church of the *Navještenje* (Annunciation) has an early Christian relief on the porch.

About 1 m. w. of the village is a 15C *Franciscan Monastery* in a mixture of Gothic and Renaissance styles, with a fortified cloister and loggia. The relief of the Madonna over the w. door of the church is by a pupil of Mino da Fiesole; a similar relief within is by Nikola Firentinac. The monastery also has plate and ex-votos donated by local sailors. Higher up the hillside is the site of *Trstenica*, with the ruined Kneževa palača and a Baroque loggia. The Gothic church of Gospa od Karmena was later converted to a Baroque edifice and contains Baroque gravestones and more ex-votos and plate. Beyond the monastery a fair gravel road leads to the neighbouring villages of *Kučišće* (Gothic chapel with bell from 1522) and *Viganj* (Dominican Monastery with cloister, 1671), which shared the management of the merchant fleets with Orebić. Captains' houses may be seen in both places; of particular interest is the Lazarević house (c. 1700) in Kučišće.

Orebić lies at the foot of Zmijino brdo and the highest peak on the Pelješac peninsula, *Sv. Ilija* (3123 ft), which can be climbed in about 1½ hrs (mountain hut).

CAR FERRY several times daily to Korčula in ½ hr; buses to Dubrovnik.

Continuing s. the Adriatic Highway passes through the village of *Djunta-Doli* (16C tower, Bogomil tombstones) and skirts the shore.

177 km. *Slano* (Admiral; Primorje; autocamp; shingle beach) is a curious village, one of whose main occupations is the gathering of medicinal herbs. At the annual fair (2 Aug) folk costumes are worn and an ancient dance called the Lindjo is performed. The Franciscan church of Sv. Jeronim (1420) contains ornamented tombstones of the Ohmučević family of Bosnia, whose pleasant summer villa stands in the village. In the hills behind Slano, at *Zavala* (14 km.), is the large limestone cave of Vjetrenica, with stalagmites and stalactites and several underground

lakes.—To the s. of Slano the grey karst gives way to more vegetation, with views across the Koločepski kanal to the Elaphite Islands (Šipan, Lopud, and Koločep). Beyond (189 km.) *Brsečine*, with a summer villa and park of the Bizzarro family, we enter the beginning of the historical purlieus of Dubrovnik.

192 km. **Trsteno** is celebrated for the excellent *Botanical Park*, the oldest in Yugoslavia, laid out in the Renaissance manner in 1502 by the Gučetić family of Ragusa. It is administered by the Biological Institute of the Yugoslav Academy of Sciences. Occupying the slope between the Adriatic Highway and the sea, the park is reached by an avenue of cedars and cypresses. The exotic species include oleander, jasmine, eucalyptus, cinnamon, camphor, magnolia, bougainvillea, etc., together with varieties of cactus and palm. A rare oak (quercus lanuginosa), 600 years old, stands behind the villa; in front of it a long pergola is covered with climbing plants. The villa, once the residence of the writer Nikola Vitov Gučetić (1549–1610), contains a small historical collection relating to the family, a small lapidary collection and an arboretum. The Baroque fountain in the park depicting Neptune with sea nymphs was erected in 1736. In the village stands a pair of colossal plane trees (platanus orientalis) said to be 400 years old and the only specimens in continental Europe. The larger of the two has a girth of 36 ft.—A painting of St Michael in the Gothic parish church is sometimes wrongly attributed to Titian.

195 km. *Orašac* until 1399 marked the boundary between Ragusa and Bosnia and was a favourite resort of the Ragusan nobility. Here are a small Dominican monastery (1690) and the former villa (1700) of the Austrian Resident in Ragusa, Filippo Saponaro. The massive ruined palace of Arapovo is said to have belonged to the Gonfalier, Pietro Doderini, of Florence. The twin villages of *Veliki Zaton* and (203 km.) *Mali Zaton*, on opposite sides of a pretty inlet, also have private chapels of the Ragusan nobility, and Mali Zaton a summer villa of the Sorkočević family.

We turn inland to follow the course of the Rijeka Dubrovačka or river Ombla (see p. 208) and return on the other side to Gruž (see p. 206) and (223 km.) **Dubrovnik** (Rte 22).

18 THE ISLAND OF BRAČ

STEAMERS daily from Split to Supetar, Postira, Pučišća, Milna, Bol, Sutivan, and Spliska; daily except Sundays to Bobovišća; four times a week to Sumartin. CAR FERRY daily from Split to Supetar.

The island of **BRAČ** (14,721 inhab.) is the most northerly of the southern Dalmatian group and the third largest in the Adriatic, 24 m. long, and 8 m. wide. It is divided from the mainland by the Brački kanal, 3½ m. at its narrowest point, and from the island of Hvar to the s. by the equally narrow Hvarski kanal. Over most of its surface Brač exhibits the typical rocky landscape of the karst region, particularly in the s., where a range of mountains rises to 2529 ft in Vidova gora, the highest island peak in the Adriatic. Although there are no springs, the island is relatively fertile in the centre and E., and produces morello cherries, almonds, figs, and olives in abundance. Its goats' milk cheese was praised by Pliny and its wines are renowned, particularly the white Vugava and the red Murvica. Brač limestone, quarried along the N. shore, is remarkable for the purity and durability of its whiteness and was utilized for Diocletian's palace, the cathedral tower at Split, and the cathedral at Trogir. It was chosen, after much research, for the Canadian Vimy Ridge Memorial in Flanders. Ponies and mules still provide the chief mode of transport in the interior. They are pastured for much of the year in a semi-wild condition and rounded up periodically in colourful fashion.

In spite of its size and relatively large population the island has never had a town, although Supetar was recently designated the administrative centre and is a town in name. The inhabitants are more rural and conservative than on neighbouring islands and have preserved ancient customs, dialects and a way of life which differ from other parts of Dalmatia. The strong indigenous tradition of stone carving can be seen in dozens of cemeteries and small churches scattered about the island.

History. Brač has been continually inhabited since Neolithic times. To the Greeks it was known as *Elaphos* for the stags found on it, while the Latin name of *Brattia* may derive from *brentos*, the Illyrian word for stag. The chief settlement in ancient times was on the site of Škrip, but in the early middle ages, owing to the danger from pirates, the entire population withdrew inland and the centre shifted to Nerežišća. Brač passed to Byzantium and in the 11C was occupied by the Neretvans. It passed to the Kačići of Omiš, to Split (1240), Hungary, Bosnia and finally to Venice in 1420, under whose greater security the population began to move back to the coast. For much of this time Brač was administratively united with the neighbouring island of Hvar. All but two of the main settlements on the island date from after the 15C. During the 16C Brač received numbers of refugees fleeing from the Turks on the mainland, particularly from the small republic of Poljica. With the fall of Venice, Brač passed to Austria, was for a while a base for the Russian fleet and after a brief period of French rule returned to Austria. It was united to Yugoslavia in 1918.

Natives include Trifun Bokanić (1575–1609), the stone mason and builder; the sculptors Ivan Rendić (1849–1932) and Branko Dešković (1883–1939); and Vladimir Nazor (1876–1949), the poet, novelist and critic.

The principal settlement, **Supetar** (*Jadran; Palma*), usually the first or second port of call of the steamer from Split, has daily bus services to all parts of the island, and local boats to the villages on the N. coast. Supetar is a modern little town (1500 inhab.) that originated as the port for Nerežišća and later, thanks to its proximity to Split, replaced it as the island's administrative centre. The parish church retains Baroque west doors (1733), the central one surmounted by a statue of God the Father blessing. Inside is a Baroque Venetian painting of the Virgin and St Anne, a portrait (in the sacristy) of the parish priest by a local painter, F. Tironi (1783), and in the treasury a Renaissance monstrance. The painted processional standards lining the walls, with representations of saints at the top, are guild emblems. An ornate Baroque wellhead (1734) stands in an adjoining courtyard.

A pleasant promenade runs W. of town to the beach (cabins, showers), with a pebble foreshore and sand beyond, and thence to the wooded headland of Sv. Nikola with the town's *Cemetery*. Among the fine headstones are a number of apprentice works by Ivan Rendić, notably the Franasović Memorial with a good pietà. The cemetery is dominated by the exotic Petrinović Mausoleum by Rendić's contemporary, Toma Rosandić, an uneasy blend of Byzantine and oriental elements. Two early Christian sarcophagi against the N. wall are decorated with low relief crosses.

From Supetar a gravel road lined with cypresses runs W., parallel with the N. shore, to (7 km.) the quiet village of *Sutivan* (Vesna). On the waterfront are an abandoned windmill, the Baroque Palača Kavanjin (1705), now used as a hotel, the fortified Renaissance Palača Natali (1505) and the Kaštel Marjanović (1777), all of modest pretensions and with later additions and alterations. In the Baroque parish church of Sv. Ivan a mannerist work depicting Our Lady of the Rosaries (17C Italian) is of interest. The handsome Baroque bell tower with an onion dome is by P. P. Bertapelle (18C).

In the opposite direction from Supetar a similar road runs E. to (6 km.) *Spliska*, a delightful small village set in pine woods at the head of its own bay. In the centre the massive Kaštel Cerineo (1577), with machicolated corner towers, contains a Madonna by Bernardino dei Conti (c. 1500), a pupil of Leonardo da Vinci, and a 16C portrait of Mauro Cerineo Morruso. A Madonna and Saints signed by Leandro Bassano adorns the high altar of the parish church. From the harbour the stone for Diocletian's palace was shipped and the quayside is now usually piled with Brač limestone awaiting despatch. The quarries lie about 15 mins walk inland; in *Rasohe* quarry is an unusual 4C Roman relief of Hercules cut in the rock.

A tortuous narrow gravel track leads uphill inland from Spliska to the hamlet of *Škrip* (3 km.) the oldest settlement on the island. On the E. side of the village is the 18C parish church of *Sv. Jelena* with a good Baroque w. front, though the effect of a fine wheel-window has been somewhat spoiled by the addition of other windows. A statue of the Madonna and Child occupies a niche over the w. door and on top of the gable is the Risen Christ. The aisleless interior has a stuccoed apsidal chapel enclosing the high altar, while four Baroque side altars bear paintings by Palma Giovane. The bell tower exhibits styles from Gothic to Baroque. Adjoining is the much altered *Kaštel Cerineo* (1618), with fortified towers at opposing corners (view). Three Roman sarcophagi stand beside the castle. To the E. of the church is the single tower of the *Kaštel Radojković*, with a vaulted lower story which is largely Roman. Beside it can be seen the massive masonry of a *Cyclopean Wall* thought to have been constructed by the Illyrians (? 3C B.C.). In the near-by cemetery is the curious Romanesque church of *Sv. Duh* (11–12C), to which a double bell cot was added in the 14C and aisles in the 16C. Ornately carved gravestones of the Cerineo family can be seen inside the church, and in the cemetery the simpler stones of various artisans and craftsmen, bearing carved emblems of their trade.

Beyond Spliska the coastal road continues to (9 km.) *Postira* (Park, sandy beaches), a large village spread out on a hillside with an attractive fishing harbour and waterfront. The parish church of Sv. Ivan Krstitelj (John the Baptist) has a curious fortified apse with embrasures and machicolations dating from the 16C, when the Turkish threat was most imminent. The house in which Vladimir Nazor was born (plaque) has Renaissance elements. A favourite excursion is to the lovely sandy bay of *Lovrečina* about 1¼ m. to the E., where the ruins of an early Christian basilica, with an unusual ground plan, preserve two sarcophagi. The hamlet of *Dol*, lying 2 m. inland, is pleasantly reached on foot by a steep gravel track, through olive groves. The pre-Romanesque church of Sv. Mihovil with shallow blind arcades in the interior and a w. door constructed from a sarcophagus is one of the oldest of this type on the island (? 11C). The Gothic church of Sv. Petar retains its 14C bell. The parish church has a late but surprisingly pure Baroque w. front (1866) and the fortified Renaissance Palača Gospodnetić a fine Baroque escutcheon over the main gate.

THE MAIN ROAD from Supetar runs inland to serve the remaining villages on the island. Leaving Supetar on good gravel we quit the Spliska road after 1 km. and wind up through olive groves with retrospective views to the Brački kanal and mainland. A feature of the landscape here as elsewhere in Brač are the turret-like heaps of stones known as *gomile*, removed from the land by the peasants, a mute testimony to the struggle to maintain a viable agriculture.—6 km. The roofless pre-Romanesque church of *Sv. Luka* stands just off the road. On the inside w. wall, N. of the door, is a rare 11–12C graffito of a sailing ship cut into the plaster, the oldest such drawing in Dalmatia; two smaller ones can be seen on the N. wall.—At 7 km. a T-junction offers a short cut (l.) to Nerežišća (see below), but we bear right to (9 km.) *Donji Humac*, set on a low hill. The parish church of Sv. Fabijan i Sebastijan has a Romanesque nave with Gothic elements dating from a reconstruction in the 14C and aisles added in the 18C, when Ignacije Macanović of Trogir worked on the bell tower (1766). A marble reredos shows the Madonna with SS Fabian and Sebastian and above the apse is a 13C Romanesque fresco of Christ Enthroned, with the Madonna and St John the Baptist. In the treasury is a silver-gilt Renaissance processional cross with saints on the four arms.

The little pre-Romanesque church of *Sv. Ilija*, standing about a mile w. of Donji Humac, incorporates re-used Roman material (part of a Roman memorial in the s. wall). The remains of a sizeable Roman mausoleum can be seen outside the N. wall.

From Donji Humac a road leads w. through the hamlet of *Dračevica* to (8 km.) *Ložišća* where the late Baroque parish church (1820) has an elaborate bell tower designed by I. Rendić; to the N.E. of the village is the Romanesque chapel of Stomorica (11–12C)—9 km. *Bobovišća* consists of a picturesque small harbour and the village c. ½ m. inland. The parish church contains two Venetian paintings in the sacristy, a Pietà (school of Palma Giovane) and Our Lady of Mt. Carmel (18C), while the treasury contains a Renaissance processional cross and fine 18C lace of local workmanship. On a hill overlooking the village is the 14C church of Sv. Martin with a Renaissance reredos carved in relief by a follower of Nikola Firentinac. Beside the harbour of Bobovišća the large fortified Palača Marinčević-Gligo has Baroque details to relieve the plain exterior.

16 km. **Milna**, a growing community (1300 inhab.), situated on a fine natural harbour, was founded in the 17C. In 1807 during the Napoleonic wars, it served for a time as a Russian naval base. The large *Parish Church* (1783) is an excellent example of Dalmatian Baroque with an impressive w. front (statue of the Assumption in the central niche) and an exuberantly stuccoed interior. Cherubs emerge from half-open doors on the key-stone and sideposts of the triumphal arch, a motif borrowed from the chapel of St John in Trogir cathedral. A good Venetian Annunciation (18C) adorns the high altar. The detached 17C bell tower with open upper stories derives from an earlier church. In the centre of the village is the fortified mansion known as *Anglešćina*, errected in the 17C by the Cerineo family. The name derives from a tradition linking mansion and family with a 14C English crusader.

Turning S.E. from Donji Humac we shortly reach (11 km.) **Nerežišća**, a sprawling village, until 1828 the administrative centre of Brač, known for its wine and goats' milk cheese. On rising ground stands the Baroque parish church of *Gospa od Karmena* (1752) by Ignacije Macanović, the cluttered w. front an adaptation of an earlier façade (1593).

The contemporary bell tower anachronistically recalls the Romanesque towers typical of Dalmatia. On the sumptuously Baroque altar is a 17C Venetian painting of the Madonna with SS John and Catherine. The N. aisle has a Madonna of the Rosaries by Carlo Ridolfi and a 17C Annunciation. In the square in front of the church stands a stone flag-pole (*štandarac*), decorated with the Lion of St Mark, and there is large but damaged relief of the Venetian lion on a nearby wall (1545), flanked by the arms of two local governors, Alvise Tiepolo and Giovanni Morosini.

Over another low hill behind the parish church extends the oldest quarter, with many picturesque houses with courtyards, outside staircases and attractive balconies; the largest, the Baroque *Palača Harašić*, has a fine balcony enclosing the s. and E. sides. Near-by are the tiny Gothic chapel of *Sv. Rok*, and, in the grave-yard, the 14C Gothic church of *Sv. Nikola*, with an attractive rose window. In the newer quarter at the bottom of the hill, are two Gothic churches, Sv. Margarita and Sv. Petar, the latter containing a good sculptured reredos depicting the Madonna and Child by Nikola Lazanić (1578), a local artist. Two similar reliefs may be seen just outside the village in the pre-Romanesque church of Sv. Juraj (on a hill to the N.) and (s.) in Sv. Jakov.

Beyond Nerežišća the road climbs higher to the barren karst plateau in the centre of the island. At 14 km. a narrow gravel road forks right to the summit of *Vidova gora* (2529 ft) with superb views over the island and s. to Hvar and Korčula. Excursions may be made to the mountain from Nerežišća, on foot or horseback.—24 km. *Pražnice* is gradually being depopulated as its inhabitants move to the coast. In the modern parish church two reredos illustrate the excellence of the local stone-carving tradition. An early Renaissance relief (1467) adorns the 14C Gothic church of Sv. Ciprijan in the cemetery, and a somewhat cruder one of Pope Clement (1535) the small church of Sv. Klement.

In Pražnice the road divides left for Pučišća (7 km.) and right to the E. and s. areas of the island.

Pučišća, the largest settlement (1680 inhab.) on the island, is today the main source of Brač building stone, with three large quarries near-by and a fine natural harbour, on an inlet 2 m. from the open sea. The modern *Parish Church* has over the high altar a wooden relief of St Jerome by Franja Čiočev, part of an older alter (1578). On the fine wooden Baroque altar of St Anthony is a painting of St Roch by Palma Giovane; and, in the treasury, a processional cross of silver-gilt and an embroidered chasuble (1629). The small Renaissance church of *Gospa od Batka* (Our Lady of Batko, 1533) contains the graves of members of the Bokanić and Radojković families, active throughout Dalmatia in the 16–17C as sculptors and builders. On the high altar is an Renaissance reredos in stone relief attributed to Nikola Radojković, and in the chapel of Sv. Juraj at *Velika Bračuta* just outside the village a relief of St George of similar period. The war memorial by Valerija Michieli, a local sculptor, is the best of its kind on the island.

The right branch beyond Pražnice passes the abandoned hamlet of *Straževnik*, where the early 12C Romanesque church of Sv. Juraj has a bell cot thought to be the oldest in Dalmatia. The unusual Romanesque and Gothic w. door, with six stylized acanthus leaves carved on the lintel and a cross in the tympanum, was added in the 14C. The reredos has two stories, the upper part (Christ with angels) Renaissance work by a pupil of Nikola Firentinac (15C) and the lower (St George and the Dragon) dating from about a century later.—28 km. *Gornji Humac* is another inland village with a dwindling population. In the cemetery church of Sv. Marija a good reredos of three relief panels from the school of Firentinac shows the Madonna and Saints; a Baroque wrought-iron gate divides the chancel from the nave. Over the entrance to the parish church is a late Gothic relief of St Michael, part of an earlier triptych of which a second portion, depicting the Madonna, is kept in the small church of Sv. Rok.

In Gornji Humac the road divides again, the left branch (comp. below) continuing E. We turn right and traverse the ridge of mountains dividing the interior from the s. shore, descending by sharp hairpin bends. About 2 m. beyond Gornji Humac we pass (l.), some distance off the road, the small Gothic church of *Sv. Mihovil*, which contains a Renaissance reredos of St Michael and the dragon. With the high peak of *Draževo brdo* (2038 ft) on our right we swing gradually w. parallel with the shore.

41 km. **Bol**, the only major settlement (1000 inhab.) on the s. shore, is an attractive small resort famous for its golden beach, *Zlatni rat* (*Bijela kuća*, 100 R; *Zlatni rat*; rest.; cinema). The charming small square above the harbour is flanked by the small medieval church of *Sv. Ante* (late Gothic monstrance in the treasury). Adjoining is the 15C Gothic *Palača Lode*, also known as the Kaštil. A short distance behind the square is the parish church of *Gospa od Karmena* (1785), with a good Baroque gable. At the E. end of the village, beyond the hotel Bijela kuća, stands the *Dominican Monastery* (1475). The Gothic church (enlarged in the 17C) has a painting of the Madonna and Child with Saints on the high altar (workshop of Tintoretto) and a choir ceiling decorated with Baroque paintings by Tripo Kokolja (1713). Inserted above the entrance to the cloister is a pre-Romanesque Tympnum from Sv. Ivan (see below). The monastery includes among its paintings an icon of the Adoration of the Magi and a copy of Titian's St John the Baptist, and possesses an extensive numismatic collection. In the treasury is a Baroque chalice from Florence (1666). Near the monastery is the pre-Romanesque church of Sv. Ivan with a w. front and apse altered in the 13C.

At the w. end of the village an avenue of pine trees leads to the pleasant shaded beach of Potočine (pebble and shingle) and in about 10 min to *Zlatni rat, a tongue of fine pebble and shingle beach projecting 600 metres into the sea. The beach while remaining more or less constant in length, is remarkable for changing its shape and direction as affected by the currents of the Hvarski kanal and by wind and wave. Its unique shape assures bathing in calm water irrespective of wind direction. Hotels, comp. above.
To the w. of Bol are a number of pleasant smaller places best visited by boat. The hamlet of *Murvica* (6 km.) has an excellent shingle beach and good inn and is the starting point for walks into the hills to the picturesquely sited nunnery of *Stipančić* (c. ½ hr), now abandoned, and *Dragonjina* (or *Zmajeva*) *špilja*, a near-by cave with medieval monsters and animals carved in the rock (? 15C). A little farther w. and reached by a separate footpath is the ruined hermitage of *Dračeva. luka*, founded in 1519 by Marin de Capitaneis of Split, with its church situated in a cave. The hermitage was fired by the Italians during the Second World War, The more interesting hermitage of *Blaca*, farther w. still, can be reached only by by taking a boat to the tiny bay of Blaca (c. 1½ hrs from Bol) and walking up the valley. The hermitage, founded in 1588, occupies a beautiful situation at the head of the valley beneath vertical cliffs. The last resident, a keen astronomer, left a fascinating collection of old clocks. Among many pictures are lithographs by Poussin. During the war Blaca was used for a while as a British radio station and military hospital; and, on 15 Feb 1961, it provided astronomers with an admirable view of total solar eclipse.

From Gornji Humac the left branch leads through the narrow cultivated valley of *Guča Dol* to the E. tip of the island.—41 km. *Selca* occupies a striking situation at the head of the long narrow bay of Radonja and is an important centre of stone quarrying. In the main square is the colossal unfinished parish church being built by local masons to designs by Adolf Schlauf of Vienna. Projected in 1925 and begun in 1942, the neo-Romanesque building provides a graphic illustration of island pride and local stone-masons' craft. A bronze representation of the Heart of Jesus by Meštrović (1956) stands behind the high altar. On a hill outside the village stands the pre-Romanesque church of *Sv. Nikola*, an excellent example of early Croatian architecture with a cupola and a suspended arch projecting over the w. door. At the seaward end of the bay is the little port of *Sumartin*, whose Franciscan monastery preserves 17–18C Venetian paintings.

A good gravel road through groves of olive and fig trees crosses the E. tip of the island to (48 km.) **Povlja** (*Galeb*), on one arm of a many-branched bay of the same name. In the centre of the village, beside the harbour and adjoining the parish church, are the remains of a large early-Christian BASILICA (4–5C), discovered in 1960. The main body of the basilica has been preserved only in outline, though parts are incorporated into later buildings. The main apse, with an excellent three-light window, forms the base of a fortress tower, itself an adaptation of an earlier building made in the 16C as a defence against the Turks. The *Baptistery* survives complete and is still used. The immersion font is roofed with a cupola above an octagonal drum. The building was converted into a church c. 1100 to serve the Benedictine abbey of Sv. Ivan (St John) of Povlja, when the cruciform basin was used as the saint's tomb. Abbey and church were abandoned in the 14C but the church was later adopted to parochial use. During later enlargements the baptistery was reinstated to its proper use. Traces of frescoes have recently been found on the pendentives of the dome, and elsewhere of decoration from the 12C, but restoration is not yet complete. The remainder of the church is modern, but the abbey *Chapter House* has been incorporated into the present sacristy and the stone bench for the monks is still in position. The church treasury contains a simple Gothic monstrance and in the parish offices can be seen the Povaljska listina (1250), an abbey muniment that is the oldest Cyrillic document in Serbocroatian.

Off the w. coast of Brač lies the small island of *Šolta*, dotted with tiny villages (steamers daily from Split to Stomorska, Nečujam, Rogač, and Maslinica; local boats from Milna and Bobovišča, Pensions at Nečujam and Maslinica). The older settlements are all inland, and the largest, *Grohote* (982 inhab.), in the middle of the island, is the main administrative centre. Among the Roman ruins in the village are sections of mosaic floors, and beside the parish church the remains of a 6–7C early-Christian basilica. The 14C church of Sv. Mihovil just outside the village is decorated with Gothic frescoes. The coastal villages date mainly from the 16–17C, after the threat from pirates had receded. On the N.E. coast are *Stomorska* (15C Madonna and Child on the high altar of the parish church), *Nečujam* (small museum dedicated to Marko Marulić, the poet from Split) and *Rogač* the port for Grohote. At the w. end of the island is the holiday and fishing village of *Maslinica*, with a 17C fortress tower and the plain Baroque Palača Marchi (1708).

19 THE ISLAND OF HVAR

Steamers to *Hvar* daily (less frequently in winter) from Rijeka, Rab, Zadar, Šibenik, Split, Korčula, Vela Luka (Korčula), Lastovo, Dubrovnik, Hercegnovi, Budva and Bar; once a week from Venice, Silba, Primošten, Cavtat, Tivat and Kotor. To *Jelsa*, *Vrboska* and *Stari Grad* daily from Split; to *Jelsa* and *Vrboska* daily from Bol (Brač), thrice weekly from Sutivan (Brač) and once a week from Milna (Brač); to *Stari Grad* daily except Sundays from Rogač (Šolta), Nečujam (Šolta) and Stomorska (Šolta).—CAR FERRY from Drvenik 6 times daily to Sućuraj (1 hr); twice daily from Split to Stari Grad (2½ hrs).

HVAR is the longest island (43 m.) in the Adriatic and the fourth largest in size, with an area of c. 114 sq. miles. A range of mountains rising from the sparsely populated s. shore to a peak at Mt. Sv. Nikola (2034 ft), is paralleled in the N. by the flat and fertile plain of Velo polje. The majority of the population (12,150 inhab.) lives at the broader w. end of the island, and although the main towns are situated on the coast the chief occupation is agriculture. Wine, olives, figs, and honey are produced and lavender and rosemary are cultivated on a large scale. An exceptionally favourable climate gives Hvar the highest number of hours of sunshine in the Adriatic and mild winters, so that the island, sometimes compared with Madeira, is both a summer and a winter resort.

History. Abundant archeological finds on Hvar have given name (Hvarska kultura) to the early-Neolithic culture centred in Dalmatia. Circa 385 B.C. Syracusan Greeks founded a colony (Pharos) on the site of Stari Grad, and another colony, Dimos, grew up at Hvar. Curiously the Slavonic name for the island has always been Hvar, derived from the Greek, whereas the Venetian and Italian name, Lesina, is from a Slavonic root meaning 'woody'. After a short period under the Illyrians, during which Hvar was ruled first by King Agron and then by Demetrios (husband of Queen Teuta), the island passed to Rome in 219 B.C. The mixed Roman and Illyrian population did not survive after the arrival of the Slavs in the 7C and the island was subsequently disputed between the Neretvans and Byzantium. In the 11C Hvar acknowledged the sovereignty of the Kings of Croatia and thereafter of Venice (1145–64), Byzantium (1164–80), and Hungary–Croatia (1180–1278). In 1278 she accepted the protection of Venice. The city of Hvar replaced Stari Grad as the capital, being granted its own statute in 1331. In 1358, by the Treaty of Zadar, the island passed to Hungary again. After another period of uncertainty at the beginning of the 15C Hvar passed decisively to Venice (1420) and prospered as an agricultural producer and an important naval station midway between Venice and Corfu. In spite of several popular revolts during the 16C and fearsome destruction at the hands of the Algerian Bey, Uluz-Ali, in 1571, this prosperity survived well into the 17C. Decline set in by the 18C, and the final blow came in 1776, when Kotor superseded Hvar as a naval station. In 1797 Hvar passed to Austria, France (1805–12) and even England (1812–13) before reverting to Austria, again until 1918. After an illegal Italian occupation, which lasted until 1921 Hvar became part of Yugoslavia.

A notable feature of Hvar society during the 16C and 17C was its devotion to literature and the theatre, and the number of writers it produced. Chief among them were Hanibal Lucić (1485–1553), author of 'Robinja' (The Slave-girl), the first secular drama in Croatian, and Petar Hektorović (1487–1572), whose eclogue on fishing 'Ribanje' had considerable literary influence. Others included the 16C historian, Vinko Pribojević, the poets, Jerolim Bertučević and Mikša Pelegrinović (d. 1563), Marin Gazarović (Gazzari), and Martin Benetović (d. 1607). Hvar was also the birthplace of Gian Francesco Biondi (Ivan Franjo Biundović, 1574–1645), the Venetian diplomat and author who spent many years at the court of James I. Apart from numerous novels Biondi wrote a history of the Wars of the Roses (1637) that was immediately translated into English. The Hvar theatre was built in 1612.

The city of **Hvar,** the principal settlement and administrative centre (1900 inhab.), is a delightful small port at the foot of twin hills near the

w. end of the island. Extensive rebuilding after the Turkish sack of 1571 gave the town a strong Venetian flavour and it maintains the spacious atmosphere of a prosperous past. It is one of the most popular Yugoslav holiday resorts.

Hotels. Adriatic; Dalmacija (d); Palace (a), incorporating former Park Hotel; Pharos, 170 R with bath or shower, kavana; Slavija (c); Galeb.

Restaurants. *Gradski restauran*, *Stara obala*; *Palma* (fish); *Skuša*. —Kavana. *Loža*, Gradski trg; *Slavija*; *Mornar*.

Post Office, Nova Obala.

Information Offices. *Turistički biro*, Nova Obala; *Dalmacijaturist*, Stara obala.

Bus Station. Trg Dolac, for buses to Stari Grad, Vrboska, Jelsa and Sućuraj.

Amusements. *Gradsko kazalište* (theatre) and Kino (cinema), both in the Arsenal. Open Air Theatre (cinema) at Veneranda.—Amateur Drama Festival annually (end July and early Aug).

Beaches. Gradsko kupalište (cabins, showers) at Veneranda; Pokojni dol (sand), 1 m. s.e. of town; Palmižana (sand) on the island of Sv. Klement; nudist bathing on the island of Jerolim.

The **Harbour** comprises a modern quay along the e. shore and the tiny *Mandrać*, an enclosed basin for smaller boats constructed before 1459. The name suggests an affinity with 'Mandraki' the Greek diminutive (literally 'sheepfold') commonly used for such small harbours in the Dodecanese. At right angles to the quay and completely bisecting the town the long and spacious **Pjaca** extends from the Mandrać to the cathedral. In Roman times this space formed an inlet of the sea which in the middle ages became the *Campo* dividing the fortified city (*Grad*), on the steep hill to the N., from the newer suburb (*Burg*) in the s. It was fully paved only in 1780 and is now the largest square in Dalmatia, over an acre in extent. A large circular well (1520) in the centre is still used.

The Hotel Palace, in the N.W. corner of the square, occupies the site of the Governor's Palace, demolished by the Austrians. The magnificent 16C *Loža survives, however, with graceful arcades, decorative Corinthian columns and a lion of St Mark in the upper balustrade. The obelisks on the roof were added in the 17C. In 1868 the loggia was enclosed and now serves as a café to the hotel. Another survivor is the clock tower, *Leroj*, formed in the 15C from the s.e. tower of the city walls, and reconstructed after hurricane damage in 1725. The bell on the roof dates from 1562, but the clock was replaced during 19C restoration. The white marble base of the *Štandarac* (municipal flagpole; 1735) stands before the Loža.

On the N. side of the square stands the Gothic *Palača Gazzari*, restored in the 19C. Just before it opens (l.) *Gradska vrata*, the main gate into the Grad, surmounted with machicolations, a feature generally of the 13–14C City Walls that enclose the **Old City** on all sides. To the left the spectacular Venetian Gothic façade of the unfinished *Palača Hektorović* (15C) rests on the city wall. Its interior is gained through a vaulted arch inside the gate, and gives access to the tiny derelict church of *Sv. Kuzma i Damjan* with a coffered Renaissance ceiling. From the Gradska vrata steep steps rise through the heart of the medieval town to the castle on top of the hill, with fascinating narrow streets leading off to either side.

Immediately on the right in the street which follows the line of the city wall parallel with the main square a number of patrician houses were built into the wall when fortification was no longer necessary under the Venetians. These houses then marked the southern limit of the city and overlooked the main square. The nearest is the large Venetian Gothic *Palača Lucić-Paladini* (15C), with the Lucić escutcheon over the door and a fine Gothic façade to the s. (go through main door to garden to view). Note especially the *Balcony. Adjoining are the modest house of the poet, Petar Hektorović, and the *Palača Gazzari*, part of which straddles the street on a vaulted arch. In front of its ruined N. portion (14C) is a large octagonal wellhead (1475) bearing a Lion of St Mark with a closed book. The street bends to reach the massive Renaissance *Palača Jakša* just above the *Vrata kod katedrale* (1454), another town gate.

We pass (r.) the *Old Bishop's Palace* (15C) and in the cross street (l.) the 17C Baroque church of the Benedictine nuns, where the altarpiece (Madonna and Saints) is by Liberale Cozza (1750). Their convent occupies the former mansion of the poet, Hanibal Lucić, on the next corner. We come to the main E.–W. artery of the old town, at the w. end of which the 14C *Vrata od Gojave* has curiously fashioned sides constructed to allow the passage of pack animals. In the same street, to the right, are a small Gothic and Renaissance house that bears the arms of the Piretić family and the 15C church of *Sv. Duh* (Holy Spirit), in late Gothic style with a Romanesque relief of a Saint in the tympanum and a wheel window above. In the interior (key from house next door) are a Madonna with St Nicholas, by Padovanino, and a small Descent of the Holy Ghost by the Spanish-born painter, Juan Boschetto (1523). At the far end of the street is the 14C *Vrata od Dolca*, the East Gate. The road beyond affords a fine *View of the crenellated walls ascending the hillside.

To the N. of the main street the remaining houses soon give way to rocky terraces planted with cypress, agave, and pine trees, through which paths wind to the handsome **Kaštil**, known also as **Španjolo**, on the summit of the hill (354 ft). The original castle was erected in 1551, but the present building, with a massive redoubt projecting to the s.E. and round towers at the corners, dates from a re-building in 1551. In 1571, during the raid by Uluz-Ali, much of the population took refuge in the castle and survived unharmed. The castle retained its strategic importance until the first half of the 19C when the Austrians built the barrack-block that stands gaunt and ruined within.

The **Cathedral of Sv. Stjepan** was begun in its present form in 1560 but, delayed by the Turkish incursions, was completed only in the first half of the 17C. An earlier cathedral on the site, mentioned in 1326, started as a Benedictine abbey in the 12C, probably when the bishopric was founded. Portions of the old church and its furnishings survive in the choir. The W. Front, already Baroque in feeling, imitates the composite Dalmatian style of Šibenik Cathedral. The *Campanile*, built by Nikola Karlić and Milić-Pavlović of Korčula in 1532, is in a severely retarded form of Romanesque.

The aisles are furnished with eleven Baroque marble altars (17C). To the left of the entrance (w. wall) is a large Gothic reredos, with a small panel above of the Scourging of Christ (perhaps a copy by Nikola Jurjev, a local pupil, of Juraj Dalmatinac's relief at Split). N. Aisle. A pietà by Juan Boschetto is incorporated into a larger canvas by A. Gradinelli, 1728. The Baroque chapel of Bishop Andreis (1678) contains the sarcophagus of St Prosperus. The entrance to the CHOIR is flanked by unusual Ambones incorporating miniature altars below. The elaborate Gothic stalls (15C, restored 1579) are of walnut. On the high altar: Palma Giovane, Madonna with St Stephen. In the S. Aisle are a 13C icon of the Pisan school and a number of carved gravestones set into the floor.

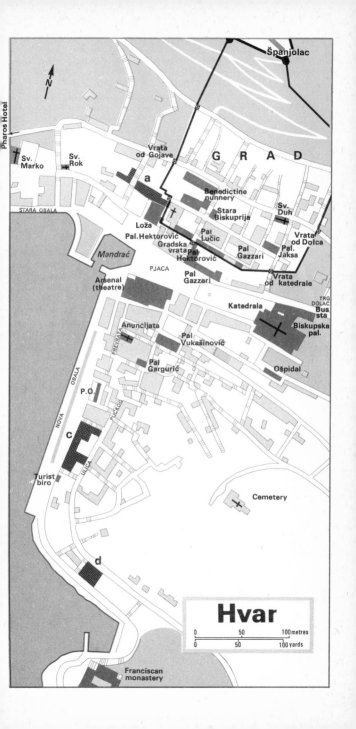

Hvar

0	50	100 metres
0	50	100 yards

The much rebuilt *Bishop's Palace*, adjoining the cathedral on the N. side, now houses the cathedral TREASURY (open daily, 9–11, 5–6). Of prime interest is the sumptuously ornamented *Pastoral staff of Bishop Pritić (Patrizius, 1509–22) in gilt brass, the work of Pavao Dubravčić, a local silversmith; the church plate includes a Gothic monstrance and chalice, both the gifts of Bp. Tomasini (15C), a 16C pax, and a number of Baroque vessels and chalices. Vestments include a rare 15C *Cope embroidered with the heads of saints, and a crimson and gold chasuble dating from the end of the 18C. The lace garments (16–18C) are numerous and there is a 16C figure of St Michael in stone.

A little behind the cathedral is the small square of Dolac (wellheads) from which the island buses depart. The old Put Grablje leads to the 16C Renaissance summer *Villa of Hanibal Lucić*. The interior now houses part of the Institute of Conservation; the surrounding park (wellhead with the Lucić and Gazarović escutcheons) has been laid out as a botanical garden. On Mt Sv. Nikola, above the road for Stari Grad and reached by a gravel track, stands *Fort Napoleon*, erected by the French in 1811.

Facing the harbour at the s.w. corner of the main square, stands the fine **Arsenal**, completed c. 1559 with a large vaulted arch forming a covered dock for the city galley. The building was fired by the Turks in 1571 and completely renewed in 1611 under Governor Pietro Semitecolo. An inscription over the E. door recording this date also calls it "the first year of peace", a reference to a serious rebellion which Semitecolo had resolved in the previous year. In 1612 an upper story was added to the Arsenal in the form of the **Kazalište**, the oldest theatre in Yugoslavia and one of the earliest still extant in Europe, and in the same year a *Belvedere* was added on the N. side with a spacious terrace overlooking the square. This wing was subsequently adapted as a granary and named Fontik. The Arsenal proper has been turned into a cinema. The theatre may be visited (daily 10–12) and has a charmingly painted Baroque interior (restored 1800) and covered galleries. The painted wooden figurehead of a dragon in the vestibule is from the galley sent by Hvar to the Battle of Lepanto (1571).

Behind the Arsenal, steps lead up to the huge Baroque *Palača Vukaš-inović* (17C), now a children's home. *Nova Obala*, the pleasant palm-lined promenade and steamer quay, runs s. from the Arsenal past the Post Office and travel agencies to the hotels Slavija and Dalmacija. UL. PUĆKOG PREVRATA, the main street of the old *Burg*, running parallel, presents a fascinating medley of architectural styles. From it a maze of narrow alleys, staircases, cul-de-sacs and small squares lead off to the east. Beyond two fine Gothic and Renaissance houses (l.) we come to the small Renaissance church of *Anuncijata*. The relief of the Annunciation in the tympanum is attributed to Nikola Firentinac; inside are a 16C icon (on the high altar) and four 18C processional candlesticks with Rococo wood carvings. We pass a cluster of Gothic and Renaissance houses, then below the 15C Venetian Gothic *Palača Gargurić* (l.), and, at the Hotel Slavija, descend steps to the promenade.

Beside a small bay (bathing) at the s. end of the promenade is the **Franciscan Monastery**, founded in 1461. The elegant Campanile, is identical with that of Sv. Marko (see below) and resembles that of the cathedral save that it terminates in an octagonal lantern topped with a small cupola, less harmonious and effective. It was completed c. 1507 by Blaž Andrijić and Franjo and Nikola Španić of Korčula. The simple Gothic church, dedicated to *Gospa od Milosti* (Our Lady of Mercy), was completely renovated after being burnt by the Turks in 1571. The relief of the Madonna in the tympanum of the graceful w. door is attributed to Nikola Firentinac. The church is entered from the attractive Renaissance cloister built by the mason Rade of Šibenik (1489) and consists of a single nave divided from the raised choir by a screen. In the choir are Renaissance Stalls by Franjo Čiočić and Antun Spia (1583) and the floor is paved with memorial stones, of which the most interesting are those of the Lucić (dated 1575), Kačić, and Hranotić families. A large and over-restored polyptych by Francesco da Santacroce (1583) on the Baroque high altar encloses a small painting of Our Lady of Mercy said to ante-date the foundation of the monastery. Paintings by Santacroce also decorate twin altars at the w. end of the choir. Six scenes from the Passion on the upper part of the screen are the work of the 16C dramatist and poet, Martin Benetović, who was also organist. On the N. side of the church stands the beautiful Gothic chapel of Sv. Križ with altar rails by P. Andrijić and a crucifixion by Leandro Bassano. On the 2nd altar on the s. side is a painting by Palma Giovane of St Francis receiving the Stigmata (1617). The *Refectory*, housing the treasury and museum, is dominated by an enormous *Last Supper, an outstanding painting traditionally attributed to Matteo Rosselli but now thought to be by Matteo Ingoli. Other paintings from the 16–18C are on display with a selection of illuminated church books, a Ptolemy atlas (1524) and coins, plates (two Gothic chalices), vestments, and lace.

STARA OBALA, or *Fabrika*, a jetty, constructed in the 16C, now forms the beginning of a beautiful promenade encircling the wooded headland of **Veneranda** that protects the town on the west. Behind the Gradski restaurant the ruined Dominincan church of *Sv. Marko* fell into decay after 1806, leaving only the bell tower, a replica of the Franciscan tower on the other side of the bay. The shell of the church, containing the gravestones of many Hvar notables, has been adapted to house a small archaeological collection. Continuing along the shore we pass the old Venetian military hospital (*Ospedal*) and come (r.) to the ruined monastery and church of *Sv. Veneranda*, partially destroyed by a Russian naval bombardment in 1808 and afterwards fortified by the French. It has been transformed into an open-air theatre. Still farther round the headland the promenade brings us to the principal formal bathing place (concreted foreshore, sand, and pebble beach, café). Above, amid fine pine woods, stands the Hotel Pharos.

The **Pakleni otoci** (lit. Hell's Islands) extend for about 7 miles s.w. of the harbour and protect it from the open sea. Of the 11 islands in the group none is permanently inhabited, but there are seasonal settlements on *Sv. Klement*, the largest, with a good sandy beach (Palmižana) and the islands are growing increasingly popular with tourists. *Jerolim* is reserved for naturists. On *Galešnik*, the nearest of the islands, an Austrian fort of 1836 has been turned into a highly successful café and night locale.

A winding road runs inland from Dolac square to the outlying towns and villages. Climbing through the hills behind the town it traverses pinewoods, olive groves, and delightful fields of lavender and rosemary to the N. coast. As far as Stari Grad the road was engineered during the Napoleonic occupation.

20 km. **Stari Grad** (*Helios*, 150 R, all with bath or shower; *Adriatic; Jadran; Starigrad*), the second largest settlement (1500 inhab.) was founded by the Greeks (as Pharos) c. 385 B.C. and remained the island's chief town until in the 12–13C it was displaced by Hvar. Strikingly situated at the E. end of a five-mile long fjord in natural surroundings of great beauty, it has recently developed as a popular tourist resort.

In a small square behind the waterfront stands *Tvrdalj* (c. 1520) the fortified mansion of Petar Hektorović, the Renaissance poet. Tvrdalj is a delightful and idiosyncratic creation, with a charming fishpool as its centrepiece, enclosed by a vaulted and arcaded terrace. The sides of the pool are embellished with reliefs and Latin inscriptions and in addition to a tower with a dovecote there is also an unusual 'sparrow-cote', expressive of the deigner's whimsical intention. A small ethnographical collection has been arranged in one wing. The square is adorned with a bust of Hektorović by I. Mirkovic (1956). In the street adjoining the Tvrdalj on the w. side, a house in the Austrian 'Jugendstil' (1896) contains a small *Maritime Museum and Art Gallery* displaying works by Meštrović, Rendić, and Juraj Plančić (1899–1930), who was born in Stari Grad. The Hektorović family chapel of *Sv. Rok* (1569) stands in the street to the E. which leads uphill to the fortified *Dominican Monastery*, founded in 1482 and rebuilt in the 16C after Turkish depredations. The church contains an Entombment by Tintoretto and St Hyacinth by Baldassare d'Anna, also (at the w. end) a crucifixion by Giacomo Piazzetta (1703) of Venice. In the monastery is a catalogued lapidary collection and upstairs in the library two paintings by Giov. Crespi and a number of votive paintings donated by sailors. The 15C Gothic church of *Sv. Nikola*, farther up the hill, has a wooden Baroque high altar by Antonio Pori (17C) bearing life-size figures of SS Nicholas, Andrew the Martyr, and Antony.

The Baroque parish church of *Sv. Stjepan* (1605) contains a good triptych by Francesco da Santacroce, a 16C font and a rococo organ loft. The 18C bell tower incorporates Greek masonry and a stone relief of a Roman vessel. Parts of a *Cyclopean Wall* of Greco-Illyrian date can be seen in nearby Kiklopska ul. (inquire at Turističko društvo). In the small square, just s. of the parish church, is the Romanesque and Gothic church of *Sv. Ivan*, thought to occupy the site of the island's first cathedral. Foundations of an early-Christian baptistery (5–6C), recently discovered beside this church, have been covered up again until the site can be opened to view.

From Stari Grad a good asphalt road continues E. through *Veliko polje*, the most fertile plain of the island, given over mainly to vineyards. A small grass airstrip runs parallel to the road. A by-road to the s. serves the two large villages of *Vrbanj* (altarpiece by Baldassare d'Anna in the parish church) and *Svirče*, with attractive rustic houses dating back to the middle ages.

30 km. **Jelsa** (*Adriatic;* Autocamp) the main settlement (1450 inhab.) on the N. coast, is spread out on both sides of a fine natural harbour, with a pleasant park, good beaches and unusually green surroundings. On the w. shore stands the newer quarter, the result of a minor 19C shipping boom. The old quarter embraces the head of the bay to the s.

At its head just behind the promenade, in a beautiful little square, stands the fine Baroque church of *Sv. Ivan* (16C) with a wheel window in the w. front. In the area behind the church are a number of old houses, notably those of the Skrivaneli and Kačić families. A short walk brings us to the parish church of *Sv. Fabijan i Sebastijan*. The original church dating from before 1331 was heavily fortified in 1535 and became the choir of a larger building with a nave and aisles; the w. front and bell tower were added during the last century. The lofty Gothic Choir has a painted ceiling and a magnificent Baroque Altar in painted wood by Antonio Pori (17C). The treasury contains a Gothic crucifixion in wood, a late Renaissance crucifixion in silver-gilt and vestments (16–18C). On the E. side of the harbour a pleasant promenade leads to the wooded peninsula and sandy bathing beach of *Mina*, beyond the cemetery and 17C church of the former Augustinian monastery.

The sloping hills behind Jelsa offer numerous walks. With a local guide visits may be made to the well-preserved foundations of a former Greek look-out *Tower* (5–4C B.C.); a ruined Roman fort called Grad or Galešnik, farther E. (both about an hour's walk); and near the summit of the mountain ridge to the s., *Grapčeva špilja*, a large cave from which the rich finds date back to 3000 B.C. Another excursion (bus or car) may be made to the picturesque old village of *Pitve* and thence viâ a rough tunnel (just under 1 m. in length) that pierces the mountains and emerges on the steep, sparsely populated s. shore of the island. From here the road serpentines down the mountainside (views offshore to Šćedro and Korčula) to the hamlet of *Zavala*, with a small café and pleasant beaches.

Vrboska (*Adriatic; Madiera; Villa Anna*), in a deeply indented bay 4 km. to the N.W. of Jelsa, can be reached from Jelsa by bus or boat. The long inlet curves into the heart of the picturesque village, which, with its island and three bridges linking the opposite banks, resembles a corner of old Venice, an impression strengthened in the oldest quarter by the survival of 15C houses in Venetian Gothic. The remarkable fortified church of Sv. MARIJA, a massive crenellated building, has huge semicircular bastions at the E. end and a spur bastion attached to the N.W. corner. The fortifications, erected c. 1580 round a church dating from the previous century, were designed as a refuge for the populace in the event of attack by pirates or Turks. In the interior are numerous 17C paintings; the floor is paved with grave slabs. From the sacristy the ascent may be made to the roof for a closer look at the fortifications and for the view. A short distance to the w. stands the Baroque parish church of *Sv. Lovrinac* with a polyptych of St Lawrence by Paolo Veronese (c. 1575) on the high altar, a Madonna of the Rosaries by Leandro Bassano, and three paintings by Celestin Medović (19C). The w. front of the Gothic chapel of *Sv. Petar* (1469) on the waterfront bears a small statue of St Peter by a pupil of Nikola Firentinac.

From Jelsa a fair gravel road traverses the length of the island (views to the Biokovo Mts. on the mainland) to (81 km.) *Sućuraj*, the small fishing village whence a car ferry plies to Drvenik on the mainland (see p. 156).

20 THE ISLAND OF KORČULA

STEAMERS to Korčula daily in summer (4 times weekly in winter) from Rijeka, Rab, Zadar, Šibenik, Split, Hvar, Dubrovnik, Hercegnovi, Budva, and Bar; twice weekly from Venice and Opatija; once a week from Pula, Silba, Primošten, Cavtat, Tivat, and Kotor. To Vela Luka daily from Split, Hvar, and Lastovo.

CAR FERRY to Korčula six times a day from Orebić.

KORČULA, the most southerly of the major islands of the Adriatic is in many ways the most attractive. Geologically it is a continuation of the Pelješac Peninsula, from which it is separated by a channel ¾ m. in width. It is the sixth largest island in the Adriatic, 29 m. long from E. to w., with the N. and s. shores almost parallel 3 m. apart. It is also the most thickly populated, with 22,000 inhabitants. Except at either end the settlements are inland and though never more than 2 m. from the sea are rarely within sight of it. The island is clothed with extensive pinewoods, and in the past had a strong tradition of shipbuilding, but this has been superseded by agriculture and, in postwar years, by tourism. Stone quarrying and carving is another traditional pursuit and quarries are still in use at the E. end of the island. Korčula is the only island in the Adriatic on which the wild jackal has survived.

History. *Korkyra Melaina* was founded as a Greek colony by the 4C B.C. The epithet 'black' in reference to dense pinewoods, passed with the island (Corcyra Nigra) to the Romans in 33 B.C. after two centuries of bitter struggle with the Illyrians. About the 6C Korčula became subject to Byzantium and in the 9C was colonized by the Slavonic Neretvans. In A.D. 1000 Korčula, after strong resistance, submitted to Doge Pietro Orseolo II and was occupied by Venice for a time. Shortly afterwards it acceded to Croatia and after 1102 to Hungary-Croatia, but was reoccupied for Venice in 1125 by Popone Zorzi, who became governor of the island. In 1180 the island reverted to Hungary-Croatia and in 1214 established its own independent statute, said to be the oldest in Dalmatia. The Zorzi family, with Venetian aid, returned in 1254 and attempted, without success, to establish themselves as hereditary rulers, though the governorship did pass from father to son until the Venetian departure in 1358. During this period of Venetian rule there took place off Korčula the great naval battle (1298), in which Venice suffered the greatest defeat in her history at the hands of the Genoese Admiral Doria, when Marco Polo was captured by the Genoese. By the Treaty of Zadar in 1358 Korčula was ceded to Hungary and during the next half century owed allegiance to many masters, including Stjepan I Tvrtko of Bosnia and the Republic of Ragusa; in 1420, in common with Dalmatia, she returned to Venice. A period of great prosperity followed during which were erected most of the public buildings in the city of Korčula, but the protectionist policies of Venice later damaged the island's principal industry, shipbuilding, and this with the depredations of the plague led eventually to decline. After the fall of Venice in 1797 Korčula went through turbulent times, being occupied successively by Austria (1797–1805), France (1806), Russia (1806), France (1807–13), and Great Britain (1813–15) before reverting to Austria (1815–1918). During the First World War the island was occupied by Italy, which prolonged its occupation until 1921, when Korčula was joined to Yugoslavia, and again during the Second World War by Italy and Germany.

Natives include the Andrijić family of architects, sculptors and masons (notably Marko and Petar), who were active in the 15–16C; Petar Kanavelić (1637–1719), the poet; and the modern sculptors Frano Kršinić (born 1897) and Petar Palavičini (1887–1958). Korčula also claims on slender evidence to be the birthplace of Marco Polo.

The administrative centre (2800 inhab.) and the principal town, although not the largest, is **Korčula,** a delightful medieval city occupying a tiny peninsula at the E. end of the island. The old town, less than ¼ m. in length and only half that distance in width, is extraordinarily small for the wealth and importance it enjoyed in former times (6000 inhab. in its prime) and is even more cramped on its small peninsula than the average town of the period. It stands on a low conical hill, which gives it an almost symmetrical appearance on the seaward side. Within the almost elliptical shore the streets are laid out to a plan, a main street running for three-quarters of its length down the middle like a central spine, with regularly spaced side streets placed like ribs at a slight angle. All but two rise in steps and are angled to catch the morning and evening sun, while avoiding the hot rays of midday and the prevailing winds. Korčula has preserved almost intact its medieval aspect, with over a quarter of its houses Gothic and a significant proportion Renaissance; and although the plague caused large areas of the town to be deliberately burnt in the 16C which have remained semi-derelict ever since, many interesting details remain to be seen.

Hotels. In the old town: **Korčula** (a), modest, Obala bratstva-jedinstva. By the town beach: **Ljubljana; Park; Sarajevo; Skopje; Beograd; Zagreb.** Outside the town: **Bon Repos,** 180 R, own beach; **Masline** (chalets).

Autocamp, 2 m. from town on the road to Lumbarda.

Restaurants. *Planjak,* Trg 19 Aprila 1921; *Plaža,* at the town beach; *Gradski podrum; Riblji restoran* (fish).—KAVANAS. *Korčula; Planjak;* and at *Hotel Park.*

Post Office, outside main gate.—INFORMATION OFFICE. *Turistički biro,* Plokata. TRAVEL AGENT, *Marco Polo,* Plokata.

Bus station. Plokata, for buses to all parts of the island.

Festivals. Moreška (see below), annually on 27 July.—Procession with candles round the town on Good Friday evening and on Easter morning.

Beach. Gradsko kupalište on the E. side of town (cemented foreshore and shingle), cabins, showers.

On 27 July a knightly ritual dance, the *Moreška, is performed in the city of Korčula symbolizing the struggle between the Moors and Turks, a survival of a traditional Mediterranean ritual that came into being probably in the 16C. The participants are recruited as boys and the performance is athletic and spirited. Visitors in summer are often granted a sight of practice dances.

The **Walls,** which formerly girdled the city, were erected by local masons in the 14–16C and partly dismantled in the last century. A good idea of them and of the shape and extent of the town can be gained by first walking round the outside. We start from the s. end of the *Yacht Harbour* where the massive cylindrical *Kula Balbi* (late 15C), now used as a reservoir, has patriotic inscriptions recalling recent tyrannies in place of its original lion of St Mark. This is overlooked by the taller, more slender *Torjun,* or Kula Lombardo (1449), with a double ring of stone brackets round the top, on which depended the defence of the governor's palace. Continuing N. we pass the Lučka Kapetanija with the Jadrolinija offices beneath a rebuilt arcade, and the town well, still the only water supply for many houses, and come to a broad neo-Baroque *Staircase* (1907) which mounts through the vestigial walls to the w. side of the town. The staircase is flanked by twin obelisks raised in honour of governors Alviseo Jelani (1589) and Pelegrin Pasqualigo (1680). A truncated square tower on the s. side contains the former *Morska vrata* (Sea gate; 15C), adorned with escutcheons. On the inner side is an inscription placed by Governor Leoni in the 16C erroneously attributing the foundation of Korčula to the Trojan hero, Antenor (1200 B.C.). Beyond the staircase stands an open **Loža** (1546) with a wooden roof supported on columns. A palm-lined promenade leads past the *Hotel Korčula*, opposite the steamer quay, to *Kula Barbarigo* (1485–88), a handsome, machicolated tower, with the Barbarigo escutcheon displayed on the wall.

Passing inside the walls we see (r.) the *Palača Kanavelić*, in 15C Venetian Gothic, with its courtyard enclosed by a crenellated wall, and (l.) the *Kula Zaherian* (or Tiepolo; 1481–83), with excellent views across the strait to the Pelješac Peninsula. On the E. side of the town the walls have been lowered to form a mere balustrade along which the Kanavalićevo šetalište runs as a tree-lined esplanade above the rocks. The little angled lane on the right has splendid Venetian fragments. The esplanade takes us past the Renaissance *Palača Andrijić*, the home of the well known family of masons and sculptors (note also the fine sculptured arms on the adjacent house to the s.), to the little guild church of **Svi sveti** (All Saints; 1306).

On the high altar is an expressive *Pieta in carved and painted wood by a Venetian Mannerist (? L. Begarelli), which is enclosed by a 15C Baldacchino with a pyramidal roof in imitation of the larger one in the cathedral. The ceiling is covered with paintings (c. 1713) attributed to Tripo Kokolja of Perast in the Boka Kotorska, but more interesting are the Christ and twelve apostles on the gallery, by a local artist.

A stone bridge crosses the street from within the N. side of the church to the adjoining Gothic *Guildhall*, a plain, rectangular building with a paved floor, timbered roof resting on Gothic stone brackets, and a late-Gothic ambry set into the N. wall. The hall has been restored and contains a collection of the guild's treasures notably nine late-Byzantine Icons believed to have been brought from Crete at the end of the Candian War (1699). Note especially *St George (? 17C), Christ Pantocrator (? 15C) and Christ and the Virgin Mary with SS Anne, John the Baptist and Joachim (? 16C). Adjacent stands the upright of a large painted Cross attributed to the School of Dubrovnik (late 14C). At the far end of the hall is a large canvas of the Last Supper by a local artist (17C), while at the opposite end stands a flag-standard surmounted by an excellent Gothic *Crucifix of beaten silver, by Ivan Progonović (1430–5), the Dubrovnik silversmith. Documents, processional candlesticks, furniture and a painted wooden Crucifix in Byzantine style (17C) are displayed left of the entrance door. On the wall outside can be seen two reliefs showing guild members adoring the cross, one Gothic (14C), the other Baroque.

At the round *Kula Cappello* (1493–99) with its old cannon, we turn right to arrive at the main entrance to the town.

The entrance is approached by a stone bridge erected in 1863 to replace a wooden one that spanned the former moat separating the town from the mainland. The bridge and its scarp provide the main venue of the Moreška dances. The **Kopnena vrata** (main or land gate), is surmounted by the massive rectangular tower of *Revelin* (14C), the oldest part of the fortifications still standing, with the lion of St Mark and various escutcheons displayed on the outer face. Inside opens the miniature TRG MARŠALA TITA, a tiny square proportionate to the cramped scale of Korčulan streets. Looking back we see the Baroque *Triumphal Arch* erected on the inner side of the main gate (1650) to honour the victories of Leonardo Foscolo, the Venetian Governor-General during the Candian War. To our left is the *Vijećnica*, or Town Hall (1520), with a graceful Renaissance loggia on the ground floor (a second story was added in 1866), complete with stone benches and the judge's table. The fluted column standing in front was erected in 1569 to Governor Ivan Michieli, who paved the square in that year. On the opposite side of the square stands the small guild church of *Sv. Mihovil*

(St Michael; 1603), with a charming triple bell cot. Inside are a Renaissance pulpit and an altarpiece attributed to the 18C Venetian painter Dom. Fedeli ('Maggiotto').

The narrow main street, Glavna ul., rises by steps to the narrow, elongated cathedral square (Trg Sv. Marka or Strossmajera), with its *štandarac* or stone flagpole (1515) standing at the near end. Immediately on our left is the Renaissance *Palača Gabrielis* (early 16C) with a handsome balcony, now the home of the **Gradski muzej** (Town Museum, open daily, 8–12, 5–7). The rather thin collection includes a plaster cast (original in Zagreb) of a Greek inscription (4C B.C.) found at Lumbarda; ethnographic, lapidary, and nautical displays; and a room devoted to the wartime resistance movement that includes photographs of the British military mission to Korčula. In the lower hall is a fine bronze Door Knocker by Tiziano Aspetti (16C) depicting Neptune between two lions.

The **Cathedral of Sv. Marko** (15–16C), an attractive hybrid of varying styles of Gothic, fills most of the E. side of the square.

The building was begun early in the 15C on the site of an earlier Romanesque edifice, of which only the three apses have remained. Hranić Dragošević, a local mason, had completed by 1426 much of the church and the first two stories of the bell tower. Bonino da Milano seems to have been associated with him. The work was continued by Ratko Ivančić of Korčula and the Dubrovnik mason, Ratko Brajković, who by 1440 had finished the third story of the bell tower and thereafter shared in work on the interior. In 1441 Giacomo Correr of Trani in Apulia assumed direction of the building and is thought to be responsible for the final plan. He may also have sculpted the w. door. The Korčulan mason, Marko Andrijić, finished the main building, adding the sumptuous decoration of the w. gable end and the double lantern on the top of the bell tower. In 1525 the chapel of St Roch, in the form of an extra aisle, was added to the N. side by Marko Milić Pavlović, another local mason.

EXTERIOR. The w. front consists of a conventional gable end to the nave and s. aisle but with the N. aisle displaced by the bell tower and an extra, flat-roofed extension attached to the N. side. The cramped effect is accentuated by the acute angle at which the front stands in relation to the s. wall, but the result is not unharmonious. The façade is enlivened by three magnificent features. The Italian Gothic W. Door, with cabled jamb shafts and moulded brackets bearing lions couchant, with the naked figures of Adam and Eve on the underside, has a figure of St Mark (? by Bonino da Milano) in the tympanum. An excellent, traceried wheel-window has four heads set in the rim. The *Cornice to the gable, by Marko Andrijić, is decorated with a profusion of fantastic beasts and Gothic blind arcading filled in with scallop shells. This unusual mixture of late-Gothic and Renaissance elements culminates in a rich finial at the apex, beneath which is a female bust, the identity of which has excited much fruitless speculation. The Campanile is topped by an arcaded parapet of trefoiled arches from which rises a sumptuously decorated octagonal lantern with a smaller lantern on top.

The rather gloomy **Interior** consists of a nave and aisles only five bays in length, of which one and a half bays in the N. aisle are occupied by the baptistery in the base of the campanile. This and the fact that its E. and w. walls are not at right angles to the sides gives an overcrowded air to the whole. The unusual timbered roof, which had been plastered over at the beginning of the 19C, was renovated in 1961. An excellent Gothic and Renaissance *Baldacchino by Marko Andrijić(1486), shelters the high altar, behind which, difficult to see, is an early painting by Tintoretto of St Mark with SS Bartholomew and Jerome.

S. AISLE: altarpiece of the Holy Trinity by Leandro Bassano; sarcophagus of Bishop Malombra with a full length figure of the bishop and the arms of Malombra and Bishop Niconisius; a Byzantine icon of the Madonna and Child (? 13C); a rack of halberds, dedicated in 1483, said to have been carried by the women of Korčula when Uluz-Ali, the Bey of Algiers, was deflected from attacking by a ruse.
N. AISLE: the Renaissance Giunio chapel in the N. apse; a remarkably handsome Gothic door to the sacristy (? Antoine de Vienne; 14C), with a relief of St Michael in the tympanum and lintel brackets portraying boys playing musical instruments. In the chapel of St Roch on the N. side are three paintings of saints by Carlo Ridolfi (1642) and on another altar carved wooden figures of saints and a Madonna by a local sculptor, Franjo Čiočić-Čučić of Blato (1576).

Just to the S., opposite the town museum, stands the large *Biskupska palača* (Bishop's palace), originally built in the 14C but with a Baroque façade added some time in the 17C. The palace now houses the well-arranged and labelled **Opatijska riznica** (Cathedral treasury, open daily, 8–12, 3–7). At the top of the stairs in the *Entrance Corridor* are hung drawings by Italian and German artists of the 17–18C, notably by *Tiepolo*, *Carracci* and *Palma Giovane*. Cupboards display church plate and jewellery from the 15–18C, a fragment of a Byzantine cross from the 4C and a collection of medals. *Room* 1 is devoted mainly to works by Dalmatian painters. On the right-hand wall is a *Polyptych with 5 panels by *Blaž Trogiranin* (1431). On the opposite wall, paintings of the Madonna and Child and St Damian, both of the school of Dubrovnik (late 15C). Also exhibited in this room are two panels from an altar painting by *Pellegrino da San Daniele* and illuminated manuscripts (one 12C). A side door leads to the private chapel of the Bishops of Korčula, with reliquaries, and a terrace with a small lapidary collection. *Room* 2 contains mainly works by Italian painters of the Renaissance, including a Painting of a Young Man by *Vitt. Carpaccio*, a Madonna and Child by *Giov. Bellini*, the Virgin and Saints attributed to the school of Titian, the Annunciation attributed to the school of Veronese, and the Mystical marriage of St Catherine by the 17C Neapolitan, Bernardo Cavallino. Also here are two 15C English alabaster reliefs, a remarkable ivory statuette of Mary Stuart (said to be 18C) and a marble relief of the Virgin Mary (school of della Robbia). *Room* 3, devoted to the Baroque, is adorned with painted arms, of the various bishops and contains a portrait of Bp. Spanić by *Tripo Kokolja* (c. 1700). In *Room* 4 are displayed embroidered *Vestments, of which the 15C dalmatics are outstanding.

In the street to the s. (second door left) a large kitchen has been re-equipped with period furniture and displays a quantity of amphorae raised from the sea.

The plain church of *Sv. Petar* behind the N. apse of the cathedral is the oldest in Korčula. Originally Romanesque, it was reconstructed in 1338 and later given a Renaissance door. It contains wooden figures of the 12 apostles (17C Venetian) and a rustic crucifixion (17C) by a local sculptor. In the adjoining street is the house displayed to visitors as *Marco Polo's House*, in reality a mainly 17C dwelling of no particular interest.

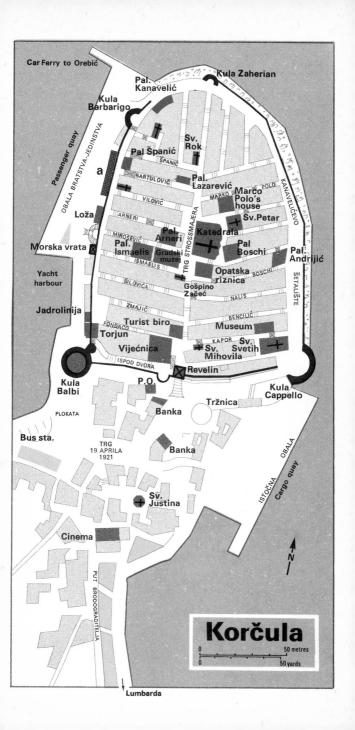

The most notable of the private houses is the *Palača Arneri* opposite the cathedral, its Gothic portion largely derelict, but with excellent façades on three sides and a fine Renaissance courtyard in the side street. A statue of Leonardo Foscolo stands in a niche in one corner, brought here from the triumphal arch inside the main gate. Opposite the entrance to the Palača Arneri is the ruined Renaissance *Palača Miloš;* in the next street to the N., the Gothic and Renaissance *Palača Lazarević*, now in use as flats; and behind the Town Museum the Renaissance *Palača Ismaelis* or Šilovića dvor (formerly an orphanage), with the ornate family escutcheon over the entrance and an excellent courtyard with a double-tiered gallery round all four sides.

The suburb to the s. of the town walls, which began in the 16C and grew in the 17C when many inhabitants fled the plague, is now the shopping and administrative centre of Korčula. On the s. side is the small Baroque rotunda of *Sv. Justina*, which contains parts of a 16C polyptych attributed to Pellegrino da San Daniele; from here a pleasant seaside walk leads round to the open-air swimming pool, beach, and hotel quarter. Another shore walk leads w. from Plokata past the hospital to the Dominican monastery and church of *Sv. Nikola* (1509); a parallel street climbs steeply by steps, continued through pleasant pinewoods to *Fort Wellington* (or *Sv. Vlah*), an imposing tower (rfmts.) built by the British in 1813 (views of the town, and across Pelješac strait to Orebić).

The road to the town beach (comp. above) continues to *Lumbarda*, a quiet village 6 km. to the E., a favourite place for excursions with good sandy beaches and a modest restaurant. The road leads past (2 km.) *Sv. Antun na Glavici* (1420), a small medieval church, which is reached by stone steps between an avenue of cypresses 250 years old and of great beauty (views). Lumbarda was the birthplace of two of Croatia's best known modern sculptors, Frane Kršinić (b. 1897) and Ivan Lozica (1910–43), and is the home of a third sculptor, Ivan Jurjević Knez (b. 1921), whose studio and workshop may usually be visited on request. A few of Kršinić's works may also be seen at the house in which he was born (plaque). Lumbarda may also be reached by boat (c. 1 hr), through part of the archipelago of small islands known as the Skoji. Of these the most interesting is *Badija*, with its former Franciscan Monastery founded in 1392 by refugee monks from Bosnia. The beautiful *Cloister (1477), is one of the finest in Dalmatia, in which late Gothic and Renaissance elements are mixed in perfect harmony. The church has a w. front in imitation of the cathedral at Korčula, but the ornament is of inferior workmanship. Gravestones in front of the church, engraved with the emblems of various trades, include that of Hranić Dragošević, one of the architects of the cathedral. The monastery is now a holiday residence for physical training instructors, but may be freely visited (restaurant). *Vrnik*, another island closer to Lumbarda, has quarries of which one is still worked.

A good road (mainly asphalted) leads from Korčula through the centre of the island, linking the main settlements. Climbing steadily out of Korčula we pass through the inland villages of (5 km.) *Žrnovo*, with views N. to the Pelješac Peninsula, and (14 km.) *Pupnat*, the oldest settlement on the island, before emerging briefly on to the s. coast at *Pupnatska luka.*—23 km. *Cara*, another old settlement, was a favourite summer resort of Korčula nobles, whose villas can still be seen, notably the Kaštil Španić (16C). In the parish church is an altarpiece attributed to one of the Bassano family and in *Gospa u polju* (Our Lady in the Fields), a medieval chapel about 1 m. from the village, are five good English alabaster reliefs (? 14C or 15C).—26 km. *Smokvica* has a fine loggia in front of the church and is the centre of the district in which the excellent white wine *pošip* is produced.

39 km. **Blato** (*Lipa*), the largest place on Korčula, is a country town (5100 inhab.) with a surprisingly continental atmosphere for an island settlement so close to the sea. The town is bisected by a magnificent avenue of lime trees that passes the town park, with a monument to National Hero Ivan Cetinić by V. Mačukatin (1959). In the centre of the old quarter in a large square stands the parish church of *Svi Sveti* (All Saints). To the original Gothic church (14C) the nave and aisles were added in the 15C, while the w. and s. fronts and campanile were rebuilt more than a century later. The high altar has Baroque furnishings and two paintings by Girolamo da Santacroce (All Saints, and Madonna and Child). The chapel of St Vincent has a Baroque altar by Petar Bertapelle of Vrboska. The handsome *Loggia* at one end of the square, replacing an earlier one, was largely the work of Spaso Foretić (1700–30). On 23 April the 'Kumpanija', a knightly ritual dance with swords, is performed in the main square to accompaniment of bagpipes and drums. Not far from the square the modest Baroque Arneri house (1699) contains a small historical museum.

46 km. **Vela Luka** (*Jadran; Dalmacija; Istra*), a busy little port and light industrial centre (4300 inhab.), lies on a deeply indented bay between heavily wooded peninsulas at the w. extremity of the island. A small museum illustrates with ship models the maritime history of Korčula. On the islet of *Glavica* in the bay stands the 14C Gothic church of Sv. Ivan. The main attraction of Vela Luka, however, lies in the beauty of its surroundings.

21 THE OUTER ISLANDS (Vis, Lastovo, Mljet)

A. Vis

STEAMERS to Vis and Komiža daily except Sundays from Split, and every Wednesday from Hvar.

The island of **Vis** is the farthest from the Dalmatian coast (27 m.) and although only 35 sq. m. in area has over 8000 inhabitants. The shores of the island are steep and difficult of access, except for the bays of Vis in the N.E. and Komiža in the s.w., and the interior is crossed by two mountainous ridges running parellel with the axis between these bays. Mt. Hum, s.E. of Komiža, is the highest point (1908 ft). The benign climate is conducive to sub-tropical flora, including palms, eucalyptus, agave and cactus, and citrus fruits; the fertility of its valleys has encouraged the growing of early fruits and vegetables. Vis wines have been lauded since ancient times, and Plavac, Opolo, and Vugava are known throughout the country.

History. Vis became the site of the first Greek colony in the Adriatic when, in the early 4C B.C., Dionysios the Elder of Syracuse here founded the colony of *Issa*. Later an independent *polis*, Issa minted its own money and founded further colonies at Lumbarda (Korčula), Trogir, and Stobreč (near Split). In 47 B.C. the island fell to Rome and after the division of the empire passed to Byzantium, being colonized by the Slavs during the 8C. Venice attacked it for the first time in 997, acquired it by purchase, together with the rest of Dalmatia, in 1420, and ruled it peacefully from Hvar until the republic's demise in 1797. Austria was succeeded in 1805 by Napoleonic France and the island's strategic position midway between Italy and the Dalmatian coast became of importance; this, allied with its impregnable cliffs and isolation, made it a natural site for a naval base, a fact first realized by the British. In 1811 a British force dislodged the French in a naval battle and fortified Vis harbour; Austria, to whom it was handed over in 1815, made it the 'Malta of the Adriatic'. A battle off Vis in 1866 between Austria and Italy was one of the biggest of the 19C, resulting in complete victory for the Austrian fleet (manned largely by Slavs) under Admiral Teghethoff. Vis came to prominence again during the Second World War, when from 1943 it became the general staff H.Q. of Tito's National Liberation Front and the centre of the Allied military effort in support of Yugoslavia (comp. Sir Fitzroy Maclean's 'Eastern Approaches').

The main town also called *Vis* at the head of a deeply indented bay on the N.E. coast, is still a garrison town (2850 inhab.) and closed to foreign visitors. The boat for Komiža does enter the harbour, however, and from its decks may been seen, among other things, the ring of fortresses built by the British in 1811–14 (George, Wellington, Bentinck, and Robertson). The small island of *Host* at the entrance to the harbour is named for Capt. William Hoste, who commanded the small British force that defeated the French here in 1811.

Komiža (*Biševo*), on the w. side of the island, is a prosperous small fishing town (2470 inhab.) backed by an amphitheatre of high mountains and spread out round a broad sandy bay. Although it was first settled by the Benedictines from Biševo (see below) in the 13C, its appearance was determined mainly in the 16–17C by the many balconied houses lining its streets.

On the quayside in the centre of the town is the machicolated *Kaštel* built by Venice in 1585, with a clock tower rising above one corner. Here a small art gallery (open 10–12, 7–8) has been arranged to display paintings of Djuro Tiljak (1895–1965), a former pupil of Kandinsky. Just s. of the Kaštel and beside the cannery is the small Baroque church of *Sv. Rok*, adapted from a lookout tower. A broad palm-lined promenade curves N. round the shore to the market place, overlooked by the Renaissance *Palača Zanetova* (16C) with a Madonna and Child in a niche in the façade. Ul. Marinkovića leads past the lobster and crab farm on the seashore (*jastužero*), which may be visited on request, to the Hotel Biševo and main bathing beach (pebble). The tripartite Renaissance church of *Gospa Gusarica* (late-16C), with a triple bell cot, just beyond the beach, is entered through a yard with an octagonal well-head (1705) decorated with reliefs showing religious subjects. The interior furnishings are Baroque except for a polyptych of 11 panels on wood (probably 16C).

On a hill behind the town stands the *Benedictine Monastery* surrounded by a defensive wall with a fortress tower (1645). A second tower forms the base of the campanile (views). The church of *Sv. Nikola*, also known simply as *Mustar*, has a Gothic nave by Andrija Vitaljić and a Romanesque aisle remaining from earlier buildings, but is otherwise of the 17C. Inside are Baroque altars of painted wood and gravestones decorated with escutcheons and relief carvings. A small museum behind the church contains 16–17C vestments, Baroque paintings and statuary, and an ethnographical collection.

AN EXCURSION may be made (daily at 8 a.m. in summer taking 45 min; a boat hired locally takes approx. 2 hrs) from Komiža to the small island of *Biševo* lying about 4 m. offshore, whose chief attraction is the beautiful *MODRA ŠPILJA (Blue Grotto). This is a large cave 100 ft long, 55 ft wide and 60 ft high, but with an entrance only 5 ft by 8 ft, and can only be entered by small boat on a calm day (or by swimming). It is best visited between 10 a.m. and 12 noon, when the sun is near its zenith. The reflection of the sun's rays from the seabed imparts to the water in the cave a silvery blue phosphorescent light of great brilliance, while objects within are bathed in an ethereal aquamarine that flickers in the play of the ripples. In beauty it compares with the more famous grotto on Capri.

Excursions can also be made from Komiža to the tiny outlying island of *Svetac*, 15½ m. to the w. of Vis, with one small fishing village (50 inhab.). Nearby is the uninhabited islet of *Brusnik* and, a further 15 m. to the w., the uninhabited islet of *Jabuka*. Both have an indigenous species of lizard (Lacerta taurica melisellenisi), are volcanic and contain enough iron ore to deflect compasses, and have rich grounds for tunny and especially lobster fishing.

B. Lastovo

STEAMERS daily to Ubli from Split, Hvar, and Vela Luka (Korčula).

Lastovo, a small island 5½ m. s. of Korčula, from which it is separated by the Lastovski kanal, lies at the centre of an archipelago of 45 uninhabited islets extending to E. and w. Roughly rectangular in shape, it is c. 5 m. long and 3–4 m. in width. The shores of the island are rocky and difficult of access, while the interior is heavily wooded and dotted with fertile valleys growing vines, the characteristic wines being plavac and maraština. Olive, almond, and walnut trees grow in profusion and the climate is favourable to citrus fruits, palms, and subtropical species. Owing to steady depopulation over the last two centuries inhabitants number only c. 2000, most of whom live in the village of Lastovo.

History. Known to the Greeks as *Ladesta*, the island was later colonized by the Romans, who founded their town on the site of present-day Ubli. In the early middle ages this became Byzantine *Lastobon*, to which the Slavs migrated in the 8C, but in 998 the town was destroyed by Doge Pietro Orseolo II and the inhabitants fled to the far side of the island. Except for a short interval under Hungary-Croatia, Lastovo now formed part of the small state of Zahumlje (in the area of present-day Hercegovina) until in 1252 it acceded to the Republic of Ragusa. Under the terms of its statute (1310) as an autononous commune it had strict laws of inheritance by which it was forbidden for any outsider (even from Dubrovnik) to settle on the island, while women had equal rights of inheritance with men. As a result Lastovo has the most purely Slavonic population of any of the islands. In 1808 the French took over the island, then the British (1813–15) and subsequently Austria (1815–1918). By the Treaty of Rapallo (1921) Lastovo was one of the few islands in the Adriatic to be granted to Italy and did not become part of Yugoslavia until after the Second World War.

Thanks to its isolation and self-sufficiency Lastovo preserves a number of folk customs, of which the most colourful is the annual Lenten Carnival or *Poklad*, a ritual pageant performed in the streets in February. On this occasion national costume is worn.

The best known native of Lastovo was Dobrić Dobričević (Boninus de Boninis; 1454–1528), pioneer printer and Venetian diplomat, whose most important works were published at Brescia in 1483–91.

The steamer ties up (always after dark) at *Ubli*, whence a minibus transports visitors two miles over a bumpy track to the island's sole hotel, the Solitudo, set in pinewoods at the N.E. tip of the island. Ubli (250 inhab.) is a nondescript village overrun by soldiers from the local barracks. An early-Christian basilica (5–6C) has recently been excavated and restored and a number of sarcophagi are displayed on one side of the site.

A bus leaves daily in the morning for Lastovo and returns at lunch time, taking a winding gravel road that affords ever changing views of the N. coast and the offshore islands, culminating in a striking view of Lastovo itself, spread out on a steep hill and tumbling down to the valley below.

10 km. **Lastovo,** the principal settlement (1700 inhab.), lies in a natural amphitheatre on the lower slopes of Glavica hill, and although adjacent to the sea is all but cut off from it by steep cliffs to the N. The village looks inward and S. to face the broad fertile valley from which it draws its livelihood. The narrow precipitous streets and hundreds of steps winding up and down the hillside give it a peculiar charm, made somewhat melancholy by the evident decay resulting from depopulation.

The majority of the 29 churches still standing on Lastovo are in this village, though only a few are of interest. The road enters the village at the Turistički biro, opposite which is the small 16C church of *Sv. Rok* built as a talisman against the plague, with a good Renaissance reredos and a painted wooden statue of St Roch by Fran Čiučić of Korčula (1576). A few steps up the hillside is the larger church of *Sv. Vlaho* (St Blaise), endowed by Ragusa as the republic's official church on the island. A side chapel and new W. front were added to the original 14C Gothic chapel in 1719. The stone seats and terrace in front of the church were for the Ragusan governor and his aides at official ceremonies, while similar seats for the governor and three judges can also be seen in the main apse. The Baroque altarpiece of St Blaise with SS Cosmas and Damian is by Anton Sciuri (1605).

Continuing along the main street we pass a large mansion incorporating fragments of the former governor's palace and the 14C church of *Sv. Ivan,* which is being adapted to hold a small museum.

The handsome parish church of **Sv. Kuzma i Damjan,** on the right, is surrounded by a spacious terrace. The main Gothic building dates probably from the late 15C, the Renaissance side chapels and W. door from a century later; the triple bell cot, decorated with lions' heads, dragons, and the head of a man, was erected by Jerolim Pavlović in 1734. This unusually late appearance of Gothic decoration is thought to have been inspired by the W. front of Korčula cathedral and there seems little probability in the persistent legend that the head represents King Uroš I of Serbia. The neo-Gothic bell tower was built by the Italians in 1942.

The most striking features of the interior are the twin altars in the side aisles enclosed by stone Baldachinos with pyramidal canopies (early 16C) in imitation of that in Korčula cathedral. On the N. altar is an icon of the Madonna and Child probably painted in Dubrovnik (? 15C), and on the S. altar is a good 16C Pieta (? by Juan Boschetto). The painting of SS Cosmas and Damian on the high altar is by Giovane Lanfranco. At the W. end of the church are a Renaissance font and a bronze urn for holy water, the gift of Dobrić Dobričević.

The treasury (apply sacristan) includes 15–16C objects of Ragusan workmanship. Among the best are a silver-gilt chalice with a portrait of St Blaise; a silver-gilt processional cross by Marul Ivaneo (1574); two censers of beaten silver; two small reliquaries of silver and glass; two silver reliquaries of the legs of SS Boniface and Constant and one of the arm of St Valentine; a Renaissance pyx. Among Baroque works are monstrances and a pax with a relief showing the Deposition.

On the far side of the terrace is a small rustic loggia (18C), around which can be seen some of the chimneys characteristic of Lastovo. Steps beside it lead down to the little 15C Gothic church of *Sv. Marija ua Grži*, with a triple bell cot and a triptych on wood in the Byzantine manner on the high altar (school of Dubrovnik, 16C). On the E. side of the village the guild church of *Sv. Antun* consists of a 14C Gothic chapel forming the choir and an attractive Baroque W. end added in the 17C. From the open space behind the church there is an impressive *View down to the Pržina valley, with its vineyards and olive groves and up to upper Lastovo and the French fort on the hilltop, now a meteorological station. Steps and narrow streets descend to lower Lastovo at the foot of the hill. Beyond the modern winery (visits arranged on request) is the cemetery with late-15C church of *Sv. Marija u polju* (St Mary in the Field). The altarpiece is a painting of the Madonna and Saints by Francesco Bissolo; the figure kneeling in the left foreground is probably the donor, Dobrić Dobričević.

C. Mljet

STEAMERS daily except Sundays to Polače, Kozarica, Sobra, and Okuklje from Dubrovnik, Koločep, Lopud, Šipan, Žuljana (Pelješac), and Trstenik (Pelješac).

Mljet, the most southerly of the larger Dalmatian islands, lies parallel with the s. half of the Pelješac Peninsula, from which it is divided by the Mljetski kanal, 5 m. in width. Nowhere exceeding 2 m. across, but 20 m. long, it is relatively sparsely populated (2000 inhab.) and is noted for the unspoiled character of its landscape, three quarters covered with virgin Mediterranean forest. This is particularly luxuriant at the N.W. end (mainly Aleppo pine), around the twin lakes of Veliko and Malo jezero, which forms a national park. The larger villages are all inland and the principal occupation is agriculture, but in modern times there has been a gradual migration towards the coast with a resultant increase in fishing. Mljet is the only European habitat of the mongoose, which was imported here from India to rid the island of poisonous snakes.

History. In Roman times the island, known as *Melita*, is thought to have been used as a place of exile and there is a theory that this rather than Malta, is the Melita on which St Paul was shipwrecked on his way to Rome. In the 6C Mljet came under Byzantium, was later occupied by the Neretvans and became a part of the Slavonic states of first Zahumlje and then Bosnia. In 1333 Ban Stjepan of Bosnia sold the island to the Republic of Ragusa, whose fate thereafter it shared.

Most visitors land at the hamlet of *Polače*, which has become the main disembarkation point for the two lakes and the national park. The name is taken from a Roman palace inside whose ruins the present settlement stands; parts of the walls and two defensive towers can still be seen (? 3–4C A.D.). According to early Ragusan sources this was the palace of Agesilaius of Anazarbo, who was exiled here by Lucius Septimius Severus and later freed by Caracalla at the urging of Oppian.

From Polače an asphalt road runs across the narrow neck of the island to (2 km.) *Govedjari* and *Veliko jezero, a beautiful salt water lake surrounded by dense pinewoods. On the far side of the lake, on a small island, the *Hotel Melita* occupies the former *Benedictine Monastery*, founded by monks from Apulia in 1151 under a bequest by Župan

Desa of Zahumlje. The two-storied building has a Renaissance cloister and a machicolated tower at one corner. The monastery church (*Sv. Marija*) is a good example of Apulian Romanesque, though it was enlarged with the addition of a Renaissance loggia and bell tower in the early 16C (Gundulić escutcheon on the loggia). The w. front and eaves are decorated with blind arcading. The narthex has Gothic relief carvings of St John the Baptist and angels. Inside is a painting of the Vision of St Benedict attributed to Petar Mattei-Matejević (1701). Among the many Dubrovnik notables who were members of the order were the writers Mavro Vetranović (1482–1576) and Ignjat Djurdjević (1675–1737), who left a description of Mljet in his long poem 'Marunko'.

A poor gravel road leads E. from Polače to the remaining villages on the island, most of which are at the E. end.—18 km. **Babino polje** (800 inhab.), at the foot of the island's highest mountain, *Veli Grad* (1670 ft), is the largest settlement and the former capital, with a number of interesting old churches. These include the pre-Romanesque church of *Sv. Andrija* with a richly ornamented transenna, the pre-Romanesque and Gothic church of *Sv. Mihovil*, the 13C Gothic churches of *Sv. Pankracija* and *Djurdje* (St George) and the 15C parish church with Renaissance and Baroque additions (Romanesque processional cross in the treasury). Several Baroque houses in the village include the former *Knežev dvor* (Governor's Palace).

The Gothic church of Sv. Trojica (Holy Trinity) in (26 km.) *Prožura* was built by the Benedictines from Lokrum (15C) and has a bronze Romanesque crucifix in the treasury. There is also a 17C defensive tower in the village.—In (33 km.) *Korita*, at the end of the road, are the 15C Gothic church of Sv. Vid (Gothic chalice), a 17C defensive tower and a number of Baroque houses from the 18th century.

22 DUBROVNIK AND ITS ENVIRONS

DUBROVNIK occupies a small rocky peninsula at the foot of Mt. Srdj with modern suburbs fanning out to E. and w. and over the lower slopes of the mountain. Although comparatively small (23,000 inhab.), it is the most famous city of Yugoslavia, a distinction it derives from its long history as the independent republic of *Ragusa*. The exceptional beauty of its streets and buildings moved even Bernard Shaw to hyperbole, and it stands high among the most attractive cities of the world, being rivalled in the Adriatic only by Venice. Its people, devout, hospitable, good-natured, and endowed with common sense, are heirs to a long tradition of civilized life. Two centuries of economic decline saved the town from the architectural philistinism of the 18–19C, and though prosperity has returned with tourism, good taste has so far kept its excesses to a minimum. The old centre constitutes one of the most perfectly preserved medieval entities in Europe, made incomparably more enjoyable by the exclusion of motor traffic.

Airport at *Čilipi*, 21 km. s.e.; bus servicè to J.A.T. air terminal at Pile (Put Maršala Tita 3). Direct services to London (also viâ Zagreb); Rome; Corfù and Athens; Belgrade; Split, etc.

Steamers from *Gruž*, 3 km. w. of the centre, to most Adriatic and E. Mediterranean ports.—LAUNCHES from Town Harbour to Lokrum and other neighbouring islands.

Railway Station in Gruška obala at Gruž; narrow-gauge line to Sarajevo, more suited to railway enthusiasts than travellers.

Hotels. In the old town: *Dubravka* (b), Ul. od puča, modest with good restaurant. —At *Ploče*: Argentina (f), 160 R; Excelsior (c), 200 R with bath, covered swimming pool, both these first class with private beach; **Villa Dubrovnik** (d), small; **Villa**

Orsula (e), with catering school, all Put F. Supila.—At *Pile:* Grand Hotel Imperial (a), 125 R, Ul. Miše Simoni, first class with garden.

At *Gruž:* Stadion (g), 100 R, open-air swimming pool, pension terms only; Petka (h), 100 R, Gruška obala, noisy but convenient for the steamer quay; Bellevue (i), Put P. Čingrije, with beach; Gruž (j), Gruška obala, modest.

At *Lapad:* Kompas (k), all R with bath, swimming pool, Dalmatinski put; Park (l), 160 R with bath, Aleja I. L. Ribara; Adriatic (m), 225 R with bath; Splendid (n), double R only, with bath, both Masarykov put, with beach; Neptun (o), 215 R, beach, Dalmatinski put; Sumratin (p), Zagreb (q), both Aleja I. L. Ribara; Komodor (r), Masarykov put; Lapad (s), Lapadska obala.

PRIVATE ROOMS may be booked through tourist agencies or by arrangement.—AUTOCAMP. *Adria-Stop* at Babin Kuk, Lapad.

Restaurants. In the old city: *Jadran*, Poljana Paška Miličevića; *Jug*, Izmedju Polača; *Prijeko*, Prijeko (fish); *Riblji restoran* (fish), Široka ul; *Višnjica*, Miha Pracata.—At Pile: *Dubravka*, Brsalje 1; *Mimoza*, Put Maršala Tita 13; *Ocean*, opp. the last.—At Ploče: *Revelin*, Put F. Supila.—At Lapad: Restaurant-Grill *Ivica Vujičić*, at the Tennis Club.   Also at the hotels, particularly the Dubravka, the Argentina, and the Imperial.

Kavanas. *Gradska kavana*, in front of the old harbour; *Stradun*, Placa; *Polače*, Izmedju Polača; *Dubravka*, Brsalje 1, at Pile; *Slavica*, Put Maršala Tita, at Boninovo.

Post Offices. *General* at Pile (Put Maršala Tita 14); at Gruž (Gruška obala); at Lapad (Aleja I. L. Ribara 5a).

Information Office. T.I.C. (Turistički informativni centar), Placa 1.—TRAVEL AGENCIES. *Atlas*, Pile 1; *Kompas*, Put Maršala Tita 12; *Putnik*, Generalturist, both Put F. Supila; *Yugotours*, Sučanica 1.

Bus Station, behind Stadion Hotel (Gruž) for all long-distance buses (most main towns in Yugoslavia).—From Ploče to *Mlini* and *Plat*, every 1½ hr; to Cavtat, every 2 hrs; less frequently to *Komolac, Gruda* and *Karasovići;* to Hercegnovi, Vodovadja, Vitaljina, Brgat, and Buići (market buses); also to Ston, Trpanj, and Orebić (Pelješac) vià Zaton and Trsteno.

Tramways. 1 Pile—Put Maršala Tita—Gruž—Kolodvor (Rly. stn). 2 Pile—Put Maršala Tita—Lapad—Uvala. TOWN BUSES (same nos.), Ploče—Pile—Gruž, and Ploče—Pile—Lapad. The route is almost circular between Ploče and Gruž owing to the one-way street system.

Beaches. *Gradsko kupalište*, Put F. Supila, Ploče; *Ispod Lovrijenca*, Pile; *Sumratin*, Aleja I. L. Ribara, Lapad. Also informally at Sv. Jakov, Dance, and Boninovo.—SAILING, Jedriličarsko društvo 'Orsan', Šetalište N. I. M. Pucića 19, Lapad.—TENNIS CLUB, Aleja I. L. Ribara, Lapad.

Amusements. THEATRE. *Narodno kazalište*, Prid dvorom.—CINEMAS. *Sloboda*, Luža; *Gruž*, behind Petka Hotel; *Jadran* (open air), Ul. iza Roka; *Slavica* (open air), Put Maršala Tita; *Lapad* (open air).—MUSIC. The City Orchestra (Gradski orkestar) plays two or three times a month: in winter in the Sala doma sindikata (Sv. Klara); in summer in the court of the Rector's Palace. The DUBROVNIK SUMMER FESTIVAL, with national and international orchestras, ballet, opera, and theatre companies, annually 10 July–25 Aug. For information and tickets apply to Ul. od Sigurate 1, or local travel agencies.

Excursions are organized in Apr–Oct (apply to travel agencies) by coach to *Mostar*, to *Ćilipi;* to *Trebinje;* to *Kotor* and *Cetinje;* by 'plane and coach to *Sarajevo* (2 days); and by launch to *Cavtat;* to *Trsteno;* to *Mljet* and *Korčula;* and to the *Elaphite Is.* A 7-day excursion into Albania was inaugurated in 1968. There are also guided tours of the city.

Religious Festivals on feast of St Blaise (3 Feb) with candlelight procession of the relics round the town and up the mountain.

History. When the Greco-Roman city of Epidaurus (today Cavtat) was sacked by the Avars and Slavs (early 7C) its population took refuge on the small rocky island of Lausa (later Rausa and then *Ragusa*), which was separated from the mainland by a narrow channel. At about the same time Slavs settled on the wooded slopes of the mainland side of the channel, whence the name *Dubrovnik* (from *dubrava*, a glade). In time the intervening channel was filled in and the two halves united and encircled by defensive walls. The city remained nominally under the suzerainty of Byzantium, having beaten off attacks by the Saracens (886–87), the Macedonians under Tsar Samuilo (988) and (in alliance with William II of Sicily) the Serbs (1184). A see was founded in 990. As a result of the sack of Constantinople by the Fourth Crusade, Ragusa was forced in 1205 to acknowledge the supremacy of her Adriatic rival, Venice. In 1292, the city, still constructed largely of wood, was ravaged by fire; the present urban plan stems from the major rebuilding that followed. Venetian dominion ended in 1358, when the whole of Dalmatia, together with Ragusa, was ceded to Hungary-Croatia. Ragusa by superior diplomacy, won better terms from her new overlords and after 1420, when Dalmatia was sold back to Venice, became independent in all but name, retaining a nominal link with Hungary as a safeguard against Turkish or Venetian aggression until 1526, after which an agreed annual tribute was paid to the Turks. Benefiting from valuable trade concessions as intermediary between Turkey and the Mediterranean, Ragusa's prosperity was such that the word 'argosy' (derived from Ragusa) entered the English language as a synonym for a treasure ship. By the 17C however, wars, and the shift of trade to the New World were affecting Ragusa and Mediterranean prosperity generally. On 6 April 1667 a catastrophic earthquake killed over 5000 citizens (including the Rector) and levelled most of the public buildings. The ruins had to be defended against looters from the South. Though with great effort a measure of recovery was achieved, the Republic was only a shadow, when, in 1797, like Malta, it attracted the cupidity of Napoleon's eastbound fleet. Menaced in 1806 by a Russian advance from Corfù to bases in the Boka Kotorska, Dubrovnik surrendered to a French force from Makarska. A month's siege by the Russo-Montenegrin fleets (during which 3000 balls fell on the city) was lifted by a French force from Split. Marmont arrived as governor and in 1809 the Republic's independence was formally ended by Napoleonic decree. In 1815, by the terms of the Treaty of Vienna, Dubrovnik passed to Austria until 1918.

The territory of the Republic of Ragusa extended from Klek-Naum in the N. to Sutorina (Boka Kotorska) in the S. and for a mere handful of miles inland. It included the islands of Šipan, Lopud, and Koločep (after 1080), Mljet (1141) and Lastovo (1216), the town of Ston (1298) and the Pelješac Peninsula (1399). Ragusa also ruled Korčula, Brač, and Hvar for a brief period (1414–17), but was forced to cede them to Venice.

The *Republican Constitution* of Ragusa, like that of Venice, was strictly aristocratic. The population was divided into three classes: nobility, citizens, and artisans or plebians. The last had no voice in government and citizens were permitted to hold only minor offices, all effective power being concentrated in the hands of a small hereditary nobility. No intermarriage was permitted. The supreme governing body was a Grand Council (Veliko vijeće or Consilium majus), on which every noble took his seat at the age 18. Executive power was vested in the Minor Council (Malo vijeće or Consilium minus), consisting at first of eleven members and (after 1667) of seven, chief among whom was the *Knez* or Rector. Both bodies had come into existence by 1235 and in 1253 a consultative body, the Senate (Vijeće umoljenih or Consilium Rogatorum), was added, consisting of 45 invited members (over 40 years of age) and including the members of the Malo vijeće. Under Venice the knez was Venetian, but after 1358 always a Ragusan, and to prevent any abuse of power he held office for only a month, becoming eligible for re-election only after two years.

The government of the Republic was liberal in character and early showed its concern for justice and humanitarian principles. In 1272 the laws, based on Roman practice and local customs, were codified into a single statute (including town planning and quarantine regulations), in 1301 a medical service was introduced, in 1317 a pharmacy, in 1347 a refuge for old people, and in 1432 a foundling hospital, while in 1418 slave trading was abolished. Having lost 11,000 lives during the Black Death of 1348, the city survived the epidemic of 1430 thanks to organized quarantine and cremation of infected corpses. After Constantinople fell to the Turks, Ragusa became a refuge for numerous wealthy and noble families from Macedonia, Serbia, Bosnia, and Croatia.

The cultural life of the Republic, though wide and varied, did not equal its political and mercantile achievements. No native artist ever achieved international recognition but evidence of good taste in the employment of architects and sculptors from other parts of the Adriatic coast or from Italy is everywhere apparent. The literary tradition is respectable if seldom brilliant. Ilija Crijević (Elius Lampridius Cervinus; 1463–1520) was crowned poet laureate in Rome in 1482 for his study of Virgil and a cycle of love poems in Latin, and other Latinists, such as Jakov Bunić (Bona Bonus), achieved recognition. Of greater importance was the considerable body of work in the Dubrovnik dialect of Serbocroatian, created between the Renaissance and the 18C. Although mainly imitative of Italian models this literature did produce two writers of more than local interest, Marin Držić (1508–67), author of a large oeuvre of Renaissance pastoral dramas and comedies (notably Skup—The Miser, and Dundo Maroje—Uncle Maroje), and Ivan Gundulić (1589–1638), author of Osman, a long epic poem on relations between Turks and Christian Slavs. Other leading figures were Šiško Menčetić (1457–1527), Džore Držić (1461–1501), Mavro Vetranović (1482–1576), Dinko Ranjina (1536–1607) and Dinko Zlatarić (1558–1609) from the earlier period, and from the 17C Junija Palmotić (1606–57), Dživo Bunić Vučić (1594–1658), Stijepo Djordjić (1579–1632) and Vladislav Menčetić (? 1600–66). The last Dubrovnik writer of any note was Ignjat Djurdjević (1675–1737).

The natural sciences produced two outstanding men in Marin Getaldić (Marino Ghetaldi; 1568–1626), who determined the specific weights of metals, and Rudjer Bošković (1717–87). Mathematician, physicist and astronomer of genius, author of Theoria Philosophiae Naturalis (1758), Bošković founded the Observatory of Milan and was a member of the French Academy. In London as a Fellow of the Royal Society, he made the acquaintance of Dr. Johnson, Boswell, and Sir Joshua Reynolds. Juraj Dragišić (Georgius Argenteneusis Salviatus; ? 1450–1520), was tutor to the sons of Lorenzo de' Medici and defending counsel for Giovanni Pico della Mirandola against the Inquisition. Benedikt Kotruljić or Kotruljević (1400–68), a minister at the court of Aragon, was author of one of the first scientific treatises on trade and commercial practices. A more recent native of Dubrovnik was the Croatian playwright, Ivo Vojnović (1857–1929), who wrote several works about the decline of the ancient Republic.

I The Old City

The riches of Dubrovnik are concentrated into a small compass, but even so visitors whose time is limited are advised to begin with the area between the Jesuit Church and the Ploče Gate at the E. end of the town, with perhaps a walk round the walls to gain some idea of the whole layout.

Most visitors will approach for the first time from the w., arriving at the irregular open space of PILE (comp. p. 204), where the air terminal, the reversing point of the two tram routes, a taxi rank, and the offices of the Atlas travel agency contribute to the invariable air of arrival and departure. An excellent preliminary view of the massive walls encircling the city may be gained from a few paces up Put iza grada on the landward side. Steps lead down beside the bridge to a pleasant small park in the former moat, which descends to the water's edge (view of forts Bokar and Lovrijenac).

A stone bridge with twin Gothic arches, designed by Paskoje Miličević (1471), the Republic's official architect, leads viâ a wooden drawbridge to the **Pile Gate,** one of the two main land entrances to the city. A statue of the city patron, St Blaise, is set over the arch and on the inner side can be seen the heavy iron balls and windlass that used to operate the drawbridge. The entrance to Fort Bokar (see p. 192) is just inside the gate. Within the outer gate a flight of steps and a ramp provide alternative descents to the Gothic inner gate (1460), which was modelled on the Fishmarket Gate in the old harbour. The Balustrade of the steps and a second statue of St Blaise set in a niche are both the work of Ivan Meštrović. A small gate gives access to the moat (comp. above). Immediately inside the inner gate we find ourselves at the w. end of Placa, the main artery of the old city (see below).

Those who wish to gain some idea of the city's extent and general plan before exploring it in detail, are well advised to make a tour of the *City Walls* (open 8–12, 4–7; 3 din.), access to which is gained by a flight of steps to the left. Another entrance is to be found at the Ploče Gate on the E. side of the city.

The **City Walls** of Dubrovnik are among the finest and most complete in Europe and majestically symbolize the strength and stability of the ancient republic. They comprise an inner and an outer section. The inner ring, with a circumference of just under 1¼ m. and rising to a maximum height of 72 ft, with a thickness attaining 18 ft in places, is furnished with 3 round and 12 rectangular towers, 5 bastions, 2 corner towers and one major fortress. On the landward side, this is protected by a lower outer wall having 10 semicircular bastions and the casemated fortress of Bokar, with a moat running round the outside.

The walls were begun when the city was founded and the earliest remaining fragments date from the 10C, although the first complete enceinte was thrown up only in the 12–13C. In the 14C the works were extended on the Ploče side and 15 square towers added. The fall of Constantinople in 1453 led to a reappraisal of system, during which the curtain walls were trebled in thickness and many of the towers rebuilt. A century later in answer to threats from Venice, some bastions were added on the seaward side, together with the fortress of Revelin, and the last reconstruction took place (1647–63) as a response to the Candian War between Venice and Turkey. Among the numerous architects and builders involved, the most prominent were Jean de Vienne (1381–87), Michelozzo Michelozzi (1461–64), Juraj Dalmatinac (1465–70) and Ivan Giorgi (1668–71).

Walking N.E. along the top of the steeply rising wall flanking the Franciscan Monastery, we soon reach the magnificent round tower of *Minčeta* (rfmts), built in 1455–61 to designs by Michelozzi and Dalmatinac. It rises from the highest and most massive of the corner towers. The battlements afford one of the finest *Views of the old city. From the N. wall we have a constantly changing panorama of the landward side of the city, with its regular streets running almost N. and s. Beyond the N. entrance gate to the city, we come to the semicircular tower of *Sv. Jakov*, once the N.E. corner tower of the walls. Its present shape dates from the 16C. The projecting complex of bastions that enclose the Dominican Monastery (comp. p. 201) was added in the 14C and brings us to the Old Ploče Gate. A further short section of wall takes us to the 13C tower of *Sv. Luka*, the oldest tower still standing; farther on, beyond the triangular bastion in which the Labirint nightclub is situated, the tower of *Sv. Dominik* (1387), opposite the s. door of the Dominican church, overlooks the harbour. Beyond the roof of the Gradska kavana, the footway is blocked.

We descend to the street behind the Clock Tower, pass between the Rector's Palace and the Cathedral (comp. p. 198), and regain the walls by steps just inside the *Vrata od Ponte*, on the far side of the harbour. A straight section of wall skirting the s. side of the harbour takes us to the massive *Tvrdjava of Sv. Ivan* (comp. p. 200) the largest single component of the walls, erected in four stages between 1346 and 1557. From here a massive chain used to be stretched across the harbour to the tower of Sv. Luka. We now traverse the s. walls with excellent views out to sea. The bastions of *Sv. Spasitelj* (1647–57) and *Sv. Stjepan* (1658–63), facing s.E. and enclosing the oldest quarter of the city, were the last to be rebuilt. From the high bastion of *Sv. Margarita*, beyond a re-entrant angle, we command the exterior of the sector just traversed, which rises from jagged rocks. This section, that following, and the bastion of *Zvijezda* (Star), suffered heavily from the earthquake of 1667 and parts had to be repaired afterwards, though the largest fortification on this side, the *Mrtvo zvono* (1509–74), designed by Paskoje Miličević, was not affected. We descend to the tower of *Sv. Marija*, with views ahead of Fort Lovrijenac and the coast, and come to *Kalarinja* (completed 1430) the s.w. corner tower, with Bokar fortress below. We turn N.E. to the large rectangular *Puncijela* tower (1305–50), with an unusual pillared stair (good view of Pile), beyond which the cloister of the former nunnery of St Clare (Jadran rest.) is well seen, and regain the Pile Gate.

An entrance within the Pile Gate gives access to **Fort Bokar** (open 8–12, 4–7), a handsome round fortress (1461–1570) designed by Michelozzi that stands just below Kalarinja on an outcrop of rock. It is said to be the oldest casemated fortress in Europe and contains a small lapidary collection and numerous cannon.

Within the Pile Gate an open space called POLJANA PASKOJE MILI

ČEVIĆA extends on the right. In the centre stands the *Velika česma*, a sixteen-sided reservoir and drinking fountain by Onofrio di Giordano della Cava, which formed part of the town waterworks, designed and partly constructed by this Neapolitan architect in 1438–44. The dome was added later. In the corner of the square and next to the Pile Gate is the delightful small church of *Sv. Spas* (St Saviour), designed in thanksgiving for deliverance from the earthquake of 1520 and built in 1520–28 by Petar Andrijić of Korčula, with a typically Dalmatian Renaissance w. front (wheel-window) and a Gothic interior. Above the w. door is a painting of the Ascension by Pietro Antonio da Urbino (1528).

Adjoining is the **Franciscan Monastery**. We visit first the CHURCH (open daily 8–12, 4–8), erected in 1343. The fine late-Gothic *South Portal*, by the brothers Petrović (1499), facing the Placa, has a good Pietà in the tympanum, flanked by SS Jerome and John the Baptist, and surmounted by God the Father. The detail of the elaborately crocketed finial and windblown acanthus decoration is admirably emphasized by the plain wall. The Gothic *Campanile* (1424) was given an unfortunate cupola after the earthquake had toppled its spire. The lofty INTERIOR (reputed once to have had ceiling paintings by Titian) was reconstructed after the earthquake of 1667. To the left of the high altar is the *Sacristy* with a good lavabo and vestment cupboards of walnut with inlaid portraits of Christ and saints. It is extended E. by the beautiful little Gothic chapel of the Bunić (Bona) family (1472). A huge Gothic ambry for reliquaries surmounts the altar; its triple doors, painted as a triptych, form the altarpiece.

The *CLOISTER is entered from the passage between the w. front and Sv. Spas. A remarkably original creation by Mihoje Brajkov of Bar (1317–48), it escaped damage in the earthquake and remains the chief glory of the monastery. Each bay of the covered walk is enclosed by an arcade of six closely set round arches borne on coupled octagonal columns. The joint capitals of the paired columns display a variety of fantastic beasts, monster, and mythological creatures in the best traditions of Romanesque art. The tympana above have circular openings, the central one of each side surrounded by a rich border of acanthus leaves, the remainder containing a quatrefoil. The elegant ornamented balustrade above is the work of Ratko Brajković (1433). A richly decorated Gothic sarcophagus of the Gučetić family is set into the wall of the S.E. corner. Two-light windows flank the door into the Gothic *Chapter House*, which is now used as the monastery TREASURY (open 10–11 only). The well-labelled exhibits include a 15C silver-gilt cross and silver thurible, and an interesting display from the monastery's extensive library (30,000 volumes, 20 incunabula, 1500 MSS), notably the manuscript of Gundulić's epic poem 'Osman', a first edition of 'Judita' by Marko Marulić (Venice, 1521), a 15C copy of the Statute of Zadar, an illuminated martyrology (1541) by Bernardin Gučetić (Gozze) and illuminated psalters. Among the pictures is one of Rudjer Bošković (see above) painted in London in 1760. The Gothic chapel of the Djordjić family contains a charming fragment of a reredos and the adjoining niche a 16C wooden statue of St Nicholas. The *Pharmacy*, or apothecary's shop, established in 1317, the oldest to survive in

Europe, has been restored, with early ceramic jars (Faience and Delft), apparatus, furniture, and 16C pharmacy registers.

The beautiful wide street of **Placa,** or *Stradun* (c. 300 yds; pedestrians only) runs from the Pile to Ploče gates, following the line of the channel that once bisected the town. The street came into being in the 12C, was paved in 1468 and reconstructed after the earthquake of 1667. The marble pavement, polished by five centuries use, shines like glass after rain. The Placa is the main street and traditional venue of the evening corzo. The houses on either side, though preserving an ancient ground plan, also, date from the 17C, their elevation and style being uniform. Their shops mostly have the characteristic 'na koljeno' combined door and counter.

The 'na koljeno' consists of a door and window in a single frame spanned by a semi-circular arch. The door was kept closed and goods handed over the sill, which served as a counter. The recipient took them on to his knee (hence the name 'on to the knee'). The distinctive shape of the 'na koljeno' with its stone frame is to be found in many parts of the Kvarner (comp. p. 70) and Dalmatia, but particularly in Dubrovnik, where it has been adopted almost as a local trade mark.

The irregularly shaped LuŽA, the hub of public life in the days of the old republic, makes a fitting architectural climax to the walk down the Placa and is a favourite meeting place for natives, visitors, and pigeons alike. The N. side of the square is occupied by the striking *Palača Sponza,* a harmonious blend of Gothic and Renaissance architecture probably inspired by the Rector's Palace near by. A graceful loggia stands forward of the façade.

As the ancient custom house, mint, and main warehouse (variously known at different times as the Fontik, Divona or Dogana) this was one of the most important buildings in the city and remained in continuous public use until the end of the 19C. For many years the first floor was used also for social gatherings and the meetings of learned and literary societies. The palace dates from 1516–22, when plans by Paskoje Miličević were executed by the Andrijić family from Korčula, notably the sculptor Petar Andrijić. Authorities differ as to whether it was designed and built in a mixture of styles or whether the Gothic middle story remains from an earlier building.

The interior is built round a spacious court arranged as a double cloister, with round arches below and slightly pointed ones on the first floor. A pithy Latin inscription set in the far wall refers to the public scales that formerly stood here (Cheating and tampering with the weights is forbidden and when I weigh goods God weighs them also). The adjoining escutcheon enclosed in a wreath held by two angels is by Beltrandus Gallicus (1520). The ground floor houses a museum devoted to the National Liberation Movement and contains the original 16C mechanism and jacks of the town clock, while on the upper floors are stored the extensive Republican archives. The courtyard is used for exhibitions and festival concerts.

In the centre of the square stands *Orlando's Column,* with a statue of the Paladin Roland by Antun Dubrovčanin (1418), symbolizing a free city; from it state decrees were proclaimed. The upper part bore the Republic's standard, while the forearm of Orlando was the standard measure of the Ragusan cubit (shown more accurately by a line in the base). The Baroque church of **Sv. Vlaho** (*St Blaise*), the patron saint of Dubrovnik, was built by Marino Gropelli in 1706–14 to replace a building of 1368 lost by fire. It faces N. instead of W. The spacious interior, modelled on San Maurizio in Venice, is rectangular with a central dome, and preserves some of the treasures from the earlier church. In the reredos is a celebrated silver *Statuette of St Blaise, holding a model of 15C Dubrovnik. The painted organ loft behind the high altar is by Petar Mattei Matejević (early 18C). High on the walls are placed stone statues of SS Blaise and Jerome, by Nikola Lazanić of Brač (late 16C), and above the side door a wooden figure of St Anthony, of unknown date.

Along the E. side of Luža a continuous line of buildings extends from the Sponza across the width of the harbour, fronting upon the long open space called PRID DVOROM. A Gothic archway adjoining the Sponza marks the beginning of Put medju vratima od Ploča leading to the Outer Ploče Gate (see p. 202) and supports the **Loža zvonara**, an open loggia in which were hung bells for sounding alarms or summoning assemblies. Erected in 1463, the loggia was restored to its former appearance in 1952 after conversion by the Austrians into an admiral's residence. The graceful *Bell Tower*, 100 ft tall, dating from 1444, was dismantled and rebuilt in 1928. The modern clock, with bronze jacks in the form of soldiers that strike the hour, is a faithful copy (with the addition of a figured time indicator) of one dating from 1478 (remains in Sponza palace). The great bell in the tower was cast by Ivan Rabljanin in 1506. The adjoining *Glavna Straža* (Main Guard), incorporating a Gothic upper story of 1490 from the Ragusan admiral's house, was constructed in 1706–08, when the Baroque portal was inserted after a design by Marino Gropelli. The charming *Mala česma* (little fountain) of Onofrio, an octagonal basin with defaced sculptural panels, from which rises a 'Baroque-Gothic' column recalling the fountains of Viterbo, was completed by Pietro di Martino da Milano (mid-15C). The undistinguished *Gradska općina* (Town Hall; 1864) incorporates the pleasant *Gradska kavana*, with a loggia overlooking the harbour on the far side (comp. p. 200) and a cinema above, and the *Narodno Kazalište* (theatre).

The *Knežev dvor*, or *Rector's Palace, embodies (like the Sponza) a blend of Gothic and Renaissance styles so harmoniously fused as to epitomize Ragusan architecture at its best. Here the Rector of the Republic had his official seat and hence supreme political power was wielded.

A castle on the site, which became the early rector's residence, was destroyed in 1435 when fire exploded a magazine. A new palace was commissioned from Onofrio di Giordana della Cava and built in South Italian Gothic. This in turn was partly destroyed by another explosion in 1463 and plans for its renovation were commissioned from Michelozzi and Juraj Dalmatinac. Their Renaissance solutions were rejected, although it is probable that Michelozzi's designs formed the basis of the subsequent rebuilding of the ground floor by Salvi di Michiele in 1468. Slight damage caused by the earthquake of 1667 was made good by Jerolim Skarpa of Korčula.

The upper floor of the façade is pierced by eight graceful Gothic windows with traceried heads, probably as Onofrio built it in 1435 but reassembled during the rebuilding of 1468. The plain Gothic portions at either end are the remnants of two towers between which has been inserted the handsome loggia of Michelozzi, built by Michiele. The columns and four of the *Capitals (first, second, sixth, and seventh from

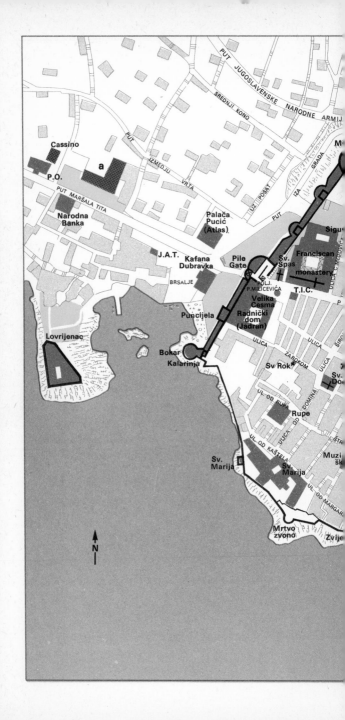

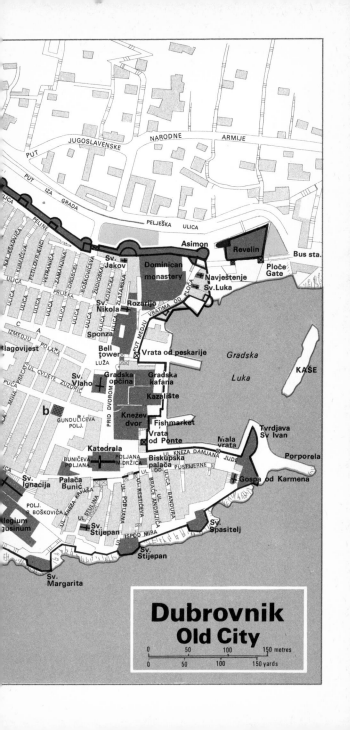

Dubrovnik
Old City

| 0 | 50 | 100 | 150 metres |
| 0 | 50 | 100 | 150 yards |

PUT JUGOSLAVENSKE NARODNE ARMIJE

PUT IZA GRADA

PELJEŠKA ULICA

ULICA NALJEŠKOVIĆA

ULICA KUMIČIĆA

PELINE

ULICA PETILOVRENCI

VETRANIĆA

ULICA ZAMANJINA

DROBCEV

IBRKOVIĆEVA

ULICA PRIJEKA

ŽUDIOSKA

KOVAČKA

ZLATARSKA

Asimon

Revelin

Ploče Gate

Bus sta.

Sv. Jakov

Dominican monastery

Navještenje Sv.Luka

Sv. Nikola

Rozarijo

VRATIMA OD PLOČA

Sponza

IZMEDJU POLAČA

CA

Blagovijest

Bell tower

LUŽA

Vrata od peskarije

PUT MEDJU

Gradska Luka

KAŠE

MIHA PRACATUL CVIJETE ZUZORIĆ

PUČA

Sv. Vlaho

Gradska opčina

Gradska kafana

Kazališče

b

GUNDULIĆEVA POLJ.

PRID DVOROM

Kneževdvor

Fishmarket

Vrata od Ponte

Mala vrata

Tvrdjava Sv Ivan

Porporela

Katedrala

BUNIČEVA POLJANA

POLJANA M.DRŽIČA

Biskupska palača

UL KNEZA DAMJANA JUDE

PUSTIJERNE

Gospa od Karmena

Sv. Ignacija

Palača Bunić

UL KNEZA KRAŠA

UL. STULINA

UL BRAĆE ANDRIJIĆA

UL OD PUSTIJERNE

UL. RESTIĆEVA

UL. POBIJANA

BANDURA

POLJ. R BOŠKOVIĆA

llegium jusinum

Sv. Stijepan

ISPOD MIRA

Sv. Spasitelj

Sv. Stijepan

Sv. Margarita

the right) are Gothic in manner, though the first depicts Asklepios in the setting of a medieval pharmacy. The loggia is vaulted with graceful Gothic ribs which spring fanwise from carved Renaissance corbels. Arcaded marble seats line the rear wall and that to the left. The Gate of Mercy, where alms were distributed, opens in the s. wall. Entrance is gained by the main *Portal*, a Gothic arch with fanciful capitals and imposts; the figure of St Blaise in the niche above is by Pietro di Martino and there is a fine bronze knocker in the shape of a lion's head.

The inner *COURT has a Renaissance arcade on three sides; on the fourth, an imposing staircase leads to an arcaded balcony. Below the stair arch are a Venetian Gothic fountain and a doorway (angel in niche above) leading to the offices of the Conservation Department in the former repository of the State Archives. The Bust of Miho Pracat (Michaeli Prazzato) by Pietro Giacometti da Recanati (1638) was the only monument to a citizen ever erected (or even allowed) by the medieval state; Pracat, a 16C merchant adventurer from Lopud, bequeathed his riches to the Republic. A small staircase leads to the mezzanine and former hall of the Lesser Council, which now houses the city's *Naučna biblioteka*, a research library of 90,000 vols (78 incunabula) and many manuscripts. Two of Onofrio's original capitals flank the entrance, one depicting Justice with a pair of lions, the other the Rector administering justice to the citizens.

On the FIRST FLOOR the *Hall of the Great Council* and the adjoining *State Rooms* house the **Gradski muzej** (open daily 9–11.30; explanatory booklet available in English). The entrance to the Hall at the head of the main staircase bears an admonitory inscription to forget private affairs and attend to public business. The State Rooms are furnished with Baroque and Rococo furniture, portraits of Republican notables, and faience. The anteroom contains Louis XVI furniture and five paintings by Annibale Carracci (1560–1609), notably Cain and Abel. The Rector's Study preserves the former state seals and keys of the city gates. The paintings include the Baptism of Christ by Mihajlo Hamzić (1509), a Ragusan pupil of Mantegna; Paris Bordone, Daphnis and Chloe; Holy Family (sch. of Tintoretto); and Maiden and Flautist (attrib. Vinc. Catena).

Exhibits illustrating daily life in the Republic occupy the EAST WING. These include Ragusan coins from 1350 to 1803, copies of the city statutes, registers of the nobility and state decrees, robes of various officials (remarkable for the great stature they indicate), and apparel, jewellery and appurtenances (mainly 17–18C).

The court and the street outside are both used for performances during the summer festival, a tradition stemming at least from 1628, when Gundulić's play 'Dubravka' was first given here.

The Baroque **Katedrala,** designed by Andrea Bufalini of Urbino and built in 1672–1713, stands in the centre of Poljana Marina Držića. Its predecessor, a 13C Romanesque basilica said to have received a benefaction from Richard Coeur-de-Lion (supposedly shipwrecked on the island of Lokrum in 1192 when returning from the Third Crusade), was destroyed in the earthquake of 1667. The cathedral is cruciform in plan, with the high altar unusually towards the w. and a high dome over the crossing. The exterior is decorated with a balustrade enclosing the roofs of the aisles and surmounted by statues of saints carved by Marin Radica of Korčula early in the present century. The interior is light and spacious. A large polyptych of the Assumption, by Titian (after 1552), occupies the wall above and behind the high altar. In the sanctuary are four paintings by Padovanino and over the entrance to the treasury a work by Andrea del Sarto. The pulpit is a fine example of the wood-carver's art. Among many altarpieces by lesser Italian masters in the nave is a Flemish triptych, which served as a portable altar when Ragusan ambassadors went to pay the annual tribute in Constantinople (they alone holding the privilege of hearing mass in Turkey).

The *TREASURY (open Tues & Thurs, 11–12), to the left of the high altar, contains some 138 reliquaries, most of which are carried in procession round the city on the feast of St Blaise (3 Feb). Entry has always been a jealously guarded privilege, in the days of the Republic needing permission of the bishop, the Grand Council, and the treasurer, each of whom kept a key to one of the three locks. The collection occupies a beautiful Baroque chapel designed by Gropelli and painted by Mattei-Matejević. The head of Christ is by Pordenone. On the altar stand the three major reliquaries of St Blaise: the *Reliquary of the Skull, in the form of a Byzantine crown of enamel and silver filigree work (1694) set with twenty-four 12C enamels; a 13C silver-gilt arm reliquary, set with nine Byzantine enamels (originally 18); and a 17C silver filigree leg reliquary with the arms of the Republic in enamel. Behind is a large late-Gothic silver *Cross enclosing part of the true cross, decorated with reliefs in silver-gilt by J. Matov (16C), and a silver statuette of St Blaise. Cases display a superb *Ewer and Basin of silver by W. Jamnitzer of Nuremberg (c. 1550), a Baroque casket enclosing a supposed fragment of Christ's swaddling clothes, another with the hand of St Bridget, a Gothic reliquary containing the lower jaw of St Stephen of Hungary, and a silver-gilt rib cage of St Blaise. A bronze English lectern with a Latin inscription reading 'Remember, Henry, that thou too must die' is said to be of the time of Henry VIII.

The former *Biskupska palača* faces the cathedral; built in Tuscan Renaissance style, it was previously the home of the Sorkočević family. In the s.w. corner of Bunićeva poljana, behind the cathedral, the *Palača Bunić* has a good portal with the Bunić (Bona) escutcheon in the tympanum and a Renaissance court within. GUNDULIĆEVA POLJANA, the larger adjoining square, accommodates the principal fruit and vegetable market (Tržnica), to which peasants from surrounding districts sometimes come in local costume. The monument to Ivan Gundulić in the centre, by I. Rendić (1893), depicts scenes in bronze relief from his epic poem 'Osman'.

Ul. uz Jesuite leads to the foot of the imposing staircase (modelled in 1738 on the 'Spanish Steps' in Rome) that mounts to Sv. Ignacija, the Baroque church of the Jesuits, designed by And. Pozzo (1725) in imitation of the Gesù in Rome. The belfry boasts a bell cast in 1355. The focal point of the spacious interior is the apse painted by the Sicilian G. Garcia (1738). The *Collegium Ragusinum*, dominating the s. side of Poljana Rudjera Boškovića (and indeed much of Dubrovnik), was designed by two local Jesuits in 1735 and is perhaps the least tasteful building in the city. In the steps leading to the main entrance is a relief (1481), thought to be from the church of Sv. Bartula (Bartholomew) which once stood at the far end of the square. According to legend St Francis slept in the vestibule of this church during a week's halt en route for Constantinople. Its portal, richly decorated with pre-Roman carving, survives in Ul. Kneza Krvaša.

Pustijerna, one of the oldest and most picturesque quarters of the city, lying to the E. between the harbour and the city walls, largely escaped the devastation of the earthquake. It repays detailed exploration, but since this involves a serpentine progress up and down its stepped streets, it is best reserved for a cool day. From the Collegium Ragusinum Ul. Krvaša (comp. above) descends past one of the oldest houses in the city, with Romanesque door and window frames, to *Vrata od Pustijerne*, the Romanesque gate that marks the extent of the 10–11C walls (also reached from behind the cathedral by steps). In Ul. Stulina, which mounts again almost parallel, are two town houses of the Restić (Resti) and Saraka families and, at the top, the ruined church of *Sv. Stjepan*. The original building, dating from the 8C or earlier, is mentioned by Constantine Porphyrogenitus in his account of the founding of Ragusa; only the lower courses of this remain. Over the s. door is a pre-Romanesque carving of a cabled double arch enclosing twin crosses. The narrow winding Ul. ispod mira runs inside the walls at the head of delightful small streets lined with old houses. On the corner of Ul. Pobijana is the Renaissance *Palača Bunić*. In Ul. Restićeva are the Gothic *Palača Zamanjina* and the Renaissance *Palača Skočibuha*, built by the brothers Josip and Ivan Andrijić (1549–53) to designs by Antun iz Padove. Perhaps the finest street of Pustijerna is Ul. Braće Andrijića where Gothic and Renaissance mansions make up the complex *Palača Restić*. The pleasant Baroque church of *Gospa od Karmena* (Our Lady of Mt Carmel; 1628–36) lies at the end of Ul. ispod mira in the shadow of the fortress of Sv. Ivan, with the city escutcheon over its w. door. The interior (key from Bishop's Palace) contains 17C paintings by minor Italian artists.

Dominating the entrance to the old harbour is the **Fortress of Sv. Ivan.** On the ground floor an *Aquarium* is stocked with fish from various parts of the Mediterranean. On the next floor is the *Pomorski muzej*, a maritime museum in which the four sections are devoted to the Republican period; the age of steam; the Second World War; and to techniques of sailing and navigation. One floor higher, the *Etnografski muzej* displays folk costumes, musical instruments, and bygones illustrating the life of the surrounding countryside.

From Ul. Kneza Damjana Jude, occupied by carpenters' shops, the plain *Mala vrata* gives access to the old harbour (comp. below), but it is more interesting to return to the Cathedral by UL. OD PUSTIJERNE, an almost subterranean street spanned by numerous vaults and lined with ancient houses. In Ul. Bandureva, a narrow cul-de-sac, are the handsome Renaissance town houses of the Kaboga and Sorkočević (Sorgo) families (l.) and the Bunić family (r.).

Between the Cathedral and Rector's Palace, the *Vrata od Ponte* (1476) gives access to the peaceful **Old Harbour,** now used only by little fishing boats and pleasure craft. The breakwater (*Kaše*) was built by Paskoje Miličević in the 15C, but by the 16C the harbour had already been superseded by Gruž. To the right a narrow way along the walls leads round Fort Sv. Ivan to the *Porporela*, a favourite swimming place of the local youth. The Veliki arsenal, built to house four state galleys, was demolished in 1863 to make way for the Gradska općina (p. 195), but parts of it, incorporated into the Gradska kavana, are still visible. Beyond the cafe, opposite the mole whence excursion boats ply to Lokrum, the Harbourmaster's Office occupies the site of the former Mali arsenal.

The Gothic *Vrata od ribarnice* (or peskarije), erected in 1381–87 as the second of the original gates (with a statue of St Blaise on the harbour side), readmits to the town by the narrow PUT MEDJU VRATIMA OD PLOČA, the street linking the inner and outer Ploče gates (as its name states). Just to the left steps lead up to the walls (comp. p. 191); we turn right, between the high city wall and the side of the Sponza palace.

A stone staircase with a Renaissance balustrade mounts left to the **Dominican Church and Monastery.** The Church was erected before 1315 but had to be rebuilt after the earthquake of 1667 and again after the French occupation, when it was used as a stable and storehouse; its last renovation was in 1883. The plain interior consists of a huge single nave with a triple Gothic arch near the E. end opening into the sanctuary and two side chapels, the only part of the original building that survives. The fine **Rood comprises a 14C crucifixion by Paolo Veneziano, flanked by paintings of the Virgin Mary and St John by Lorenzo di Marino Dobričević (15C).

S. WALL. The Annunciation, with an 'argosy' in the centre panel of the predella, by Nikola Božidarević (1513); two altarpieces by Francesco di Maria (17C). The Romanesque s. door (13C) has a Gothic frame added in 1419. A 15C statue of St Vincent Ferrer surmounts the next altar. A large 17C painting of the Assumption (signed A.B.D.) incorporates in the lower centre the best extant representation of Ragusa before the earthquake of 1667. Below is a reclining effigy of a bishop with an inscription of 1393. The Renaissance chapel of the Lukarević (Luccari) family, adjoining the high altar, contains a triptych by Mihajlo Hamzić (1512). Behind the high altar is a Gothic portal (damaged) with the Mečetić (Menze) escutcheon in the tympanum and arms of the Zamanjina, Držić, and Restić families round it. The Gundulić Chapel, by Luka Paskojev (1536), left of the high altar, contains a triptych by Nikola Božidarević (after 1485).

N. WALL: Descent of the Holy Ghost by Giorgio Vasari, not his best work; altarpiece, Miracle of St Dominic by Vlaho Bukovac (a local 19C work in the Sicilian manner); a late-Gothic stone pulpit (15C); altarpiece, Mary Magdalen with St Blaise and the Archangel Raphael, by Titian (c. 1554), including a portrait of the donor, a member of the Pucić family. The w. wall incorporates a curious Renaissance triple arch with scalloped semi-domes, by Ludovik Maravić of Korčula, into the base of which are built carved Gothic tomb-slabs.

The Gothic *Sacristy*, built by Paskoje Miličević (1485), contains a fine contemporary lavabo, a huge 16C cross, and a magnificent wall-press for vestments (16C). It opens into a similar *Chapel* built by Marko Andrijić (1470) to a design by Bartolomej Gracianus, with an early-16C polyptych of the Dubrovnik school (? by Lorenzo Dobričević). The graceful late-Gothic CLOISTER, erected by local masons to a modified design of Maso di Bartolomeo of Florence, has interesting bosses in the vault and tomb-slabs in the walls, but is somewhat marred by the over-clever interlaced ornament in alternate tympana and in the balustrade above. The s. side was surmounted by a balcony in 1520 inscribed with the date and the words of the Te Deum. The garth is planted with orange trees; the Venetian wellhead in the centre of 1559 was given a

Renaissance superstructure in 1623. In the corner, over the sacristy, rises the *Campanile*, begun in 1390 and completed in 1531 in a curiously retarded Romanesque style, continued somewhat unfortunately by the later Baroque lantern. The CHAPTER HOUSE was divided in 1668 into an outer (Djurdjević) chapel and an inner treasury. The chapel has a splendid altarpiece, Madonna enthroned with saints and donors, by Nikola Božidarević (1513), with a pietà in the gable above. Among many tomb slabs is that of Dinko Ranjina, the 16C poet.

Items from the *Treasury* are in course of arrangement in an adjacent chamber (to be opened in 1969). These include a 14C silver cross inscribed to Uroš II Milutin of Serbia by Gregorije, Bp. of Raša; a 15C English alabaster relief; a 16C thurible in the shape of a Ragusan galleon; a diptych of Christ and the Virgin Mary by the 15C Avignon painter Enguerrand Charonton; and the Holy Family, in the manner of Lor. di Credi. The display will also include items from the fine monastic *Library* of 16,000 vols, with 217 MSS, many illuminated, and 239 incunabula, notably the illustrated chronicle of Pleydenwurff and Wolgemut (1493) and the speeches of Savonarola (1497).

Adjoining the Dominican church is the former Renaissance church of *Sv. Sebastijan* (1466–69), transformed into a prison by the French (note the barred windows on the street façade). Facing is the deconsecrated church of *Rozarijo* (apply to Konzervatorski zavod in the Rector's Palace for admission), built in 1594 and restored after a fire in 1642. The French turned it into a salt store but it was restored in 1962 as the headquarters of the Društvo prijatelja Dubrovačke starine (Society of Friends of Old Dubrovnik). The beautiful interior is divided by two tall Renaissance arcades, ornamented with heads of nuns and angels, while an ornate portal, probably the entrance to a vanished chapel, stands within the vestibule.

Put medju vratima od Ploča slopes uphill past the s. door of the Dominican church (l.), its Romanesque style disguised by the florid ogee arch in which it was later framed. Beyond the *Labirint* night-club, we come (r.) to the tiny church of *Sv. Luka*, of pre-Romanesque foundation. The Gothic figures of saints in the tympanum are attributed to the brothers Petrović (late 15C); the lintel gives the date (1786) of the last renovation. Adjoining is the larger chapel of *Navještenje* (Annunciation), built by Petar Andrijić in 1536 in a mixture of late-Gothic and Renaissance styles (good brattice and blind arcading on the gable; restored 1910). The altarpiece is an Annunciation by Mattei-Matejević. A few steps bring us to the twin-angled arches of the *Inner Ploče Gate*, the first (Romanesque) through the wall of *Asimon Tower*, the second widened by the Austrians. The framed statue of St Blaise over the outer arch is the oldest of many in the city. A stone bridge (1449) across the moat takes us through another arch and along the foot of the massive **Revelin**, one of two vast fortresses built outside the walls to protect the city from surprise attack. A small belvedere (Trg oružja) at its foot affords a marvellous view of the old harbour and town and accommodates a war memorial by Franjo Kršinić (1954).

Revelin, entered from Put iza grada, was begun in 1463 (it is said as a preparation for the landing of Pius II's projected crusade from Ancona), and completed c. 1500, but in 1538 new plans drawn by Antonio Ferramolino, an engineer sent from Genoa at Ragusa's request, were implemented and the fortress finished in eleven years. Under Austria the building was adapted as barracks but it has been restored for use as a theatre; its enormous terrace also makes a fine natural stage for performances in summer.

We pass out of the Old City by the fortified and embrasured *Outer Gate* of **Ploče,** built by Miho Hranjac in 1628, and over a wooden drawbridge and twin-spanned stone bridge (15C) by Paskoje Miličević similar to those at Pile gate.

From the square in front of this gate depart buses for Cavtat. Just beyond, along a gravelled cul-de-sac to the right, extends the former **Lazaret** (16C), altered in 1627, and restored in 1968–69. The far end had been adapted as changing accommodation for the town beach (*Gradsko kupalište*), but this is being removed to new buildings on the beach itself and the lazaret is destined to become a covered market. Put Frana Supila leads past the prominent grammar school and a modern art gallery to the Excelsior Hotel, the *Villa Orsula*, now a catering school, and the Argentina Hotel. Here the main road rises (l.) to join the Adriatic Highway (one way only in the downward direction), while a branch continues (r.) past the *Villa Shahrazade*, built as a harem by an eccentric millionaire (magnificent walled garden; entered from Argentina) and the *Villa Dubrovnik*, used as a residence for official visitors, to the former monastery of *Sv. Jakov*. Here the Institute of Arts and Sciences have established research laboratories into corrosion of sea water and desalination methods. The cloister (12C) has charm but the church is dilapidated. The road ends at the Hotel Belvedere.

By the side of the Rozarijo (comp. above) a narrow passage leads to the street and northern quarter of the city known as **Prijeko,** the original Slavonic settlement on the mainland of the dividing channel. The little pre-Romanesque church of *Sv. Nikola*, on the left, has a Renaissance w. front of 1607 and preserves a Gothic figure of St Nicholas in wood, a 15C painting, and a stone slab with pre-Romanesque carving that serves as the altar frontal. Zlatarska ul. in front of the church mounts to *Sv. Jakov na Pelinama*, the only Romanesque church to have survived, which sheltered the Dominicans in 1225–28 on their first arrival. Within (key from Gradski muzej) is a 15C painting of the Madonna.

Ul. Peline runs w. inside the walls along the top of the quarter's narrow stepped streets. Žudioska ul. is named for the Jewish ghetto that once stood here and has, in its lower section, an unobtrusive 15C synagogue, said to be the oldest in the Balkans, which functioned throughout the Second World War. At the top of Boškovićeva ul. a modern opening in the walls leads into Put iza grada (comp. p. 191). By Boškovićeva, named for the birthplace (plaque) of the scientist Rudjer Bošković, we may descend again to PRIJEKO which, running parallel to Placa, is lined with balconied houses. Most date from after the earthquake, in which this district was hard hit, but two Gothic mansions mid-way along survived. A short distance up Ul. od Sigurate is the *Sigurata* (Transfiguration), a little pre-Romanesque church with later aisles and a Baroque w. front. We descend beside the Franciscan monastery to Poljana Paskoje Miličevića (comp. p. 192).

Enclosing its s. side is the former nunnery of SV. KLARA, founded in 1290. Restored after damage in 1667, it was dissolved by the French in 1806 and used as barracks. Under Austria the church too was occupied by the military. Since the last war the whole complex has been rearranged to accommodate the *Radnički dom* (trade union house, with a congress hall) and the Jadran cinema. The Renaissance cloister with double arcades has been excellently restored to house the *Jadran Restaurant*, in the centre of which stands a profusely decorated wellhead from the former prefect's residence on Lastovo.

The busy Ul. od puča, parallel with Placa to the s., is the principal shopping street. About half way along (l.) the ugly Serbian orthodox church of *Blagovijest* (Annunciation; 1877) displays Byzantine and

Italo-Cretan icons; four doors farther along is the parish office with a *Museum of Icons* (open daily, 10–12; donation). The collection, well displayed and labelled, consists mainly of provincial work (15–18C) of various schools; also portraits of Dubrovnik worthies, including eight works by Vlaho Bukovac, a 19C painter from Cavtat. Turning back we repass the Serbian church and, beyond the small Baroque church of *Sv. Josip*, built to replace an earlier one destroyed in the earthquake of 1667, turn left. At the top of Široka ul. stands the attractive Baroque church of *Domino* (1707) with an angled façade. It preserves as its sacristy an aisle of an earlier building destroyed in 1667. The church, reopened for worship in 1968, contains a St Jerome by And. Vaccaro and the Annunciation by B. Linterino. There is also a wooden statue of St Apollonius attrib. to Petar Bogdanović (1550).

In Ul. za rokom near by, the small 16C church of *Sv. Rok*, turned into a warehouse by the French, was restored around 1900, and has an altarpiece of the Annunciation by Mattei-Matejević.

The steep Ul. od Domina mounts by steps to a highly picturesque quarter with many houses of the 13C and 14C. In Ul. od Rupa stands **Rupa,** an enormous granary built in 1542–90 (restored 1940), with 15 huge storage chambers hewn from the rock which give a steady temperature of 17.5°C. The cavernous interior with a vaulted ground floor and arcaded upper stories houses the *Lapidary Collection* (open daily 9–12, 5–7) of the Gradski muzeji, comprising fragments from the many churches that suffered in the earthquake and from the former town loggia. Examples of pre-Romanesque stone carving show a more pronounced Mediterranean influence than is found farther north, and there are Roman pieces from Cavtat.

Ul. od kaštela passes through the oldest part of Dubrovnik, settled by the first refugees from Epidaurus. Between the street and the walls is the former Benedictine nunnery of *Sv. Marija*, used as barracks after its dissolution by the French and now turned into flats. Over the entrance is a late-Gothic relief of the Annunciation with the arms of the City and of the Pucić (Pozza), Gučetić (Gozze), and Buchia families, while higher still stands a Baroque statue of St Catherine. The outline of the former churches of Sv. Marija and Sv. Srdj can be seen inside. Another dissolved nunnery, *Sv. Katarina* of the Dominican order, stands in Štrosmajerova ul.; it is now the MUZIČKA ŠKOLA and is frequently used for musical performances in the summer festival. Two fine reliefs by the brothers Petrović (c. 1500) occupy the tympana of the two entrance gates. In the garden the picturesque ruins of the Benedictine monastery of Sv. Šime (Simon) command from their upper terrace an excellent view of the city. A recently excavated crypt in the grounds is thought to have belonged to the church of *Sv. Petar Veliki*, Dubrovnik's first cathedral (? 7–8C). Štrosmajerova ul. will return us past the *Palača Gučetić* to the Jesuit church and the Cathedral.

II The Western Suburbs

We may now take a more detailed look at the square outside the Pile Gate (comp. p. 191). On the N. side stands the Baroque *Palača Pucić* (Pozza), now the headquarters of the Atlas travel agency. Off the s. side opens *Brsalje* (i.e. Bersaglio) the former shooting range, a large open space shaded by plane trees, with the Kavana Dubravka on one side. A fountain by I. Rendić (1900) stands in the centre, decorated with figures from the Gundulić play, 'Dubravka'. Steps lead down from the far side of Brsalje to the picturesque little suburb and harbour of PILE, whence several flights of steps mount to the formidable fortress of *Lovrijenac on its gigantic spur of rock. It is probable that this rock was fortified in the 11C, but the fortress, first mentioned in 1301 was radically reconstructed twice in the 15C. It acquired its present form in 1571–76, partly from plans by Giovanni Battista Zanchi of Pesaro. Since 1866 it has been successively an Austrian barracks, a hotel, and an Italian prison. It was restored in 1933 for the International Pen Club Congress of that year and again in 1950, and now serves for performances during the festival. Entrance is gained (9–12, 4–7) through a narrow door with a locally famous inscription on the lintel: NON BENE PRO TOTO LIBERTAS VENDITUR AURO. The triangular interior contains three stories, of which the ground floor consists of a handsome courtyard ringed with Renaissance arcades. The upper terrace just under the battlements affords excellent views of the old city and the coastline to the N.W.

In the small bay to the W. of Lovrijenac is the modest beach of *Pile* (cabins, shower), beyond which a flight of steps leads up to the charming park of *Gradac* with its Aleppo and marine pines. The terrace at the entrance also acts as an open-air stage during the summer festival. Perched on rocks at the water's edge and reached by a footpath from the park is the little votive church and Franciscan nunnery of *Gospa od Danača* (Our Lady of Dance). The Gothic and Renaissance church (1457), with a triple bell cot, has a good W. door with ornately decorated capitals to the jambs, beside which is an inset stoup with a relief showing God the Father. In the tympanum of the S. door is a relief of the Madonna. In the interior (entered through the nunnery) are two good paintings: a polyptych on the high altar by Lovro Dobričević (1465), depicting the Madonna flanked by SS Blaise and Antony (l.) and SS Nicholas and Julian (r.), with God the Father above; and on the N. side a triptych by Nikola Božidarević (1521), showing the Madonna flanked by Pope Gregory (l.) and St Martin (r.). A self-portrait of the artist is incorporated in the panel of St Martin as a reflection in the saint's sword-blade. A high relief of the Madonna and Child removed from the tympanum of the W. door serves as an altar. In former times the church was particularly associated with the shoemaker's guild, whose gravestones can be seen in the adjoining cemetery. The open and unspoiled peninsula of *Danče*, where the Jug swimming club have their headquarters, offers excellent rock bathing and opportunities for skin diving. An asphalt road returns to Put Maršala Tita opposite the *Post Office* and *Hotel Imperial*.

Gruž and Lapad may be reached via Put Maršala Tita on foot or by one of the antiquated but colourful trams. Passing (l.) the Renaissance *Palača Crijević* (or Pucić), now the headquarters of the physical education club, and the General Hospital (Opća bolnica), we breast the hill to the district of BONINOVO, with a pleasant clifftop walk amid sub-tropical vegetation, commanding views out to sea. On the right are the open-air cinema and Kavana Slavica, beside which a path leads to Donji kono and the large *Palača Skočibuh-Bonda* (1576–88), now the Army Club.

The Russians exploded a barrel of gunpowder in the palace in 1806 and it was restored somewhat ineptly in 1938. The chapel in the grounds (1627) was intended to be a copy of the Santa Casa of Loreto. The road divides.

To the left, Put Pera Čingrije passes the bathing beach of Boninovo (Hotel Bellevue) to branch left though the centre of the Lapad peninsula or right to cross the lower slopes of *Velika Petka* (636 ft). Just beyond this second fork is the little church of *Gospa od Milosrdja* (Our Lady of Mercy), with votive pictures donated by local seamen, and on the lower slopes of Velika Petka the ancient church of *Sv. Mihajlo* (? 12C) with its interesting old graveyard.

Put Maršala Tita descends past the Hotel Stadion, built round an open-air Olympic swimming pool, to BATALA, where the road divides.

To the left (Lapadska obala) is the *Palača Majstorović* and the Renaissance *Palača Getaldić* (Ghetaldi), with boathouse and raised chapel, a few yards farther on. Midway along the shore, opposite the steamer quay of Gruž, is the handsome **Palača Sorkočević** (Sorgo; 1521), which now houses the *Historical Institute of the Yugoslav Academy of Sciences*. The palace, typically Ragusan in style (Renaissance below and Gothic above), has a beautiful *Forecourt with spirally fluted columns overlooking a large fish pool. The great salon, with a fine carved lavabo, opens at either end into two small rooms decorated in period style. An open loggia, adorned with Baroque murals, connects with a later wing where the fine library is situated; it overlooks a pretty garden court, enclosed by the family chapel where the altar is adorned by a statue of St Blaise by Juraj Dalmatinac. The spacious terraced garden is planted with orange trees. A little beyond is the smaller *Palača Pucić* (Pozza) in a similar style, but without the courtyard and garden. At the far end of the shore road is the Orsan yacht club, beyond which a narrow gravel road leads to the small bay of Solitudo; Aleja I. L. Ribara, crosses the peninsula of **Lapad** to the bay of Sumratin with its beach and numerous hotels.

The road to the right at Batala continues as Gruška obala to **Gruž,** the busy main harbour and steamer quay for Dubrovnik. On the right, rather hidden by their high walls, are several former summer residences now turned into flats and somewhat dilapidated. The Gothic and Renaissance *Palača Gradić* (Gradis) is conspicuous since its boathouse, with a chapel above, still spans the older part of the road. An entrance beyond the arch gives access to the main reception hall with a stuccoed ceiling, decorated with the escutcheons of prominent Dubrovnik families, and a small selection of the original furniture. About 30 yds farther is the *Palača Bunić* (Bonus), with small boathouse, and farther still, behind the pharmacy, the imposing PALAČA GUNDULIĆ (1521), with a most attractive loggia over the boathouse and a partly Gothic chapel (1507). This loggia is used during the summer festival for performances of the play, 'Na teraci' (On the Terrace), part of the Dubrovnik Trilogy by Ivo Vojnović (1857–1929). By the small *Tržnica* (market) the road divides round a small park. To the right the Renaissance *Villa Natali*, a summer residence of the Sorkočević family, has a pleasant arcaded façade. Opposite the Hotel Petka are the coastal steamer quays with the international quays beyond, in front of the guild church of *Sv. Nikola* (1527). From here it is a few minutes to the railway station (*Kolodvor*).

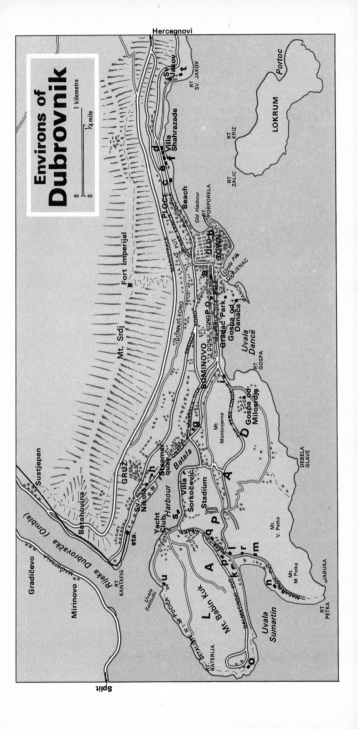

EXCURSIONS FROM DUBROVNIK

To the Rijeka Dubrovačka (R. Ombla), 5 km. (infrequent local bus; best by hired boat). The **Rijeka Dubrovačka** is an indented sea-water creek or estuary (formed from a sunken valley) immediately to the N. of Gruž, into which the *Ombla* an underground karst river, flows at its E. end. The estuary ($2\frac{1}{2}$ m. long) was once a favourite resort of Ragusan nobles who built many summer villas here, and is a pleasant backwater with its reedy banks, neglected parks and crumbling mansions, many of them now empty and abandoned. Little of the vanished splendour remains, and the atmosphere is somewhat melancholy and nostalgic, but charming details survive. In sequence along the s. bank, in *Bata-hovina* are the Palača Kaboga and Palača Stay; in *Sustjepan* the Roman-esque church of Sv. Stjepan (11–12C) with a triple bell cot and a triptych by Frano Milović (1534); in *Čajkovići* the Palača Bozdari; in *Komolac* the Palačas Gundulić, Sorkočević, Getaldić, and Bizzarro. Between Komolac and Rožat on the opposite bank is the 'source' of the river Ombla (really a continuation of the river Trebišnjica in Hercegovina), which issues from the cliff in most impressive fashion. The general view, however, is obstructed by a hydro-electric power station constructed since the Second World War. Along the N. bank in *Rožat* are a Fran-ciscan Monastery (1393, restored 1704), with a 16C Renaissance cloister, and the Palača Restić; in *Obuljeno* the Palača Sorgo-Gučetić; in *Mokošica* the Palača Zamanja and Palača Gučetić-Djordjić; in *Gradićevo* the Palača Gradić; and in *Marinovo* the Palača Bucinjolo. Freshwater fishing is possible at the mouth of the Ombla.

To Mt. Srdj ($12\frac{1}{2}$ km. by asphalt and gravel road or $2\frac{1}{4}$ hrs on foot). By car take the Put iza grada, then the Put jugoslavenske narodne armije above the suburb of Ploče. Where the road (2 km.) divides we fork left to join (3 km.) the main Adriatic Highway, along which we continue to the village of (5 km.) *Dubac*. Turning left along the road for Trebinje we turn left again at (8 km.) *Brgat* and take a winding road to the summit of (10 km.) *Žarkovica* (1017 ft) with restaurant and superb views of Dubrovnik, the coast and the offshore islands. Hence a narrow gravel track leads to the top of ($12\frac{1}{2}$ km.) **Mt. Srdj** (1340 ft) crowned by the *Fort Imperial*, built by the French in 1808.—Alternatively we may walk up to the Gornji kono from the gate behind the church of Sv. Jakov and thence by a steep winding path to Mt. Srdj ($2\frac{1}{2}$ hrs) and Žarkovica (3 hrs).

To Trebinje, 32 km., asphalt road; frequent service and excursion buses from Ploče. Trebinje is the nearest town of Hercegovina to Dubrovnik and is much visited for its oriental quarter and relics of Turkish rule. To (8 km.) *Brgat* see above. In (22 km.) *Duži* we turn right and continue beside the railway line to (32 km.) **Trebinje** (*Leotar*), a small town on the river Trebišnjica in a fertile plain. The old fortified town was built at the instigation of Sanjakbey Osman-pasha Resulbe-gović in 1706, soon after Trebinje had become the capital of the Sanjak of Hercegovina, and stands with most of its walls and gates intact. The architecture is a mixture of oriental and Mediterranean elements, since Dubrovnik masons were employed. Within the walls are the two mosques of *Careva džamija* and *Osmanpašina džamija*, a clock tower (Sahat-kula) and the Sanjakbey's residence, but their condition and that of the Turkish quarter generally is poor and only one mosque and the bey's house (museum) are open to the public. About 2 m. E. of Trebinje is the Arslanagić Bridge, a fine Turkish structure.

To CAVTAT, 19 km. by asphalt road (bus) or by steamer from Gruž in 50 min. Put jugoslavenske narodne armije climbs steeply to the Adriatic Highway. Beyond Dubac we pass inland of the three small resort villages of (9 km.) *Kupari*, (10 km.) *Srebreno* (Orlando; Motel Zupa; Srebreno; autocamp) and (12 km.) *Mlini* (Mlini; autocamp) with sandy beaches and a growing tourist trade. In Kupari is the miniature castle, Toreta (1623), of the Djordjević family and in Mlini the Renaissance Palača Stay. Beyond *Plat* (Plat), with its hydro-electric power station worked by water from the river Trebišnjica, we fork right from the main road.

19 km. **CAVTAT** (*Albatros, Cavtat, Epidaurus, Tiha, Inex Macedonia*) is an attractive holiday resort, noted for luxuriant trees and exotic shrubs. Cavtat was the Greek and later Roman colony of Epidaurus until its sack in the 7C by the Slavs and Avars. Its dispossessed inhabitants founded the city of Ragusa and the old city (Civitas vetus) was subsequently incorporated into the Republic. The central **Kapetanov dvor** (1555–58), or Captain's residence, is now a museum containing the collections bequeathed by Baltazar Bogišić (1834–1908), lawyer and bibliophile. More than 10,000 engravings include works by Lucas Cranach the Younger, Martin Rota-Kolunić, Andrea Medulić (Schiavone), Stefano della Bella, Chodowiecki, and Natale Bonifazio; the excellent library contains early printed works by Boninus de Boninis (Dobrić Dobričević, 1454–1528) of Lastovo, and Andrija Paltašić (Andrea de Paltasichis, 1450–1500) of Kotor. The house and studio of Vlaho Bukovac (1855–1922), a native of Cavtat, has been turned into a small museum and gallery of his works, and there are further paintings by him in the Baroque church of *Sv. Nikola* (1732). The *Franciscan Monastery*, with a Renaissance cloister, and the church of *Sv. Vlaho* both date from 1483; in the latter is a large polyptych of St Michael (1509–10) by Vicko Lovrin of Kotor, in a richly carved gilt frame, the sole surviving work of this gifted Renaissance painter. On a hill overlooking the harbour and monastery is the town cemetery beautifully planted with cypresses and dominated by the grandiose *Račić Mausoleum* by I. Meštrović (1920–22).

The district of Konavli, immediately S.E. of Cavtat, is noted for the fertility of its fields and the rich costumes of its inhabitants, often seen in the market at Dubrovnik.

To THE ISLAND OF LOKRUM, 15 min by boat from the old harbour. **Lokrum,** a small island covered for most of its area by dense pinewoods, is a favourite spot for picnics and swimming excursions. Its shores are rocky and in many places steep, however, and suited only to good swimmers.

A legend persists that Richard Coeur de Lion was wrecked on the island in 1191 while returning from the crusades. In gratitude for his rescue, it is said, he offered to endow a church on the island but was persuaded to divert his funds to the first cathedral of Dubrovnik. In later centuries the island was repeatedly claimed by

Venice, who even landed troops in 1631, but their withdrawal was effected by cannonade from Dubrovnik. In the 19C Lokrum belonged for a while to the Habsburg Archduke Maximilian and later to the heir-apparent, Rudolph, who often stayed on the island.

Boats usually ply to the small bay of *Portoć* whence a footpath ascends to the ruined *Benedictine Monastery*, founded in 1023. The ruined church incorporates the N. wall and apse of the earlier Romanesque basilica, a Gothic w. front and part of a semicircular Renaissance chapel, together with pre-Romanesque and Romanesque fragments from two earlier churches. Adjoining the 16C cloister is the residence built by Maximillian, now the *Prirodoslovni muzej* (Natural History Museum) with a botanical garden containing sub-tropical and Mediterranean species. On the highest point of the island is the ruined *Fort Royal*, built by the French in 1806 and later extended by the Austrians. There is a small lake, *Mrtvo jezero*, at the s. end of the island

To the Elaphite Islands (Koločep, Lopud, and Šipan). By boat (daily) from Dubrovnik to Koločep (25 min), Lopud (50 min), and either Sudjuradj (1¼ hr) or Luka Šipan (2 hrs).

The **Elaphite Islands**, a group of seven islands between the s. end of Pelješac Peninsula and Dubrovnik, are separated from the mainland by the narrow Koločepski kanal. Settled by both Greeks and Romans, the islands were subsequently incorporated into the medieval Slavonic state of Travunia and passed in the 11C to Ragusa. From 1457 the islands were ruled by a separate knez or rector and remained an important part of the Republic until its fall in 1806. Koločep was an important centre of coral fishing until the 18C with trading posts as far afield as France and the Levant. Lopud was noted for its mercantile enterprise and at the height of its prosperity in the 16C its ships accounted for a quarter of Ragusa's fleet; her galleys participated in Spanish raids on Tunis, Algiers, Portugal, and particularly the armada against England. During the Napoleonic wars, England occupied the islands from 1813–15.

Only three of the islands are inhabited, of which **Koločep** (from the Greek Calaphodia) is the smallest (250 inhab.) and closest to Dubrovnik. The steamer arrives at *Donje Ćelo* (Koločep) the larger of the two villages on the island, with a pleasant park and a good shingle and sandy beach. The Gothic parish church (13–15C) has Roman and pre-Romanesque sculpted fragments in its walls and is overlooked by a 16C fortress built to repel the Turks. Beside the footpath leading to Gornje Ćelo is the village cemetery with the pre-Romanesque church of Sv Nikola, and farther on the little church of Sv. Antun Opata (St Antony Abbot) containing a Gothic Polyptych (1434–35) of the Crucifixion, the only surviving work of the Ragusan painter, Ivan Ugrinović (d. c. 1461). In the bay of Raca at *Gornje Ćelo* is the 12C pre-Romanesque church of Sv. Antun Padovanski (St Antony of Padua) with a cupola over the nave and bell cot at the w. end. The bell (1586) is decorated with reliefs.

The central island of **Lopud** (*Grand*, 200 R; *Villa Slavica, Pracat, Dubrava*), the most important of the three, has been developed as a comfortable small holiday resort (400 inhab.) with modern amenities. From 1457 to the fall of the Republic it was the seat of the Ragusan knez for the islands. The name derives from the Greek Delaphodia.

Most of the interesting buildings on the island date from the 16–17C, when it is said to have had 30 churches, two monasteries and innumerable residences and summer villas erected by both local and Dubrovnik nobles.

Two 16C castles (now in ruins) give the place a picturesque air, one ᵤo the narrow peninsula to the w. of the town (known at one time as the 'English' castle) and the other on the hill to the E, (known as the 'Spanish' castle). A short distance away from the latter is the abandoned *Franciscan Monastery* (1483) with a pleasant but overgrown Renaissance cloister and 16C fortifications. The Gothic monastic church of Sv. Marija od Špilice (Mary of the Cave) is now parochial. Among its paintings are an excellent polyptych on the high altar by Pietro di Giovanni (1523) of Venice, a triptych from the workshop of N. Božidarević, parts of a polyptych by Girol. da Santa Croce, a Crucifixion by one of the Bassano family of Venice, a 17C garlanded Madonna, and a Mannerist work depicting St Antony of Padua. The 15C Gothic stalls are the work of local craftsmen, as are the Gothic altar rails. The church plate, kept in the parish office, includes a large Gothic chalice (15C) with an elaborately decorated base and flying angels attached to the sides, a 15C silver processional cross and a silver-gilt monstrance of later date.

On a hill in the highest part of the town is the 15C late Gothic *Knežev dvor* (Rector's Palace), now abandoned; a number of noble residences in various states of repair include the *Palača Djordjić*, with a pretty garden, the *Palača Brantić* (16C), and the ruined summer residence of Lopud's most famous citizen, the merchant Miho Pracat (see p. 198). On the w. side of town is the abandoned *Dominican Monastery* and church of Sv. Nikola (1482) with belfry, and by the harbour the small 17C Baroque church of *Sv. Trojstvo* (Holy Trinity), endowed by the ship owner, Vice Bune, who is buried here.

The 15C Gothic church of GOSPA OD SUNJA (with 17C additions), once the principal church of the island, is situated on the s. side of the island about ½ hr walk from Lopud. There is a good late Renaissance high altar of painted wood (16C), which a curious erroneous legend links with Henry VIII of England, and contemporary side altars. The high altar is also set off by Gothic altar rails and there is a Renaissance font. The paintings mostly in poor condition include a large Madonna attributed to Palma Vecchio, a Madonna attended by Saints attributed to Nataline da Murano, a painting of the Holy Family signed A.B.D., an Annunciation by an unknown Umbrian artist and several pieces of a large polyptych by the Ragusan Matej Junčić (1452), the only work extant by this artist. Of the many pre-Romanesque churches scattered about the island, the small church of *Sv. Ivan* with primitive cupola and lesenes (beside the path to Sunj) is the best preserved and contains a number of examples of pre-Romanesque stone carving.

Šipan (700 inhab.), the largest of the Elaphite Islands, has two main settlements with smaller villages in between. The larger of the two is *Šipanska Luka* (Dubravka) with the handsome Gothic Knežev dvor (Rector's Palace, 1450) built by local masons, the 15C Gothic Palača Sorkočević and the massive Palača Pracat. The parish church of Sv. Stjepan contains interesting paintings. Beside the gravel track that leads to Sudjuradj is the 16C summer residence of the archbishops of Ragusa, of which one half, with wall paintings, has recently been restored. This part was originally erected (1557) by Abp. Becadelli, a friend of Michelangelo. The ruined castle in the nearby hamlet of *Renatovo* is said to have been built by René of Anjou, king of Naples. A little farther along the track is the unusual fortified church of Sv. Duh (1577) with towers and battlements.

5 km. *Sudjuradj* is an attractive small fishing village. It derives its name from the Romanesque church of Sv. Djurdje (George), which has a loggia attached to the w. front. Behind the harbour are the Palača Skočibuh (1539), with a machicolated tower (1577) and paintings by G. Vasari, and the Palača Sagrojević,

another fortified mansion. The parish church of Sv. Marija is situated in *Pakljena* about ½ m. E. of Sudjuradj. Built in 1323, it was enlarged in the 16C; on the high altar is a triptych of the Assumption in imitation of Titian by the Ragusan Hristofor Nikolin (1552–54), and on other altars a Madonna and Child by an unknown French artist (15C), a painting attributed to the school of J. Cornelis van Oostsanen (16C) and a polyptych by a Dubrovnik painter. Skočibuh, Stjepović, and Sagrojević tomb slabs adorn the church. Adjoining is the ruined Benedictine monastery of *Sv. Mihajlo*, with a 16C tower and fragmentary carvings of the pre-Romanesque to Gothic periods.

V THE MONTENEGRIN COAST

23 FROM DUBROVNIK TO KOTOR

ROAD, 97 km. (60¼ m.), traversing some of the finest scenery of the Yugoslav coast. 27 km. *Čilipi*.—50 km. *Hercegnovi*.—67 km. *Kamenari*.—79 km. *Risan*.—83 km. **Perast**.—97 km. **Kotor**.

STEAMERS from Dubrovnik, once weekly (Sun), call at *Cavtat*, *Hercegnovi*, *Tivat*, and *Kotor* (4½ hrs), returning same evening (stay of c. 4¼ hrs).

From Dubrovnik to (17 km.) *Zvekovica*, see Rte 18. We continue straight on through the fertile valley of Konavli, passing on our left (21 km.) the airport of Dubrovnik. Traversing (27 km.) *Čilipi*, where the inhabitants wear national costume to church on Sunday, we accompany the abandoned narrow-gauge railway line parallel with the coast to the point, at 44 km., where the road divides on the boundary between Croatia and Montenegro. The main road branches left and runs high above the shore to Hercegnovi (see below), while a by-road continues straight on to the narrow peninsula of *Prevlaka* (12 km.) at the mouth of the Boka Kotorska.

The ****Boka Kotorska** (Gulf of Kotor), the grandest natural feature of the Adriatic coast, is a deeply indented and irregularly-shaped fjord surrounded by steep and lofty mountains that rise ever higher towards the interior. The contrast between the intense green of the luxuriant vegetation at sea level and the denuded rock of the mountains is enhanced by the changing colours of the sea, particularly striking effects being gained in winter when the higher mountains are clothed in snow. The abrupt changes in height give the region a violent and changeable climate with an unusually heavy rainfall and frequent thunderstorms. A good road encircles the shores of the gulf (see below), but by far the finest impression of its majesty is gained from the water. The passage can be made either by regular steamer service or by excursion from near-by resorts.

BY STEAMER TO KOTOR. The entrance to the gulf lies between Oštri and Mirišta points, from which it is a little under 20 m. to Kotor at the far end. On the E. side of the fairway is the island of *Mamula*, named for General Lazar Mamula, a former Austrian governor of Dalmatia, who fortified it in 1850. During the First and Second World Wars it was used as a prison camp by the occupying forces. A mile-wide channel leads into the *Bay of Hercegnovi*, with Hercegnovi itself visible on the far side, whence the narrow strait of *Kumburski tjesnac* (812 yds) gives access to the broad, triangular and apparently landlocked *Bay of Tivat*, with the town of Tivat directly ahead. As the boat proceeds, with bare limestone mountains descending in folds to the shore on either hand, it becomes apparent that in the N.E. corner there is an even narrower passage. The mountains part to reveal the channel of *Verige* (325 yds), whose name, meaning 'chain', has led to a tradition that it was once closed off by this method. Perast is seen framed in the opening ahead before we emerge into the innermost gulf, consisting of the twin bays of Risan and Kotor, which affords the most spectacular marine vistas in Europe outside Norway. The awe-inspiring heights of the Njegoši Mts. rise to a climax at Mt. Lovćen (5684 ft) behind Kotor.

In April 1941 King Peter was evacuated from the Gulf of Kotor in an R.A.F. flying boat; the British Minister fell into Italian hands, and an attempt at rescue by a British submarine was beaten off by German dive-bombers.

50 km. **HERCEGNOVI,** the outermost town (3800 inhab.) of the Boka Kotorska, occupies a position of romantic beauty on precipitous cliffs at the sea's edge. The town is noted for its luxuriant sub-tropical vegetation and is the leading resort in the Kotor region.

Hotels. Boka, Na plaži, Villa Jadranka, Villa Palma. In the suburb of *Topla:* Riviera, 210 R with bath or shower; Topla, 210 R with bath or shower (chalets), kafana, dancing, rock bathing.
Restaurants. *Zdravljak, Riblji restoran* (fish), *Gradski restoran*, all in the main street.—KAFANA. *Beograd*, in the main street.
Bus station, outside the Hotel Boka. Local buses to all parts of the Boka Kotorska. Long-distance buses to the main cities of the coast and to Titograd, Belgrade and the principal towns of Serbia.
Steamers daily in summer from Rijeka, Rab, Zadar, Šibenik, Split, Hvar, Korčula, Dubrovnik, Budva and Bar; twice a week in summer from Trieste, Koper, Rovinj, Pula, Mali Lošinj, Silba, Makarska and Orebić; once weekly in summer from Venice, Primošten, Cavtat, Tivat and Kotor.
Beach (by the railway station). Cemented foreshore and rock bathing, cabins, showers.

History. *Hercegnovi* was founded in 1382 by Stjepan I Tvrtko of Bosnia as a trading post and salt-producing centre. Its strategic position at the mouth of the gulf assured it a stormy history. In the 15C the town came into the possession of Herceg (duke) Stjepan Vukčić Kosači of Zahumlje, from whom it derives its name. The Turks conquered it in 1483, lost it temporarily to a Venetian expedition (aided by Spanish troops) in 1538, but regained it a year later under Khair-ed-din Barbarossa. In 1687 Venice finally drove out the Turks to hold the town until the republic's downfall in 1797. Hercegnovi was then disputed between the powers involved in the Napoleonic Wars. To the Austrians (1797–1806) succeeded Russia (1806–7), then France (1807–13), then Britain and Montenegro, both for a few months only, before in 1814 Austria gained firm possession until 1918.

Hercegnovi comprises the old walled town at the top of the cliffs and the newer district spreading w. in the direction of Igalo and down the hillside in a succession of terraces. Fortifications testify to the defensive building of various rulers. **Španjola,** the best preserved fortress, stands high on a hill overlooking the town. Begun by the Spaniards during their brief occupation (1538), it was completed in its present form by the Turks on their return. The Turks also built the walls on the N.E. side of the town, including the *Kanli Kula* (Bloody Tower), now ruined. In the 17–18C the Venetians completely rebuilt the *Forte Mare* on the seaward side and constructed the *Citadela*. The old town inside the walls has a typical Mediterranean air but is sadly dilapidated, the only building of interest being the Turkish *Sahat-kula* (Clock Tower; 1667), a machicolated tower guarding the main entrance. In the small square that opens inside the gate is the *Gradski arhiv* (Town Library), with about 25,000 volumes, including a few incunabula and a good collection of works relating to the history of the Adriatic coast.

In the suburb of Topla a spacious villa in a small botanical garden houses the *Zavičajni muzej* (Town Museum, open weekdays 8–11, 5–7). The museum has rooms illustrating the history and ethnography of the region and the National Liberation Struggle, but the most interesting room displays icons of the Boka Kotorska school (mainly 18C), notably by the Dimitrijević-Rafailović family of Risan. In the same room is a fine pre-Romanesque stone relief (11C).

About 1 m. E. of town in a lovely sylvan setting stands the Serbian Orthodox monastery of **Savina,** reached by a gravel track through pleasant groves of oak, laurel, and cypress (or by the main road and an uphill walk just before Meljine). The monastery was founded by monks fleeing from Tvrdoš near Trebinje in 1694 and takes its name from St

Sabas (Sava), the most revered saint of the Serbian Orthodox church. Petar I Petrović Njegoš, Prince-Bishop of Montenegro, stayed in Savina while attending school in Hercegnovi. The larger of the two churches attached to the monastery, harmoniously combining Baroque and Byzantine elements, was built by Nikola Foretić of Korčula (1777–79), and contains a good iconostasis by Simo Lazović of Bijelo polje (1797). The smaller Gothic church was refurbished for monastic use in 1694; the iconostasis dates from various times in the 18C, the Royal Doors being the work of Daskal Dimitrije of Risan (1703), father of the Dimitrijević-Rafailović family of icon painters, while the icon of the Ascension is by his son, Rafailo (1750). The church now houses the TREASURY (open daily, 9–12, 4–7), a good collection of work done in the Byzantine tradition set out in showcases round the walls.

The oldest piece is a crystal Cross edged with silver (1219), supposed to have belonged to St Sabas himself. Later works include an unusual silver and enamel Server (*petohljebnica*) made in Požarevac (1648); a silver model of the original monastery at Tvrdoš (1685); a silver thurible of similar age; two pierced silver lamps and a chalice (17C); a wooden patriarchal Cross with deep relief carvings in miniature (16C); another, bound in silver and enamel (1657); and a silver reliquary of a hand (1759), supposedly of Queen Jelena, wife of Stefan Dušan the Mighty. Vestments and frontals include a beautiful *Brocade embroidered with scenes of the Passion in silver and gold thread (1659), another design made in Russia (18C), a Greek Epitrachelion (? 14C), and two 18C omophoria, one of which is embroidered with a pietà. The LIBRARY in the main building preserves many historical manuscripts, including decrees on parchment by medieval Serbian monarchs (Stefan Dečanski, Uroš, Carica Jelena, Stefan Lazarević, etc.), the *Savina krmčija*, a nomocanon of the 16C, and a liturgical book (octoechos) dated 1509. Pictures here include portraits of Peter the Great and Catherine the Great of Russia and icons by painters of the Boka Kotorska school (17–18C).

Beyond Hercegnovi the lower and upper roads join at *Meljine.*— 54 km. *Zelenika*, terminus of a narrow-gauge railway from Sarajevo (recently abandoned) and a port for the export of bauxite from the interior. We continue along the shore to (51 km.) *Miočevići*, where the highway divides again, the faster road cutting through thickly wooded country higher up the hillside and the lower traversing the villages on the shore.—In (56 km.) *Baošić* the parish church of Sv. Nikola has an iconostasis by Aleksija Lazović (1805). A plaque indicates the house where Pierre Loti stayed in 1880; the village and the Boka Kotorska are described in his short story, 'Pascale Ivanović', and in his diary. Beyond *Bijela* (14C frescoes in the church of Riza Bogorodica), we reach (67 km.) *Kamenari* whence a car ferry across the strait of Verige to Lepetane (5 min; comp. Rte 24) affords the fastest route to the s., linking up with the Adriatic Highway viâ either Tivat or Kotor.

Keeping to the w. shore along the newly completed asphalt road that circles the gulf, we emerge from Verige to a breath-taking view of the inner bays of Risan and Kotor, with bare forbidding mountains rising behind. Out on the right as we turn N. are the islands of Gospa od Škrpjela and Sv. Djurdje (comp. below); Perast is seen across the bay. Just beyond *Kostanjica* the road crosses a bridge over the *Sopot Waterfall*, an unusual feature hereabouts, which gushes from the rock 100 ft above sea level.

79 km. **Risan,** the oldest settlement in the Boka Kotorska, at the far end of the bay of Risan, is only a village (1200 inhab.).

Risan (Rhizinion) is linked by legend with the story of Cadmus and Harmonia, who, according to Appian and Euripides, went to reign over Illyria. Historically it was, at any rate, one of the chief towns of the kingdom of Illyria and for a while, under Queen Teuta, its capital. Teuta is thought to have committed suicide here after being defeated by the Romans in 229 B.C. In 167 B.C. the town placed itself under Roman overlordship, subsequently becoming a *colonia* (Iulium Risinium) attached to the province of Dalmatia. Sacked by the Saracens in 865, the Illyrico-Roman city is said to have been finally destroyed by a landslide or an earthquake. In the 10–14C the medieval community was ruled by various local powers and in 1451 passed to the Republic of Ragusa. The Turks occupied it from 1539 to 1687 when it passed to Venice. In Risan the Dimitrijević-Rafailović family of icon-painters was active in the 17–18C. Among many archaeologists to dig here was Sir Arthur Evans (1882–85).

Few traces remain of the remote days of Risan's greatness, though archaeological finds have included Greek, Illyrian, and Roman coinage and abundant fragments of Roman temples, statues, sarcophagi, as well as bronze statuettes and a 2C mosaic floor depicting the god Hypnos. Some of these, within the foundations of the Illyrico-Roman city, can be seen on the hill of *Carina*, while other Roman remains are said to be visible deep in the water at the edge of the bay. The two fortresses on adjacent hills, Grkavac and Ledenice, were erected by Venice (17–18C) as a defence against the Turks.

Risan is the starting point for excursions to *Mt. Orjen* (6159 ft), the highest mountain on the Adriatic coast, and the mountainous region of *Krivošija*. The inhabitants of Krivošija, now mostly shepherds, are noted for their fierceness and pride and achieved a certain notoriety when they raised two rebellions against Austria (1869–70 and 1881–82) and emigrated en masse to Montenegro rather than submit to military conscription.

Continuing s. from Risan we pass almost immediately the Orthodox monastery of *Banja*, founded in the middle ages and rebuilt in 1720 after destruction by the Turks. In the treasury is an embroidered epitrachelion made for Župan Stroja Buzescu in Rumania (1606), and the iconostasis is by Petar Rafailović (1775).

83 km. **Perast** is an attractive Mediterranean township (500 inhab.), neither quite village nor city, with a charming air of faded elegance and wealth. Because of its relatively short period of prosperity, it presents an unusually homogeneous architectural whole, almost entirely Baroque in the restrained tradition characteristic of the Adriatic coast. There are few buildings of outstanding merit, but almost none that are ugly or inelegant.

Parestum is first mentioned in 1326 and later in the same century assisted the Venetians to capture its mother city, Kotor, against whom it was in constant rebellion. Both cities passed from Hungary-Croatia to Venice in 1420 and in the 16C Perast emancipated itself from Kotor to become an independent commune. It built up a large merchant fleet and for the next 200 years enjoyed prosperity. With the coming of steam it sank to the status of a large village. Throughout its history Perast was renowned for loyalty to Venice and its sailors enjoyed the distinction of guarding the republic's gonfalon in time of battle. Its strong maritime tradition began with the foundation of a shipyard as early as 1367 and a nautical school in the 16C and gained European status when Peter the Great of Russia sent 17 young noblemen here in 1698 to train for his embryo navy. Distinguished natives include Matija Zmajević (1680–1713), admiral of Peter the Great's Baltic fleet; the hydrographer, Anton Grubaš (18C); and the Baroque painter, Tripo Kokolja (1661–1713).

The town, strung out along the narrow strip of land between the mountains and the sea, has no distinct centre. At the N. end stands its finest single building, the Baroque *Palača Bujović* by G. Fonta (1694), with an open loggia on the ground floor and an immense balcony running the length of the façade above. Once the residence of the Venetian Captain, it now houses the ZAVIČAJNI MUZEJ (Town Museum, open weekdays, 9–1, 3–6). Downstairs is a small lapidary collection; on the first floor the many banners include a Venetian gonfalon and the naval banner presented to Admiral Zmajević by Peter the Great. Paintings include portraits of Zmajević and V. Bujović by Tripo Kokolja, and (on the second floor) a self-portrait by Kokolja and icons by the Dimitrijević-Rafailović family of Risan. A balcony on the s. side of the museum offers an excellent view over Perast.

Plaques mark the Naval School (*Nautika*) of Capt. Marko Martinović just to the N. and the house in which Admiral Zmajević was born to the s. Steps mount to the monumental but ruined *Biskupija*, the palace of Abp. Andrija Zmajević (1670), with a fine Baroque portal and open loggia (view) and damaged wall paintings by Kokolja. Adjoining is the Baroque chapel of *Gospa od rozarija* (Our Lady of the Rosaries) where Zmajević lies buried (escutcheon, 15 medallions by Kokolja), which has an octagonal Baroque bell tower of great charm. Returning to the shore we pass the house of the Cizmai family (escutcheon) and come to the handsome *Palača Smecchia* (1760) with its vaulted boathouse; the family chapel of Sv. Marko (1740) is ornamented with a Lion of St Mark and statues of Christ and SS Peter and Paul. Beyond the former *Palača Mazarović* (rest.) and the *Palača Marković* (1622), with wrought-iron balustrade, is the small town square with the former town hall on the N.E. side. The parish church of **Sv. Nikola**, founded in the 15C, was rebuilt in its present form in the 17C, when an ambitious new church was also begun to designs by Giuseppe Beati. The lofty *Campanile* was completed (1691), the tallest in Montenegro (179 ft), and the enormous apse of the unfinished church, abandoned for lack of funds, stands beside the older building.

In the interior of Sv. Nikola are a good Baroque font and marble pulpit, the gift of Abp. Zmajević. In the TREASURY (apply to parish priest) plate includes the large Ren. silver Cross of Abp. Zmajević; a silver tablet depicting the Battle of Perast against the Turks (1654); a silver-gilt chalice decorated with filigree work (18C), the gift of Anton Bašić; a large silver censer and a cross of the order of Alexander Nevsky, both presented by Admiral Zmajević. The fine Vestments include the robes of Abp. Zmajević, and *Lace of the 16–19C. An oriental silk canopy may have come from the tent of Mehmed-aga Rizvanagić, leader of a Turkish attack on Perast, or have been taken in the Candian War. The bronze bust of Kokolja in front of the church is by Vanja Radauš, a Croatian sculptor.

Steps left of the campanile ascend to the abandoned fortress of *Sv. Križ* (view over the Boka Kotorska), built by the Venetians c. 1600. The neighbouring small church of *Sv. Ana* has a mural painting by Kokolja.

The main street leads s. from the town square parallel with the waterfront and is lined with the mansions of former captains and ship owners. On the right, the *Palača Visković* (1718) has a Baroque portal and loggia and a small private museum (portraits, weapons). Adjacent stands the Baroque *Palača Krilović*. Opposite are two similar mansions, of which the farther one is the large *Palača Balović*. A second mansion of the Krilović family stands further down on the left, and at the far end of the street is the complex *Palača Bašić* with a relief of the Annunciation (1507) built into the façade. The coast road, built by the Austrians during the 19C, leads back to the town, affording a view of the mansions as they originally looked from the sea.

Offshore two small islands can be reached in about 5 min by local boat. *Sv. Djordje* (St George), a picturesque cypress-clad island, had a Benedictine abbey as early as the 12C but was plundered by the Turks and suffered heavily in an earthquake in 1667. The church, reconstructed in 1914, preserves dozens of memorial slabs engraved with the arms of Perast nobles and sea captains. The fortifications are mainly French and Austrian.

The artificial island of *Gospa od škrpjela* was built in 1452 on an underwater reef. The manner of construction is commemorated each year on 22 July by the 'Fašinada', when a gaily decorated procession of boats arrives from Perast to deposit stones around the island to the accompaniment of folk songs (national dress is now a rare occurrence). The present Baroque church of Gospa od škrpjela (1630) was enlarged in 1720–25 by the addition of an octagonal presbytery with a cupola. The *Interior, both walls and ceiling, are covered by 68 paintings on wood and canvas by Tripo Kokolja. This, his magnum opus, accomplished under the direction of Abp. Zmajević during the last 15–20 years of the 17C, makes an overwhelming first impression. Greater familiarity reveals that the lower band of paintings around the walls, devoted to scenes from the Old Testament, is considerably inferior to the four large canvases above (Christ in the Temple, Descent of the Holy Ghost, Dormition of the Virgin and Coronation of the Virgin), and these in turn are surpassed by the exuberantly painted ceiling. A multiplicity of New Testament scenes, interspersed with still lifes, are divided by a network of moulded and gilt frames and culminate in the centre in a monumental Ascension of the Virgin. Between the upper and lower paintings is a band of 2500 little votive plaques. Donated by sailors during the past three centuries, they are engraved with portraits, realistic scenes of Perast life, heraldic emblems and above all ships. The Icon of the Madonna on the high altar is by Lovro Marinov Dobričević of Kotor (15C). A procession similar to the Fašinada is held on 15 Aug when the icon is taken to Perast for the winter. This commemorates the victory over the Turks in 1654 and one of the boats always contains armed men.

Beyond Perast we drive E. along the shore of the Kotorski zaljev, passing through (86 km.) *Drazin Rt*, with the house of Bajo Nikolić-Pivljanin (1672), a celebrated warrior against the Turks, and (88 km.) *Orahovac*, with 15–16C frescoes in the Orthodox church of Sv. Djordje. Swinging s., with the mountains on our left descending almost sheer into the sea, we come to a chain of little villages along the shore, known under the collective name of Dobrota.

90–96 km. **Dobrota** (1313 inhab.) was an independent settlement in Roman times (*Debratha*) and remained so until 1351, when it was absorbed into Kotor. Four centuries later it was granted the status of an independent commune by Venice (1704) during a period when, like Perast, it prospered as a merchant shipping centre. A number of interesting buildings remain from this period. *Sv. Stasija* (St Eustace; 1773) in the hamlet of Ljuta is a good example of the so-called Jesuit style, with painted walls and ceiling and a number of paintings, including the Blessed Virgin by Carlo Dolci. In the treasury are trophies captured from the Turks in battle, also vestments and lace, which is a local speciality. The church of *Sv. Matija* (1670), also Baroque, farther s. at Tomići, contains a Madonna and Child by Giovanni Bellini, St Nicholas by Pietro Novelli, a 16C silver-gilt Reliquary in the shape of a pyramid from Venice, and 17–18C vestments. The shore is lined with Baroque mansions erected by former ship owners, especially the Tripković, Ivanović, and Dabinović-Kokota families (all 18C) of which the largest is the *Palača Milošević* (early 19C). The small 15C church of *Gospa od vrta* (Our Lady of the Garden) contains a contemporary fresco and a painting of Our Lady with St Dominic by Tripo Kokolja.

97 km. **KOTOR**, the chief town (4840 inhab.) of the Boka Kotorska, huddles on a narrow spit of land at the foot of Mt. Lovćen (5685 ft), by which it is so overshadowed that the afternoon hours of sunshine are curtailed. Though in its history Kotor follows much the pattern of the Dalmatian cities farther N., its unusual site and greater proximity to the medieval Slavonic states of the interior (and especially the kingdom of Montenegro) have given it a marked individuality. The old quarter is surrounded by a system of CITY WALLS, begun under Byzantium (9–11C) but largely rebuilt in their present form by Venice (15–18C), which is one of the most extensive and complete in Yugoslavia. They climb the steep mountainside behind the town to the Fortress of Sv. Ivan (845 ft), enclosing an area several times greater than the town itself, with a perimeter of 2¾ m. and a total extent nearer four miles. They reach a height of just under 50 ft and a maximum breadth of 32 ft. Kotor retains its medieval character and is second only to Dubrovnik in the completeness of its preservation. An infinite variety of vistas is afforded by twisting streets and small squares, a typical E. Mediterranean feature here developed to a striking degree.

Airport (summer only) at Tivat, see p. 225.

Steamers twice weekly from Venice, Split, and Dubrovnik; weekly from Pula, Opatija, Rijeka, Korčula, Bar, Corfù, Itea, and Piraeus.

Hotels. Fjord, 115 R with shower, beach, kafana, dancing, on N. bank of R. Škurda; **Slavija**, beach, at Škaljari.—PENSIONS. Vardar, Graz, both in the old town.—AUTOCAMP at Dobrota (3 km.).

Restaurant. *Vardar* (fish), behind the Palata Bizanti.—KAFANA. *Gradska kafana*, beside the Morska vrata.

Post Office at Škaljari.—INFORMATION OFFICE. *Turistički biro*, Trg oktobarske revolucije.

Bus station at Škaljari. Local buses thrice daily to Budva, Bar, and Ulcinj; four times daily to Prčanj, Tivat, Perast, Risan, Kamenari, and Hercegnovi. Long-distance buses to Titograd, Skopje, Belgrade, Zagreb, and main towns on the Adriatic coast.

Beach, shingle with grassy foreshore.

Amusements. THEATRE (amateur), *Gradsko pozorište*, Ul. 29 og novembra.—REGATTA, *Bokeljska noć*, usually first week in August, featuring local naval customs.—WATER POLO (1st div. team).

History. Greek *Acurion* and Roman *Acruvium* were succeeded by the *Decadaron* of Byzantium, from which the present name of Kotor (Ital. *Cattaro*) is derived. In 867 the town was ravaged by the Saracens and in 1002 was sacked by King Samuilo of Macedonia, after which it became part of the Serbian kingdom of Duklja (later Zeta). When Zeta was incorporated into the larger Serbian kingdom of Raška by Stefan Nemanja (1186), Kotor flourished as its chief port. Kotor's status as an independent commune complete with Grand and Lesser Councils of nobles, Senate and coinage dated from Byzantine times, and during its association with Serbia it profited from special trade and political privileges, coming to rival Ragusa as a commercial power and provoking the jealousy of Venice. Raška declined and in 1370 Kotor sought the protection of Hungary-Croatia, but after an attack and temporary occupation by the Venetians under Vittore Pisani (1378) turned to King Tvrtko of Bosnia (1385). In 1391, Kotor attempted to equal its rivals by proclaiming an independent republic, but Turkish advances deprived the city of its hinterland and in 1420 Kotor was forced to seek the protection of Venice. It contrived to prosper despite the establishment of a Turkish *sanjak* on the N. shore of the Boka Kotorska (1483), but Turkish sieges in 1539 and 1657, earthquakes in 1563 and 1667, and a plague in 1572 contributed to a steady decline. From 1797 Austria occupied the city, save for brief periods during the Napoleonic Wars under France (1807–13), England (1813) and Montenegro (1813–14), until in 1918 Kotor became a part of the newly founded Yugoslavia.

The Kotor sailors' guild (Bokeljska mornarica) is one of the oldest in Europe with an unbroken tradition from A.D. 809. Natives include Fra Vita, builder of the

Serbian monastery church of Dečani; Lovro Marinov Dobričević and Vicko Lovrin, 15C painters; and Andrija Paltašić a pioneer 15C printer.

From the Quay the main entrance to the old town is through the Renaissance *Morska vrata* (Porta Marina, 1555) set in the w. wall between the Gradska kafana and the Tržnica (market). On the inner side of the gate is a relief of the Madonna and Child with SS Bernard and Tryphon (late 15C) and an inscription commemorating a Turkish defeat in 1657. TRG OKTOBARSKE REVOLUCIJE (*Trg oružja*), a spacious L-shaped square with pavement cafés, remains the social centre of the town. The w. side of the square is formed by the unfinished *Providurova palata* (Governor's Palace, 16–17C), whose ground floor is occupied by shops. At its N. end the *Vijećnica* (Town Hall), built by the French as a theatre (1808) and adapted in 1902, faces the former Venetian Arsenal, while a narrow passage between them gives access to the N.W. corner tower of *Citadela* (1540–1670), and the walk along the top of the N. wall (view of the town) beside the river Škurda. Immediately opposite the main gate is the *Gradska kula*, a rectangular tower bearing the arms of Antonio Grimani, the Venetian governor who erected it in 1602. The clock was added in 1810. The obelisk in front was the pillory. Beside the Putnik office steps mount to the w. wall, which is accessible as far as the s. gate. The *Lapidary Collection* at the foot of the steps includes the original 12C wheel-window from the cathedral, an inlaid marble Reredos with a relief of St Tryphon, and a fine pre-Romanesque stone sarcophagus decorated in low relief.

A narrow street leads from the s. side of the square between the Baroque *Palata Bisanti* (1694; l.), with an ornate wellhead in the court, and the *Palata Beskuća* (1776), with a superb Venetian Gothic *Portal built into the façade. At the end we emerge into the beautiful little Trg oslobodjenja (Trg brašna), bounded to the E. by the *Palata Pima* (late 16C), with a good Baroque façade and court, and to the w. by the plain *Palata Vracchien* and *Palata Buća* (16C). Another narrow street brings us to the large and irregular cathedral square, Trg pobune mornara. The small cathedral of **Sv. Tripun** (St Tryphon), basically Romanesque in construction, is given a Baroque aspect by its projecting w. towers, between which a balustrated arch forms a porch.

The first cathedral of Kotor, a rotunda, was erected c. 809 under the patronage of Andreacci Saracenis, to house the newly purchased relics of St Tryphon. This was replaced in 1116 by an aisled basilica with a cupola over the nave and twin towers at the w. end, the basis of the present church. After the earthquake of 1667 a completely new w. front was constructed and the cupola, removed earlier, was not replaced. Reconstruction and repairs to the remainder were effected with the original materials.

The plain interior is divided into three double bays, massive piers alternating with Roman columns of marble and granite (probably from Risan) with damaged Corinthian columns. The E. bays are unrestored. The outstanding feature is the beautiful Gothic *Ciborium(? 1362), with a delicate pyramidal canopy resting on four octagonal columns of red marble, and scenes from the life of St Tryphon carved on the architrave. The high altar is a copy of an earlier 14C mensa and has a Baroque reredos worked in silver-gilt by 17C Venetian smiths. On the wall of the central apse hang three sections of a large polyptych in silver-gilt, the

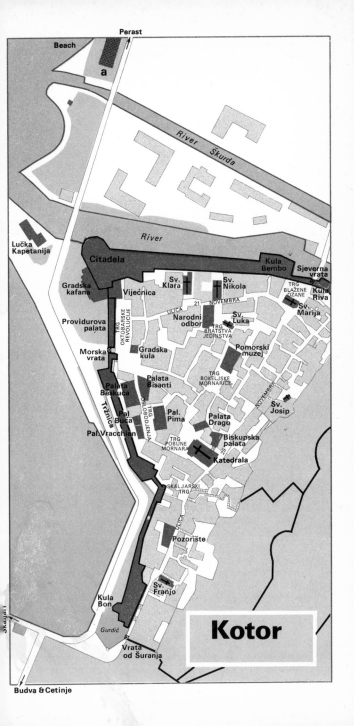

central section by Hans of Basle (1440), the others by local masters. In the s. aisle is the Tomb (1532) of Bishop Tripun Bisanti with a full length effigy.

A door left of the high altar admits to the SACRISTY, into which has been built a fine pre-Romanesque Ciborium (? 809) from the first cathedral. Here are kept chalices, monstrances and pastoral crosses. A marble staircase leads to the octagonal RELIQUARIUM above (1652), decorated by Francesco Cabianca of Venice (1704–8). The paintings here include St Bartholomew by Girol. da Santacroce, a 15C icon painting on both sides, and The Ecstasy of St Francis by Tripo Kokolja. In one corner is a small sarcophagus, supposedly the original repository of the relics of St Tryphon. A Baroque marble sarcophagus, by Cabianca, with a kneeling figure of St Tryphon on the lid, and scenes from his martyrdom depicted in relief on the sides, holds a 17C Venetian casket in silver-gilt containing the saint's relics, a Reliquary of the head (of Gothic workmanship), and a 16C crystal Cross. The remaining reliquaries, about 50 in number, housed in glass cases around the walls, date mainly from the 17–18C. The large Gothic crucifix of wood, said to be the gift of Jelena, consort of Uroš I of Serbia (13C), is probably of much later date. More interesting is a missionary cross used to bless the army of Jan Sobieski before the decisive defeat of the Turks at Vienna in 1683.

A narrow passageway divides the N. wall of the cathedral from the bishop's palace (numerous escutcheons). Built into the wall is the sarcophagus of the cathedral's first patron, Andreacci Saracenis (d. c. 850). An excellent Romanesque three-light window, possibly by Fra Vita, is set into the wall of the main apse.

Passing the *Palata Drago* (16C), which has notable Renaissance windows, we leave the square by the N. side and emerge almost immediately into the Trg Bokeljske mornarice. The Baroque *Palata Grgurina* (18C) on the far side houses the POMORSKI MUZEJ (open daily except Mondays, 8–1), devoted mainly to the history of the Kotar Sailors' Guild (later the Boka Kotorska Navy). Note in particular the armoury, the excellent ship models, and the traditional costumes of the Kotor sailors. The narrow Ul. Karampane passes between the museum and the delightful little square of Karampane with a 17C well and the Baroque *Palata Lipovac* (18C), to Trg bratstva-jedinstva, bounded on the w. side by the 19C *Narodni odbor* (Town Hall). In the centre stands the ancient little church of *Sv. Luka* (1195), Romanesque in conception but with a dome over the nave of Byzantine inspiration. Originally Roman Catholic, it passed to the Orthodox church in 1657 and in 1747 the chapel of Sv. Spiridon was added on the N. side. The interior (key from sacristan of Sv. Nikola) contains two iconostases, the smaller of which, in the side chapel, is attributed to Vasilije Rafailović of Risan (18C). The Orthodox *Cathedral of Sv. Nikola* on the N. side of the square was designed in the traditional Serbo-Byzantine style by Kiril Iveković (1902–9), and contains a collection of old icons soon to be opened to the public (inquire locally).

Ul. 21 novembra leads w. to *Sv. Antuna*, the much altered church of the convent of St Clare (16–17C), with a Baroque marble altar by Francesco Cabianca (c. 1700), and E. past the ruined Venetian Gothic Buća and Drago houses to the Trg Blažene Ozane in front of the North Gate. The church of **Sv. Marija** or *Collegiata* (1221), with its alternating courses of pink and white stone, octagonal dome and semicircular apse and blind arcading, successfully fuses Romanesque and Serbo-Byzantine styles of architecture despite the addition of a N. aisle (1434) and bell tower (1771). On the exterior can be seen a fine Romanesque two-light window in the apse, a Byzantine arch over the s. door and a 17C wooden crucifix hanging beneath a projecting arch on the s. wall. Inside are a

14C stone Pieta and a 15C wooden crucifix. The N. aisle contains the richly carved sarcophagus of Blažena Ozana (Blessed Osana), a local saint beatified in 1930, with scenes from the saint's life carved in bas-relief by the Croatian sculptor, Antun Augustinčić.

The *Sjeverna vrata* (North Gate), across the square, was erected in 1540 to celebrate the previous year's defeat of Khair-ed-din Barbarossa (inscription). On the w. side of the gate is the *Kula Bembo* (1538), from which the walk on the city wall leads to the Citadela (see above); to the E. is the handsome *Kula Riva*, best seen from across the bridge over the river Škurda. Riva houses an open-air cinema during the summer months.

Leaving the square by the s. side, we see on our left the entrance to the upper system of city walls, with a medallion bearing a stylized Lion of St Mark (1760) on the archway. Hence a steep path leads up the mountainside to the 15C church of *Gospa od zdravlja* and the fortress of Sv. Ivan (views). Beside the gate a plaque commemorates a former apothecary's shop, one of the earliest in Southern Europe (1326). Ul. 29 novembra farther E. passes the Romanesque chapel of *Sv. Ana* (12C; r.) with a variety of medieval sculpture on the s. front, and comes to (l.) the bell tower and church of *Sv. Josip* (1631), with a Baroque high altar and a painting by Angelo Coster. Farther on, the Romanesque door of the disused church of *Sv. Pavle* (1266) faces the street. We pass behind the E. end of the cathedral into Škalijarski trg, whence flights of steps on the left lead up to another section of the city walls, with alternative paths to the church of Gospa od zdravlja and fortress of Sv. Ivan.

The quarter s. of here, known as **Šuranj**, is the oldest part of Kotor and in spite of neglect amply repays exploration. Gothic and even Romanesque houses still stand and good architectural details abound. Ul. 29 novembra narrows past the *Narodno pozorište* (Popular Theatre), adapted from a Venetian military hospital (1769), to reach the ruined *Franciscan Church and Monastery*, a part of whose cloister (17C) can still be visited. A short distance beyond we come to the triple gate of *Vrata od Šuranja*, the inner arch 16C Baroque, the middle one Gothic (? 14C) and the outer arch 18C, with drawbridge mechanism attached. Beside the gate *Kula Bon* (1473), a round corner tower, affords views of the s. part of the town; a walk follows the top of the w. wall to the main gate. Below the tower is a large pool formed by a freshwater spring called *Gurdić*, and beyond the bridge the modern suburb of *Škaljari*.

EXCURSION TO LOVĆEN AND CETINJE, mountain road (48 km., asphalt). Turning left at the road junction in Škaljari we ascend by a steep winding road to the pass and village of (6 km.) *Trojica* (view of the bays of Tivat and Kotor), where we quit the Adriatic Highway. After about 3 km. the road begins to climb the side of the mountain in stupendous zigzags, disclosing at every turn a wider vista of the Boka Kotorska.—22 km. *Krstac* provides a superb **View of the entire gulf.

A rutted gravel road runs s. from Krstac, providing an alternative route to Cetinje (26 km.). From the village of Vuči Do (3 km.) a footpath leads to the summits of *Lovćen* (5544 ft), *Štirovnik* (5684 ft), and *Jezerski vrh* (5395 ft; Hotel Lovćen), the last with the tomb of Petar II Petrović Njegoš (1813–51), the poet and prince-bishop of Montenegro. Jezerski vrh can also be reached by a turning from this road, midway between Krstac and Cetinje.

From Krstac the main road continues downhill to the village of *Njeguši*, birthplace of Petar II, with his former summer residence left of the road. The road now climbs again in a series of zigzags to the pass of *Bukovica* (4140 ft) and then descends to (36 km.) *Čekanje*, where it is joined by a gravel road from Grahovo and Danilovgrad.

48 km. **Cetinje** (*Grand Hotel*), the former capital of Montenegro, lies on a barren and forbidding plateau (2000 ft) ringed with mountains, and snow-bound at least five months of the year. Although founded in the 15C by Ivan Crnojević, the first ruler of Montenegro, the city today is quite modern and interesting more for the majesty of its surroundings and its historical association than for any architectural merit. The locals still carry pistols; the atmosphere is Balkan and the Adriatic seems very distant. A short distance from the hotel is the former palace of Prince Petar II, the mighty black-bearded prince-bishop, poet, and crack-shot. The low fortified building is called the **Biljarda** (1838) because a billiard table was hauled up for it direct from the sea. It now houses three museums: the *Njegoš Museum; Ethnographical Museum;* and *Museum of the Liberation Struggle*. A large relief model of Montenegro is displayed in an annex alongside. Behind the Biljarda is the *Monastery*, founded by Ivan Crnojević in 1484 but destroyed and rebuilt repeatedly over the centuries. In the treasury are good icons, vestments, and a gospel of 1493, one of the first books to be printed in the Cyrillic alphabet. The tiny cruciform chapel contains the sarcophagi of three former Princes of the Njegoš dynasty, Danilo, Mirko, and Petar I. From *Kula Tablja*, the ruined tower overlooking the monastery, the heads of executed Turks used to be displayed as a symbol of undying hatred. The modest *Royal Palace* of the later kings of Montenegro, in Trg Maršala Tita, last occupied by King Nicholas (d. Antibes, 1921), preserves intact some of the state rooms. In the park beside the road for Budva the *Umjetnička galerija* (Art Gallery) has a selection of works by modern Yugoslav artists.

From Cetinje the main road continues to (94 km.) *Titograd;* an alternative return to the coast from Cetinje may be made by another wild and beautiful road to *Budva* (35 km.), see Rte 24.

24   FROM KOTOR TO ULCINJ

ROAD, 122 km. (75¾m.). 18 km. *Tivat.*—44 km. **Budva.**—63 km. *Petrovac.*—80 km. *Sutomore.*—89 km. **Bar.**—122 km. *Ulcinj.*

An alternative route to Budva via Trojica, avoiding Tivat and saving 14 km. leaves our road left just outside the town. The road is mountainous for the first 6 km., offering views back to the bay of Kotor and w. over the Bay of Tivat, then levels out across the plain of Grbalj and joins the Tivat-Budva road 12 km. from Budva.

Leaving Kotor viâ the suburb of *Škaljari* we leave the more direct road to Budva (comp. above) on our left. Rounding the head of the inner bay of Kotor we follow the w. shore to (7 km.) **Prčanj** (900 inhab.), a village that straggles over the hillside and along the water's edge. Like other places in the Boka Kotorska, Prčanj has a pronounced nautical tradition and prospered mainly in the 16–19C. The sailors of Prčanj ran the first regular postal service on the E. Adriatic coast (1625–1806), plying between Venice, Zadar, Kotor, and Corfù; Capt. Ivo Visin of Prčanj became the first Slav to circumnavigate the globe

(1852–59). Sturdy sea captains' houses testify to its former prosperity, but the pride of the village is the colossal neo-Renaissance parish church of *Rodjenje bogorodice* (Birth of Our Lady), erected between 1784 and 1909 to designs by Bernardino Macaruzzi of Venice. The interior has been liberally adorned with works of art. A good Italo-Cretan icon forms the main altarpiece; there are paintings by Palma Giovane, G. B. Piazzetta, and Ant. Balestra; and three angels sculpted by G. M. Morlaiter (1746). Works by many leading modern Yugoslav artists include I. Meštrović and T. Rosandić. On a terrace in front of the church there are busts of Abp. Strossmayer and Prince Petar Petrović II Njegoš by Meštrović.

Continuing N. from Prčanj along the W. shore of the bay of Kotor we round Rt Gospa at the tip of the Vrmac peninsula and enter the Verige narrows, on the S. side of the strait.—14 km. *Lepetane* is linked by car ferry (continuous throughout the summer; 5 min) with Kamenari (see Rte 23) on the N. shore of the Boka Kotorska. Turning S.W. and S. we follow the shore of the bay of Tivat.

18 km. **Tivat,** the second largest town (3420 inhab.) on the Boka Kotorska, is sheltered from N.E. winds by Mt. Vrmac (2458 ft). Its pleasant climate early attracted summer villas of the nobility of Kotor, now mostly ruined, and sub-tropical vegetation is abundant. Tivat is well supplied with sandy beaches, to the N. around Rt Seljanovo and the hamlet of Donja Lastva, and to the S. around Kalimanj, and is developing into an attractive little resort.

Airport at *Soliosko polje* 3 m. to the S.E. (summer only). Flights from Belgrade, Zagreb, Skopje, Sarajevo, and Bari.

Steamers once a week from Rijeka, Silba, Zadar, Šibenik, Primošten, Split, Hvar, Korčula, and Dubrovnik. Daily from the main towns on the Boka Kotorska.

Hotels. Mimoza; Lastva; Park. —AUTOCAMP at Pržno.

Buses to places on the Boka Kotorska and to the main towns on the Montenegrin coast.

The luxuriant *Town Park* contains many botanical rarities. In the centre of the town the small Gothic church of *Sv. Antun* (1373) has the arms of various Kotor nobles painted on the walls and an inscription mentioning King Tvrtko I of Bosnia. The remains of the *Palata Buća* (1548) and a few private chapels survive from their former pleasure palaces. The church of *Sv. Rok* in Donja Lastva contains a good icon of St Tryphon by Ilias Moschos, a 17C Greek artist.

In the S. corner of the Bay of Tivat are the three small islands of Prevlaka, Stradioti (or Sv. Marko), and Otok. *Prevlaka* has excavated remains of a 13C Benedictine Monastery. The 15C Franciscan Monastery on *Otok* occupies the site of a Benedictine foundation of the 9–11C (ruined church), the seat (1219–c. 1300) of the primate of the medieval kingdom of Zeta. A gravel road traverses the salt flats of *Soliosko polje*, which have been in continuous use for 2000 years, to serve the little known peninsula of **Luštica**, which descends to the open sea in many deserted sandy beaches. The small bay of *Pržno*, 14 km. from Tivat, is already attracting tourists and has an autocamp on the shore. The inhabitants of Luštica are predominantly Orthodox, and the churches, though plain, sometimes have good iconostases. Among the most interesting are those in Sv. Petar (by Daskal Dimitrije; 1704) and Sv. Lazar (Petar Rafailović; 1771), Sv. Andreja and Sv. Nedjelja (both Djordje Rafailović; 1802) at *Zabrdje*. The little church of Sv. Tripun at *Klinci* has 17C wall paintings.

From Tivat a new section of the Adriatic Highway takes us past the airport, skirts Soliosko polje (comp. above) and crosses the plain of

Grbalj. The shore is hidden and inaccessible behind a range of low hills. We traverse the green Zupa valley to rejoin the coast at (44 km.) Budva

BUDVA (2000 inhab.), with excellent sandy beaches, a tempered climate and an old walled quarter of typically Mediterranean aspect is the most popular holiday resort in Montenegro. Enjoying particular favour with the English it is rapidly acquiring a modicum of sophistiation.

Airport at Tivat (see above).
Steamers daily (June–Sept) from Rijeka, Rab, Zadar, Šibenik, Split, Hvar, Korčula, Dubrovnik, Hercegnovi and Bar; once weekly (June–Sept) from Trieste, Koper, Rovinj, Pula, Mali Lošinj, Silba, Makarska, and Orebić.
Hotels. Avala (with annexes), 230 R kafana, dancing, open all the year; **International,** 300 R; Slavija, 290 R, these two sharing open-air swimming pool; **Splendid,** 210 R; **Adriatic,** 115 R; **Plaza,** 150 R; **Mogren**; all these closed in winter.
Autocamp at *Bečići.*
Buses from Belgrade, Skopje, Titograd and all the main cities of the Adriatic coast. Also local buses to the Boka Kotorska and to all points on the Montenegrin coast.

History. *Budva,* like Risan, is linked by legend with the name of Cadmus, king of Phoenicia, and was Greek, Illyrian, Roman, and Byzantine by turn. In the 9C the town was sacked by the Saracens and in the 11C joined the medieval Serbian kingdom of Duklja, while preserving its municipal autonomy. A century later Duklja was absorbed into Raška (Serbia) by Stefan Nemanja and in 1371 Budva, by statute, confirmed its status as a self-governing commune similar to the cities of Dalmatia. With the decline of the Nemanjas, however, dynastic quarrels led to the disintegration of Raška and after 50 years of turbulence Budva acceded to Venice in 1443, becoming the most southerly Venetian outpost on the Adriatic coast. Cut off from its hinterlands by the Turks, Budva languished, and the earthquake of 1667 wrought catastrophic damage from which it never recovered, although the city walls were partially repaired in the face of continuing danger from the Turks. With the fall of Venice (1797) Budva passed to Austria, then France (1806), against whom it twice revolted, and back to Austria again until 1918.

The old quarter is girdled with CITY WALLS, one section of which ante-dates Venetian rule, though the major portion was erected in the 15C and rebuilt in 1639. From the *Kopnena vrata* (Land Gate), opposite the Hotel Avala, with the city escutcheons of Venice and Budva over the doorway, the picturesque main street leads in a few minutes to the main square. The Catholic cathedral of Sv. IVAN in the centre, founded in the 8–9C, has been repeatedly rebuilt and acquired its Baroque appearance in the 17C. Among the pictures within are a Madonna (school of Tiepolo), a 16C Venetian painting of SS Peter and Paul, and a venerable icon with a background of beaten silver. In the Orthodox church of Sv. TROJICA (Holy Trinity) are paintings by Nicholaos Aspioti of Corfù. Adjoining the church is the open-air cinema, at the rear of which is the 12C church of Santa Maria in Punta. The former *Franciscan Monastery* adjacent to the church now contains the ZAVIČAJNI MUZEJ (Town Museum, open 8–11, 2–5), in which are exhibited Phoenician, Greek, and Roman archaeological finds from a necropolis on the site of the Hotel Avala. The tiny medieval church of *Sv. Sava,* where in former times the altars were shared between Orthodox and Catholic worship, is being adapted as a further section for the museum. The *Citadela* overlooks the sea on the s. side of town, affording views E. and w. of the coast. Hence access may be had to a walk round the top of the walls.

About 1½ m. N. of Budva, beside the road to Cetinje, is *Maine* the village where Šćepan Mali, the 18C pretender to the Montenegrin throne, first made his appearance posing as the murdered Tsar Peter III of Russia. The village has two Orthodox monasteries of which the more interesting is the fortified Podostrog, now somewhat dilapidated but to be restored. The small basement chapel of Sv. Gospodja (Our Lady) is completely covered with 17C frescoes, of which those in the narthex are the easiest to see; the large 18C church beside it contains the tomb of Vladika Danilo, founder of the Petrović-Njegoš dynasty of Montenegro, who died here in 1735. Prince Petar II Petrović Njegoš wrote part of his famous epic poem, 'Gorski vijenac' (The Mountain Wreath), while staying in this monastery. In the court a fine wellhead is decorated with a relief of the royal arms of Montenegro (two-headed eagle holding a snake in its claws). The nearby monastery of Podmaine was burnt down in 1869, but the surviving church is decorated with wall paintings by Rafailo Dimitrijević of Risan (1747) and has an iconostasis by Nicholaos Aspioti. Dositej Obradović (1742–1811), pioneer Serbian scholar and encyclopaedist, spent several months at this monastery.

The road to Bar traverses a beautiful stretch of coast quite unlike anything farther N. A ridge of low, green mountains known as *Paštrovske gore* in the district of Paštrovići runs parallel with the shore where long stretches of sand or shingle beaches are interspersed by craggy headlands and beetling cliffs. The scenery, by comparison with the remainder of the coast, is both restful and varied.

Leaving Budva we follow the long pebble and shingle beach of *Slavenska plaža*, with the offices of the Zeta and Lovćen film companies on our right, and many striking modern hotels. On the headland, Rt Zavala, at the far end of the beach, can be seen the small 15C burial chapel of Stevan Štiljanović, the last duke of Paštrovići. A mountain road to Cetinje (33 km.; comp. Rte 23) swings away to our left. Passing the sandy beaches of *Bečići* (autocamp; views ahead of the mountains and coast), *Kamenovo* and *Pržno*, we bear right from the main road for Sveti Stefan.

54 km. Sveti Stefan (*Sveti Stefan*, 115 R with bath, night-club, casino; *Miločer*, with annexes, 230 R with bath, swimming pool. Steamers once a week in summer from Venice, Ravenna, Šibenik, Split, Korčula, Dubrovnik, Bar Corfu, Itea, and Piraeus), is a charming island fishing village that has been expropriated and converted into a luxury hotel colony, to shoreward of which is developing an associated holiday resort. The village was founded in the 15C by the Paštrovići, who maintained their own autonomous district under Venice, and was fortified in the 16C against the Turks. A sand-bar joins the village, once an island, to the mainland and visitors are admitted (fee) to view its narrow crooked streets and two tiny churches of *Sv. Stefan* (15C) and *Preobraženje* (The Transfiguration; 1693).

To the N. along the shore the *Hotel Miločer*, formerly the summer residence of the Yugoslav royal family, stands in a beautiful park with Mediterranean and sub-tropical trees and flowers. Hence a narrow gravel track leads uphill (15 min on foot; practicable by car) to the Orthodox Monastery of Praskvica. The iconostasis of the main church of Sv. Nikola is by Nicholaos Aspioti (1863). A Gothic chapel (1413) with frescoes survives from an earlier church. The treasury preserves a 16C copy of the gospels, with engraved silver covers and miniature reliefs; a silver-gilt chalice presented by Tsar Paul of Russia (18C); and a large 16C icon. A few steps away is the small *Sv. Trojica* (Holy Trinity), the oldest church in the region (? 1050). The interior is covered with frescoes (1680–81) by Radul, the Serbian painter, best in the apse.

The road beyond Sveti Stefan affords excellent retrospective views of the wide bay of Budva.—At 59 km., just off the road (r.), is the Orthodox monastery of *Reževići*, said to have been founded by Tsar Dušan the

Mighty of Serbia. The older of its two churches (enlarged in 1714) has 17C frescoes and an iconostasis by Aleksija Lazović (1833). Reževići used to be the seat of the 'Bankada', or Grand Council, of the autonomous district of Paštrovići, elections to which were held at the nearby cove of Drobni pijesak.—At 62½ km., where the Titograd–Petrovac road crosses the Adriatic Highway, we turn right.

63 km. **Petrovac-na-moru** (*Oliva; Palace; Petrovac; Sutjeska.* Autocamp. Steamers from Dubrovnik and Ulcinj; buses from all parts of the Montenegrin coast and from Cetinje and Titograd) is a small modern resort (550 inhab.) set in splendid natural surroundings with dense olive groves almost to the water's edge. Popular with the people of Titograd (only 58 km. away by a good asphalt road), Petrovac is laid out with a pleasant promenade and rapidly acquiring the amenities of a pleasure resort. Roman finds have been made in the neighbourhood, of which a 4C mosaic floor (inquire locally for directions) is the most interesting example.

The Adriatic Highway continues s.e. above the broad sandy beach of *Buljarica*, passing (2 km. beyond Petrovac) the ruined Orthodox monastery of *Gradište*, with two early churches. Both the larger Gothic church of Sv. Nikola (rebuilt 1620) and the older church of Uspenje (The Assumption) are decorated with good frescoes by Strahinja of Budimlje, a Serbian painter whose Byzantine style is modified by strong western influences. The church of Sv. Nikola also has an iconostasis by Vasilije Rafailović of Risan (1796).

At the far end of Buljarica bay we pass a large bentonite quarry and processing plant before striking inland through beautiful hilly country covered with pine woods and olive groves.—77 km. the spectacular ruins of *Haj-Nehaj* castle, built by the Venetians and later adapted by the Turks, stands on a dizzy spur of rock.

80 km. **Sutomore** (*Korali*, 325 R with bath or shower; *Južno more* 235 R with shower, kafana, dancing, cinema, both open Apr–Sept. Railway station for connections with Bar, Titograd, and Belgrade) is a modern resort village (800 inhab.) strung out along a sand and pebble beach that extends for more than a mile. The 12C church of *Sv. Tekla* has twin altars, one for the Catholic rite, the other for Orthodox services. At the s.w. end of the beach on the headland of Ratac, stand extensive ruins of the ancient Benedictine monastery of *Our Lady of Ratac* (11–13C), including a two-storied burial chapel of early-Christian type.—At 88 km. a T-junction offers the choice of turning right to Bar or left to Stari Bar.

Bar (1 km.; *Agava; Rumija*. Railway station for trains to Titograd and Belgrade. Car ferry daily to Bari in summer. Steamers daily in summer from all the main cities of the Adriatic coast, also regular services to Greece, Turkey, Italy, and the Near East), at the s. end of the wide bay of the same name, is a modern industrial port (2500 inhab.) expanding rapidly to handle the import and export traffic of Serbia and Montenegro.

For the old town we turn left, passing (89 km.) a poor gravel road to Virpazar and take the next gravel road left.—92 km. **Stari Bar**, just off the main road, is little more than a ghost town whose romantic ruins, huddling picturesquely at the foot of Mt. Rumija (5008 ft) give little idea of its former wealth and importance.

After being both a Greek and a Roman colony (*Antibaris*), the town became an important military and trading post under Byzantium and in 1089 was elevated to an archbishopric. In the 12–14C it acknowledged the Nemanja dynasty of Raška and after dynastic squabbles passed to Venice in 1443, by whom it was fortified. In 1571 it was captured by the Turks and remained in their possession until 1878, when it was liberated by Montenegro.

The town is encircled by 15–16C Venetian walls. On the N. side can be seen the well preserved *Aqueduct* (16–17C) that used to bring water to the town. The former *Cathedral* and the church of *Sv. Nikola*, were blown up by explosions of gunpowder in 1881 and 1912. *Sv. Veneranda* and *Sv. Katarina* are both Gothic (? 14C) and an 11–12C Romanesque chapel on the N.W. side of town has been incorporated into the Venetian Fortress. A large medieval mansion on the W. side of town, with traces of frescoes is thought to have been the *Archbishop's Palace*. The Turks left relatively few marks on the town, in general adapting existing structures, but a large 17C *Hamam* (Bath House) bears witness to their long stay.

Beyond Stari Bar the road becomes narrow, winding and difficult to negotiate. Although asphalted, it is the only section of the Adriatic Highway not rebuilt and widened since the war. Its course lies at first close to the shore, enveloped in dense and attractive olive groves of great antiquity. There are said to be over half a million trees on the lower slopes of the Rumija mountain range and specimens are estimated to be between 1500 and 2000 years old. We begin to head inland and climb to barren, rocky foothills of typically karstic appearance.—At 99 km. a narrow and badly surfaced gravel road (r.) offers a slightly shorter route to Ulcinj (see below).—At 107 km. a similar gravel road branches left for Skadar (Shkoder) in Albania. Glimpses may be caught of the occasional village mosque, while the peasants in the fields are frequently in national dress, the women in Turkish trousers and vividly embroidered aprons.

122 km. **ULCINJ** the most southerly town (6000 inhab.) of the Yugoslav coast, is unique on the coast in its oriental appearance and flavour, though this is fast disappearing. Its popularity as a tourist resort is enhanced by unmatched beaches (with iodine content) and a growing complex of hotels and modern facilities. About three quarters of the population is Albanian.

Hotels. **Metropol**; **Mediteran**, 330 R, kafana, dancing; **Galeb**, 145 R, kafana; **Jadran**; **Republika**; **Lido**, 240 R.

Buses from Belgrade, Sarajevo, Titograd, Dubrovnik and all parts of the Montenegrin coast.

History. The Greek and Roman colony of *Olcinium* was somewhat to the N.W. of the present town, but gave its name to the Byzantine settlement which arose on the present site in the 9–10C. In 1181 Ulcinj acknowledged the sovereignty of the Nemanjas of Raška and remained in Serbian hands until 1421, when it transferred its allegiance to Venice. In 1571 it was captured by the Turks and during the 16C became notorious as the seat of the sought-after renegade and pirate, Uluz-Ali, Bey of Algiers. Its fleet was captured and burnt by Turkish forces in 1675, but Ulcinj remained a pirate centre until well into the 18C. In 1878, after a protracted seige, Ulcinj was captured by Montenegro and after brief occupations by Austria (1916–18) and Italy (1918–20) was joined with Yugoslavia.

The town is spread out amphitheatrically over three hills round a sandy bay and harbour. To the E. lies the newest hotel and tourist quarter; in the centre the modern section of the town with shops and administrative offices; and in the w. is the old fortified citadel, best reached from the beach by taking the ascending path beside the harbour. The massive *Walls*, dating from the 13C but extended and rebuilt by the Venetians and Turks, are imposing on their high cliffs, but are virtually all that is left of the medieval city, for the inside was reduced to rubble by the Montenegrin artillery in 1878. Entering by the *Istočna vrata* (East Gate) we follow the inside perimeter of the walls left to a raised platform, commanding good views w. into the cove of Liman. A few steps farther on, stone vaults mark the site of the Turkish market, opposite which is the shell of a 14C church and mosque. For religious reasons, the Turks reversed the w. door, so that the lintel now forms the threshold and the Gothic capitals can be seen upside down near the ground. The stump of a ruined minaret adjoining the church and to the left is the ruined *Balšićeva kula*, a tower erected by one of the last of the Serbian kings. Following the main street e. with houses in a mixture of Venetian and Turkish styles, we regain the e. gate and footpath.

The central part of the town is grouped around the main street, which runs uphill at right angles to the beach and promenade. On the left is the oldest of seven small mosques, the *Pašina Džamija* (Pasha's Mosque, 16C) adjoining which is a small contemporary *Hamam* (Bath House). Beyond the 18C Turkish *Sahat-kula* (Clock Tower), at the top of the street is the colourful market place, particularly busy on Wednesdays and Fridays.

Pleasant excursions may be made to the *Velika plaža* (Great Beach), 4 km. e. of town, which extends for an impressive 12 km. from Rt Djeran to the mouth of the river Bojana (forbidden zone) on the Albanian border. It can be reached on foot from behind the Hotel Galeb ($\frac{3}{4}$ hr); or by road (bus) turning right at the petrol station to cross the edge of Ulcinj plain. Before the beach we come to *Porat Milena*, a narrow canal leading inland to the extensive salt flats of Solila. An interesting feature here are the fishing devices known as *kalimera*, consisting of a net on the end of a long pole that is lowered into the water on a cantilever principle. The Velika plaža, of fine grey sand, slopes gradually to the sea. Although several hotels are projected here, the greater part of the beach remains natural and untouched and it is unwise to stray too close to the Albanian frontier.

A boat trip to the peaceful bay of Valdanos, w. of the town, affords excellent views of the walls and extensive olive woods for which Ulcinj is noted. The bay itself is deeply indented, with a lovely shingle beach backed by pinewoods; it was here in 1675 that the Ulcinj pirate fleet was waylaid and destroyed.

LIST OF THE PRINCIPAL ARTISTS

whose works are referred to in the text, with their birthplaces or the schools to which they belonged.

ABBREVIATIONS:

A. = architect engr. = engraver G. = goldsmith
Mil. Engin. = military engineer P. = painter
S. = sculptor W. = woodworker Flor. = Florence
Ven. = Venice

ACQUA, PIO AND VICKO DELL' (18C), S., Ital. — 113, 116, 119

ALBERT, MASTER (15C), P., Istria — 41

ALEŠI, ANDRIJA (c. 1430–c. 1504), A. & S., Drač (Durazzo, Albania). — 78, 105, 115, 116, 125, 145, 148

ANDRIJIĆ, BLAŽ (Vlahuša; 15–16C), Mason, Korčula. — 173

ANDRIJIĆ, JOSIP AND IVAN (son of Josip; 16C), Masons, Korčula. — 200

ANDRIJIĆ, MARKO (d. c. 1509), Mason, Korčula. — 179, 180, 201

ANDRIJIĆ, PETAR (15–16C), Mason, Korčula. — 173, 193, 194, 202

ANGELI, GIUS. (c. 1709–98), P., Ven. — 16

ANTON OF PADOVA (Antun iz Padove; 16C), P., Kašćerga (Istria). — 19, 41, 200

APPIANI, ANDREA (1754–1817), P., Lomb. — 118

ASPETTI, TIZIANO (1565–1607), S., Padua — 3, 179

ASPIOTI, NIKOLAOS (19C), P., Corfù. — 226, 227

BAKOTIĆ, FULGENCIJE (c. 1720–92), W., Raštel Gomilica. — 131, 149

BALDASSARE D'ANNA (Melchisedecco Baldissera; 1560–c. 1639), P., Ven. — 88, 174

BALESTRA, ANT. (1666–1740), P., Verona — 225

BARTOLOMEO, MASO DI (1406–c. 1456), Bellfounder, Capannole. — 201

BASSANO (Leandro da Ponte; 1557–1622), P., Ven. sch. — 163, 173, 175, 180

BASTIANI, LAZZ. (1449–1512), P., Ven. — 93

BELLINI, GIOV. (1430–1516), P., Ven. — 180, 218

BERTAPELLE, PETAR PAVAO (1763–1817), S. & A., Vrboska. — 163

BISSOLO, PIER FR. (c. 1470–1554), Ven. sch. — 187

BLAŽ OF DUBROVNIK (16C), P., ? Dubrovnik. — 41

BLAŽ JURJEV TROGIRANIN (early 15C), P., Trogir. — 95, 125, 144, 180

BOJKOVIĆ, IVAN (17C), W., Šibenik. — 118

BOKANIĆ, TRIFUN (1575–1609), A., Brač. — 124

BONAZZA, GIOV. (fl. 1695–1730), S., Padua. — 18, 19

BONIFACIO, NATALE (1548–92), Engr., Šibenik. — 209

BONIFAZIO VERONESE (or de' Pitat; 1487–1553), P., Ven. — 36

BONINO DA MILANO (d. 1429), S., ? Milan. — 114, 116, 139, 179

BORIČEVIĆ, MATEJ AND LUKA (16C), G., fl. Zadar. — 102

BOSCHETTO, JUAN (16C), P., Spanish. — 170

BOŽIDAREVIĆ, NIKOLA (Niccolò Raguseo; c. 1460–1517), P., Kručica (Lastovo). — 201, 202, 205

BRAJKOV, MIHOJA (14C), A., Bar. — 193

BRAJKOVIĆ, RATKOV (15C), Mason, Dubrovnik. — 179, 193

BUDČIĆ, ANDRIJA (15C), Mason, fl. Šibenik. — 113

BUFALINO, PIETRO AND. (fl. 1656–73), A. & Engr., Urbino. — 198

BUKOVAC, VLAHO (1885–1922), P., Cavtat. — 201, 204, 209

BUNIĆ, ŽUPAN (15C), Mil. Engin., South Slav. — 158

BUSATO, ANT. (15C), A., Ven. sch. — 114

BUVINA, AND. (13C), W., fl. Split. — 139

CABIANCA, FR. (1665–1737), S., Ven. — 222

CAFFA, MELCHIOR (18C), S., Ven. — 31

CALIARI, CARLO (son of Paolo Veronese; 1570–96), P., Ven. — 159

CAMPSA, PAOLO (c. 1497–1539), P. & W., Ital. — 72

CAPOGROSSO, MARCO (1628–?), P., Split. — 119

CAR, ZVONKO (b. 1913), S., Crikvenica. — 56

CARPACCIO, BEN. (d. c. 1560), P., Ven. — 4

CARPACCIO, VITT. (c. 1455–1526), P., Ven. — 4, 95, 180

CARRACCI, ANNIBALE (1560–1609), P., Brač. — 198

CHARONTON, ENGUERRAND (c. 1410–66), P., Laon. — 202

CIMA, G. B. (da Conegliano; 1460–1518), P., Ven. sch. — 6

ČIOČIĆ, FRANO (Čučić; 16C), S. & W., Korčula. — 173, 180, 186

CLERIGIN OF KOPER (15C), P., Koper. — 19

COLERO, P. (15C), silversmith, Ital. — 67

CONTARINI, GIOV. (1549–1606), P., Ven. — 22

CONTI, BERNARDINO DEI (fl. 1496–1522), P., Castelseprio (Varese). — 163

CONTIERI, IAC. (17–18C), S., Padua. — 44

CORREGGIO (Ant. Allegri; 1489–1534), P., Emilian sch. — 3

CORRER, GIAC. (15C), A., Trani. — 116, 179

COSSA, FR. DEL (c. 1438–77), P., Ferr. sch. — 90

231

INDEX

Topographical names are printed in **bold** type; names of eminent persons in *italics*; other entries (including subordinate indexes) in Roman type. In this index c and č follow c; š follows s; ž follows z. But dj, lj, and other compound letters are arranged as though in English, not according to their order in the Cyrillic alphabet.

235

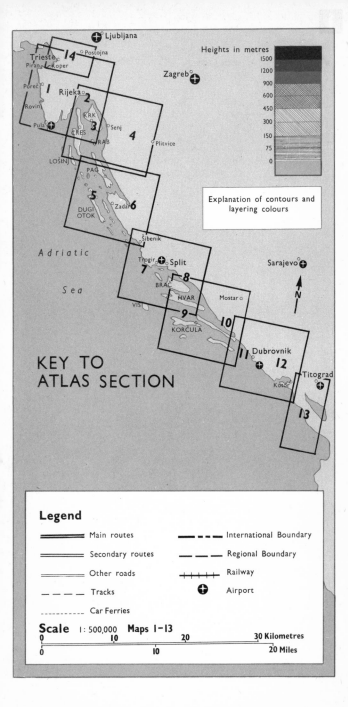

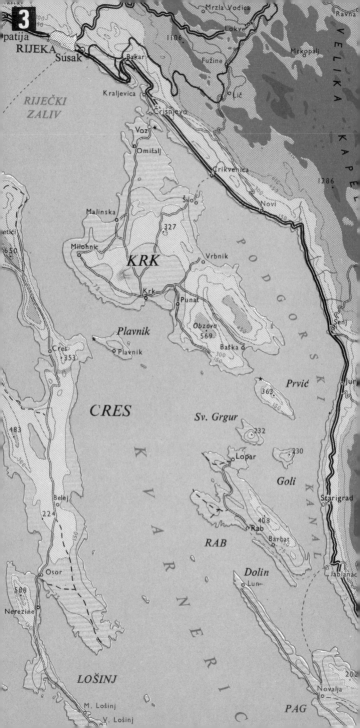

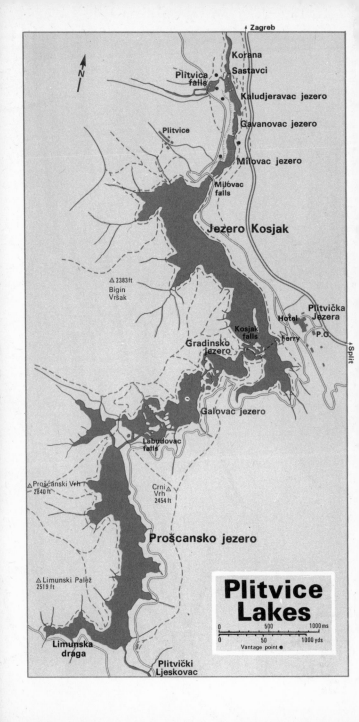